Identification in Psychoanalysis

This fascinating book offers an in-depth exploration of the gradual development of the concept of identification as it has evolved in the Freudian tradition of psychoanalysis.

Featuring a detailed review of the key Freudian texts, referencing them in their original German, this volume demonstrates how psychoanalysis sheds light on the richness and complexity of the identification process in human psychology, at both the individual and collective levels. The author closely follows the various reformulations of the theory – undertaken by Freud in the course of three different periods – and contextualises them within her clinical experience with various pathologies and her observations of the development of individuals, revealing throughout the great extent to which this fundamental process is unconscious.

Providing a critical examination of a fundamental Freudian concept, this volume is not only a teaching manual serving specifically to train psychoanalysts and psychotherapists but is also an important read for anyone interested in human sciences, philosophy and the history of psychoanalysis.

Jean Florence is a *psychothérapies* based in Belgium. As a professor at the UCL between 1973 and 2007, he taught psychology, the psychology of dramatic art, and clinical psychology and psychoanalysis and became Professor Emeritus in 2007. He was President of the Belgian School of Psychoanalysis from 1982 to 1990 and from 1993 to 1997.

This book covers new ground within psychoanalytical scholarship. As few psycho-analysts, if any, have written systematically about this subject, Professeur Flor-ence's work fills an important gap in the literature.

Brett Kahr, practising psychoanalyst, UK

Identification in Psychoanalysis

A Comprehensive Introduction

Jean Florence
Translated by Agnes Jacob

Routledge
Taylor & Francis Group

LONDON AND NEW YORK

First edition published 2021
by Routledge
2 Park Square, Milton Park, Abingdon, Oxon, OX14 4RN

and by Routledge
52 Vanderbilt Avenue, New York, NY 10017

Routledge is an imprint of the Taylor & Francis Group, an informa business

British Library Cataloguing-in-Publication Data
A catalogue record for this book is available from the British Library

Library of Congress Cataloging-in-Publication Data
Names: Florence, Jean, 1942- author.
Title: Identification in psychoanalysis : a comprehensive
   introduction / Jean Florence.
Other titles: Identification dans la théorie freudienne. English
Description: Abingdon, Oxon ; New York, NY : Routledge, 2021. |
   Originally published in 1978 as: L'identification dans la théorie
   freudienne. | Includes bibliographical references and index.
Identifiers: LCCN 2020045163 (print) | LCCN 2020045164
   (ebook) | ISBN 9780367722487 (hardback) | ISBN
   9780367354855 (paperback) | ISBN 9781003154426 (ebook)
Subjects: LCSH: Identification (Psychology) | Psychoanalysis. |
   Freud, Sigmund, 1856–1939.
Classification: LCC BF175 .F5513 2021 (print) | LCC BF175
   (ebook) | DDC 150.19/5—dc23
LC record available at https://lccn.loc.gov/2020045163
LC ebook record available at https://lccn.loc.gov/2020045164

ISBN: 978-0-367-72248-7 (hbk)
ISBN: 978-0-367-35485-5 (pbk)
ISBN: 978-1-003-15442-6 (ebk)

Typeset in Times New Roman
by Apex CoVantage, LLC

Contents

Introduction

This book, the result of extensive and lengthy academic research, published in 1978 and then re-edited in 1984, presents an exhaustive examination of the emergence and development of the identification concept in Sigmund Freud's work.

This concept, initially based on the meaning of the term *identification* as it is commonly used in German, gradually became one of the fundamental concepts of psychoanalytic theory, closely tied to a series of other concepts developed in parallel, such as ego, repression, symptom, splitting, idealisation and sublimation. In common usage, the term *identification* refers both to the transitive form of the verb *to identify* – recognise, distinguish, designate a person or a thing – and to the reflexive form, which refers to the act of basing one's behaviour, feelings, words and even thinking on a model provided by another person. In the latter case, identification resembles empathy, pity, sympathy or the unconscious ability to share in the emotional life of other people, understand them and be receptive to a whole range of influences, from the everyday sharing of someone's feelings to individual or collective mental alienation.

Identification is also what allows us all, from early childhood, to play various roles, what enables the actor to bring to life a character, making it possible for the audience to live all kinds of imaginary lives. Identification is at work wherever the social link exists. What interested Freud and other psychoanalysts was pinpointing the psychic genesis and the ramifications of this human process essential for our personal development, extending in all directions, beneficial or harmful. Freud's investigation started with the enigmas of neurotic suffering, dreams, artistic and spiritual creation, slips and all sorts of neurotic and psychotic symptoms. He investigated childhood, subjective origins and the genesis of individuals and of societies. But he never developed an overall conception of this vast and complex question of identification. Thus, these questions – these aporias – have been passed down to us. How does psychoanalysis, which encompasses this complex question of identification, contribute today to the issue of social and political links, to the genesis of morality, to the debate on identity, to the approach to the difference between the sexes, to the question of gender?

After Freud, his disciples have contributed in various ways to pass on these questions. Without attempting to provide a complete list of contributors to Freud's theory, I shall name some of his successors, to whom we acknowledge our debt. Karl Abraham, interested in the suffering related to melancholia and manic depression, contributed the notion of incorporation; Sandor Ferenczi, mindful of the handling of the analytic relation, revealed the relation between transference and introjection; Melanie Klein, following in the footsteps of her two forerunners, greatly elucidated early identification and projection processes and formulated the notion of projective identification to explain primitive psychotic states. By doing so, she drew attention to the archaic dimensions of transference and countertransference, sharpening her colleagues' awareness of them. Anna Freud, who enriched the doctrine by including all the ego defence mechanisms, contributed the concept of identification with the aggressor, clearly seen in children and in social interactions.

Our own university and psychoanalytic training was influenced, at the end of the 1960s, by Jacques Lacan's reading of Freud's work, closely connected with human sciences and philosophy. Lacan started out by approaching identification from the perspective of his theory of the mirror stage, a stage prior to language acquisition, when the child sees his image in the mirror and shows, through his facial expression, that he recognises himself in this image, thus creating the prefiguration of an imaginary form of the ego. This identification, called specular, serves as the basis for all recognition of similarity, for games of imitation, for rivalry. But the "ego" is not the "subject"; a status of subject, no doubt inherited from the Cartesian tradition as reconsidered by Lacan, is fundamental in his view. The subject has no figurable representation as such because he is the product of the appropriation of speech, of "signifiers", which inscribe him in the humanising order of familial relations and thereby in social life. This is what we call symbolic identification, which identifies the subject with a signifier that renders him distinct by naming him and integrates him into the symbolic order of consecutive generations whose vector, it might be argued, is the paternal function. This underscores the fundamental dependence of the subject on the desire of the Other, whose message he must always decipher. We might say that this is a literal illustration of the paradox so wonderfully condensed in Arthur Rimbaud's poetic phrase "I is another". Throughout his teaching, Lacan looked for logical and topological reformulations of this paradox.

Although structuralism in linguistics and anthropology (F. de Saussure, Roman Jakobson, C. Lévi-Strauss, Alain Greimas, Julia Kristeva) placed great emphasis on the importance of speech, of language and of symbolic relations in the construction of the subject, philosophy and in particular the contribution of the phenomenological approach (E. Husserl, Martin Heidegger, M. Merleau-Ponty, Paul Ricoeur, Alphonse De Waelhens, Jacques Derrida) and the viewpoint of Anglo-Saxon philosophy (J. L. Austin, L. Wittgenstein, Noam Chomsky) also helped provide analysts with a better understanding of the logical and clinical realities of interlocution.

These various sources of inspiration, often close in nature to a dialogue with artists, playwrights, poets and writers, have greatly expanded the scope of clinical thinking. I am particularly indebted, in this respect, to Octave Mannoni, André

Green, Piera Aulagnier and Alain Didier-Weill. We must also stress the importance of the essential contribution of Jean Laplanche and Jean-Bertrand Pontalis to psychoanalytic conceptualisation as a whole, both Freudian and post-Freudian. Their book *The Language of Psycho-Analysis* (1973) is an essential work of reference for anyone wishing to understand the origin and development of psychoanalytic concepts. Moreover, it is important to note how methodically Jean Laplanche submitted Freudian and Lacanian concepts to renewed scrutiny of the effects of parental messages charged with signification, messages which sometimes remain enigmatic, lacking translation and creating splitting and unsymbolised affects in the subject.

In the course of years of analytic practice and reflection, our affinity with Donald Winnicott never ceased to grow. His brilliant concepts of potential space, transitional space and transitional object; his conceptualisation of play and of care, based on the paradigm of early interactions between the "good enough mother" and her baby; as well as his ability to speak frankly and in great detail about the difficulties and failures of psychotherapy and psychoanalysis, whether they concern infants, children, adolescents or adults, have brought a refreshing perspective to the thought, work and theory of psychoanalysts who appreciate his likeable and original personality. Winnicott renders palpable the fact that identification is a concrete, living reality, constantly inventing that which should emerge as a "self" out of random affective trials and traumas requiring the elaboration and artifices of a false self that engenders suffering and devours energy. My access to the Winnicottian universe was greatly facilitated by the stimulating work of Adam Phillips, author of fascinating biographies of Winnicott and Freud, as well as of works in which he questions, in a most original manner, the clichés and "ready-made" concepts of psychoanalysis. This testifies to his freedom of mind and independent thinking and to his ongoing relation with literature and with language. (He has edited a new translation of Freud.) I am also indebted to Heitor O'Dwyer de Macedo who, in his analysis of Winnicott's work (*De l'amour à la pensée*, 1994) develops a theory of what takes place and what strives to emerge in an analysis. De Macedo associates the effects of identification and disidentification with a phenomenon of friendship and love related to the living ties of transference.

The question of identification has been further broadened by a return to the realities of war and history, beyond Freud's "Why War?" and *Civilization and Its Discontents* and his hypotheses on the entanglement and disentanglement of life and death drives. The co-authored work of Françoise Davoine and Jean-Max Gaudillière deals with forms of madness and trauma caused by wars and with the brutality of imposed silence and deathly denial in family histories and in the history of societies. Undoubtedly, transgenerational transmission is a fundamental aspect of identification processes which has not yet been sufficiently investigated. These two authors also make use of literature (Robert Musil, Laurence Sterne, Jonathan Swift, Cervantes), of philosophy (Plato, Wittgenstein, Locke) and of anthropology and psychiatry (Devereux, Bion, Binswanger, Aby Warburg, Benedetti), keeping alive an open and curious type of psychoanalysis.

Such is the rich field – still lending itself to investigation – which sprung from the notion of identification applying to all aspects of human life, connecting the individual with the collective, the private sphere with the public sphere, the intimate space with the institutional space. This field invites us to explore together the genesis and structure of a subject in the process of becoming, in his most secret inner being as well as in the most political aspects of his existence.

I hope that the journey this book proposes, to shed light on the slow development of the concept of identification, a phenomenon ever present in our lives and so important to analysts, will stimulate the reader's interest in all the aspects of identification we have explored.

Foreword
Symptoms, transferences, identifications*

Beginning again

The point of origin of psychoanalysis cannot be definitively located in the phenomenology of a primordial science associated with a precise date or in the timeless logic of an epistemological redirection. Analysis teaches us that this point of origin can only be identified at the start of a new analysis. Every analysis necessarily repeats the inimitable origin – the birth of psychoanalysis and of Freud as an analyst. Every analysis brings up, in unforeseeable ways, the question of analytic work as contrasted to medicine.* This necessary return to the origin brings into play the psychoanalyst's identification as such. This identification must remain subject to constant scrutiny; I am not speaking of the analyst's identity. This question is intimately tied to others: ethical questions because this identification determines the manner of responding to the patient's request and symptom and questions of method because identification allows, in the singular and the plural, transmission of the object, its metamorphosis into a cause and its long-term transformation into an ideal.

If we believe that the origin of psychoanalysis is repeated, and even created anew, with each new analysis, it follows that its difference from medicine emerges every time: to be exact, its differentiation* because, once again, nothing is established once and for all. Indeed, analysts have come to believe that psychoanalysis has become distinct from medicine, just as it has freed itself from hypnosis and suggestion. Yet the medical continues "to return", be it in the analyst's language, never free of psychiatric terminology, or in his objectives, which he cannot define without reference to healing, to the disappearance of symptoms, to the therapeutic effects of what he still calls "the treatment".

Moreover, the medical persists throughout the analytic process, both for the analyst and the analysand, because the aim of this process is to create a desire for "treatment" to be received or provided.

In preparation for writing a thesis, I engaged in a lengthy and attentive study of the conceptualisation of the identification process in the Freudian oeuvre. I set out to follow the original text step by step, keeping at a respectful (or respectable) distance all established theories so as to proceed from a position of "ignorance".

My long-term objective was to reconstitute what Lacan had developed on this subject, particularly in a seminar that I only obtained after my thesis had been completed. It was only later, when I conducted analysis, that I understood the real consequences of identification theory. The vast conceptual framework had to be linked with analytic practice; in other words, identification and transference had to be connected.

Here I am, once again, where I first started. This gives me the opportunity to point out some exceptional moments when difficulties or failures in the treatment demand a return to the initial choices which founded a practice or a theory.

I will first examine these questions by looking at Freud's initial practice. Forced by the subterfuges of neurosis to learn the ways of interpretation through the symptom and through dreams, Freud involuntarily distanced himself from his medical identification. He wrote that he was very surprised, in the therapeutic work, by the extent of his identification with his patients, by the degree to which he experienced through all sorts of inhibitions or somatic manifestations his own reaction to this "school of suffering" constituted by transference. He described these symptoms to Fliess: his letters show how the change in his subjective position modifies his approach to neurotic symptoms and that an identification process is always at work in symptom formation. Therefore, we must look at transference in clinical work to understand the specificity of the psychoanalytic theory of symptom formation, originally closely bound to identification theory.

From symptoms to transference

In my opinion, Dora's unfinished treatment is a perfect illustration of what can be learned from a return to the beginnings. Dora's analysis took place between October and December 1899. Freud gave a first account of it to Fliess a year later (January 1901). He described it as a fragment of an analysis of hysteria. The interpretation work focuses on two dreams, so it is really a clinical continuation of his book on dream interpretation.

As he says himself, "it is the subtlest thing I have so far written, and will put people off even more than usual".[1]

It was five years later, in 1905, that he published these observations in a psychiatry and neurology journal. In the prefatory remarks, he wrote:

> The title of the work was originally "Dreams and Hysteria", for it seemed to me peculiarly well-adapted for showing how dream-interpretation is woven into the history of a treatment and how it can become the means of filling in amnesias and elucidating symptoms.

And he adds:

> I must once more insist. . . that a thorough investigation of the problem of dreams is an indispensable prerequisite for any comprehension of the mental

processes in hysteria and the other psychoneuroses. . . . The treatment was not carried through to its appointed end, but was broken off at the patient's own wish when it had reached a certain point.[2]

Psychoanalysts generally consider this result rather limited, in view of the real problem of hysteria – the question of femininity, beyond what Freud himself was able to recognise subsequently, in Dora's homosexual ("gynecophile") attachment to Frau K. It seems that this recognition did not come until much later, in 1923.

Repressed homosexuality in the formation of neuroses became increasingly important in Freud's subsequent investigations and was closely connected with one of Fliess's old ideas on bisexuality. We know what violent controversy this question provoked in psychoanalytic circles, in Freud's lifetime and afterwards, particularly as it concerned the definition of femininity. Among psychoanalysts, this question functions as a symptom; it brings into question their identification: that is, their sexual identity itself, inevitably and continuously brought under scrutiny by transference in the analysis. The last part of Freud's account of the treatment deals specifically with the relation of sexuality with the symptom and with transference.

Freud makes it clear that sexuality does not intervene punctually, like a "deus ex machina", in the processes which characterise hysteria; it is, rather, the "motive power" (*Triebkraft*) of each symptom and every single manifestation of a symptom. It might be said that the symptoms are the sexual activity of the neurotic. It is a general rule: sexuality is the key to the problem of the neuroses. Nothing has been found to contradict this idea or limit its scope. "What I have hitherto heard against it have been expressions of personal dislike or disbelief. To these it is enough to reply in the words of Charcot: '*Ça n'empêche pas d'exister*'".[3]

Analysis transforms pathogenic psychic material into normal material; that is, it transforms unconscious sexual representations into "normal" modes of expression whose content becomes conscious. Satisfactory results are obtained if the symptoms are formed and maintained solely by internal conflict opposing impulses concerned with sexuality. But the analysis proceeds altogether differently if the symptoms are enlisted in the service of external motives (like Dora's symptoms in the two years preceding treatment). It is surprising and misleading to see that her condition does not show noticeable improvement despite the progress made in analysis. In truth, this is not very serious; the symptoms do not disappear while the analysis proceeds but a little later, when she breaks off her ties with the doctor. Indeed, the postponement of recovery or improvement is caused exclusively by "the physician's own person".

Here, Freud makes an observation whose import is considerable for the question we are examining. He writes:

It may be safely said that during psycho-analytic treatment the formation of new symptoms is invariably stopped. But the *productive powers of the neurosis* are by no means extinguished; they are occupied in the creation of a special class of mental structures, for the most part unconscious, to which the name '*transferences*' may be given.[4]

What are these transferences? "They are new editions or facsimiles of the impulses and phantasies which are aroused and made conscious during the progress of the analysis; but they have this peculiarity. . . that they replace some earlier person by the person of the physician". Indeed, some transferences are stereotyped reprints, copies of their model. Others are like works of art; they have undergone a moderating influence or sublimation, and they may even become conscious by using some real peculiarity of the physician or his circumstances. In that case, transferences are revised editions, rather than new impressions.

If the theory of analytic technique is gone into, it becomes evident that transference is an inevitable necessity. Practical experience, in all events, shows conclusively that there is no means of avoiding it and that this latest creation of the disease must be combated like all the earlier ones. This happens, however, to be by far the hardest part of the whole task. It is easy to learn how to interpret dreams, to extract from the patient's association his unconscious thoughts and memories and to practice similar explanatory arts for the patient himself will always provide the test. Transference is the one thing the presence of which has to be detected almost without assistance and with only the slightest clues to go on while, at the same time, the risk of making arbitrary inferences has to be avoided. Nevertheless, transference cannot be evaded since use is made of it in setting up all the obstacles that make the material inaccessible to treatment and since it is only after the transference has been resolved that a patient arrives at a sense of conviction of the validity of the connections which have been constructed during the analysis".[5]

This passage throws a bright light on the specificity of the analytic experience. A little further, Freud differentiates it from medical practice. Although he compares the work of the interpreter to that of the translator and uses metaphors referencing printing and editorial techniques to define transference, he warns the reader at once about the limitations of such figures of speech and stresses unambiguously the originality of analytic work. Neuroses are not texts or statements that translation skills can elucidate. Deciphering them requires placing the decipherer under scrutiny, through the thousands of points of emphasis and pleas for help the narrator of the text of associations addresses to the analyst. Each of these appeals to the other constitutes an instance of "transference". Transference cannot be avoided; it must be undone, deconstructed.

Transferences are new symptom formations during the analytic process; they are expressions of its "creativity". Like symptoms, they are the unconscious sexual activity of the neurotic. The latter has no access to the "normal" text of instinctual representations except through repetition: that is, in concrete terms, through the reiteration of his sexual demands. The analysis becomes the very setting of the displacement of the neurotic's questioning. The resistance which tends to put off the elucidation of his enquiries exerts its effect in the transference and serves to maintain the displacement of the question of neurosis itself. Transforming an unconscious text requires this detour or this passion. The analyst must identify the outstanding elements of this itinerary, must sense them in time (*erraten*), with no help from the analysand. But it is only through analysis of the transference that the analysand's work exerts its effect retrospectively, and the accuracy of "textual" reinterpretations can be recognised. Thus, the end of the analysis exerts its action from the beginning.

Transferences and identifications

Let us go back to Freud's prefatory remarks.

Some critics may point out that transference, this new reality created by the treatment, can only be an additional hindrance to the analytic process, which is difficult enough. The handling of transference complicates the therapeutic work since it produces pathological formations of a different type. It could even be claimed that analysis, which creates transference, is harmful to the patient, who is already suffering from his neurosis. Freud counters objections rooted in a medical perspective by saying that transference does not increase the labour of the analyst because, in any case, this work must overcome a certain tendency of the subject, whether it focuses on the analyst or on someone else. Moreover, the analysis does not demand – by reason of the transference – any effort the patient would not have been required to make otherwise in order to heal. Some neuroses are cured in institutions where no psychoanalysis is practiced; it has been said that hysterics have been cured not by the method but by the physician and that a sort of blind dependence and permanent attachment usually connect the patient with the doctor who cured him through hypnosis. The scientific explanation for this resides in the "transference" patients regularly develop towards the person of the physician. The psychoanalytic process does not create the transference; it only reveals it. This is where psychoanalysis must be differentiated from other forms of therapy. In the course of medical treatment, the patient normally calls up nothing more than affectionate and friendly transferences to help bring about his recovery. If he cannot call them up, he leaves as quickly as possible, avoiding the influence of a physician he dislikes. In psychoanalytic treatment, on the other hand, in addition to a different motivational structure, all incitements, even hostile tendencies, are solicited and placed in the service of the analysis by being rendered conscious; this causes the transference to be destroyed over and over. Freud concludes his answer to such objections by saying "Transference which seems ordained to be the greatest obstacle to psycho-analysis, becomes its most powerful ally, if its presence can be detected each time and explained to the patient".[6]

What can be called the didactic value of Dora's analysis consists of this phenomenon of transference. It was Freud's failure at handling the transference which explains the young girl's sudden departure. But this failure turned out to be enlightening since it led to the publication of a detailed account of the analysis: "I did not succeed in mastering the transference in good time", Freud says.

> Owing to the readiness with which Dora put one part of the pathogenic material at my disposal during the treatment, I neglected the precaution of looking

out for the first signs of transference, which was being prepared in connection with another part of the same material – a part of which I was in ignorance. At the beginning it was clear that *I was replacing her father in her imagination*, which was not unlikely, in view of the difference between our ages. She was even constantly comparing me with him consciously, and kept anxiously trying to make sure whether I was being quite straightforward with her, for her father "always preferred secrecy and roundabout ways".[7]

   In his interpretation of the first dream (the house on fire, her father who wakes her, her mother who wants to save her jewel case), Freud concentrated on his identification with the father. What he should have noted instead was the intention of the dream, which served as a warning: Dora's desire to leave the treatment as she had once left Herr K.'s house. Freud now states what his response to Dora's dream should have been:

> "[I]t is from Herr K. that you have made a transference on to me. Have you noticed anything that leads you to suspect me of evil intentions similar (whether openly or in some sublimated form) to Herr K.'s? Or have you been struck by anything about me or got to know anything about me which has caught your fancy, as happened previously with Herr K.?" Her attention would then have been turned to some detail in our relations, or in my person or circumstances, behind which there lay concealed something analogous but immeasurably more important concerning Herr K. And when this transference had been cleared up, the analysis would have obtained access to new memories. Dealing, probably, with actual events. But I was deaf to this first note of warning, thinking I had ample time before me, since no further stages of transference developed and the material for the analysis had not yet run dry. In this way the transference took me unawares, and, because of the unknown quantity in me which reminded Dora of Herr K., she took her revenge on me as she wanted to take her revenge on him, and deserted me as she believed herself to have been deceived and deserted by him. Thus, *she acted out* an essential part of her recollections and phantasies instead of reproducing it in the treatment. What this unknown quantity was I naturally cannot tell. I suspect that it had to do with money, or with jealousy of another patient who had kept up relations with my family after her recovery. When it is possible to work transference into the analysis at an early stage, the course of the analysis is retarded and obscured, but its existence is better guaranteed against sudden and overwhelming resistances.[8]

   I have quoted this passage word for word because it deserves particular attention. It provides a painstaking depiction of analytic work and its specific requirements. We note the repeated insistence on the timing of the transference (or transferences): "in good time, early". The analyst must react in time to the transference, which can take countless shapes, including that of a dream. This was the case for Dora's first dream.

Strangely, in this dream, she awakens, with her father by her side, in a house on fire. Freud identifies with the father. Dora's conscious remarks prompt him to do so. But it is precisely this identification with a real person, doubly supported (by Freud and by Dora) which causes the enigmatic element encrypted in the dream to be overlooked. Dora would have to produce a second dream to try to clarify things, but Freud would once again be duped by the game of masks of identifications.

This makes it clear that resistance to analytic work comes from the analyst's identification with the objects of transference.

By imagining himself in the place of a certain person, the analyst loses sight of the function Freud designates as X, this enigmatic, mysterious trait which, as long as it remains unknown, makes the analysis a labour of recollections and phantasy. If this X factor is missed – as we saw earlier – what is created is transference as a symptom, unconscious sexual activity, repetition without recollection, continual and untransformed demand. If left unanalysed, transference, despite being a punctual event (a "unary" phenomenon) transforms the analysis into a continuous dream, into a fulfilled phantasy in which to pursue a parade of displaced people, an endless cycle of mythical figures, with nothing to bring it to an end, to cause an awakening.

As I see it, this text lays out the entire difficulty of identification in psychoanalysis. Earlier, I described neurosis as the displacement of a problem; in analysis, transference, which replaces the process of symptom formation (the creativity of neurosis) is, strictly speaking, a displacement of discourses appearing at once as the risk of its cessation and an opportunity for its conversion.

In transference, displacement of the patient's quest occurs through addressing another in a kind of blind discourse, in which the other is not so much a person (Freud often speaks of "the person of the physician") as he is an interchangeable figure, to be substituted based on the logic of a "trait": an X factor which makes this figure the signifier of an eternal question. The analyst is forced into the role of an extra, as is the ego itself, which, as Lacan says, takes itself for many things and does the same with (few) others. Neurotic discourse assigns the ego and the other specific places. Identifications in dreams, reinforced in symptomatic formations and in transference, are enactments of material acted out in phantasy.

Phantasmatic figures transformed in dreams and in the transference tend to remain stuck there. Although Dora places Freud in the role of the father, he realises, in the aftermath, that he should not have placed himself in this role, thereby allowing Dora to assign the analyst a "fixed" place. The concepts of *fixation* and *regression* are built on the reality of transference. Analysing the transference ensures the mobility of the figures by undoing identifications, which are attempts at pinning the other in place by pinning oneself in place. Identification cannot be transitive without being reflexive; there can be no statement without stating.

The psychoanalyst in his place

Dora's second dream is the one whose interpretation is interrupted when she breaks off the analysis. In this dream, the transference is manifest in several clear elements. The dream is a dense weave of multiple identifications, each one having its own particular characteristics: substitution of places (strange town, railway station, house, thick wood, cemetery), substitution of times (five minutes, two and a half hours, two hours), substitution of people (the mother, the dead father, the young man, the maid, the concierge), substitution of verbs (to wander, to enter, to ask, to penetrate, to question, to see, to be unable to wait).

> At the time she was telling me the dream I was still unaware (and did not learn until two days later) that we had only *two hours* more work before us. This was the same length of time which she had spent in front of the Sistine Madonna, and which [by making a correction and saying "two hours" instead of "two and a half hours"] she had taken as the length of the walk which she had not made round the lake. The striving and waiting in the dream, which related to the young man in Germany, and had their origin in her waiting till Herr K. could marry her, had been expressed in the transference a few days before. The treatment, she had thought, was too long for her; she would never have the patience to wait so long. And yet in the first few weeks she had had discernment enough to listen without making any such objections when I informed her that her complete recovery would require perhaps a year. Her refusing in the dream to be accompanied, and preferring to go alone, also originated from her visit to the gallery at Dresden, and I was myself to experience them on the appointed day. What they meant was, no doubt: "Men are all so detestable that I would rather not marry. This is my revenge".

In 1923, Freud added a very important note here, which testifies to the working-through of the analysis of the transference on the part of the analyst, and to how long it takes to understand:

> The longer the interval of time that separates me from the end of the analysis, the more probable it seems to me that the fault in my technique lay in this omission: I failed to discover in time and to inform the patient that her homosexual [gynaecophilic] love for Frau K. was the strongest unconscious current in her mental life. I ought to have guessed that the main source of her knowledge of sexual matters could have been no one but Frau K. – the very person who later on charged her with being interested in those same subjects. Her knowing all about such things and, at the same time, her always pretending not to know where her knowledge came from was really too remarkable. I ought to have attacked this riddle and looked for the motive of such an extraordinary piece of repression. If I had done this, the second dream would have given me my answer. The remorseless craving for revenge expressed in

that dream was suited as nothing else was to conceal the current of feeling that ran contrary to it – the magnanimity with which she forgave the treachery of the friend she loved and concealed from everyone the fact that it was this friend who had herself revealed to her the knowledge which had later been the foundation of the accusations against her. Before I had learned the importance of the homosexual current of felling in psychoneurotics, I was often brought to a standstill in the treatment of my cases or found myself in complete perplexity.[9]

Transference, like dreams, is governed by primary thought processes: condensation, identification, displacement. Like all symptom formations, it is overdetermined – synchronically and diachronically. The interpretation of the transference coincides with the interpretation of the dream.

Transference, like the dream, is a way of recollecting. But analysis creates a space where the dream and the symptom can combine in an articulation which, provided it is heard, reveals the unconscious assignment of the other to the status of object. The analyst is invited to identify with this status but is only expected to occupy this place until he "guesses" its preliminary function: it is the place to leave vacant so that awakening can come about. This awakening is never free of anxiety and hate turned towards the "object", which is not in the right place to allow jouissance.

What Freud failed to hear was the overdetermination of the transference as condensation, as constellation of contradictory figures, a vector of identifications, the origin of names and therefore of desired others. Freud believed that what was at stake in this treatment was love, love for a man (the father, Herr K., Freud, the young man); what he failed to see was desire, hidden in unexamined figures, in unanalysed identifications which safeguard repression. Freud responded to Dora's wish to replace the father by identifying with the recovered Oedipal object; his focus on love made him impervious to the idea that the locus of the analysis, its "house", could just as well be, for his young patient, Herr K. and Frau K.'s house. Analysis is not a matter of encountering each other again. But, in popular language, love is said to be a matter of finding each other. This expression allows the concept of love to preserve all its ambiguity. If we take Freud at his word and quote from *Analysis Terminable and Interminable*, we grasp the scope of his statement: "An analysis is ended when the analyst and patient cease to meet for the analytic session".[10]

The analyst cannot totally avoid narcissistic traps produced by introjection or the fear of being taken for another and functioning, for the subject, as an enigmatic signifier of instinctual demands. If he perceives these transferences "in time", he can interpret them as "thought formations", which transform reminiscences into recollections. For Freud, identifying with the father or with Herr K. meant being deceived, mistaking love for the solution to neurosis and for an impossible resolution of the transference.

Freud's clarification of the identification process through lessons learned from transference leads to the recognition that a subject who remains unconscious cannot be described. It cannot be said that he identifies with someone, with a "person", but only with signifiers representing someone. The game of neurotic transference, which, in fact, constitutes neurosis, consists of substituting the image of love (with its parental figures) for signifiers of desire. And Freud's embarrassment shows that the analyst is not immune to the error that teaches him, always too late, in what way he is still, unknowingly, a supporter of neurosis and of the concrete person.

From symptom analysis to identification theory

These considerations bring us back to the specificity of psychoanalysis. This question of the "person" designates what we shall call, as Lacan did, the "subversion of the subject".[11] Still, Freud's references to the person of the physician, the person of the patient, et cetera, are surprising. He uses this language precisely when he completely overturns psychology, and specifically the psychology of the doctor-patient relationship. Here, we come up against the limits of Freud's language, which can only be remedied by using another type of speech. Therefore, we are indebted to Lacan for introducing this kind of mega-speech (not metalanguage), particularly in the production of the distinct concepts of the ego, the subject, the other and the Other, all of them associated with the theory of the signifier.

Lacan's theory of specular identification, contributing to ego formation, is based, in hindsight, on his theory of identification of the subject with the signifier. To establish his theory, Lacan makes ingenious use of a text in which Freud enumerates the elements of his identification doctrine. This text recapitulates the lessons learned from Dora's analysis. One of the young girl's most persistent and overdetermined symptoms was, as we still remember, a nervous cough, also called catarrh. This symptom is a surprisingly significant condensation of her complex family story and one of the more troubling aspects of her "personal myth". On the one hand, Dora presents the same symptom as her mother.

This identification, originating in the Oedipus complex, designates the hostile wish to replace her mother; the symptom represents its fulfilment and expresses object-love for the father: it enacts the replacement of the mother under conditions of guilt ("you wanted to be your mother, now you are, at least as far as suffering is concerned"). On the other hand, the symptom is the same as that of the love object since Dora imitates her father. Here, identification is substituted for object-choice, the latter becoming secondary to identification. Keeping in mind that identification is the earliest form of emotional attachment, the conditions of symptom formation – repression – subject the ego to the rule of unconscious psychic processes, a realm in which to love means to devour, to assimilate in a primitive manner. In hysterics, identification takes an extremely limited form, borrowing a single trait of the chosen object (*Objektperson*). In Dora's case, two Oedipal object "traits" are present; they are the signifiers between which her desire fluctuates. But these traits are also symptoms (cough, catarrh); that is, they designate a flaw in these others, allowing Dora to deny them the function of "models".[12]

We have only to consider these few concepts to grasp the complexity of symptom formation and its connection to identification. At the unconscious level, desire is the interpretation of identification; it is fulfilled through imitation of its objects – the "unary", singular traits taken from them in accordance with the laws of dismembering, which do not respect the integrity of "persons". This dismembering is carried out according to the rules of the signifier (the primary process). The laws of desire do not coincide with the laws governing the image; Dora's enigma is not solved by repression of her love for the man, because this would be guilt-ridden love for the incomparable father; nor is it solved by her unconscious homosexual love for the woman. What the neurosis attempts to preserve is the space of "neither one nor the other", a scene which painfully prolongs the impossible dream of being the one and the other.

The meaning of the symptom and the end of the analysis

To complete our discussion of the foundations and renewed beginnings of psychoanalysis, let us return to our initial question: how is the physician's approach to the symptom different from that of the psychoanalyst?

As we know, one of the heuristic and ethical principles of analysis states that the neurotic symptom is not a sign but has a meaning: it is the enactment of the unconscious knowledge of the subject.

Freud specifies:

> It will take the strenuous labor of many months, even years, to show that the symptoms in a case of neurotic break-down have their meaning, serve a purpose, and result from the fortunes of the patient. On the other hand, the efforts of a few hours suffice in providing the same content in a dream product which at first seems incomprehensibly confused.[13]

It takes longer to recover from a neurosis than to recover from a dream, but both are the effect of the same psychic mechanisms – the therapeutic relation is governed by the same laws as the dream. This principle further differentiates psychoanalysis from the medical conception of treatment. But Freud goes even further: the purpose of the symptom is always the fulfilment of sexual phantasies. Symptoms act in the service of the patient's sexual jouissance; they are substitutes for the same type of satisfaction when the patient avoids experiencing it in ordinary circumstances. The "meaning" of the symptom escapes consciousness; indeed, the meaning must remain unconscious in order for the symptom to appear. Symptoms disappear when the neurotic *knows* what they mean. But how does he come to now? His knowledge must be founded on internal change, a change produced by the analytic work whose aim is to fill in gaps in memory and eliminate amnesias (hysteria) or to re-establish the links between memories (obsession).

> We have combined two things as the meaning of the symptom, its *whence*, on the one hand, and its *whither* or *why*, on the other. By these we mean to indicate the impressions and experiences whence the symptom arises, and the purpose the symptom serves. The "whence" of a symptom is tracked back to

impressions which have come from without, which have therefore necessarily been conscious at some time, but which may have sunk into the unconscious that it, have been forgotten. The "why" of the symptom, its tendency, is in every case an endopsychic process, developed from within, which may or may not have become conscious at first, but could just as readily never have entered consciousness at all and have been unconscious from its inception. It is, after all, not so very significant that, as happens in the hysterias, amnesia has covered over the "whence" of the symptom, the experience upon which it is based; for it is the why, the tendency of the symptom, which establishes its dependence on the unconscious.[14]

Instead of remembering, the neurotic reproduces the attitudes and feelings he has experienced through transference. These psychic materials always place themselves in the service of resistance at first, showing only hostility to the treatment.

Analysis of transference resistance is the foundation of psychoanalytic work with neurosis and justifies abandoning hypnosis, which hides resistance, keeping it repressed. Symptoms appear as a result of a psychic process which cannot achieve its ends; we will only be able to reconstitute this process at the state of dissociation when the transference undergoes interpretation. Repression prevents the process from being completed, keeping it out of the realm of reality. The symptom replaces transformation of the outside world by transformation of the body: like the dream, it produces infantile satisfaction; it relies on the pleasure principle, on a sort of "increased auto-eroticism".

Thus, analysis is a space in which "new knowledge" is constructed to replace the symptom formation. The only way to learn something from these symptoms is to let transferences play their role since they instigate and reinterpret the symptoms.

The "end of analysis" is not simply a term; it is a process which builds regular knowledge ("there are various kinds of knowing", Freud says, on the model of Molière's "*Il y a fagot et fagot*"). The patient's new knowledge takes the place of an unconscious jouissance, which is the "meaning of his symptom".

As Lacan has pointed out many times, the end of analysis is not identification with the analyst, nor is it identification with the unconscious, which remains the Other, the origin of the signifiers of the entity we call a subject. "So then, in what does this mapping out called analysis consist?" Lacan asks in his seminar. "*L'insu que sait*". And he answers:

> Might it be or might it not be, to identify oneself, to identify oneself while taking some insurance, a kind of distance, to identify oneself to one's symptom? I put forward that the symptom could be. . . the sexual partner. . . . [I]t is a fact, I put forward that the symptom taken in this sense is. . . what you know, it is even what you know best, without that going very far. . . . So then what does knowing mean? Knowing means being able to deal with the symptom, knowing how to sort it out, knowing how to manipulate it, to know, this is something that corresponds to what man does with his image, it is to

imagine the way in which you can manage this symptom. What is in question here, of course, is secondary narcissism, radical narcissism, narcissism that is called primary being ruled out on this particular occasion. Knowing how to deal with your symptom, that is the end of the analysis.[15]

The end of analysis could be to change in the way *symptom* is written; is this the extent of the change achieved by Lacan when he replaced *symptom* with *synthome*? Contrary to medicine, the aim of analysis is not, if we are to believe both Freud and Lacan, a suppression of the symptom comparable to the removal of a foreign body. Analysis is not exorcism. It is, rather, a shifting of knowledge, allowing the knowledge contained in the symptom, in dreams and in transference to be deciphered so that the underlying desire can be fulfilled: in "reality", says Freud; in "knowing how to handle it", says Lacan – but, in either case, through an act which creates otherness.

Thus, the analytic practice that deals with the symptom makes demands on the analyst. The fact that he is "the subjects-supposed-to-know", the "target" of transference, can only provoke his resistance and even revulsion. Freud observes (in "Psychoanalysis and Psychiatry", 16th lecture):

Perhaps the physician's habit of steering clear of his neurotic patients and listening so very casually to what they have to say allows him to lose sight of the possibility of deriving anything valuable from his patient's communications, and therefore, of making penetrating observations on them.

Of course, paying attention to what patients say is what any good doctor does. Analysis is different from sympathetic listening because it provides a way of dealing with what is said and doing something with it within its communication structure, which is already transferential. What is said is not only subjective information about the illness; it is a substitutive formation, the invention of a renewed mode of engaging the analyst. If the analyst is drawn in, he will experience anxiety and even horror, according to some. But this is no more than the unavoidable flip side of a process of discovery that always produces a special joy: that born of combining research with "healing".

Notes

* This is a slightly modified version of a text published in *Revue Psychiatries*, January 1984 issue. We thank the journal for permission to reproduce the text in the present work.

1 Freud, S., *The Origins of Psycho-Analysis: Letters to Wilhelm Fliess, Drafts and Notes, 1887–1902*, New York: Basic Books, 1954.

2 Freud, S., *Fragment of an Analysis of a Case of Hysteria*, S.E. 7: 1–122, London: Hogarth, 1905.

3 Ibid., p. 114.

4 Emphasis added.

5   Ibid., pp. 115–116.

6   Ibid., p. 117.

7   Ibid., p. 118. Emphasis added.

8   Ibid., pp. 118–119.

9   Ibid., pp. 119–121.

10   Freud, S., *Analysis Terminable and Interminable*, S.E. 23, London: Hogarth, 1937.

11   Lacan, J., "Subversion of the Subject and the Dialectics of Desire", in *Écrits: A Selection*, Sheridan, A. (Trans.), London: Tavistock/Routledge, 1977. In this text, which is the transcription of the seminar "Formations of the Unconscious", built around the diagram illustrating the concept of subject, Lacan shows the intertwining of the double process of identification: symbolic identification, constitutive of the ego ideal, rooting the subject in the signifier (the field of the Other), and imaginary identification, in which the ego as a form (or gestalt) is a precipitate while still manifesting its object status and reciprocal relation with the little Other. We can easily grasp the richness of the necessary distinction between the "subject" and the "ego" – a distinction already made by Freud (for instance, in differentiating the "subject" from the ego and from the ego as object – see our analysis) – in the analytic process. A new study is needed to show the extent of Lacan's efforts to rigorously maintain not only the theoretical particularity of psychoanalysis (it is not a psychology of the ego), but also its ethical character: the subject is the movement of a question. Transference lends itself as a possibility to understand this question in its very movement. Identifications are the trail of white pebbles left along the way.

12   Dora's double identification with the traits of her Oedipal objects provides a clinical illustration of Lacan's statement: "The signifier represents the subject for another signifier".

13   Freud, S., *A General Introduction to Psychoanalysis*, New York: Boni and Liveright, 1920, p. 205.

14   Ibid., p. 247.

15   Lacan, J., "Seminar XXIV", 1976–77, www.lacaninireland.com.

Exergue

In a discipline that owes its scientific value solely to the theoretical concepts that Freud forged in the progress of his experience – concepts which by continuing to be badly criticized and yet retaining the ambiguity of the vulgar tongue, benefit, with a certain risk of misunderstanding, from these resonances – it would seem to me to be premature to break with the tradition of their terminology.

But it seems to me that these terms can only become clear if one establishes their equivalence to the language of contemporary anthropology, or even to the latest problems in philosophy, fields in which psychoanalysis could well regain its health.

In any case, I consider it to be an urgent task to disengage from concepts that are being deadened by routine use the meaning that they regain both from a re-examination of their history and from a reflection on their subjective foundations.

J. Lacan*

This epigraph lends our discussion its style and its orientation; it structures its development. Indeed, our intention is to follow as closely as possible, in Freud's writing, the stages of the construction of a fundamental concept of psychoanalysis: the concept of identification.

Burdened with the meanings conferred on it by common language, this term has acquired, since the introduction of its psychoanalytic version, a surprising destiny within various terminologies in the human sciences, ranging from psychiatry to psycho-sociology. Among analysts themselves, the term seems to have put an end to the problem that always plagued Freud: that it lost its meaning through routine use. Today, the term *identification* seems to be firmly established in the conceptional inventory of psychoanalysis. There is little place left for the uncertainty of what for us remains a question and no doubt *the* question Freud had only began to formulate: the question of the "subject" – the subject in relation to the unconscious, not the subject of knowledge.

By patiently following the sequence of steps that inscribed this term in the theory based on experiencing the original effects of the unconscious, we might be able to undo, to "analyse" the intertwining of the established meanings of this term, now indissociable from similar concepts like ego, ideal, intersubjectivity, empathy, et cetera. Such an analysis would also make it possible to identify the subversive effects produced by Freud on the psychology of the ego and on knowledge in general.

Thus, identification might have constituted a secular question whose formulation became more complex when Freud connected it to its mythical origin.

This immemorial question is an intrinsic part of the riddle presented by the Sphinx to the inhabitants of Thebes. And there is only one possible answer, enacted in the birth of a subject. Oedipus. Of course, this question became somewhat lost in the hubbub of the endless discourse on the Same and the Other, identity and difference, desire and the law, the ego and the other. By making use of the term *identification*, without ever making it the object of a general metapsychological system, Freud shifted the implications of this very old concept. He took the concept as he found it in his everyday reality: in analysis, in the experience of transference.

Freud took this major concept which had always belonged to the speculative sphere of philosophy and placed it under a completely different light.

Our intention is to point out the decisive moments of this Freudian endeavour in the expansion of the concept.

Notes

* Lacan, J., *Écrits: A Selection*, Sheridan, A. (Trans.), London: Routledge, 1989, p. 25.

Identification and symptom formation

It was in the analysis of dreams and neuroses that Freud detected the work of identification. Initially, he used this concept uncritically, or innocently, as we might say. Later, when he had formulated his first theoretical questions about identification, he would give the term alternately its conceptual meaning and the meaning it has in common usage. As we shall see, this ambiguity was paralleled throughout Freud's work by indecision about the theory itself, which he never resolved and which delegated the question of identification to the periphery of the doctrine he was elaborating, without putting an end to the development and structuring of concepts related to it.

According to a remark made by Freud in a letter to Ferenczi, he believed that his productivity followed a certain rhythm:

> My good ideas actually occur in seven-year cycles: in 1891 I started working on aphasia; in 1898/9, the interpretation of dreams; in 1904/5, wit and its relation to the unconscious; in 1911/12, totem and taboo; thus I am probably in the waning stage and won't be able to count on anything of importance before 1918/1919 (provided the chain doesn't break before).[1]

We can keep this rhythm in mind as we follow Freud's thought development. His fascination with chronological cycles is no doubt rooted in his former friendship with Wilhelm Fliess, a friendship to which we owe the emergence of psychoanalysis, as Octave Mannoni so aptly remarked.[2]

It is in the correspondence with Fliess that we find the term *identification* for the first time in the large body of work at our disposal today. Lacan designates as "Freud I" the works produced by Freud in the first three cycles of his "goods ideas": that is, approximately between 1891 and 1913. He started to rethink and reshape his ideas in 1913; this period, known as "Freud II", produced the theory of narcissism, the metapsychology and the technical writings. Based on this cycle, after the First World War, the reassessment period called "Freud III" started in 1918.

This division of Freud's work into three parts seems to us to require a more systematic classification, highlighting the distinct stages of the theoretical edifice.

Identification: the first references

The Freud-Fliess correspondence records the period of redefinition of the theory of neurosis and describes the occurrence of the initial exploration of the concept of identification.

Most often, the term is used as it is defined in ordinary language, in the empirical context of interpretation of a neurotic symptom or a dream fragment.[3] Each time, Freud uses it in the description of a psychological phenomenon he observes in his patients or in his own world. Many dreams Freud partially analyses in the *Interpretation* or in his correspondence reveal the diversity of individuals with whom Freud identified: relatives, friends, mentors, professors, theories in antiquity, fictional character, writers, painters, playwrights, et cetera.[4]

Nevertheless, it is clear that, regardless of the topic, Freud presents his clinical descriptions from a perspective he considers important. Let us look at some fragments of text whose conceptual organisation and psychological context seem to point to the emergence of the concept of identification in analytic theory. If we succeed in showing that this term is only used in certain contexts and in relation to certain rather specific questions, the usefulness of this initial work of selection and differentiation, at the level of language itself, will appear evident. If, however, these occurrences are shown to form a system, it will become reasonable to foresee the development of a topic whose scope will be revealed in the subsequent theoretical discussion.

These particularly significant texts are among Freud's contributions to the psychopathology and psychotherapy of "nervous disorders" – specifically, hysteria, phobia, obsessional neurosis, melancholia and paranoia. The letters to Fliess offer the advantage of revealing the direction of the intellectual enquiry underlying the progress, hesitations, setbacks and satisfactions present in these contributions.

The letter fragments which follow are presented in chronological order; certain symptoms are underscored and the corrections between the topics discussed are pointed out.

Letter Vienna, 17–12–1896

> "Fear of throwing oneself out of the window" is a *misconstruction* by the conscious or rather the preconscious, and relates to an unconscious content in which window appears and can be dissected as follows:
> Anxiety + ... window. . . . . . ; explained thus:
> Unconscious idea: going to the window to beckon to a man *as prostitutes do*: sexual release arising from this idea;
> Preconsciousness: rejection, hence anxiety arising from the release of sexuality. . . . I have confirmed, for instance, a long-standing suspicion about the mechanism of agoraphobia in women. You will guess it if you think of prostitutes. *It is the repression of the impulse* to take the first comer on the streets – *envy* of the prostitute and *identification* with her.

From the very first time it emerges, the concept of identification is presented in the specific context of emotional conflict, and associated with the mechanism of sexual repression.

Letter Vienna, 8–2–1897

Somnambulism . . . turns out to have been correctly diagnosed. The latest result is the explanation of tonic hysterical spasm. It is the *imitation* of death with *rigor mortis, i.e., identification with someone who is dead.*

Here, the words *imitation* and *identification* are used interchangeably.

Draft L with Letter 2–5–1897

The architecture of hysteria

The aim seems to be to arrive [back] at the primal scenes.

The part played by servant-girls

An immense load of guilt, with self-reproaches (for theft, abortion, etc.) is made possible [for a woman] *by identification with these people of low morals*, who are so often remembered by her as worthless women *connected sexually with her father or brother.* . . . There is a tragic justice in the fact that the action of the head of the family in stooping to relations with a servant-girl is atoned for by his daughter's self-abasement.

Mushrooms ["Schwamm" means both mushroom and sponge]

There was a girl last summer who was afraid to pick a flower or even to pull up a mushroom, because it was against the command of God, who did not wish living seeds to be destroyed. This arose from a memory of religious maxims of her mother's directed against precautions during coitus, because they meant that living seeds are destroyed. . . . *The main content of her neurosis was identification with her mother.*

Multiplicity of psychical personalities

The fact of identification perhaps allows us to *take the phrase literally.*

The numerous characters with whom the hysteric identifies become unstable figures, a series of images in which he recognises himself and in which this self is lost. These multiple identifications are no doubt a reflection of the psychic structure itself.

Agoraphobia

Agoraphobia seems to depend on a *romance* of prostitution which itself goes back once more to this family romance. Thus a woman who will not go out by herself is asserting her mother's unfaithfulness.

A family story and imaginary, romanticised reconstruction of the first infantile attachments, form the basis of symptom formation through identification.

Draft N with letter 31–5–1897

Impulses

Hostile impulses against parents (a wish that they should die) are also an integral constituent of neuroses. They come to light consciously as obsessional ideas.

In paranoia what is worst in delusions of persecution (pathological distrust of rulers and monarchs) corresponds to these impulses. They are *repressed at times when compassion* for the parents is active – at times of their illness or death. On such occasions it is a manifestation of *mourning* to reproach oneself for their death (what is known as melancholia) or to *punish oneself in a hysterical fashion* (through the medium of the idea of retribution) *with the same states that they have had. The identification which occurs here is, as we can see, nothing other than a mode of thinking and does not relieve us of the necessity for looking for the motive.*

It seems as though this death wish is directed in sons against their father and in daughters against their mother.

Poetry and "fine frenzy"

The mechanism of poetry is the same as that of hysterical phantasies. For his *Werther*, Goethe combined something he had experienced (his love for Lotte Kästner) and something he had heard (the fate of young Jerusalem who died by his own hand). He was probably toying with the idea of killing himself and found a point of contact in that and *identified himself with Jerusalem,* to whom he lent a motive from his own love-story. By means of this phantasy he protected himself from the consequences of his experience.

So Shakespeare was right in his juxtaposition of poetry and madness (fine frenzy).

Motives for the construction of symptoms

Remembering is never a motive but only a way, a method. *The first motive for the formation of symptoms is, chronologically, libido.* Thus symptoms, like dreams, are the fulfillment of a wish. . . . *The construction of symptoms by identification* is linked to phantasies – that is, to their repression in the unconscious – *in an analogous way to the alternation of the ego in paranoia.*

These scattered observations carry the seeds of important developments that were to continue over time. But from the outset, we note the connections drawn between identification, mourning, melancholia, pity and structure of the ego. The recognition of the role of identification in the work of the writer is also worth nothing.

In his letter dated October 3, 1897, Freud describes to Fliess the discoveries he is making in his "self-analysis". This letter follows the one written on September 21, in which he wrote, "I no longer believe in my neurotica": that is, in his theory that the origin of the neuroses was to be found in the childhood experiences his patients related to him. Of course, this relativisation of the reality of "seduction scenes" presented as memories and the discovery of the reality of phantasy came about thanks to his self-analysis.

At the same time, Freud went back to reading Shakespeare, and particularly Hamlet, as well as a play by Franz Grillparzer, *Die Ahnfrau* (*The Ancestor*). But he felt that this play failed to move the audience, despite being a "tragedy of fate"; this prompted him to reflect on the riveting power of works that belonged to the classical tragic genre.

The letter dated October 15, 1897, records an auspicious moment in the development of psychoanalysis, and a critical stage in distinguishing phantasy from the Oedipal tragedy and its relation to identification:

One single thought of general value has been revealed to me. I have found, in my own case too, falling in love with the mother and jealousy of the father, and I now regard it as a universal event of early childhood, even if not so early as in children who have been made hysterical. (Similarly with the romance of parentage in paranoia – heroes, founders of religions). If this is so, we can understand the *riveting power of Oedipus Rex*, in spite of all the objections raised by reason against its presupposition of destiny; and we can understand why the later "dramas of destiny" were bound to fail so miserably. Our feelings rise against any arbitrary individual compulsion, such as is presupposed in *Die Ahnfrau*, etc. But the Greek legend seizes on a *compulsion which everyone recognizes* because he feels its existence within himself. *Each member of the audience was once, in germ and in phantasy, just as Oedipus and each one recoils in horror from the dream-fulfillment here transplanted into reality, with the whole quota of repression which separates his infantile state from his present one.*

A fleeting idea has passed through my head of whether the same thing may not lie at the bottom of *Hamlet* as well. I am not thinking of Shakespeare's conscious intention, but I believe rather that here some real event instigated the poet to his representation, in that the unconscious in him understood the unconscious in his hero. How can Hamlet the hysteric justify his words: "Thus conscience does make cowards of us all", how can he explain his hesitation in avenging his father by the murder of his uncle – he, the same man who sends his courtiers to their death without a scruple and who is positively precipitate in killing Laertes? How better could he justify himself than by the torment he suffers from the obscure memory that he himself had mediated the same deed against his father from passion for his mother, and – "use every man after his desert, and who should 'scape whipping?'" His conscience is his unconscious sense of guilt. And is not his sexual alienation in his conversation with Ophelia typically hysterical? and his rejection of the instinct which seeks to beget children? and, finally, his transferring the deed from his own father to Ophelia's? And does he not in the end, in the same remarkable way as my hysterical patients, *bring down punishment on himself by suffering the same fate as his father of being poisoned by the same rival*?

Let us draw attention to some important elements presented here in a fleeting fashion. This text is, indeed, a foreshadowing of the Oedipus complex, although its significance is only suggested through the passion and pathos created by dramatic performance in the theatre. All this contributes to the understanding of identification, although no mention of it is made in this letter. Freud was to elucidate the identification process by looking at the dramatic effect of a staged performance – be it the acting out of hysterics or classical tragedy.

The riveting power exerted by the recognition[5] of a universal compulsion relies on the spectator's identification with the drama, with what transpires, what takes place between the protagonists portrayed – and not only with a single hero. In fact, Freud uses the very terms used by Aristotle in his *Poetics*: the mimetic function of the fable, "recognition" of the events of the plot, riveting power and catharsis. But Freud stresses the unconscious nature of identification as an effect of repression; he places identification in the sphere of the imaginary ("*in der Phantasie*"). However, a long latency period would prove necessary before Freud was going to develop all the elements drawing a parallel between Oedipus and Hamlet[6] as he presents them here and in the *Interpretation of Dreams*, where they are examined in greater depth.

Letter 27–9–1898

> He is a young man of twenty-five, who can scarcely walk owing to stiffness of the legs, spasms, tremors, etc. A safeguard against any wrong diagnosis is provided by the accompanying *anxiety*, which makes him cling to his mother's apron-strings, like the baby that lies hidden behind. The death of his brother and the death of his father in a psychosis precipitated the onset of his condition, which has been present since he was fourteen. He feels *ashamed* in front of anyone who sees him walking in this way and *regards that as natural*. *His model* is a tabetic uncle, with whom he already *identified himself* at the age of thirteen on account of the accepted aetiology (leading a dissolute life).

Analysis always reveals, behind the symptom, a family story, an unconscious sexual saga played out through identifications.

Letter 9–12–1899

> I have before me the problem of "*choice of neurosis*". When does a person become hysterical instead of paranoid? A first crude attempt, made at a

time when I was trying to storm the citadel by force, put forward the view that it depended on the age at which the sexual traumas occurred [see Letter 20–5–1896]. I gave that up long ago, when a *link with the theory of sexuality* dawned on me.

The lower sexual stratum is *auto-erotism*, which does without any psycho-sexual aim and demands only local feelings of satisfaction. It is succeeded by allo-erotism (homo- and hetero-erotism); but it certainly also continues to exist as a separate current. *Hysteria (and its variant, obsessional neurosis) is allo-erotic: its main path is identification with the person loved. Paranoia dissolved the identification once more; it re-establishes all the figures loved in childhood . . . and it dissolved the ego itself into extraneous figures.* Thus I have come to regard paranoia as a forward surge of the auto-erotic current, as a return to the standpoint prevailing then.

These texts require explanation. As soon as the elaboration of psychoanalysis began, the concept of identification emerged, associated with a constellation of other concepts which together created a system. This system governed a theoretical corpus whose ramifications, instead of coming together, continued to spread in different directions as the analytic experience progressed. Having crossed the threshold thanks to the Freud-Fliess correspondence, let us trace the stages of this emerging body of knowledge.

When we read all the letters written at the same time as *Studies on Hysteria, Project for a Scientific Psychology*, the *Interpretation, The Psychopathology of Everyday Life*, Dora's case and *Jokes*, we notice a certain clustering of topics which reflect the major ideas of psychoanalysis: the sexual origin of neuroses, the role of phantasy in dream and symptom formation, the relation of phantasy to primitive scenes and to the family narrative, psychic structure and dynamics, anxiety and repression. This is the web in which identification is caught, more or less loosely.

Often, it is someone else's sexual activity which awakens, through jealousy or identification – the same sexual compulsion as in the hysteric, but a compulsion quickly repressed. The symptom (agoraphobia, shame, self-abasement, cramps, shaking) replaces the satisfaction of this compulsion, appearing as a form of self-punishment.

In this case, identification is the key to deciphering the symptom, provided the unconscious logic in which it is rooted is formulated. Identification is the "method", the path taken by this sequence of ideas – this phantasy or, better still, this unconscious story (repressed) – in its effort to find expression. Indeed, the thought or the wish is always the same: "If only I could *act like* this person: the father, the mother, the brother, the prostitute, the servant-girl". Here, the concept of identification is associated with that of imitation, and it often follows it. This pseudo-synonym status is reflected in the term *model* (*Vorbild*). But it must be made clear that in identification, the imitation is desired, dreamed of; when it is actually enacted, this is done unknowingly, through a symptom.

The last letter quoted, in which Freud formulates a general hypothesis of the neuroses, provides a different idea than earlier ones concerning the object of the identification. In a context of hysteria, this object is the rival, of whom one is jealous. This time, Freud writes that hysteria is allo-erotic and expresses itself mainly through identification with the beloved. This reveals an intriguing particularity of neurosis: the ambiguity of the subject's phantasmatic position. While the hysteric identifies with the love object and with the rival (or the envied model), identification as a "method" can serve various "purposes", including aims that are contradictory (heterosexual and homosexual).

As for paranoia, the claim is that is dissolves identifications, re-establishes the figures loved in childhood and dissolves the ego into extraneous figures. Another way to say this is: "The fact of identification perhaps allows us to take the phrase literally". Here, the problem of the ego is touched upon, but Freud does not develop the topic: the plurality of its constitution, the figures loved in the past and the "lost objects" of childhood which comprise it. Identification is a name well suited to the constitution of this essentially plural ego, fragile because it can be split and stratified.[7]

These observations highlight two questions whose interrelation will be demonstrated in our subsequent discussion. Thanks to the many shapes hysteria can take, identification can easily be seen as the staging of a phantasmatic, usually sexual, scene: the theatrical production of an action bringing together characters in a drama, in a common "crime". Hysteria introduces the "specular" dimension of sexuality and what it produces in the phantasy played out or represented in symptomatic identification. Hysterical identification provides an understanding of theatrical representation in general, of the possibilities of dramatic art and the philosophical and psychological theories that have often taken over its definition in the course of time.

The second question, highlighted by paranoia as a pathological formation, is that known as the "constitution of the ego", its genesis and its intersubjective structure. Guilt, mourning and melancholia are all related questions.

Although its contours are still blurred, this is the field we have defined so far as the object of our research. Now, we shall gather the descriptive and diagnostic elements following Freud's own method: not simply finding "modes of thinking" or "paths", but looking for the motives, the forces which promote identification.

Hysterical identification

The dream of the "witty butcher's wife"

In parallel with his proto-analytic and scientific dialogue with Fliess, Freud's trajectory leads him to explore dreams. His major work *The Interpretation of Dreams* is the logical, unavoidable outcome of his first studies of neurosis. He writes, in a letter to Wilhelm Fliess:

> [T]he dream schema is capable of the most general application. . . the key to
> hysteria as well really lies in dreams. I now also understand why in spite of

all my efforts I have not yet finished the dream [book]. If I wait a little longer, I shall be able to present the psychic process in dreams in such a way that it also includes the process in the formation of hysterical symptoms.[8]

The Interpretation of Dreams provides a complete description of the dream process, as well as a peremptory clinical illustration of the structural connection between the dream process and hysterical processes provided by the Dora case.[9]

It is important to note that the relationship between dream and hysteria is brought to light during a detailed discussion of the identification function and its connection with the general drive to wish fulfilment.

The letter excerpt that follows establishes the foundations for this discussion:

> My latest generalization holds good and seems inclined to spread to an unpredictable extent. It is not only dreams that are fulfillments of wishes, but hysterical attacks as well. This is true of hysterical symptoms, but it probably applies to every product of neurosis. . . . Reality – wish fulfillment: it is from this contrasting pair that our mental life springs. I believe I now know the determining condition which distinguishes dreams from symptoms that force their way into waking life. It is enough for a dream to be wish fulfillment of repressed thought; for a dream is kept apart from reality. But a symptom, which has its place in actual life, must be something else as well – the wish fulfillment of the *repressing* thought. A symptom arises where the repressed and the repressing thoughts can come together in the fulfillment of a wish. A symptom, in its character of a punishment, for instance, is a wish-fulfillment of the repressing thought, while self-punishment is the final substitute for self-gratification – for masturbation.[10]

This is the theoretical ground underlying the questioning that was to follow: what is the difference between dream and symptom, given that both function as fulfillers of wishes?

The fourth chapter of *The Interpretation of Dreams* deals with the most obvious and pressing question posed by dream interpretation: how and why does "*Entstellung*"[11] deformation come about?

What is their use, and who benefits from these distortions, these absurdities present in dreams? Of course, these questions are dealt with at length in a subsequent chapter, "The Dream-Work". For the moment, we are asking what element is affected by this transposition: what aspect "suffers" this violence in the dream? The dream is a text, a sequence of thought, a series of statements: *Wünschen* (wishes or desires). For the proposition put forth in the previous chapter to be validated by resisting attacks from possible objectors, it is imperative to produce, through a kind of counter-work – specifically analysis – the supposed original text, presumably distorted by the dream: the "literal meaning" whose "figurative" version is presented by the dream.

An objection to Freud's view of the dream is raised by a dreamer: her cleverly structured dream strongly contests the validity of Dr. Freud's theory, which makes a generalisation. No, her dream is not the fulfilment of a wish.

Here is the dream of the witty butcher's wife[12] in her own words:

> "You are always saying that a dream is a wish fulfilled", begins a witty lady
> patient. "Now I shall tell you a dream in which the content is quite the oppo-
> site, in which a wish of mine is not fulfilled. How do you reconcile that with
> your theory? The dream was as follows: I want to give a supper, but I have
> nothing available except some smoked salmon. I think I will go shopping,
> but I remember that it is Sunday afternoon, when all the shops are closed.
> I then try to ring a few caterers, but the telephone is out of order. Accordingly,
> I have to renounce my desire to give a supper".[13]

The subsequent transcription of the narrative of the dream focuses on the structure of its reasoning: three statements separated by *but*, reiterating the *no* held up
by "reality" to oppose the repeated desire of the dreamer. The *accordingly* which
neatly closes this irreproachable reasoning has a certain tone of insolence, for it is
clearly addressed to Freud – proving the transferential nature of the dream – and is
meant to incite the interpreter to identify the person to whom this whole discourse
is addressed.

Freud keeps his composure and invokes the technical rule: the analysis of associations is the only way to arrive at the meaning of a dream and demolish the
most seductive arguments of logic. Dividing the narrative into its constituent parts
causes the immediate collapse of the construction used by the hysteric to resist
the work inherent to the treatment. What, then, are the motives that prompted this
dream? Their traces must be found in the events of the preceding days.

The following sequence of associations came to light:

1) First, the figure of the husband, a wholesale butcher, a stout, honourable
man, expert at what he does, as we shall see. Recently, he has spoken of his excess
weight and expressed the desire to start a weight-loss diet. He has resolved to
wake early, exercise, keep to a strict diet and refuse invitations to dinner.

The patient related with some amusement an incident showing her husband's
temperament: when a painter he met while dining with other habitués at his
favourite restaurant asked him to pose for a portrait,[14] since he had an exceptionally expressive face, he answered in his usual coarse manner that he was flattered
but was sure the painter would gladly exchange his whole face for a piece of the
derrière of a beautiful damsel. She added that she was in love with her husband
and constantly teased him. She said she had also asked him not to give her any
caviar. What does this mean? Why this coy refusal?

2) Her explanation seems inadequate: she has been promising herself for a long
time the pleasure of savouring a caviar sandwich every morning, but she does not
allow herself the expense. If she asked her husband for the caviar, she would have
it at once, but, on the contrary, she begged him not to give her any, so as to prolong
the pleasure of teasing him.

Freud found this explanation unconvincing. The lack of information about
recent events reminded him of the way subjects hypnotised by Hippolyte

Bernheim tried desperately, when they awoke, to find reasons for their spontaneous and irrational behaviour while under hypnosis, instead of admitting that they had no explanation.

The witty butcher's wife's explanation involving caviar resembled these improbable fabrications. Freud comments that she felt the need to invent and have an unfulfilled wish in her life.

Her dream also shows her refusal to have her wish fulfilled.

The question is, why does she need an unfulfilled wish?

3) The day's residues.

So far, the patient's associations have been insufficient to make sense of her dream; Freud urges her to continue. After a pause indicating the resistance she has to overcome, she recounts that the previous day she visited a friend of whom she is very jealous because her husband does not tire of singing her praises. Fortunately, this friend is very thin and lanky, to her great despair, and the patient's husband likes buxom, voluptuous women. And what did this skinny friend talk about during the visit? About her desire to become plumper, of course. And she asked, "When will you invite us again? You always serve such good food".

We should point out that the patient had shown considerable resistance to revealing the relationship she and her husband had with this woman.

But the emergence of this third person gives the dream a new meaning, which Freud interprets for his patient as follows:

> It is just *as though* you had thought at [that] moment. . . "Of course, I'm to invite you so that you can eat. . . and get fat and become still more pleasing to my husband! I would rather give no more suppers!" The dream then tells you that you *cannot* give a supper, thereby fulfilling your wish not to contribute anything to the rounding out of your friend's figure. Your husband's resolution to accept no more invitations to supper in order that he may grow thin teaches you that one grows fat on food eaten at other people's tables.

The only thing lacking now is some coincidence that will confirm the solution. The smoked salmon in the dream has not yet been explained. "How did you come to think of salmon in your dream?" Freud asked.

"Smoked salmon is my friend's favourite dish", the patient replied. It so happened that Freud knew the lady in question and was certain that she grudged herself salmon, just as his patient grudged herself caviar.

Although Freud's theory of wish fulfilment was already confirmed by the first interpretation of the dream, this as yet unclarified and seemingly unimportant detail in the dream – "some smoked salmon" – sets the analytic work in motion again and leads to a brilliant breakthrough concerning the psychopathology of hysteria.

The dream now admits of yet another, more subtle interpretation, which becomes inevitable if we pay attention to the subsidiary detail of the smoked salmon. The two interpretations do not contradict one another, but rather dovetail into one another and provide an excellent example of the double entendre often found in dreams and other psycho-pathological formations. We have heard that at the time of her dream of a denied wish, the patient was impelled to deny herself a real wish (the caviar sandwiches). Her friend, too, had expressed a wish – to become fatter – and it would not be surprising for the patient to dream that her friend's wish was not to be fulfilled. Her own wish was that her friend be unable to fulfil her wish (of becoming fatter).

But instead, she dreamt that her own wish was not fulfilled.

Now, a new interpretation is possible, because in the dream, she has substituted herself for her friend; she has identified herself with her.

Freud concludes that having made this identification, she succeeded in creating, in reality, an unsatisfied desire.

This, then, is the second, more subtle meaning of the dream. While the patient dreams every night of a wish that is not fulfilled despite all her efforts, with respect to her life with her husband, she is expressing a desire by denying its fulfilment in the dream. In addition, by reporting this dream, she thought she was proving Freud wrong and creating a problem for him since the theory runs into a weighty barrier: with her analyst, she repeated the scenario she played out daily with her husband, as if attempting to gain control over him and claim the love she was so afraid of losing.

But she did not express her desires directly. She had to make a detour: the insignificant signifier revealing her fear in the dream became the symbolic signifier of the friend, and her suspicion transformed the smoked salmon into a signifier that could be substituted for the symbol of the friend: caviar.

In terms of motivation (wish fulfilment), the dream enacts a drama of jealousy – justified or not in reality – but, in any case, serving to express the psychic reality of the butcher's wife: an insatiable demand for love. It is through identification with her (imaginary) rival that she reveals this unfulfilled and unfulfillable wish; the disguised dream form is both ingenious and revealing: it shows what it attempts to cover up. The desire for love (the fragment of analysis does not tell us which love is unsatisfied) presents itself as a desire for the desire of another to remain unfulfilled because the desire of this other is precisely to replace her in her husband's life and even to become fatter by being a guest at their table. In reality, the friend's desire is impossible to satisfy because of her extreme thinness.

The patient identifies with a rival who is not one in reality. This raises the question of the husband's desire in this scenario that involves him.

What game is this bon vivant playing?

At the level of reality, the symptom becomes clearer: teasing as an entreaty that wants no response is a game in which the friend indulges; knowing that what the friend wants (to seduce the butcher) cannot be achieved without the agreement of the butcher's wife (she must invite her to dinner), we can see the vicious circle, the impasse the hysteric cannot escape.[15] Is the butcher's wife really jealous of her friend? Isn't it rather her mystery that fascinates her, the mystery of her femininity, that undefinable "something" her husband finds attractive?

The other signifiers in the dream still have to be linked up to this web: the Sunday afternoon, the telephone out of order, the closed stores – all these "refusals" coming from the outside.

But the theme of eating and the play on inflating (the friend) and deflating (the husband) are ample indicators of the orality of hysteria and of the impossible-to-fill void the hysteric creates in her body, in her "sexuality". Sexual relations are signified in the language of consuming food and drink. Stoutness alludes to pregnancy and to the promise of feminine fulfilment.

But let us go back to *The Interpretation of Dreams*. The use of the word *identification* opens the way to a digression into the psychopathology of hysteria, a field of research closely related to our discussion.

After having untangled the unconscious threads of his patient's desire, Freud asks himself, "What is the meaning of hysterical identification?"

He leaves aside the witty butcher's wife for the moment to concentrate on hysteria in general and examine more closely its typical symptom formations.

> Identification is a highly important factor in the mechanism of hysterical symptoms. It enables patients to express in their symptoms not only their own experiences but those of a larger number of people; it enables them, as it were, to suffer on behalf of a whole crowd of people and to act all the parts in a play single-handed. I shall be told that this is not more than the familiar hysterical imitation, the capacity of hysterics to imitate any symptoms in other people that may have struck their attention. . . . But this only indicates the way in which the psychic process is discharged in hysterical imitation; the way in which a psychic act proceeds and the act itself are two different things.[16] The latter is slightly more complicated [. . .]: *it corresponds to an unconscious concluded process*, as an example will show. The physician who has a female patient with a particular kind of twitching, lodged in the company of other patients in the same room of the hospital, is not surprised when some morning he learns that this particular hysterical attack has found imitations.
>
> He simply says to himself: The others have seen her and have done likewise: that is psychic infection [when] sympathy, which does not reach consciousness, is aroused: "If it is possible to have this kind of an attack from such causes, I too may have this kind of an attack, for I have the same reasons".
>
> If this were a cycle capable of becoming conscious, it would perhaps express itself in *fear* of getting the same attack; but it takes place in another psychic sphere, and, therefore, ends in the realization of the dreaded symptom. *Identification is therefore not a simple imitation, but a sympathy based upon the same etiological claim; it expresses an "as though", and refers to some common quality which has remained in the unconscious.*
>
> *Identification* is most often used in hysteria to express sexual community. An hysterical woman identifies herself most readily – although not

exclusively – with persons with whom she has had sexual relations, or who have sexual intercourse with the same persons as herself.

After this digression, Freud returns to the dreamer:

> The patient, then, only follows the rules of the hysterical thought processes when she gives expression to her jealousy of her friend (which, moreover, she herself admits to be justified, in that she puts herself in her place and identifies herself with her by creating a symptom – the denied wish). I might further clarify the process specifically as follows: She puts herself in the place of her friend in the dream, because her friend has taken her own place in relation to her husband, and because she would like to take her friend's place in the esteem of her husband.

This text from which we quoted extensively is important in the work of elaborating a psychoanalytical explanation – a metapsychology – of the processes involved in dream and hysteria. Here, on the theoretical level, identification is deliberately placed at the intersection of dream and neurosis, revealing the source of the latter.

Let us enumerate the elements of this first stage in the systematic construction of the concept of identification. Identification is a path, a method. It springs from certain motives: it is the manifestation of a mental construct. The impulse in question is libidinal – sexual – in nature and appears as a scene, a phantasy, a sexual drama unfolding among a number of characters. Identification is the means by which this drama can be staged, acted out: either in the psychic sphere of dreams, in an imaginary space, or in the sphere of human relations, in reality. But in that case, it takes the distressing form of a symptom. In both cases, the motive – the libidinal impetus – finds expression, but at the cost of a distortion, a detour through recourse to images, signifiers of one or several other characters.

It is at the topographical level that identification, as unconscious thought, differs from imitation since the hysteric is unaware of the thought process leading to his conclusion.[17] When this thought process enters consciousness, it provokes fear of an impending crisis.

At the dynamic level, the motivating forces are those of sexual phantasy. Given that "sexuality" itself is polymorphous, the form taken by the phantasy can activate any part of the sensory apparatus. But the dominant instinctual drive seems to be aimed at self-gratification.[18]

The *economic* viewpoint, which takes into account the distribution of libidinal energy investments, is not examined here directly. In Chapter V of *The Interpretation of Dreams*, where Freud connects dream identification with the primary process of condensation, this "economic" aspect of identification is presented as the "saving" of psychic energy.

Judging by the substitutions through which the hysteric enacts her phantasy – the characters in her imaginary scenario of jealousy – it seems that she can only ask her "question" (to be a man or a woman?) by presenting a scene from which she is absent. These substitute characters reveal her interpersonal positions and formulate in her place her impossible quest, her ever-deferred demand for love, at once desired and refused. But this substitution – in effect, a sort of proxy procedure – captures and mobilises the hysteric's psychic energy, spent in the detours of neurotic errancy.

Thus, hysterical identification, both as a symptom and in the dream, stages a scenario of jealousy which covers up something else. The phantasy it masks, and whose *Entstellung* (substitute) it is, could be supposed to be the "perverse" bisexual phantasy that would cause the subject to hesitate about sexual identity.

The dream and the symptom are both compromises bringing together repressor and repressed elements. But the dream provides the key to the symptom since it "fulfils", figuratively, in the beautiful butcher's wife's imagination, her wish to occupy a place that another has mysteriously acquired without occupying it.

Dream and hysteria: the Dora case

A note of apology closes this discussion:

> I myself regret the inclusion of such passages from the psycho-pathology of hysteria, which, because of their fragmentary presentation, and because they are torn out of their context, cannot prove to be very illuminating. If these passages are capable of throwing any light upon the intimate relations between dream and psycho-neurosis, they have served the intention with which I have included them.
>
> (Chapter 4, Note 7)

While writing *The Interpretation of Dreams*, Freud took into analysis a young hysteric he would call "Dora" in the description of the case he published a few years later. He spoke of her in several letters sent to Fliess.[19] He described the case in these terms:

> It is a fragment of an analysis of a case of hysteria in which the explanations are grouped around two dreams; so it is really a continuation of the dream book. In addition, it contains resolutions of hysterical symptoms and glimpses of the sexual organic foundation of the whole. It is the subtlest thing I have written so far and will put people off even more than usual.[20]

The question defined initially as that of the relations between dream formation and symptom formation is given a clinical illustration that elucidates the role of interpretation of dreams in the analytic process and explains the transformations brought about by the production of symptoms. Identification, a process inherent in both the dream and the symptom, remains at the limit between normal and pathological: this fundamental ambiguity deserves our attention.

Dora's combination of symptoms forms a constellation of identificatory traits, organised along two essential poles, with the opposing tension between them constituting the arena of a ruthless and painful game of masks. The overdetermination of symptoms facilitating the plasticity of an eminently "convertible" body lends itself to being analysed as the effect of a sexual quest – the search for her feminine identity – not yet ready to emerge.

Identifying by turns with the man and then with the woman, Dora reveals, pitifully, the conflictual nature of her unconscious desires. But it is the content of her two dreams "addressed" to Freud[21] in the analysis which makes it clear that the "pathos" of her symptoms results from this combining of the sexes.

The nervous cough,[22] or "catarrh"; the sporadic aphonia; the disgust with men; the phobic avoidance of couples who are embracing; the written threat of suicide; depression; gastralgia and appendicitis; difficulty breathing – these are the multiple signs that serve to immobilise, through their silent symbolism, through their repetition and their insistence, complicated thoughts and secret reasoning. Multiple identifications emerge as solutions to blocked paths which can only be shown in these tragicomic mimes.

Freud makes use of this profusion of symptoms to demonstrate his general theory of the psychic function of hysterical symptoms. In his discussion, he says several times that one of the meanings of a symptom is the representation of a sexual phantasy.[23] This representation is enacted like a performance, staged like a "sexual" script. Here, "sexuality" is to be understood in a structural sense: that is, as the mobilisation of infantile behaviours which follow paths inscribed in the body along a preferred erogenous itinerary.[24] Using terms that introduce the question of "psychic representation", which would become a major topic of the metapsychology a few years later, Freud writes that stimuli have a "psychical coating" from the outset, which fixates them. This coating itself is stratified. Indeed, in the phantasies of the hysteric, these layers of coating are characters which haunt her and allow her to obtain vicariously – like at the theatre – unconscious jouissance.

Thus, the hysterical symptom, as a set scene, is presented by reference to other people playing the protagonists of the sexual script of her phantasy.

The unfolding of this phantasmatic script can only be a repetition of historical or even prehistorical scenes in which the hysteric herself, as a child, acts or "sees herself acting" – her action proving to be an act of jouissance.

> She very clearly remembered that in childhood she had been a "*Lutscherin*" or thumb-sucker. Her father also remembered that he had weaned her off the habit when it continued into her fourth or fifth year. Dora herself had kept in her memory a distinct image from early childhood, in which she sat in a corner on the floor, sucking on her left thumb, while tugging with her right hand on the earlobe of her brother, who sat peacefully beside her.

Lacan attributes an essential function to his *imago*, this childhood memory: "What we seem to have here is the imaginary mold in which all the situations orchestrated by Dora during her life came to be cast – a perfect illustration of the theory, yet to appear in Freud's work, of repetition automatisms".[25]

In view of the concept he has developed of such an image in the structure of the subject, Lacan objects to the interpretation of aphonia proposed by Freud. He writes:

> We can gauge in it what woman and man signify to her now. Woman is the object which cannot be dissociated from a primitive oral desire, in which she must nevertheless learn to recognize her own genital nature. (It is surprising that Freud fails to see here that Dora's aphonia during Herr K's absences expressed the violent call of the oral erotic drive when Dora was left alone with Frau K, there being no need for him to assume she had seen her father receiving fellatio. . .). In order for her to gain access to this recognition of her femininity, she would have to assume [*assumer*] her own body, failing which she remains open to the functional fragmentation (to refer to the theoretical contribution of the mirror stage) that constitutes conversion symptoms. Now, her only means for gaining this access was via her earliest imago, which shows us that the only path open to her to the object was via the masculine partner, with whom, because of their difference in age, she was able to identify, in that primordial identification through which the subject recognizes herself as I. . . . Hence Dora identified with Herr K, just as she was in the process of identifying with Freud himself. . . . And all her dealings with the two men manifest the aggressiveness in which we see the dimension characteristic of narcissistic alienation.[26]

The analysis of dreams and symptoms revels why specific characters are chosen to cover, as it were, the characters in the past – and herself. These screen characters are endowed with a particular power of fascination; they embody a mystery: they are Dora's models (*Vorbild*), her brother and later her aunt (her father's sister) and, more enigmatically, Frau K. and the Sistine Chapel Madonna in her dreams. Their "consent" to present her wishes as being fulfilled springs from a motive originating in the Oedipal situation. Freud writes, in *Fragment of an Analysis of a Case of Hysteria*:

> [H]er preoccupation with her father's relations to Frau K. owed its obsessive character to the fact that its root was unknown to her and lay in the unconscious.
>
> Her behaviour obviously went far beyond what would have been appropriate to filial concern. She felt and acted more like a jealous wife – in a way which would have been comprehensible in her mother. By her ultimatum to her father ("either her or me"), by the scenes she used to make, by the suicidal intentions she allowed to transpire, – by all this she was clearly putting herself in her mother's place. If we have rightly guessed the nature of

the imaginary sexual situation which underlay her cough, in that phantasy she must have been putting herself in Frau K.'s place. She was therefore identifying herself both with the woman her father had once loved and with the woman he loved now. The inference was a much stronger one than she knew or than she would have cared to admit: in fact, that she was in love with him.

I have learned to look upon unconscious love relations like this – between a father and a daughter, or between a mother and a son – as a revival of germs of feelings in infancy. I have shown at length elsewhere at what an early age sexual attraction makes itself felt between parents and children, and I have explained that the legend of Oedipus is probably to be regarded as a poetic rendering of what is typical in these relations.

[Her father's] numerous illnesses were bound to have increased her affection for him. . . . [H]e had made her his confidante while she was still a child. It was really she and not her mother whom Frau K.'s appearance had driven out of more than one position.[27]

(We will soon see, in a passage of *The Interpretation of Dreams*, that the dream is excellently suited to represent this consensual relation by means of primary identification.) But the Oedipal situation to which Dora returns repeatedly through the duplicity of her identifications has not allowed her to choose a definite "position". A considerable layer of what Freud sees as the stratification of her desire consists, in fact, of her identification with her father.

In fact, her problematic relation to her father expressed in her behaviour by her constant blaming of him was what rendered her so unbearable that he brought her to be treated by Freud. We know that it is from him that Freud first learned about the incredible imbroglio in which everyone is involved and which is further complicated by Dora's illness, which appears, from the start, like a failed protest. Then Freud hears Dora's lengthy indictment of the underhanded dealings in which she figures as a victim, although before long, it turns out that she is a willing accomplice. She brings accusations; Freud will show that what she is really doing is apologising, that the blame she heaps on her father for his affair is really a form of self-reproach she covers up through projection.

With surprising lucidity, she witnesses the adults' games, unaware of the role she chooses to play. Painfully aware of the factors underlying the behaviour of others, she is blind to her own motivations. Here we have an initial effect of identification: inadequate self-knowledge and its confirmation in an inability to guess. She can see how her father, Frau K. and her cousin use illness as a pretext for the fulfilment of secret desires, but by holding on to her symptoms, she maintains her "advantage".[28]

Identification acts as a masquerade: by showing, she covers up; by bringing to light, she blinds. She is the servant of the Ego which "doesn't want to know", denies and disclaims its own games. But she is also the servant of unconscious thoughts, which she illustrates in her symptomatic transposition which is, as we have seen, an exposition of the jouissance/punishment of illness.

Where she claims to have been betrayed, she betrays herself. Her apparent passivity turns into an activity which affects her; the interpretation causes the passive to turn into the reflexive (the middle position). In the treatment, this is the moment of a first reversal, which will lead to the secondary development of her truth.[29] By coughing, like her father, she irritates her throat, like Frau K. does – at least, this is what she imagines. She betrays in a single symptom her double sexual inclination and a very old sexual phantasy. She is jealous of Frau K., who, from the first, is seen as a new Oedipal rival, because behind her is hidden the mother about whom "nothing" is said and who obviously amounts to nothing.[30] But in the final analysis, it is her own father, the unpunished seducer of Frau K. – her adorable companion in earlier times of solitude, her initiator and confidante with the splendid body – who would become the detested rival.

Homosexuality revealed: this is the second dialectical reversal, which should have led to the final development of the truth but failed to do so due to a technical error committed by Freud. Because

> the young woman and the scarcely grown girl had lived for years on a footing of the closest intimacy. When Dora stayed with the K.s she used to share a bedroom with Frau K., and the husband used to be quartered elsewhere. She had been the wife's confidante and adviser in all the difficulties of her married life. There was nothing they had not talked about.
>
> Medea had been quite content that Creusa should make friends with her two children; and she certainly did nothing to interfere with the relations between the girl and the children's father.[31]
>
> When Dora talked about Frau K., she used to praise her "adorable white body" in accents more appropriate to a lover than to a defeated rival. . . . Indeed, I can say in general that I never heard her speak a harsh or angry word against the lady, although. . . she should have regarded her as the prime author of her misfortune.[32]

The fact is that Frau K. gave her up without regret to preserve her relations with her father. Speaking of this homosexual relation between Dora and Frau K., Freud presents certain hypotheses which apply to hysteria in general:

> For behind Dora's supervalent train of thought which was concerned with her father's relations with Frau K, there lay concealed a feeling of jealousy which had that lady as its *object* – a feeling, that is, which could only be based upon an affection on Dora's part for one of her own sex.

And a little further:

> When, in a hysterical woman or girl, the sexual libido which is directed towards men has been energetically suppressed, it will regularly be found that the libido which is directed towards women has become vicariously reinforced and even to some extent conscious.[33]

And again:

> The jealous emotions of a woman were linked in the unconscious with a jealousy such as might have been felt by a man. These masculine or, more properly speaking, *gynaecophilic* currents of feeling are to be regarded as typical of the unconscious erotic life of hysterical girls.[34]

When he described this case in his 1905 text, Freud admitted:

> The longer the interval of time that separates me from the end of this analysis, the more probable it seems to me that the fault in my technique lay in this omission: I failed to discover in time and to inform the patient that her homosexual love for Frau K. was the strongest current in her mental life.[35]

This tendency was also the most strongly repressed: this could explain Dora's amnesia regarding the source of her knowledge of sexual matters and her contemplative fascination with the Madonna in the second dream.

The first dream reveals that the father – admirable paradox – serves as a cover-up to Herr K., Dora's persistent suitor, but that this is, in fact, a cover-up of himself, the Oedipal father of earlier times.[36]

The second dream shows that the Madonna she loves is no doubt the most revealing image she uses as the emblem of her own indecision: to be the mother – an accomplished woman – but a virgin – untouched, unsoiled – and to have the Phallus without submitting to the feminine condition that makes you be the object of a man's desire. This dream, which was also her farewell to Freud, would certainly have led the analysis – had it not been for Freud's omission – to Herr K., to this homosexual love that surmounted all the betrayals of the beloved.

Freud, who had seen in her attitude a triumph of "normal" love, had no doubt identified, in the counter-transference, with Herr K., for whom he clearly felt sympathy.

Let us return to the theory of the hysterical symptom and to the function of identification in the formation of dreams and neuroses.

If we use the concluding formula of the dream of the "beautiful butcher's wife", analysed earlier, we could reformulate to say about Dora that she identifies, through her symptoms (particularly the nervous cough) and in her dreams with persons with whom, in reality or phantasy, she has had sexual relations or who have had sexual relations with the same persons as herself. Her polyvalent jealousy, reversible in a sense, is expressed through these borrowed characters, these screen figures of the stratified "psychical coating". When Freud writes: "Hysteria is allo-erotic (homo or heterosexual); the main highway it follows is identification with the loved person" (letter to Fliess, December 9, 1899), he summarises the theory of hysteria which Dora's case so admirably illustrates.

What remains to be determined is whether identification as a process of stratified symptom formation and identification as a representational process fulfilling the dreamer's wishes are phenomena of the same type. What is the relation – or perhaps the difference – between hysterical identification and dream identification? This is not simply a matter of differentiating a symptom from a dream; what must be decided is whether it is possible or not to speak of something "typical" in what Freud discovers by examining hysterical symptom formation, given that all such symptoms seem to result from identification in phantasy. The question then is whether the hysterical identification process is applicable to all psychic life, hysterical or not, in the same way as the dream process lends itself to generalisation.

To deal with this question appropriately, we need additional information on the nature of the identification process in dreams. Fortunately, a passage in *The Interpretation of Dreams* can help us clarify a question that arose as soon as we formulated our commentary on the first case of hysteria.

Identification in dream-work

Chapter VI of *The Interpretation of Dreams* describes dream construction processes one by one; these processes are revealed and dismantled by the work of interpretation. After presenting the effects of condensation and displacement, Freud examines how representation itself functions. The means of representation serve much the same purpose as condensation and displacement: the aim is to show how, through these processes, the dream can transform thoughts into visual scenes and visible characters. Specifically, Freud asks himself what the dream does with the essence of the thought material: that is, its logical relations. And what role do intellectual operations play in the dream?

The dream does not present the same easy interchange between logical relations as waking thoughts do. Freud uses specific dreams to show the simplification and reduction to which these relations are subjected. Thus, causal relations are illustrated by a succession – a dream sequence or gradual transformation of images; alternative or disjunctive elements are juxtaposed in a sequence that renders them equivalent. Contradiction and antithesis are simply reduced to one of these elements.

The only logical relations dream images respect are those of resemblance, agreement, contact and "as if" situations. The dream has a great variety of ways of presenting them. Indeed, the dream excels at producing resemblances, at finding unsuspected similarities, at making connections and finding shortcuts. Freud even quotes Aristotle, who considered that the most skilled interpreter of dreams has the faculty of observing resemblances[37]:

> The screening which occurs in the dream-material, or the cases of "just as" are the chief points of support for dream-formation, and a not inconsiderable part of the dream-work consists in creating new screenings of this kind in cases where those that already exist are prevented by the resistance of the censorship from making their way into the dream. The effort towards condensation evinced by the dream-work facilitates the representation of a relation of similarity.[38]

Freud called the production of cases of "as if", of substitutes, *identification*. To avoid censorship, the dream must constantly find new means of assimilation, new symbols, because the old ones are already resisted by the censoring agency. The foremost technique of dream-work is unification. The elements of a relation of similarity, agreement and connection are contracted, unified, combined.

Thus, identification is a means of condensation; it is, as it were, the image-making involved in this process. Freud goes on to say:

> Identification consists in giving representation in the dream-content to only one of two or more persons who are related by some common feature, while the second person or other persons appear to be suppressed as far as the dream is concerned. In the dream, this one "screening" person enters into all the relations and situations which derive from the persons whom he screens. In cases of composition, however, when persons are combined, there are already present in the dream-image features which are characteristic of, but not common to, the persons in question, so that a new unity, a composite person, appears as the result of the union of these features.[39]
>
> The common feature which justifies the union of two persons – that is to say, which enables it to be made – may either be represented in the dream or it may be absent. As a rule, identification or composition of persons actually serves to avoid the necessity of representing this common feature.[40]

This is what often produces extraordinary condensations in dream content: I can avoid representing directly very complex situations involving one person by finding another person who has the same connections with a part of what they have in common. It is easy to understand how effectively this mode of presentation through identification can make it possible to escape the censorship of resistance, which creates such difficult conditions for dream-work.

> The thing that offends the censorship may reside in those very ideas which are connected in the dream-material with the one person; I now find a second person, who likewise stands in some relation to the objectionable material, but only to a part of it. Contact at that one point which offends the censorship now justifies my formation of a composite person, who is characterized by the indifferent features of each. This person, the result of combination or identification, being free of the censorship, is now suitable for incorporation in the dream-content. Thus, by the application of dream condensation, I have satisfied the demands of the dream-censorship. When a common feature of two persons is represented in a dream, this is usually a hint to look for another concealed common feature, *the representation of which is made impossible by the censorship*. Here a displacement of the common feature has occurred, which in some degree facilitates representation. . . . Accordingly, the identification or combination of persons serves various purposes in our dreams; in the first place, that of representing a feature common to two persons;

secondly, that of representing a displaced common feature; and, thirdly, that of expressing a community of features which is merely wished for. . . . In the dream of Irma's injection I wish to exchange one patient for another – that is to say, I wish this other person to be my patient, as the former person has been; the dream deals with this wish by showing me a person who is called Irma, but who is examined in a position such as I have had occasion to see only the other person occupy. In the dream about my uncle this substitution is made the centre of the dream; I identify myself with the minister by judging and treating my colleagues as shabbily as he does.

It has been my experience – and to this I have found no exception – that *every dream treats of oneself.* Dreams are absolutely egoistic. In cases where not my ego but only a strange person occurs in the dream-content, I may safely assume that by means of identification my ego is concealed behind that person. I am permitted to supplement my ego. On other occasions, when my ego appears in the dream, the situation in which it is placed tells me that another person is concealing himself, by means of identification, behind the ego. . . . There are also dreams in which my ego appears together with other persons who, when the identification is resolved, once more show themselves to be my ego. Through these identifications I shall then have to connect with my ego certain ideas to which the censorship has objected. I may also give my ego multiple representations in my dream, either directly or by means of identification with other people. By means of several such identifications an extraordinary amount of thought material may be condensed.[41]

In this text, identification is described as a means of condensation: a condensation that acts on the representation of persons. Moreover, it is a means of making the ego appear behind a screen or accompanied by the deployment of its various masks. Identification illustrates; it enacts artfully the relations between the ego and the characters with whom it is connected. As is the case in hysterical identification, this process makes it possible to conceal an unconscious relation: either the desire to be like another person or the desire to have what the other person has.

Identification in dreams and hysterical identification are both founded on an unconscious identity phantasy. The first produces a hallucinatory figure image of the phantasy; the second enacts it dramatically through a symptom in the body, which makes itself a significant ally in an interpersonal reality. In a context of hysteria, identification is acted out: it goes beyond the imaginary space of the dream, leaves this "another scene" and influences behaviour. Here, we could speak of a true "fulfillment" of desire going beyond hallucinatory enactment, through topical overflow. In both cases, the identification function serves to avoid psychical effort, to deceive the censoring agency.

What stands out in this passage of the text, which elucidates what was already said, is that the concept of identification is explicitly related to that of "ego". Indeed, the ego (dreaming/dreamt) only appears through multiple identifications.

To relate the ego to an identification function is an unusual perspective for Freud, who, at this early stage, in the *Project*, usually spoke of perceptual and motor investments.

Here we note once again Freud's hesitation about the ego. It is a different thing to describe it based on its perceptual-motor functions and by its role in identification stratification. The language of the first topography (relations between systems governed by differentiated functions) cannot describe, from its solipsistic standpoint centred on a psychic apparatus, the interpsychology implied by the concept of identification. Yet Freud did not develop the subject of interpsychology until later. The fact that a duality in the analytic discourse concerning the status of the ego is present in Freud's earliest writings justifies an in-depth reading of the seminal texts.[42]

The ego can also be described by examining dream (and symptomatic) productions, which reveal its defensive function: that of avoiding and ignoring desire.

As he continues to develop the concept of identification in the context of dreamwork – that is, to describe a deformation phenomenon – Freud also develops a theory of the ego and its function. It is noteworthy that the foundations of this theory, in these early writings, are given as part of a study on dreams and hysteria.

This brings us back to the question of the normal and the pathological. The dream (psychosis of the sleeping subject) and hysteria (neurosis) provide analytical access to ego functions because they highlight the identification process, the prevailing mode of the ego to "imagine itself", to "stage itself" and, consequently, "to reflect itself". This raises the question of whether it is essential for the ego to be perceivable – identifiable – only through this screening process: a display of stand-ins, of substitute faces. Indeed, the "subject" only becomes aware of his desires by seeing them in the traits and gestures of others. It is easy to understand how this phantasy relation to the other alienates the hysteric. We have just seen how this same game of masks tricks the dreamer. Does this mean that the ego itself is always to be taken figuratively, as a metaphor, and that its "literal sense" is always missing or lost? The greatest ambiguity is due to the fact that the ego in the dream and in hysteria was not explicitly discussed by Freud and that the categories applicable at this stage of the teachings are insufficient to allow clear reflection on the problem as a whole.

We know how much Lacan's concepts of the "imaginary" and the "symbolic" have contributed to a better definition of the term "subject" – as distinct from the notion of "ego". But that was to come later. At the stage of Freud's research we are examining now, we have a number of paths to explore. The theoretical elements presented earlier (letters to Fliess, analysis of dreams and hysteria) are now classified by themes or simply into sequences with converging characteristics relevant to our field of study. These fragments of an original theory of identification (or theory of the ego) still await systematisation. As we continue to read the texts written in this early period (1895 to 1912), the ideas will be developed in greater detail.

Identification and the comic

A question glimpsed in passing earlier, and apparently minor, can shed light on our topic. We will now look more closely at a conceptual distinction encountered in the analysis of the beautiful butcher's wife's dream: this is the distinction between identification and imitation, which Freud seemed to regard as a decisive element of his theory. He returns to it in the study of the mechanisms of humour in *Jokes and Their Relation to the Unconscious*.[43]

This perspective on the question of identification is original since the humorous exchange, wit and humour are not marginal or pathological phenomena. But Freud's essay also deserves our attention for another reason: written at the same time as *Three Essays on the Theory of Sexuality*, it expands our understanding of productions of the unconscious by adding the genealogical dimension, already glimpsed numerous times in the analysis of dreams and neuroses but described in detail here. The infantile element in adults is clearly and insistently portrayed here. The care taken to describe developments and geneses, and not only topographical systems, unavoidably leads to a relativisation of concepts. Choosing to focus on conceptual genesis, a choice imposed by clinical and theoretical experience, places the question of the Ego in a different perspective.

Freud's "aesthetic" curiosity, which impels him to explore the human production of wit, also awakens his interest in artistic works, particularly those of poets, playwrights and novelists. We shall see what the concept of identification, developed in dream interpretation and symptom formation, can help reveal concerning aesthetic productions and, inversely, how the analysis of the latter can change the understanding of the concept.

From dream to witticism

The originality of Freud's interpretation of witticism lies in the fact that he links it with dream development. He reaffirms this connection throughout the essay.[44] The great number of jokes analysed from the perspective of the technique which produces them and the tendencies which characterise them are further proof of the pertinence of the concepts formulated earlier. Condensation, displacement and indirect representation are just as much at work here as in dream and thought processes connected to psychopathological states. When he lists the "techniques" involved in producing jokes, Freud goes over the many forms taken by condensation, without ever including identification in his long and patient investigation. In this essay, Freud prefers to speak of "unification".[45] However, he does use the concept of identification, not in connection with the primary mechanism of *Verdichtung*, but as part of the structure of an intersubjective situation. This situation points to a sort of reduplication of identification. This particular identification acts like a transformer of representations, allowing them to shift topographically from the unconscious to the preconscious, based on the "logic" of the similar. (We might say "the illogical" since it cancels all differences and thereby the conditions needed for any relation.) Here, identification is used to name the phenomenon that creates in the protagonist of the joke: the "psychical correspondence" needed to construct the joke and to take in the joke. In this situation, identification also changes the course of thought, but by doing so, it brings about a real exchange, evidenced concretely by a burst of laughter.

Thus, double use confers to the word *identification* the meaning "intrapsychic operation", appearing in the unconscious as an interpsychic operation connecting "egos" by appealing to an unconscious communality.

Our task now is to understand the logic inherent to this double use. There are several reasons to think that it is neither an abuse of language nor a misunderstanding based on a homonym, but rather, that the two meanings are not completely foreign to each other. In other words, the question is "What is the difference between identifying a representation with another based on a common element (see earlier in this chapter) and identifying one's ego with another ego (also based on a common element, hidden or not)?" In grammatical terms, the question would concern the relation between the transitive and the reflexive form of the verb *to identify*.

To elucidate these questions encountered several times in our investigation, let us look at some passages in *Jokes*. First, our attention is drawn to a series of comments in Chapter III ("The Purposes of Jokes"). By examining the conflict inherent in tendentious jokes, they point out the essentially social character of wit. This particularity is only mentioned here because the tendencies of wit will be discussed in detail in the analytic portion of the essay. But this noteworthy mention foreshadows the central theme of the essay, which will be developed in the "synthetic" and "theoretical" sections.

> The woman's inflexibility is therefore the first condition for the development of smut. . . . The ideal case of a resistance of this kind on the woman's part occurs if another man is present at the same time – a third person – for in that case an immediate surrender by the woman is as good as out of the question. This third person soon acquires the greatest importance in the development of the smut. . . . So that gradually, in place of the woman, the onlooker, now the listener, becomes the person to whom the smut is addressed, and owing to this transformation, it is already near to assuming the character of a joke.[46]

And concerning tendentious jokes:

> Since we have been obliged to renounce the expression of hostility by deeds – held back by the passionless third person, in whose interest it is that personal security shall be preserved – we have, just as in the case of sexual aggressiveness, developed a new technique of invective, which aims at enlisting this third person against our enemy.[47]

And finally, this decisive passage:

> What these jokes whisper may be said aloud: that the wishes and desires of men have a right to make themselves acceptable alongside of exacting and ruthless morality. And in our days it has been said in forceful and stirring sentences that this morality is only a selfish regulation laid down by the few who are rich and powerful and who can satisfy their wishes at any time without any postponement. So long as the art of healing has not gone further in making our life safe and so long as social arrangements do no more to make it more enjoyable, so long will it be impossible to stifle the voice within us that rebels against the demands of morality. . . . The decision in this conflict can only be reached by the roundabout path of fresh insight. One must bind one's own life to that of others so closely and be able to identify oneself with others so intimately that the brevity of one's own life can be overcome; and one must not fulfill the demands of one's own needs illegitimately, but must leave them unfulfilled, because only the continuance of so many unfulfilled demands can develop the power to change the order of society. But not every personal need can be postponed in this way and transferred to other people, and there is no general and final solution to the conflict.[48]

This passage is closer to the meditations of a philosopher than to an analysis of processes and tendencies. Its tone is that of future texts of a clearly anthropological nature, such as *"Civilized" Sexual Morality and Modern Nervous Illness, The Future of an Illusion* and *Civilization and Its Discontents*.[49] The constraints and taboos imposed by society – or, in Marxist terms, by the dominant class to safeguard its ideological and economic privileges and its ideological and economic domination – are not only pathogenic factors generating neuroses but also incitements to "aesthetic" productions like the joke. What interests us here is the insertion of the concept of identification in a different context than those in which we are used to seeing it play a role. We could say, in anticipation of the theory based on relations between the individual and society, that identification is already inscribed in the phenomenon of sublimation (social resolution of internal instinctual conflicts). The conceptual connection between identification and sublimation is made, in this instance, through the concept of displacement or transference – in its oral form. It is not new to see identification play such a conflict-resolution role. What is new is its function – merely glimpsed at this stage – of maintaining individual desires and aspirations by means of a reassignment of psychic place. Identification brings about the transference of these personal demands to other people in order to transform them into collective demands, which leads to social change.

Thus, making and listening to jokes can now be seen as a covert exchange of desires, the placing in common of symbolised subjective tensions, the sharing of the hardships of daily life. Identification offers itself as the "medium" of this exchange.

Perhaps we can propose a hypothesis concerning the difference between dream and hysterical identification on the one hand and identification related to wit on the other hand. Hysterical identification "achieves", through the unconscious symbolism of the symptom, a compromise between a sexual tendency (desire to be liked) and moral or social prohibition; dream identification, whose motive is also the existence of an unconscious shared trait, censored this time, achieves a similar desire for uniformity in a roundabout way. As for identification in the comic, which "transfers individual needs", it is the detour, the deviation, the placement of these needs into a sort of "common social reserve". This deviation provides partial relief of the tensions caused by the original conflict. In this third case, desires are not satisfied, accomplished or achieved, but they are indicated, shared and exchanged to give added impetus to the "Revolution". Identification is not *Erfüllung* (fulfilment), but rather *Umuweg* (a detour). To help describe these two modes of identification, we can refer to the criteria used to compare dreams with jokes: that is, to compare a purely "selfish" production to an essentially social production. (In this context, hysteria is classified as a "selfish production" as well.)

This is how Freud summarised his discussion at the end of Chapter 6 ("The Relation of Jokes to Dreams and to the Unconscious"):

The most important difference [between jokes and dreams, two very distinct psychic activities] lies in *their social behaviour*. A dream is a completely asocial mental product; it has nothing to communicate to anyone else; it arises within the subject as a compromise between the mental forces struggling in him, it remains unintelligible to the subject himself and is for that reason totally uninteresting to other people. Not only does it not need to set any store by intelligibility it must actually avoid being understood, for otherwise it would be destroyed; it can only exist in masquerade. For that reason, it can, without hindrance, make use of the mechanism that dominates unconscious mental processes, to the point of a distortion which can no longer be set straight. A joke, on the other hand, is the most social of all the mental functions that aim at a yield of pleasure. It often calls for three persons and its completion requires the participation of someone else in the mental process it starts. The condition of intelligibility is, therefore, binding on it; it may only make use of possible distortion in the unconscious through condensation and displacement up to the point at which it can be set straight by the third person's understanding. Moreover, jokes and dreams have grown up in quite different regions of mental life and must be allotted to points in the psychological system far remote from each other. A dream still remains a wish, even though one that has been made unrecognizable; a joke is developed play. Dreams, in spite of all their practical nonentity, retain their connection with the major interests of life; they seek to fulfill needs by the regressive détour of hallucination; and they are permitted to occur for the sake of the one need that is active during the night – the need to sleep. Jokes, on the other hand, seek to gain a small yield of pleasure from the mere activity, untrammelled by needs, of our mental apparatus. Later they try to catch a hold of that pleasure as a by-product during the activity of that apparatus and thus arrive *secondarily* at not unimportant functions directed to the external world. Dreams serve predominantly for the avoidance of unpleasure, jokes for the attainment of pleasure; but all our mental activities converge in these two aims.[50]

We have said that identification in the dream and in hysteria fulfils in a hallucinatory manner in the first case and dramatically (in behaviour) in the second case, a phantasy of community, strictly "private", emerging from the unconscious and unknown to the subject who dreams it or acts it out. Identification acts as a transformer of selfish thoughts, augmenting as much as possible the least resemblances, to the detriment of all other logical or real differences. The identification involved in jokes takes place between real and different people. In fact, they must be different people in different positions (the subject producing the joke and the object of the joke and the listener who sanction the joke). This assignment of places is crucial. Here, identification does not reinforce individual phantasy; it does not reproduce figures that are just so many representations of the "ego", shut away in an imaginary gallery where there is never anything else that's "real". Identification in jokes creates solidarity, enables the successful communication of an unconscious message and creates a community – ephemeral, since it only lasts the time it takes for the joke to be told – but effective. Thanks to this identification – this transfer of desire – a kind of unconscious pact is concluded; its conscious sign is laughter.

Perhaps this differentiation brings us closer to the difference Lacan makes between the symbolic and the imaginary. Transformations in dreams and in hysteria take place within the same subject when topographical shifts occur, compromises of which neither the subject nor anyone else is aware. Transformations in jokes take place through an exchange of signs – through language – and produce inter-psychic pleasure. In the first case, there are imaginary exchanges, substitutions of equivalent terms which maintain desire in its phantasmatic form. In the second case, the exchange is symbolic and creates solidarity, but limited and partial. This type of "psychic affinity" (*Einfühlung*) is no doubt produced by an authentic work of art. The examination of texts dealing with aesthetic productions other than the comic will make it possible at a later stage to assemble methodically what might be seen as Freud's theory of aesthetic relations, or his "psychology" of art.

But first we shall continue our reading of *Jokes* to look more closely at a conceptual distinction suggested earlier in the text: the analysis of the comic, to which Freud dedicates his impressive Chapter 7, which clarifies the difference between imitation and identification.[51]

The species of the comic or the play of comparisons

From the start, Freud distinguishes jokes from the comic:

> The comic. . . can be content with *two persons: a first who finds what is comic and a second in which it is found*. The third person, to whom the comic thing is to be told, intensifies the comic process but adds nothing new to it.

> In a joke this third person is indispensable for the completion of the pleasure-producing process; but on the other hand the second person may be absent, except where a tendentious, aggressive joke is concerned. *A joke is made, the comic is found.*[52]

Freud now turns to the "naïve" as a form of the comic to show the relevance of this structural distinction. In fact, the "naïve" was going to serve as a model for the interpretation of all the other forms of the comic.

> None of the characteristics of the naïve exist except in the apprehension of the person who hears it – a person who coincides with the third person in jokes.[53]
>
> The naïve must arise. . . in the remarks and actions of other people, who stand in the position of the second person in the comic or in jokes.[54]

The pleasure produced by the naïve form of the comic occurs when the other seems oblivious to an inhibition because he does not have it and therefore overcomes it effortlessly. Faced with this unexpected economy of psychical expenditure, we act like the third person in the joke and are able to lift this inhibition spontaneously.

While the effect of the joke is subject to the condition that the person producing the joke and the person hearing it have the same internal inhibitions or resistances, the effect of the naïve resides in the fact that its unwitting "producer" has none of the inhibitions of the listener.

In both cases, the lifting of internal inhibitions is what produces pleasure. But the psychic processes involved are very different. Although Freud speaks of psychic processes, in this context he should speak of intrapsychic processes. Indeed, in the naïve form of the comic, the person receiving it always coincides with the *I* who watches the free performance given by the other and carries out a sort of arithmetic of representations. By contrast, in jokes, the words cause the listener to unconsciously take the place of the person producing the joke, to identify with him. Although the "naïve" acts like the joke in terms of its effect on the third person (lifting an inhibition), this person must be certain that the one producing the joke has no inhibitions. It is only after he is sure inhibitions are absent that the third person laughs instead of becoming indignant. The process can be described as follows: "We now look at what has been said from two points of view – once in the way it happened in the [producing person] and once in the way it would have happened to us".[55] We infringe on and compare ourselves with the other; this produces an economy of expenditure which is discharged in laughter. Freud adds:

> A mechanism of pleasure like this would seem incomprehensible to us. . . . We should be inclined to assume of [comic pleasure] quite generally that it arises from expenditure economized in a comparison of someone else's remarks with our own.[56]

From this point on, the chapter is devoted to testing this hypothesis by applying it to various species of the comic. The concept of imitation is introduced by means of an analysis of the comic of movement. The clown's pantomime, awkwardness in adults, the hesitant and awkward movements of toddlers elicit laughter because the observer considers them excessive, inexpedient or unsuitable. When I compare them with what my own movements would be in the same situation, I laugh at their disproportionate extent. But for such a comparison – in this case, of the size of movements – a common standard is needed. Freud chose for this purpose the innervatory expenditure involved in the movement. The size of a movement is learned by imitation. The impulsion to imitation develops very early: it is constitutionally linked to the perception of movement. Every perception of movement is accompanied by a kind of ideational mimetics. Freud adds that the impulse to mimicry was not originally intentional; it was not initially intended for communication with others.[57]

Imitation is pleasurable in itself. Freud admits he has no explanation other than this pleasure. He also admits that it is easier to understand the comic effect of caricature, parody, travesty or unmasking and degradation. Yet the most faithful imitation is what makes us laugh the most. To imitate the living means to transgress what constitutes the essential character of every living thing: its singularity.

> Experience has taught us that every living thing is different from every other and calls for a kind of expenditure by understanding; and we find ourselves disappointed if, as a result of complete conformity or deceptive mimicry, we need make no fresh expenditure.[58]

This disappointment takes the form of reduced tension. What we expected was an expenditure by understanding difference (our life experience has accustomed us to the diversity of the living), and the expenditure required to understand what has remained the same cancels the tension of our expectation. The comparison is pleasurable in itself; the pleasure here is the original pleasure in rediscovering what is familiar[59] and results, moreover, from a relief of intellectual work since comparisons are generally made between the less known and the better known, between the most difficult and the easiest and between the unusual and the familiar. The comic metaphor is most often an unmasking, a demystification. These forms of the comic through comparison, substitution or fusion are indeed similar to certain types of jokes. But only the nonsensical comparison is comic – the comparison which, through repeated allusions, insinuates itself into the listener's unconscious and does not lose its effect as soon as the joke has been told.

But all these considerations do not exhaust the subject of the comic. To understand its essence, we must elucidate its genealogy. Freud's reflections can be said to lead to a new theoretical undertaking which brings the question of the comic back to its true foundation: childhood. Freud's task now is to understand the comic though its psychogenesis. In this, he allies himself with Henri Bergson, on whose work he comments extensively.

> Perhaps we ought even to carry simplification still farther, and, going back to our earliest recollections, try to discover, in the games that amused us as children, the first faint traces of the combinations that make us laugh as grown-up persons. . . . Above all, we are too apt to ignore the childish element, so to speak, latent in most of our joyful emotions.[60]

In his study of wit, Freud had already traced jokes back to children's play, play with words and thoughts that critical reason rejects. The psychogenesis of the comic leads to a better understanding of the concepts governing the analysis presented up to this point. First let us look briefly at what Freud says about the psychogenesis of jokes, a discussion we postponed until now in order to present it in parallel with the discussion of the comic. The end of Chapter IV of the *Witz*, "The Mechanism of Pleasure and the Psychogenesis of Jokes", presents a historical reconstruction of the development of jokes. The first stage is the play of children: play develops when a child learns to use words and coordinate thoughts. Agreeing with Groos, Freud writes:

> [P]lay probably obeys one of the instincts which compel children to practise their capacities. In doing so they come across pleasurable effects, which arise from a repetition of what is similar, a rediscovery of what is familiar, similarity of a sound, etc., and which are to be explained as unsuspected economies in psychical expenditure. It is not [surprising] that these pleasurable effects encourage children in the pursuit of play and cause them to continue it without regard for the meaning of words or the coherence of sentences. *Play* with words and thoughts, motivated by certain pleasurable effects of economy, would thus be the first stage of jokes.[61]

A "tireless pleasure seeker", the developing human will be unable to give up the pleasures he has discovered. The jesting of adolescents introduces the second stage of the process which leads to jokes. It serves to augment the gain of pleasure from play while silencing criticism from reason. But the combination of words or the meaningless aggregation of thoughts must retain some meaning. The purpose of jokes, from the start, is to lift inherent inhibitions and to reopen access to the sources of pleasure hitherto blocked by the setting in place of inhibitions. The jest becomes a joke as soon as it is imbued with sense and is valuable. In that case, the joke can be considered to serve the major tendencies and impulses of psychical life and to assist them in their fight against repression. By seducing thought and escaping criticism, the joke offers a "bonus of pleasure", a little surplus of pleasure freeing a considerable yield of extra pleasure that would otherwise have remained inaccessible. This pleasure, serving to free even greater pleasure called "preliminary pleasure", is governed by a principle applying, for instance, to sexual caresses.

The psychogenesis of the comic is also linked with childhood, but on a different level because the child himself is not comical. He only becomes comical when compared to the adult: for example, if he pretends to be a serious grown-up, like a person wearing a disguise. Moreover, the child does not automatically have a "sense of humour". Indeed, Freud holds that the feeling of the comic originates in an economy of psychical expenditure resulting from the fact of understanding the other person.[62] The comic of movement shows this clearly, since the comparison that produces the comic difference could be formulated in the language of the conscious, as follows: "He does it this way; I would do it – I did it – differently". But the child does not yet have the standard named in the second part of this proposition. He only understands imitation and acts like he sees others act. However, the child, whom in many situations we find comical, laughs from pure pleasure. . . and Freud admits that some of the child's sources of pleasure are lost to adults, who compensate by taking pleasure in the comic.

We can hazard a generalisation: the comic always has an infantile character; it is the retrieval of the lost infantile laugh. Thus, we laugh at the difference in expenditure we observe in others or in ourselves each time we find the child in the other (or in ourselves). A complete formulation of the comic could be as follows: he does it this way; I do it differently; he does it like I did it as a child.

Let us summarise the possible sources of comic difference. They can result from 1) a comparison between the other and ourselves, 2) a comparison of a difference observed within another person or 3) a comparison that concerns only ourselves. In a note in *Jokes*,[63] Freud asserts that the most primitive form of the comic is offered by a comparison between someone else's psychic expenditure and our own.

Let us attempt to gather up these scattered elements and consolidate the various concepts into a comprehensive classification system. From the perspective of intersubjective structure, the comic situation occurs in isolation while the situation of the jokes involves several participants. The comic dyad finds its resolution in a monad: although two subjects are present, the entire process takes place in the listener's mind, where the elements of perception are engaged in a dialogue with those of preconscious memory. Comic "sympathy" is entirely solipsistic, and understanding the other is the recognition of oneself in the other: to perceive another person means to be moved, either in the fictional manner of representation or in the active manner of imitation. Imitation shows the child the amplitude of the movement that will give him access to comic pleasure later. As for the joke, it creates a sympathy allowing shared pleasure. This sharing is what ensures its success; it is what sanctions it.

From the topographical perspective, the scene of the joke is the unconscious while the scene of the comic is the preconscious. Thus, in jokes, symbolic identification is unconscious while comic comparison is preconscious. In jokes, the exchange is a sublimation of unconscious tendencies where identification transfers psychic investments outside the subject, but the latter is unaware of this process, and this lack of awareness is a prerequisite for the pleasurable effect of the joke. The comic difference results from a comparison which reveals the difference between the self and the other, but here the process is preconscious – it must escape attention, which is a product of the conscious. The joke originates in repressed drives held back by censure. The comic originates in the impulse to understand the behaviour of the other, seen as another self.

From the perspective of origination, the infantile returns both in the comic and in the joke, but in the first case, the infantile ego (the preconscious representation of this ego) serves as a point of comparison, even offering opposition and resistance to the adult ego, while in the second case, the eternal child returns, imposes himself fraudulently and makes fun of the adult. In the comic, the reasonable ego laughs at the child, but the child blithely defies the adult. The comic validates the ego's maturity and superiority; the joke reminds the ego of its infantile reality (the perverse polymorphous child).

From the economic perspective, comic pleasure, just like pleasure in jokes, emerges from an economy: the economy of the expenditure required by inhibition. In the case of the joke, this is the economy of the expenditure required by representation or investment, and in the case of the comic (in humour, the most subtle form of the comic), what is economised, is the expense required by affect. The common purpose of the joke and the comic is to offer a surplus of pleasure.

Freud concludes that "jokes, the comic and all similar methods of getting pleasure from mental activity are no more than ways of regaining [a] cheerful mood. . . when it is not present as a general disposition of the psyche".[64]

Identification is the "method" characteristic of the joke;[65] (imitative) comparison is the "method" characteristic of the comic.

Comic illusion

Theatrical metaphors have been part of our discussion of the concept of identification from the beginning. We have used an abundance of terms like "psychic scene", phantasmatic scenario, (hysterical) theatricality, theatre of dream-work, neurotic drama, masks, travesty and performers. Indeed, the language of the theatre seems unavoidable for explaining the work of identification. But the need for this theatrical metaphor appeared only secondarily; we are aware of its insistence but have not yet discovered the justification for its systematic use. Since the texts we have examined so far have enlightened us about the subtleties of "ego" substitution, about the play of masks that hides the ego behind the fictional screens of its exposed truth, we can assume the existence of a link between theatrical action and the formation of the ego, but this action requires separate analysis.

A brief article by Freud confirms our intuition. It is a little-known text, which has attracted commentary from very few sources[66] and which expands on certain concepts in *Jokes* by specifying the principles of what could be called an "aesthetics of psychoanalysis". The article is entitled "Psychopathic Characters on the Stage". Indeed, these characters provide an opportunity to deepen our knowledge of the mechanism of theatrical pleasure, which should, a priori, be impeded by the presence of the mentally ill on the stage, and to broaden our understanding of aesthetic pleasure in general.

Freud came to reflect on the psychological conditions required for enjoying theatre through his review of a (second-rate) play by Viennese playwright Hermann Bahr, titled *Die Andere* (*The Others*).[67] The play presents a morbid personality entangled in a complicated love affair. Freud, the spectator, was not convinced by the play. Was this due to the subject of the play itself – mental illness – or to the inability of the playwright to deal effectively with such a delicate subject? Freud analyses the problem at the simplest level. Dramatic effectiveness concerns first and foremost the soul of the spectator: this is Aristotle's undisputed hypothesis in his *Poetics*. In his article, Freud follows in the philosopher's footsteps but uses the language of psychoanalysis.

From the outset, he adopts the Aristotelian theory of catharsis. It is the function of drama to bring about catharsis.[68] Just as wit does, tragedy initiates a flow of eminent and pathetic signs carrying a hidden truth, which shatters the secret depths of our being. The dramatic arts, the art of tragedy in particular, resort to a veritable science of the human soul.[69]

Freud then discusses the finality of drama: that is, the striking effect it is intended to have on the spectator. But who is this spectator? Freud answers: "a 'Misero' to whom nothing worthwhile can happen", stuck in prosaic dullness, obliged to moderate his ambition, who dreams of undertaking great feats but has resigned himself to limiting his desires to the imaginary sphere. And now, the playwright and his actors give him the opportunity to step out of his solitary gloominess, offering him an experience in which he can both lose himself and be saved. This illusory experience is the opportunity to identify himself with a hero – and this is the source of his enjoyment.

Theatre becomes a sphere where life is played out differently, the "elsewhere" where desire triumphs, another reality more powerful than "real life", in which impulses are no longer suppressed. Effective illusion leads to catharsis. What remains to be elucidated is the link between illusion, identity, catharsis and pleasure.

To do this, we must make a detour since it is the tragedy itself that produces a cathartic effect. It derives this power from the passions (*pathèmata*) which it directs, even acting as their therapist, if tragedy is indeed a "treatment of the passions". What distinguishes tragedy from other poetic forms,[70] such as lyric and epic works, is that it explores the depths of the soul in areas close to suffering and death.[71]

This is the essential paradox at the heart of the discussion: a suffering that generates pleasure. What are the conditions that make this illusion possible? For indeed, all the great classical tragedies deal with a form of suffering, resulting from man's conflicts with the gods, with the city and its officials; with members of his family; or with his own conflicting impulses. Dramatic intensity is greater if such conflicts are unconscious; in that case, the neurotic man and the normal man have very different reactions.[72] A good example is needed to develop this idea.

Freud's undisputed choice is *Hamlet*, one of the great creations of tragic poetry, by "the greatest of poets".[73]

Hamlet is undoubtedly the first "modern" tragedy because it portrays psychological suffering: in other words, mental illness.[74] Of course, Freud has not chosen this example at random since he has long recognised in Hamlet the paradigm of the modern Oedipus. He acknowledges the radical meaning of both Sophocles's and Shakespeare's tragedies in his well-known apperception of "typical dreams" in Chapter V of *The Interpretation of Dreams*.[75]

The fact that Hamlet[76] interests the spectator, although he draws him into the uncanny strangeness of his madness, means that he holds the key to the aesthetics of tragedy. The secret of the fascination he exerts resides in these three guiding principles: 1) Hamlet is not psychopathic at the start but becomes so because of the task required of him in the course of the action. 2) The repressed impulse in Hamlet is an impulse we have all repressed in the course of our personal development. 3) This impulse continues to exist under the surface, unnamed and unnamable; it escapes the attention of Hamlet's consciousness and our consciousness as spectators, which is entirely occupied with the pathos of his destiny. It is only in the aftermath that this impulse can be named. . . and Freud goes so far as to say that he had to come along to recognise it and give it a name.

Inversely, and as if to confirm these three rules of tragedy by the absurd, Freud explains the failure of Hermann Bahr's play by showing how it systematically breaks these rules. Bahr's heroine is neurotic from the start; the love affair which destroys her is highly improbable; finally, there is nothing to discover – everything is exposed and therefore flattened.

This detour – the most direct road for the reading of the tragic – allows us to consolidate the concepts presented here into a general statement to be regarded as a fundamental "aesthetic" hypothesis of psychoanalysis. The central question is one of empathy, a recurring theme in the comic and the joke. Cathartic pleasure springs from identification.

Through unconscious identification with the (instinctual) dramatic conflict taking place in the character who displays the signs or symbols of our own impulses, we are freed of the anxiety connected with instinctual pressure and the fragility of our own ability to repress our instincts; we economise resistance – the type of resistance that ordinarily causes us to refuse any encounter with neurosis (that is, repressed material). Identification causes us to espouse the fate of the other and creates the illusion of an experience which, although fictional and imaginary, provides real pleasure and whose value is recognised. Indeed, if the spectator is seduced by this "bonus of seduction", this "preliminary" pleasure granted by the poet's technique (like that of the troubadour or – why not? – the composer of jokes), his "ego" gains access to deeper sources of pleasure, which, however, do not reveal themselves as such.

This being so, we can now attempt a more complete systematisation of identification functions.

In the dream, identification incites substitutions for the self, presenting them as imaginary figures; in hysteria, it fulfills the desire to be the other (or to have what he has in order to be like him) by using the symptom itself as the substitution; in the joke, it symbolises shared desires that are sublimated; in a theatrical performance, it creates the illusion of a liberating knowledge-ignorance through terror and pity: that is, our strange solidarity in the face of our mortal human condition. This points to a series of identification functions: identification-hallucination, identification-symptom, identification-sublimation, identification-illusion. In this sequence, two modalities are apparent: the prevalence of a space, an "imaginary" element in the case of the dream and hysteria, and the emergence of a symbolic space where a (hidden) truth comes to light (in the case of the joke and theatre, particularly tragedy).

We would like to add an observation which contributes an important nuance. Freud speaks of identification with a hero. His discussion clarifies this statement, giving it a more precise meaning: the hero grips the spectator's attention because he is caught in a drama: that is, a conflict made evident in the action of the play by signs and symbols. For example, suffering can only result from contradictory signs. The spectator does not know exactly which is the "trait" he shares with the hero, the trait on which empathetic substitution is based – the *Mitleid*. This underscores a difference pointed out earlier between identification and imitation: one imitates a model, a hero; one identifies with what he unconsciously represents. The theatrical context with the conventions governing the performance, which create the illusion,[77] does not lend itself to imitation, which requires mental or actual movements or expressions. In theatre, there is a comic relation not limited to the comic genre. But dramatic identification involves impulses and functions through its signs and its "productions" which succeed in avoiding censure. This observation alone clearly eliminates any imitative conception of identification which reduces it, as it were, to a psychology of the ego or, from the topographical point of view, to a psychology of the preconscious. One imitates a fully constituted ego; one identifies with what occurs between subjects struggling with impulses.

Notes

1 *The Correspondence of Sigmund Freud and Sandor Ferenczi: 1908–1914*, Falzeder, E., and Brabant, E. (Eds.), Cambridge, MA: Harvard University Press, 1993. (Letter July 9, 1913).
2 Mannoni, O., "L'analyse originelle", in *Clés pour l'imaginaire*, Paris: Editions du Seuil, 1969, pp. 115–130.
3 Freud, S., *The Origins of Psychoanalysis: Letters to Wilhelm Fliess, Drafts and Notes, 1887–1902*, New York: Basic Books, 1954.
4 In his book *Freud's Self-Analysis*, Didier Anzieu (International Universities Press, 1986) highlights the personal drama of the discoverer of psychoanalysis as it is revealed in the self-analysis addressed to Fliess. In it, Freud refers to constructive identifications with writers, artists and historical figures like Zola, Goethe, Moses, Michelangelo, Leonardo da Vinci, Shakespeare, Schiller, Signorelli and Brutus and

ambivalent identification with superiors or colleagues like Brücke, Meynert, Fleischl, Breuer, Königstein, Oscar Rie, Nothnagel and Fliess. These two major types of identification reveal Freud's ambiguous attitude towards his developing oeuvre and explain why this oeuvre wavered between art and science.

5   Recognition (the German word *Anerkennung* is a reminder of the Hegelian term) is discussed by Aristotle in a passage (1454 and continued) where its different forms are described: recognition by signs, recognition invented at will by the poet, recognition through a memory, recognition by a process of reasoning and recognition which arises from the incidents themselves.

6   In the *Interpretation of Dreams*, the corresponding passage is in Chapter 5.

7   In his analysis of Schreber (1911), Freud wrote: "Paranoia decomposes, just as hysteria condenses. Or rather, paranoia resolves once more into their elements the products of condensations and identifications which are effected in the unconscious".

This note on paranoia anticipates far in advance the content discussed by the Freudian theory of the "ego" in 1920 (*Group Psychology and the Analysis of the Ego*), in 1923 (*The Ego and the Id*) and in 1938 (*Splitting of the Ego in the Process of Defence*), a theory of the ego generally associated with Freud's second topographical model.

8   Letter to Fliess, January 3 and 4, 1899, in Freud, S., *The Origins of Psycho-Analysis: Letters to Wilhelm Fliess, Drafts and Notes, 1887–1902*, op. cit.

9   The prefatory remarks to the *Fragment of an Analysis of a Case of Hysteria* reaffirm the importance of the relation of the dream to the neuroses: "The preparatory labor of investigating thoroughly the problem of dreams [is] an indispensable pre-requisite for any comprehension of the mental process in hysteria and the other psycho-neuroses".

10 The letter goes on to give a clinical illustration: "This key opens many doors. Do you know, for instance, why X.Y. suffers from hysterical vomiting? Because in fantasy she is pregnant, because she is so insatiable that she cannot bear being deprived of having a baby by her last fantasy lover as well. But she also allows herself to vomit, because then she will be starved and emaciated, will lose her beauty and no longer be attractive to anyone. Thus the meaning of the symptom is a contradictory pair of wish fulfillments". Letter to Fliess, February 19, 1899. Freud calls this "compromising" function of the symptom *overdetermination*.

11 The use of the word *Entstellung* is particularly interesting: *Ent* – the equivalent of the Latin prefixes *de*, *trans*, *ex* – conveys the notion of an abrupt break, of radical change. As for *stellen*, it recalls the earliest meanings of the verb "to do" – place, set up, lay out, construct – in a reflexive form; *sichstellen* can mean "to pretend", "to feign", "to impersonate". It is not a coincidence that the term *identification* appears in connection with "distortion" since it is indeed a phenomenon of deformation. The double idea contained here is that of an abrupt change of place on the one hand and a disguise on the other.

12 The expression "witty butcher's wife" originates in Jacques Lacan's enthusiastic duplication of Rabelaisian candor in his remarkable commentary of Freud's text, titled "The Direction of the Treatment and the Principles of Its Power", specifically the section "Desire Must Be Taken Literally", Lacan, J., *Écrits*, Fink, B. (Trans.), New York: W.W. Norton, 2006, pp. 489–542.

13 See Standard Edition, Volume 4, Chapter 4, for the analysis of this dream in *The Interpretation of Dreams*.

14 Freud delights in the man's humour and goes on to mention a personal association with the expression *Dem Maler Sitzen* (sitting for the painter) and Goethe's lines: "*Und wenn er keinen Hintern hat Wie kann der Edle sitzen?*" (And if he has no backside, how can the nobleman sit?)

15 But how can another woman be loved (isn't it enough that her husband appreciates her, for the patient to think of love?) by a man who would find her lacking – this man who

speaks of a piece of a woman's derrière? This is the question developed here, a question that applies in general to hysterical identification.

16 This opposition between processes (*Wege*) and motives (*Motive*) is constant in Freud's thinking. See letter of May 31, 1897, quoted earlier, as well as the following texts related to Dora's analysis: *Fragment of an Analysis of a Case of Hysteria*, S.E. 7, London: Hogarth, 1905; *Jokes and Their Relation to the Unconscious*, S.E. 8, London: Hogarth, 1905.

17 The dream of the witty butcher's wife, as we have reported it, looks like a syllogism. A little further in the text, Freud referred to "rules of the hysterical processes of thought". This rational metaphor indicates Freud's interest in mental processes, as well as the influence the philosophical and psychological texts of the Empiricists have had on him.

18 "*Die Identifizierungistnicht simple Imitation, sondern Aneignung auf Grund des gleichenätiologischen Anspruches . . .*" "*An-eignung*" (translated in the Standard Edition to "assimilation" (Vol. 4, p. 150) can be translated to the words "assimilation" and "acquisition", as well as "appropriation" and "usurpation". The term "*eignung*" is etymologically derived from "*eigen*", meaning "own", one's own, whose Gothic root is the verb "*eigen*" – "*oe*" in English – the archaic form of "owe". "*Aigen*" means "to have", "to possess". It is English which has kept the closest connection between property and possession: the verb "to own", identical to the adjective "own", means "to have or hold as property", as well as "to acknowledge as one's own" and, finally, "to recognize, to admit, to confess" (*Webster's Dictionary*).

19 See letters 139, 140, 141: October 14, 1900, January 25 and January 30, 1901, respectively. (*The Origins of Psycho-Analysis*).

20 Letter 140; and in letter 141: "'Dream and Hysteria' should not disappoint you, so far as it goes. The chief thing in it is again psychology, the utilization of dreams, and a few peculiarities of unconscious mental activity. There are only glimpses of the organic background – in connection with the erotogenic zones and bisexuality. But bisexuality is mentioned and specifically recognized once and for all, and the ground is prepared for detailed treatment of it on another occasion. It is hysteria with tussis nervosa and aphonia, which can be traced back to pronounced sucking tendencies, and the chief issue in the conflicting mental processes is the opposition between an inclination towards men and towards women".

21 When she recounts her dreams to Freud, Dora uses them to show him something else about the transference. She "produces" these dreams which are intended for "the other" (the analyst), just as her illness is intended for others. Freud wrote, in fact, that "morbid states are usually directed to a particular person".

22 "The cough, which no doubt originated in the first instance from a slight actual catarrh, was, moreover, an imitation of her father (whose lungs were affected), and could serve as an expression of her sympathy and concern for him. But besides this, it proclaimed aloud, as it were, something of which she may then have been still unconscious: 'I am my father's daughter. I have a catarrh, just as he has. He has made me ill, just as he has made Mother ill. It is from him that I have got my evil passions, which are punished by illness'" (*Fragment of an Analysis of a Case of Hysteria*).

23 Freud, S., *Fragment of an Analysis of a Case of Hysteria*, S.E. 7: 1–122, London: Hogarth, 1905.

24 "Let us next attempt to put together the various determinants that we have found for Dora's attacks of coughing and hoarseness. In the lowest stratum we must assume the presence of a real and organically determined irritation of the throat – which acted like a grain of sand around which an oyster forms its pearl. This irritation was consequently well fitted to give expression to excited states of the libido. It was brought to fixation by what was probably its first psychical coating – her sympathetic imitation of her

father – and by her subsequent self-reproaches on account of her 'catarrh' [in its double sense: pulmonary and genital]. The same group of symptoms, moreover, showed itself capable of representing her relations with Herr K.; it could express her regret at his absence and her wish to make him a better wife. After a part of her libido had once more turned towards her father, the symptom obtained what was perhaps its last meaning; it came to represent sexual intercourse with her father by means of Dora's identifying herself with Frau K. I can guarantee that this series is by no means complete".

25 Lacan, J., *Écrits: The First Complete Edition*, Fink, B. (Trans.), New York: W.W. Norton, 2006; "Presentation on Transference", p. 180.

26 Ibid., pp. 180–181.

27 Freud, S., *Fragment of an Analysis of a Case of Hysteria*, op. cit.

28 Ibid.

29 In his commentary on the Dora case, Lacan shows that the rhythm of the treatment follows that of the transference. Thus, he reveals the dialectical structure of the analytic process and the technical conditions needed for the truth to develop. See "Presentation on Transference" in *Écrits*. We are borrowing this language, with the terms "reversal" and "development of the truth".

30 The famous scene by the lake where Herr K. makes his "declaration" to Dora was what triggered her neurosis. Herr K. is puzzled by Dora's reaction, when after his first words – "*My wife means nothing*" – she slaps him and hurries away. The quasi-magical power of these few words was due to the very particular meaning they had for Dora. A governess in the K. household had already heard Herr K. say the same words with the plaintive intonation of an unhappy husband. But this governess, who was in love with him, was soon disappointed. She left the household when she realised that she had nothing more to expect from Herr K. Dora had listened to the confidences of the seduced and then abandoned governess; this is what she thought when she heard the declaration by the lake: "Does he dare to treat me like a governess, like a servant?" Wounded pride added to jealousy and to conscious motives of common sense – it was too much, Freud told her. "To prove to you how deeply impressed you were by the governess's story, let me draw your attention to the repeated occasions upon which you have identified yourself with her both in your dream and in your conduct. You told your parents what happened. . . just as the governess wrote and told *her* parents. You give me a fortnight's warning, just like a governess. The letter in the dream which gave you leave to go home is the counterpart of the governess's letter from her parents forbidding her to do so". Lacan maintains that the slap, which was Dora's only answer to Herr K.'s laments, had another cause, which involved Frau K. This is what Dora might have thought: "*If she is nothing to you, what can you be to me?*" This shows the overdetermination of this surprising reaction, which might have shocked Dora herself and which she probably regretted afterwards. Her appendicitis nine months after the scene by the lake is her way of correcting her error at the level of phantasy. It could represent a phantasy of pregnancy, expressing regret at not letting Herr K. pursue his propositions.

31 Freud, S., *Fragment of an Analysis of a Case of Hysteria*, op. cit.

32 Ibid.

33 Ibid.

34 Ibid.

35 Ibid.

36 See the substitutions identified by the interpretation of this dream: Herr K. taking the place of the father and Frau K. the place of the mother. The dream shows Dora's desires clearly, as well as the defences she mounts against them.

37 Freud, S., *The Interpretation of Dreams*, S.E. 4–5, London: Hogarth, 1900, chapter VI.

38 Ibid., chapter VI (c).

39 Ibid., "The Means of Representation in Dreams".

40 Ibid.

41 Ibid.

42 Duyckaerts, F., "Conscience et prise de conscience", *Éditions Mardaga*, 1974.

43 Freud, S., *Jokes and Their Relation to the Unconscious*, S.E. 8, London: Hogarth, 1905.

44 "[F]or our investigation of jokes we brought with us an instrument of which no one else had hitherto made use – a knowledge of the dream-work" (p. 181).

45 "[T]he aspect of 'unification' can also be stressed here – the eliciting of a more intimate connection between the elements of the statement than one would have had a right to expect from their nature" (p. 39). Unification, described in Chapter 1, is a modality of the multiple-use technique (discussed earlier). It usually relies on the verbal assonance that provides the "unpredictable relation", the unsuspected point in common between two trains of thought. See Tzvetan Todorov, *Theories of the Symbol*, Ithaca, NY: Cornell University Press, 1984.

46 Freud, S., *Jokes and Their Relation to the Unconscious*, op. cit., p. 99.

47 Ibid., p. 108.

48 Ibid., p. 110.

49 Freud, S., *"Civilized" Sexual Morality and Modern Nervous Illness*, S.E. 8: 76–99, London: Hogarth, 1908; *Civilizaton and Its Discontents*, S.E. 19, London: Hogarth, 1930; *The Future of an Illusion*, S.E. 21: 5–56, London: Hogarth, 1927.

50 Freud, S., *Jokes and Their Relation to the Unconscious*, op. cit., pp. 179–180.

51 Chapter 7 of *Jokes*: "Jokes and the Species of the Comic".

52 Freud, S., *Jokes and Their Relation to the Unconscious*, op. cit., p. 181.

53 Ibid., p. 185.

54 Ibid., p. 182.

55 Ibid., p. 187.

56 Ibid., pp. 187–188.

57 Freud speaks of a primitive impulsion to imitation, an initial movement of the psychic apparatus that impels it to reproduce what it perceives, to repeat it. In the child, this imitative repetition is the foundation for his essential adaptive automatisms, but imitation is also a source of pure pleasure, independent of any utilitarian adaptation or desire to communicate. This illustrates an aspect of the primary process characterised by identity of perception. Thus, imitation seems to be, initially, a compulsive and necessary activity, producing primary pleasure. Secondarily, it seems to be an instrument in the mastery of the body, which takes place in parallel with learning to understand others.

58 Ibid., p. 209.

59 The original pleasure in rediscovering the same thing is referenced here as something obvious, a fact Freud does not bother to discuss: that is, to place into the conceptual framework he is elaborating. He writes: "It seems to be generally agreed that the rediscovery of what is familiar, 'recognition', is pleasurable". A quote from Groos confirms this: "Recognition is always. . . linked with feelings of pleasure. . . . If the act of recognition thus gives rise to pleasure, we might expect that men would hit on the idea of exercising this capacity for its own sake – that is, would experiment with it in play. And in fact Aristotle regarded joy in recognition as the basis of the enjoyment of art" (p. 121). Freud explains this pleasure occasioned by recognition by the reduction of psychic expenditure. It is another way to define the mechanism of pleasure he described, for example, in Chapter 8 of *The Interpretation of Dreams*. We might note that in everyday language "to recognise" means "to identify". The expression "to recognise oneself" implicitly carries the double meaning of identification: to identify oneself (find one's identity based on certain traits), and to identify with another (find oneself

in him). This brings to mind Hegel's dialectic of recognition in *The Phenomenology of Mind*: the struggle for recognition.

The pleasure in rediscovering the same thing relies on the "identity of perception" belonging to the primary process. (Thought identity belongs to the secondary process.) Thus, we can make the connection with what Freud has said about identification in dreams: the dream only deals with relations of likeness and shows them through identification, which is the most direct road to the fulfilment of wishes, as a hallucination.

See Laplanche and Pontalis: *The Language of Psycho-Analysis*, "Perceptual identity/Thought-Identity". What's more, the question of pleasure and recognition, closely tied to that of primitive imitation, is not unrelated to the concept of repetition compulsion, devised in 1920.

60 Bergson, H., *Laughter: An Essay on the Meaning of the Comic*, Eastford, CT: Martino Fine Books, 2014, chapter II.

61 Freud, S., *Jokes and Their Relation to the Unconscious*, op. cit., p. 128.

62 Ibid., p. 236.

63 Ibid., p. 231, Note 1.

64 Ibid., p. 219.

65 Another way of describing the joke is presented in this formulation, which underscores its intersubjective nature: "An urge to tell the joke to someone is inextricably bound up with the joke-work" (p. 143).

66 Octave Mannoni was one of the first to draw attention to this text in a lecture published in 1959 in *La Psychanalyse*, No. 5, Paris: Presses Universitaires de France, pp. 195–216, under the title: "Le théâtre du point de vue de l'imaginaire" and reprinted under a slightly different title: "L'Illusion comique ou le théâtre du point de vue de l'imaginaire", in *Clefs pour l'imaginaire*, Paris: Editions du Seuil, 1969, pp. 161–183. André Greene referred to it as well, without quoting it specifically, in *Un oeil en trop, le complexe d'Oedipe dans la tragédie*, Paris: Les Éditions de Minuit, 1969. An English version of this article, by Dr. Max Graf, Freud's friend, was published in the *Psychoanalytic Quarterly*, Volume II, 1942.

67 Freud summarized the play in a brief note in "Psychopathic Characters on the Stage", S.E. 7: 310.

68 The history of esthetics abounds with reformulations and commentary on this Aristotelian concept, which is repeatedly distorted based on moral, religious, medical and psychological considerations.

69 We are well aware of the close affinity between psychoanalysis as a processing of truth and the tragic. In *The Interpretation of Dreams*, when Freud discusses his "typical" dreams, which led him to recognise in Oedipus's tragic faith the compelling story of all dreamers and of all men, he writes: "The action of the play consists in nothing other than the process of revealing. . . a process that can be likened to the work of a psychoanalysis – that Oedipus himself is the murderer of Laïus, but further that he is the son of the murdered man and of Jocasta" (S.E. 4: 279).

70 In *Basic Concepts of Poetics*, University Park, PA: Penn State University Press, 2008, first published in Zurich in 1946, Emil Staiger offers a phenomenological analysis of poetic styles that it would be interesting to compare to the psychoanalytic definition of the three traditionally recognised "genres": lyric, epic and dramatic. Freud connects lyric art with feelings and sees dance as a uniquely special form of the lyric; epic art transmits the joy of heroic triumph; dramatic art touches the deepest layers of emotional life because it unfolds in the sphere of misfortune and suffering.

71 This was the original meaning retained in the German term *Trauer-Spiel* (tragic play). The characteristic feature of tragedy is this paradoxical mixing of play and mourning (Freud, S., *Creative Writers and Day-dreaming*, S.E. 9: 143–153, London: Hogarth, 1908).

72 The normal man uses the defences again and consolidates the repression of the revealed impulse; the neurotic man sees the effort needed for the defensive formation economised by the acting out of the impulse on the stage, in a play with which he identifies and in which he loses himself. The art of the playwright consists of the ability to trigger identification, not resistance.

73 This is what Freud called Shakespeare in "Some character-types met with in psychoanalytic work", S.E. 14: 312.

74 It is noteworthy that theater enters "modernity" through the dramatic introduction of madness on the stage. What is modern is the new relation between the normal and the pathological, between reason and insanity. See Foucault, M., *Madness and Civilization*, New York: Vintage Books, 1988.

According to Foucault, Shakespeare introduces the tragic conscience of madness: chapter *Stultifera Navis*.

75 Freud, S., *The Interpretation of Dreams*, op. cit., S.E. 4: 278.

76 After Freud, Ernest Jones attempted to make his own study, perhaps more "psychological" than psychoanalytic, of the portrayal of Hamlet and, through him, of Shakespeare. See *Hamlet and Oedipus*, New York: Norton Library, 1976.

77 The term *illusion* is used throughout this work without being classified or otherwise situated in the conceptual framework constructed. Nevertheless, this "quasi-psychoanalytic" concept has yet to emerge from layers of unformed theoretical clay. For we are aware of the importance of this notion which so closely links the themes of play (illusion: in-ludus), phantasy liberated by the theatrical performance, reality which it denies while seeking support in it (like the child who, in play, reworks fragments of the real to create the truly playful space of his hesitant mastery) and, finally "aesthetic" sublimation.

But illusion, as an ambiguous psychic formation which subtly allies dream and reality, is a subject discussed earlier in another context. Indeed, the relation between the spectator and the performance involves identification and illusion: it produces an "as if". We have seen that the dream is good at enacting relations of likeness, of similitude, but ignores the differences inherent in the very structure of resemblance, of "like", so that the akin is transformed into the same, into the un-different. But on the stage, where enactment takes place as well, the theatrical work consists of bringing about identification – a transgression of difference – but within certain bounds. The operation preventing any possibility of fusion and confusion is a sort of negation. Negation is what provokes the reaction "it's theatre" or "it's only theatre". The hysteric identifies with the actor himself – the real person – and not the action for which he is the sign, the living text, the animated hieroglyph (to quote Antonin Artaud); this is because the neurotic is unable to conform to the convention of play, where to play is both to be and not to be. Illusion provides a peculiar pleasure: the ego almost loses itself in it each time, and the movement through which it recovers, enriched and as though satiated with terror and pity, is the triumph of its autarkic character. Clearly, this question opens numerous possibilities: Freud's theory of the Ego as he formulated it in the *Project* shows itself, once again, inadequate to explain a series of experiences where the ego is lost or in danger of being lost, as a delimited, fortified and defended space – a psychological fortress – and as master of its own movements. Of course, something like a psychological "ego" is needed for an "illusion" to occur (or, as we have said, for the enjoyment of jokes). But both sublimation in jokes and theatrical illusion, unrelated to pathology, are suspensions of the ego and, at the same time, positive social experiences. In spheres other than the world of dreams and neurotic phantasy, identification has a dissolving-synthesising function: it is instrumental in creating communities in the Real.

Lastly, let us note that the concept of illusion is not included in Laplanche and Pontalis's *The Language of Psycho-Analysis*. Indeed, Freud only defined the meaning he attributed to this concept on a single occasion, in his text *The Future of an Illusion*, a critique of religion (S.E. 14). Freud's text differentiates illusion from *error*, on the one hand, and from *delusion* on the other:

"What is characteristic of illusions is that they are derived from human wishes. In this respect they come near to psychiatric delusions. . . . In the case of delusions we emphasize as essential their being in *contradiction with reality*. Illusions need not necessarily be *false* – that is to say, unrealizable or in contradiction to reality. . . . Thus we call a *belief* an illusion when a wish-fulfillment is a prominent factor in its motivation, and in doing so we disregard its relation to reality, just as the illusion itself sets no store by verification" (S.E. 14: 31).

The theorisation of the concept of illusion in psychoanalysis was yet to unfold in works dealing with the omnipotence of ideas, superstition, delusional formations and hallucinations and belief in general. The more recent discussion related to the analysis of the self completed the picture by bringing in other correlated concepts (splitting, denial, projection). On the relation between illusion and play, see Winnicott, D. E., *Playing and Reality*, London: Routledge, 1971.

II

Identification and narcissism

As our reading continues, the question of identification becomes more complex and branches out in different directions. The first discussions of the concept, dealing with the hysteric's particular relation to his love objects and to sexual rivalry, extends to include human love life in general, whether it be that of the hysteric, the pervert or the normal subject. The analysis of the identification process in dream-work, whose relation to the process of symptom formation we already examined, leads to the elaboration of a metapsychology, a systematic theory of all these psychic processes. Finally, advances in the practice of analysis and new analytic material stemming from the analysis of phobias, obsessional neuronal and psychoses associate the work of identification with ambivalence, totemism, castration and death.

This complexity makes it more and more difficult to establish a chronological sequence of texts on identification. Repetitions, return to earlier texts, hesitation and anticipation typical of any clinical-theoretical reflection cause some confusion and make it improbable that a well-ordered chronology can be restored.

The present chapter examines an exceptional moment in the Freudian elaboration: the passage from the first topography to the second,[1] a transformation of the conceptual structure of psychoanalytic theory dictated by the advent of new experiments, hypotheses and areas of interest. Therefore, we shall associate texts that were sometimes published at different periods but are closely related in their subject matter.

Identification, orality and object-choice

Freud's reflection on human sexuality reached its most detailed development in *Three Essays on the Theory of Sexuality* in 1905. The numerous new versions of this text, re-edited one after the other between 1905 and 1925, testify to the importance Freud attached to this central theme of psychoanalysis.

The investigation of sexual development introduces a new context in which to define the concept of identification: the context of a genetic pattern of psychosexual development. In his attempt to reconstitute this genesis of sexuality, Freud needs the appropriate concepts: first, he must define the concept of instinct itself, a definition which produces a constellation of related concepts: source, energy, aim, object. This construction must make it possible to conceptualise what is intermediary (between the biological and the psychical), to find the language that can best express approximately this "emotional" character of sexuality as a pathway in the historisation of the subject. The use of terms like *stages* and *phases* can cover over what occurs in the elaboration of the theory: that is, the fortuitous nature of instinctual impulses dispersed in their partial and fragmented searches, the construction of an erotogenic body bit by bit, the precarious unification of impulses into adult sexual organisation. It is within the tentative conceptual reconstruction of these phases and psychical locations of sexuality that the concept of identification was inserted in a different theoretical space than dream and hysteria.

A genealogy of identification

A passage added to the second essay ("Infantile Sexuality") in 1915 defines the contours of this space and confirms the gap beginning to appear between the first topography and the second.

> We shall give the name of "pregenital" to organizations of sexual life in which the genital zones have not yet taken over their predominant part. . . . The first of these is the *oral* or, as it might be called, *cannibalistic* pregenital sexual organization. Here sexual activity has not yet been separated from the ingestion of food; nor are opposite currents within the activity differentiated. The object of both activities is the same; the sexual aim consists in *incorporation* of the object – the prototype of a process which, in the form of *identification*, is later to play such an important psychological part. A relic of this constructed phase of organization, which is forced upon our notice by pathology, may be seen in thumb-sucking, in which the sexual activity, detached from the nutritive activity, has substituted for the extraneous object one situated in the subject's own body.[2]

These lines deserve our complete attention. They seriously complicate the questions examined so far and point to the polymorphous, multi-dimensional character of identification. This term, used in the theory as an explanatory concept – one of many mechanisms – is now considered on its own, in its genesis; its genealogy is revealed. Indeed, from this point on, Freud's attention turns more and more to questions of genesis, particularly the genesis of the ego. The text we just quoted illustrates this preoccupation with beginnings, indicated by an investigation of "infancy": the infancy of sexuality, of the personality, of processes. Let us look at some key terms.

When he speaks of the pregenital organisation of sexual life, he is referring to a phase when "the genital zones have not yet taken over their predominant part".[3] He adds: "We have hitherto identified two such organizations, which almost seem as though they were harking back to early animal forms of life". This remark indicates interest in a biological perspective. Indeed, in *Three Essays*, Freud attempts to place biology in perspective, and it is thanks to the inevitable questioning prompted by considering the role of instincts that he succeeds in identifying the specific object of psychoanalysis: sexuality as the driving force of psychic genesis, as a departure from biology. The question of the nature of identification is closely linked to this debate, and the debate finds, in the question of identification, the key element and strategic sphere of its analysis. But to pre-empt a simplistic understanding of the notion of genesis, Freud is careful to explain how he came to postulate it.

> The study, with the help of psycho-analysis, of the inhibitions and disturbances of this process of development enables us to recognize abortive beginnings and preliminary stages of a firm organization of the component instincts such as this – preliminary stages which themselves constitute a *sexual regime* of a sort.[4]

What exactly is the pregenital organisation called oral? It is the first level of organisation in which an instinct can be recognised as such: that is, "organised" into source, energy, object, aim – terms defined in the first essay. This is the foundation of a sort of "sexual regime": something starts to operate, to make itself heard, to take shape, to take hold. A mythic moment when that which will be a "body" is drafted out of the dispersion of erotogenic zones and the thrust of desire. Feeding behaviour and sexual behaviour are distinct entities in law but not in fact. They have only one path open to them: the mouth – which is also the channel of breath and of cries. This is a cannibalistic phase because what is consumed – what emerging sexuality takes in and what serves to sexualise vital nourishment – is originally flesh: the breast with its milk. Two different activities, but the object of one is also the object of the other. The aim of feeding is, of course, absorption, which for a time eliminates the pressure of hunger; the sexual aim (Freud does not allude to a feeding aim, which is obvious) is incorporation of the object. Is there any difference between these two aims?

The only answer Freud provides is found in an opposition: "*the incorporation of the object – the prototype of a process which, in the form of identification, is later to play such an important psychological part*". What is specifically sexual in incorporation is the psychical component being prepared. Thus, incorporation functions in two modes – a feeding mode and a sexual mode – which can only be recognised as such through reference to what will happen later. It is clear to see here the ambiguous status of this oral instinctual regime: sexual and not yet sexual, the status of a pre-figuration, a prototype, a model. Indeed, Freud notes the "virtual" (*Fiktive*) existence of this phase of organisation, which has no other purpose than to confer meaning to psychopathological phenomena.

If we consider the same phase from the perspective of the residue it leaves – that is, sucking – we have a better idea of the gap opened between the feeding function and the sexual function. The sucked thumb, which acts like a substitute for the breast, consecrates, we might say, the definite loss of the object common to both activities and, by separating them, initiates the series of specifically sexual objects, starting with a part of one's own body. There is layering (*Anlehnung*)[5] of the sexual on the non-sexual based on an initial communality of the object, but this communality has to be broken in order for the sexual as such to emerge (in the form of auto-eroticism): that is, to set in motion the process of psychic development, whose onset is signalled by the production of a substitute. In other words, the "psychical" or the "sexual" is the play of substitution as an elaboration of the loss of the object.

This being so, could we not hazard the following interpretation: does not psychic activity which follows the oral stage receive from this initial mode of functioning the imprint of its "cannibalistic" destiny? To love is to devour. To love is to assimilate the object. These could be the mottos of oral-phase love and sexual activity in its primitive form. This is the sense to be made of the relation of the so-called prototypic process to a later process. Although all activities invoked in loving retain the mark of orality, identification appears to be a psychic elaboration of oral sexuality: it "oralises" or "cannibalises" the love object. When seeing, feeling, touching, caressing and speaking are sexualised, they serve this incorporative sexual purpose. Thus, psychic cannibalism may well be the original but also the permanent objective, leaving its archaic mark on the movement of subsequent stages of organisation. All subsequent identifications belonging to more elaborate sexual systems are destined to contain this devouring tendency.

But this passage from the second essay is itself a foreshadowing: it points to an orientation in the research as if by a flash of lightning. But nothing in the theoretical context of *Three Essays* allows any productive development of this idea of archaic identification.

The work of puberty

At the other end of libidinal development, the function of puberty is to organise the polymorphous structure of the partial organisations of sexual impulses. Puberty is a period when decisive transformations occur, reorganisations ushering in adult sexuality. This is how Freud summarises the trajectory followed by sexuality:

> At a time at which the first beginnings of sexual satisfaction are still linked with the taking of nourishment, the sexual instinct has a sexual object outside of the infant's own body in the shape of his mother's breast. It is only later that the instinct loses that object, just at the time, perhaps, when the child is able to form a total idea of the person to whom the organ that is giving him satisfaction belongs. As a rule the sexual instinct then becomes *auto-erotic*, and not until the period of latency has been passed through is the original relation restored. There are thus good reasons why a child sucking at his mother's breast has become the prototype of every relation of love. *The finding of an object is in fact a refinding of it.*[6]

Finding the sexual object is, therefore, a rediscovery. This succinct formulation provides the key to understanding how sexuality develops. The unfolding of this development will depend on the vicissitudes involved in the process of choosing the object. The "original" choice must be repeated, and puberty is the time of this deferred repetition. The choice of the object occurs in two stages.[7] The first time, the object was "given":[8] the child takes the breast and incorporates it; he gives it up through a separation brought about by a certain totalisation based on the organisation of the visual field: an image of the other takes the place of the dispersed functioning of auto-eroticism. The work of puberty consists of taking back the object, finding the lost object (partial object before totalisation). To rediscover the necessary object, the subject must recover the lost object by performing a series of substitutions. A few pages further on, Freud specifies that the choice of the object

> is accomplished at first. . . in the world of ideas; and the sexual life of a maturing youth is almost entirely restricted to indulging in phantasies, that is, in ideas that are not destined to be carried into effect.[9]

The sexual functioning of phantasy (phantasm?) is to provide imaginary objects – substitute objects – for the sexual impulse at the height of its reorganisation. The identification function supplements the task of object-choice. But Freud gives no explicit description of this connection in the present context. To show it, we must take a circuitous route by looking at several other texts.

The two methods of choosing a sexual object

The sexual object "rediscovered" in the choice of a love object of adulthood reveals the structure of the initial loves subsequently lost. This choice of adulthood can be made using one of two methods (*Wege*). A note added in 1915 to *Three Essays* describes these methods:

> Psycho-analysis informs us that there are two methods of finding an object. The first, described in the text, is the "anaclitic" or "attachment" one, based on attachment to early infantile prototypes. The second is the narcissistic one, which seeks for the subject's own ego and finds it again in other people. This latter method is of particularly great importance in cases where the outcome is a pathological one, but it is not relevant to the present context.[10]

This note is clearly based on the reasoning laid out in 1914 in the pivotal text *On Narcissism: An Introduction*. The text describes the two methods of choosing a sexual object as follows:

A person may love: –

1)   According to the narcissistic type:
    a   what he himself is,
    b   what he himself was,

    c   what he himself would like to be,
    d   someone who was once a part of himself.

2)   according to the anaclitic (attachment) type:

    a   the woman who feeds him,
    b   the man who protects him, and the succession of substitutes who
        take their place.

    This inclusion of case c of the first type cannot be justified till a later stage
of this discussion.

    And he adds, "the significance of narcissistic object-choice for homosexuality
in men must be considered in another connection".[11]
    In fact, Freud had already considered this question earlier, in an essay in which
he makes an analysis of Leonardo da Vinci's phantasm. The third chapter of *Leonardo da Vinci and a Memory of His Childhood*[12] is crucial to our discussion. It
presents hypotheses from which the text on narcissism follows directly. Freud's
discussion of Leonardo's substitute sexual choices includes the relationship
between identification and narcissism. Surprisingly, the concept of identification
is never mentioned in the theoretical text on narcissism, although we know that
Freud had already acknowledged that identification is a desirable development of
the narcissistic libido.
    A passage on the genesis of masculine homosexuality, closely related to a long
note on homosexuality in the first of the *Three Essays*,[13] provides the following
explanation:

> In all our male homosexual cases the subjects had had a very intense erotic
> attachment to a female person, as a rule their mother, during the first period
> of childhood, which is afterwards forgotten; this attachment was evoked or
> encouraged by too much tenderness on the part of the mother herself, and
> further reinforced by the small part played by the father during their child-
> hood. . . . Indeed it almost seems as though the presence of a strong father
> would ensure that the son made the correct decision in his choice of object,
> namely someone of the opposite sex.
>   After this preliminary stage a transformation sets in whose mechanism is
> known to us but whose motive forces we do not yet understand. This child's
> love for his mother cannot continue to develop consciously any further; it
> succumbs to repression. The boy represses his love for his mother: he puts
> himself in her place, identifies himself with her, and takes his own person as
> a model in whose likeness he chooses the new objects of his love.[14] In this
> way he has become a homosexual. What he has in fact done is slip back to
> autoeroticism: for the boys whom he now loves as he grows up are after all
> only substitutive figures and revivals of himself in childhood – boys whom he
> loves in the way in which his mother loved *him* when he was a child. He finds

the objects of his love along the path of *narcissism*, as we say; for Narcissus, according to the Greek legend, was a youth who preferred his own reflection to everything else and who was changed into the lovely flower of that name.[15]

The repression of love through identification makes it possible to keep this love intact in the unconscious. Unconsciously, the homosexual remains faithful to the woman who was his first love object. The repression can only be lifted at the cost of forgetting this early love.

The phantasm of the vulture, around which Freud constructs his entire interpretation of Leonardo's curious contradictions, is a coded representation of this old attachment, a manifestation of the return of this unforgettable repressed material. It seems clear that, at the level of sexual development, this identification with the mother prevented successful identification with Leonardo's father, who was absent for the first five years of his life and relatively present afterwards but no doubt "too late".

> No one who as a child desires his mother can escape wanting to put himself in his father's place, can fail to identify himself with him in his imagination, and later to make it his task in life to gain ascendency over him. When Leonardo was received into his grandfather's house before he had reached the age of five, his young step-mother Albiera must certainly have taken his mother's place where his feelings were concerned, and he must have found himself in what may be called the normal relationship of rivalry with his father. As we know, a decision in favour of homosexuality only takes place round about the years of puberty. When this decision had been arrived at in Leonardo's case, his identification with his father lost all significance for his sexual life, but it nevertheless continued in other spheres on non-erotic activity.[16]

Vasari, the biographer cited by Freud, lists the attributes which show Leonardo's identification with his father: a taste for luxury, for opulence, for fine clothes, for a multitude of servants, for horses. Freud sees this mimetism as a veritable compulsion to imitate and surpass the father.[17] He adds:

> There is no doubt that the creative artists feel towards his works like a father. The effect which Leonardo's identification with his father had on his paintings was a fateful one. He created them and then cared no more about them, just as his father had not cared about him.
>
>   But if his imitation of his father did him damage as an artist, his rebellion against his father was the infantile determinant of what was perhaps an equally sublime achievement in this field of scientific research.[18]

Leonardo was the first since the ancient Greeks who dared to challenge their authority and investigate the secrets of nature. His unquenchable thirst to see and to know was no doubt rooted in his infantile attitudes. The ancients and their authority represent his father, and nature takes the place of the good and tender mother who nurtured him. He had had to do without the support of a father during his early explorations; he had learned to do without him. The boldness and independence of his subsequent scientific research presuppose infantile sexual investigation with no opposition from a father. Later, the investigation continued in fields other than the sexual. Not subjected to intimidation, free of any complex in his filial relations, he never had to find a substitute father in belief in God. His contemporaries testify to the fact that he was irreligious.

What is particular in Leonardo's story is that his relationship with his parents was characterised by a split: he did not find himself in an Oedipal situation until relatively late, and this belated triangle, displaced, deferred, involving another mother (the adoptive mother who had replaced the birth mother, abandoned by the father because of her modest extraction) did not exert the effect of a "normal" Oedipal situation. This hiatus explains Leonardo's sexual inhibitions and his inconsistent behaviour in his artistic activities.

Having been subjected early to the seductive influence of an abandoned mother who saw him as her unique and "complete sexual object",[19] her only consolation, exposed too early to sensuality in the form of passionate kisses (the oral content of the vulture phantasm testifies to this), Leonardo no doubt entered too early a period of infantile sexual activity. Passive repression of this explosive erogeneity led, at puberty, to an aversion to real sexual activity and to a preference for platonic relations with young boys whom he protected, it has been said, like a mother. Genital sexual impulses were subjected to repression, but partial, infantile sexual impulses escaped this fate; thanks to the early expression of uninhibited sexual curiosity, the impulse to see and to know was sublimated into a thirst for scientific knowledge. Thus, sublimation appears to be another path for impulses to take, instead of repression. A very small part of Leonardo's libido remained oriented towards sexual aims; his atrophied adult sexual life – that of a quasi-asexual adult – took the form of homosexuality rooted in repression through identification.

This brief presentation of the "Leonardo case" invites us to reflect on the role of identification.

Identification with a perfectly attentive and seductive mother is described as a means employed by Oedipal repression. By identifying with his mother, Leonardo rids himself of his incestuous libido, only to conserve it that much better in the unconscious. The love which he was forced to give up (when his father married Dona Albiera) was "forgotten" and transformed, by the play of identification, into an unconscious libidinal position which kept him faithful to the image of the lost mother, despite all his homosexual attachments. Identification is the process that converts the oral object libido into libido which takes as its object the disguised ego, transformed on the model of the abandoned object. This process can only be detected through Leonardo's homosexual love objects: the second phase, that of puberty, is the most revealing. It is as if the loss of this adored mother constitutes such a great libidinal catastrophe that the subject, forced to let her go, only gives the appearance of resigning himself to this abandonment while, in fact, holding on to the lost relationship by playing it out in the other context, where it escapes conscious censure.

Here, identification is placed in the service of repression; it seems to be a means of resolving Oedipal conflict when identification with the sexual rival cannot take place for lack of a father. This association of repression with sexual identification is, indeed, what we have repeatedly observed in the hysterical process. The love object desired by the hysteric proves to be impossible to obtain, inaccessible, cancelled, prohibited; this repressed object is maintained, but in a sphere other than conscious reverie. The hysteric can indulge in unconscious sexual activity, experience the desired satisfaction, play out in phantasy the erotic scenarios he longs for, but this sexual activity can only be maintained by becoming a symptom: satisfaction followed by punishment. The sexual objects remain the same but only in the precarious sphere of fiction; exacerbated erotism manifests itself freely, but always in the shadows of unawareness.

The hysteric identifies with the love object, with the sexual rival: the model reveals libidinal quality and the type of object-choice repeated in these symptoms. Freud asked himself if the root of hysteria might not lie in a hesitation regarding sexual position, when latent homosexuality is discovered, since this is the most deeply repressed tendency in the unconscious of hysterics. Thus, we can say that homosexuality and hysteria develop in similar ways, at least in terms of the paths and means they use to preserve an infantile relation. This is the function of the identification process: to maintain – at the cost of a change in topographical context – a relationship of which reality has deprived the subject.

We now have to examine the nature of Leonardo's identification with his father. Its main characteristic is that it is rooted in a sphere other than the erotic. The father was not originally part of young Leonardo's libidinal attachment configuration; he was not in the role of the other who prohibits and intimidates. For Leonardo, to take the place of the father was not going to mean to replace him as the woman's lover, to identify with him in his sexual role; it would mean, more likely, imitating the father rather than identifying with him, to remain true to the technical terminology presented earlier. A taste for luxury, et cetera is an imitation; rivalry with the father, independent of any role in the child's sexual attachment to the mother, takes the form of pure revolt, an independent spirit, the challenging of authority, irreligiosity.

These observations are far from totally satisfactory: Leonardo's identification with the Oedipal father remains unexplained. Freud only commented clearly on the identification with a lost sexual object, identification as work of transformation accomplished by the sexual impulse. In what circumstances does the relation of rivalry become sexual identification rather than mere revolt? What are the differences between identification with the mother and identification with the father? In what circumstances does their association or dissociation in the organisation of infantile sexuality prove to be pathogenic? We are now faced with what Freud was to call later the delicate description of the "complete Oedipus complex",[20] but the conceptual framework Freud had at his disposal when he wrote *Leonardo* was insufficient for reconstituting the whole process precisely.

The considerations on the work of puberty and the double path of the choice of a sexual object, in their relation to the identification process, allow us to advance the following conclusions: first, masculine homosexuality illustrates, through the nature of sexual choices at puberty, the type of choice of a narcissistic object; identification with the mother reproduces the lost infantile love object since the subject playing the role of the other loves his own self in the reproductions of his own childhood ego, represented by young boys, (case b of type 1 described earlier). Secondly, such an identification plays a role in repression: the incestuous child remains so, by means of self-transformation based on the maternal model; incest continues to be committed in the protected and unknown sphere of the unconscious, where the different roles are redistributed: I am still the one she, who has become me, loves. Thirdly, identification appears to act as a mechanism which converts the libido and preserves archaic object-choice: in hysteria, the acting out increases in complexity given the ambiguity of this choice of the object (the man and/or the woman); in masculine homosexuality, the preserved object, the loved object, is the unforgettable *I*. It is as though the homosexual makes a decision, by means of a clearer narcissistic regression, regarding something about which the hysteric can't bring himself to decide. Finally, in the fourth place, the difference between Leonardo's relationship with his father and his relationship with his mother suggests the usefulness of looking more closely at the possible distinction between sublimation type identification (Leonardo's scientific researches, rivalry, challenge and artistic creation) and repression-oriented identification (choice of homosexual position in puberty, hysterical symptom, dream representations, etc.). This second obstructive mechanism is the one we formulated after our discussion of the connection of dreams with hysteria and with jokes. In the first case (identification-sublimation), the process is seen as transforming sexual impulses and leading to desexualisation; in the second case (identification-repression), the process is seen as the repetition of an unforgettable primary relationship, stored and preserved safely in unconscious phantasy, when the subject has no other means than such a fictional reproduction to overcome the loss of an object (be it the ego in narcissistic love or the parents in attachment-type love).

"Totemic" identification

The discussion of incorporation in *Three Essays on the Theory of Sexuality* suggested that Freudian investigation of origins – the origins of perversion, neuroses, sexuality and love in general – would proceed in a manner similar to the investigation of the origins of processes. This implied a relativisation of the theoretical concepts attempting to explain these processes. During this period of major reformulations based on the introduction of the concept of narcissism as it relates to the concepts of the stages of libidinal organisation, choice of object and identification, Freud's writings were concerned with defining as clearly as possible the idea of psychic genesis: that is, the genesis of psychic energy, understood to be "sexual". The cannibalistic origins of identification, mentioned in this text in passing, actually hold a strategic position in Freud's elaboration of his edifice.

Freud's reasoning constantly relates the time of origins to the effects manifest at the stage of retroaction: that is, to pathological phenomena. This back-and-forth movement between current neurosis and a time of origins is also at work in an analysis, where interpretation obliges the subject to recreate the past. Nowhere is this working through by means of interpretation, which turns out to be a descent into Hell every time, described more eloquently than in the clinical and theoretical writings of this extremely productive period between 1912 and 1917. We believe this productivity was the result of an increasingly well-structured elaboration of a series of connections intuitively established based on analytic practice: the series child-neurotic-primitive.

While this theoretical series constitutes the foundation of what we have called Freud II, *Totem and Taboo* is the paradigm for the hypothetical productions governed by this series. The book itself serves to make the transition between Freud I and Freud II, which coincides with the first manifestations of dissidence and with the start of taking psychoanalysis beyond the limits of treatment.[21] We shall see that *Totem and Taboo* marks a crucial stage in the exploration of the identification process.

Identification and projection: magic as a model

Animism is the starting point. It is a "spontaneous" theory of identification, we might say. Of all systems of thought developed by man since the beginning of time, animism is the most consistent and complete, the one which "allows us to grasp the whole universe as a single unity".[22] The original nucleus of the animistic system is psychological in nature. The innumerable "spirits" inhabiting the world are "souls" that have made themselves independent of "bodies"; the "souls" of animals, plants and inanimate objects are perceived as constructed on the analogy of human souls. This body/soul duality, the foundation on which the animistic system is based, is the answer to the problem of death.

"What primitive man regarded as the natural thing was the indefinite prolongation of life – immortality. The idea of death was only accepted later, and with hesitancy. Even for us it is lacking in content and has no clear connotation".[23] The practical need to gain mastery over the world and over death inspired this system of thought, which includes a whole series of instructions concerning the actions necessary to control men, animals and things or, rather, the "spirit" of men, animals and things. Witchcraft and magic constitute these concrete practices: they are the technique of animism. Freud focused on magic because it was the most primitive and most important part of animistic technique.

E. B. Tylor formulated the principle of magic as "mistaking an ideal connection for a real one". Freud proposed eliminating the value judgment implied in this formulation and simply saying "taking an ideal connection for a real one".[24] Indeed, in this context the categories "true" and "false" (mistaken) are irrelevant. The magic art replaces the real with reflection, based on a dominant and widespread conviction: the omnipotent character of wishes. The reality to be mastered is first and foremost this reality of desire, and magic, with its techniques, provides means – paths – leading to the fulfilment of pressing desires. Magic does this through a series of displacements. These magical paths deserve closer examination: indeed, the techniques of magic make it possible to reveal the "logic" which the psychic apparatus obeys when subjected to the omnipotence of desire, a "logic" persisting in the unconscious of those who had to capitulate in the face of omnipotent reality.[25] In our opinion, the identification process is a favoured technique, a magical path ideally suited to serve desire. While reflecting on the techniques involved in magic, Freud discovered the "techniques" of unconscious thought – including identification.

Homeopathy and telepathy: the wish, the act and the thought

Let us look more closely at the ideas outlined here. Freud approached the problem of magic from the perspective of the efficacy of its techniques.

One group of magical techniques obtains its efficacy through ritual actions imitating the desired event. Referring to Frazer, Freud calls this first type of magic imitative or homeopathic. "If I wish it to rain, I have only to do something that looks like rain or is reminiscent of rain".[26]

And he gives the following illustration:

> [In] some part of Java, at the season when the bloom will soon be on the rice, the husbandman and his wife visit their fields by night and there engage in sexual intercourse to encourage the fertility of the rice by their example.[27]

The example shown by a human act of reproduction induces by magic the fertility of the earth. But incestuous sexual relations are banned or dreaded because of their adverse effect on the fertility of the soil. A trace of this magical belief is to be found in Sophocles' *Oedipus Rex*. Another example: by building the effigy of an enemy or declaring that a particular object represents his image, I can harm this enemy by beating the thing which imitates him.

A second group of magical acts relies on a principle other than that of similarity.

> There is another procedure by which an enemy can be injured. One gets possession of some of his hair. . . or even a piece of his clothing, and treats them in some hostile way. It is then exactly *as though* one had got possession of the man himself; and he himself experiences whatever it is that has been done to the objects that originated from him. In the view of primitive man, one of the most important parts of a person is his *name*. So that if one knows the name of a man or of a spirit, one has obtained a certain amount of power over the owner of the name. . . . In these examples the place of similarity is evidently taken by affinity.

The higher motives for cannibalism among primitive races have a similar origin.

> By incorporating parts of a person's body through the act of eating, one at the same time acquires the qualities possessed by him. This leads in certain circumstances to precautions and restrictions in regard to diet. . . . The magical power is not affected even if the connection between the two objects has already been severed or even if the contact occurred only on a single important occasion.[28]

This last example is one of contagious magic, whose effective principle is spatial contiguity or, rather, imagined contiguity – the recollection of it. As if "real" contiguity itself were created by magical thinking, which alone granted its value and efficacy.

But we know that similarity and contiguity are the two essential principles of the association processes. Magic obeys the laws of association: this is what explains the extravagance, the folly of magical observances. Psychoanalysts are familiar with this extravagance, which they encounter daily in dream content. We must go beyond this observation. Similarity and contiguity are only the paths along which magic proceeds; we must still find the true essence of magic, that which leads to its extravagance: what is this misunderstanding, this false idea, which causes it to replace the laws of nature with psychological ones?

What is lacking in associative theories of magic is clearly the dynamic factor. To uncover these motives for magic, we have only to rely on this associative theory, provided we subject it to closer examination. Imitative magic – simpler and more important than contagious magic – will be our guide in this search for the motives leading men to practice magic. Why does Freud assert this priority of the principle of imitation over that of contagion? He provides the answer himself, summing it up as follows:

> It is easy to perceive the motives which lead men to practise magic: they are human wishes. All we need to suppose is that primitive man had an immense belief in the power of his wishes. . . . To begin with, therefore, the emphasis is only upon his wish.[29]

We are left with the task of reconstructing the theoretical genesis of this production of magic Freud defined as being motivated by wishes and the desire to satisfy them. The psychoanalytic understanding of magic adds another link to the chain of psychic formations already identified. This understanding reveals a new branch of the genealogical tree of desire. Magic, dream, children's play, neurotic thought, art, science and religion: a true anthropological structure is taking shape, revealing Freud's ambition to elaborate a unified system.

But let us look at the genesis of this development, starting with this sentence that sets its orientation: "To begin with. . . the emphasis is only upon [the] wish".

Children are in an analogous psychical situation, though their motor effi-
ciency is still undeveloped. I have elsewhere put forward the hypothesis that,
to begin with, they satisfy their wishes in a hallucinatory manner, that is, they
create a satisfying situation by means of centrifugal excitations of their sense
organs. *An adult primitive man* has an alternative method open to him. His
wishes are accompanied by a motor impulse, the will, which is later destined
to alter the whole face of the earth in order to satisfy his wishes. This motor
impulse is at first employed to give a representation of the satisfying situation
in such a way that it becomes possible to experience the satisfaction by means
of what might be described as motor hallucinations. This kind of representation of a satisfied wish is quite comparable to *children's play*, which succeeds
their earlier purely sensory technique of satisfaction. [The fact that] children
and primitive man find play and imitative representation enough for them. . .
is the easily understandable result of the paramount virtue they ascribe to
their wishes, of the will that is associated with those wishes and of the methods by which those wishes operate. As time goes on, the psychological accent
shifts from the motives for the magical act on to the measures by which it is
carried out – that is, on the act itself. . . .

It thus comes to appear as though it is the magical act itself which, owing
to its similarity with the desired result, alone determines the occurrence of
that result. There is no opportunity, at the stage of animistic thinking, for
showing any objective evidence of the true state of affairs. But a possibility
of doing so does arise at a later time, when, though all of these procedures
are still being carried out, the psychical phenomenon of doubt has begun to
emerge as an expression of a tendency to repression.[30]

Thus, the enactment of desire, the magical – playful – fulfilment of a wish,
the recourse to imitative methods are formulations of desire. At the start, there
is desire, a spontaneous "wish". Magic expands on this initial bursting through
of the wish; the magical extension brings the pure production of a wish into the
realm of myth. Satisfaction does not follow upon the simple emergence of a wish.
First, there is a picturing of it and a mimicking of its fulfilment.

Through this imitation, the child/primitive man avoids acknowledging realities other than his own psychic reality: he acts as if he were omnipotent. Desire,
motive, has been transformed into an action, for better or worse, through a picturing, an imitative staging. Wish has become will – a will still magical, of course,
subjected to the psychical overvaluation of omnipotent "wishing". The child, in
his sensorial hallucination – in a dream – and then in motor hallucination during
play, becomes an actor, the agent of desire; because he is searching for magical
paths and means, and all his psychic energy is directed to these paths, he becomes,
as it were, the stage manager or director of the wish, like primitive man who
practises magic.

But isn't this the very act of identification, of a metamorphosis through recourse to "as if"? The transformation of the wish into an act changes the actor: he is not like "before", like "at the start"; that is, he is no longer purely a desiring force. Frazer's statement describes this situation perfectly: "Imitative magic" – identificatory magic – is homeopathic. Indeed, homeopathy consists of healing illness through illness (dosage being key). In play and in magic, homeopathy consists of enacting desire and an imitation of its fulfilment. It is the first "processing" of the desiring impulse by psychical inflation, by the narcissism of desire.

We shall see that so-called contagious magic, whose technique differs from homeopathic magic, is governed by the same principles. Freud says:

> The fact that it has been possible to construct a system of contagious magic on associations of contiguity shows that the importance attached to wishes and to the will has been extended from them on to all those psychical acts which are subjected to the will. A general overvaluation has thus come about of all mental processes – an attitude towards the world, that is, which, in view of our knowledge of the relation between reality and thought, cannot fail to strike us as an overvaluation of the latter. Things become less important than ideas of things: whatever is done to the latter will inevitably also occur to the former. Relations which hold between the ideas of things are assumed to hold equally between the things themselves. Since distance is of no importance in thinking – since what lies furthest apart both in time and space can without difficulty be comprehended in a single act of consciousness – so, too, the world of magic has a telepathic disregard for spatial distance and treats past situations as though they were present.[31]

This initial description of the stages of human evolution ends with a remark concerning the question Freud raised earlier about the primacy of imitative magic.

> [T]he two principles of association – similarity and contiguity – are both included in the more comprehensive concept of "contact". Association by contiguity is contact in the literal sense, association by similarity is contact in the metaphorical sense. The use of the same word for the two kinds of relation is no doubt accounted for by some identity in the psychical processes concerned which we have not yet grasped. We have here the same range of meaning of the idea of "contact" as we found in our analysis of taboo.[32] By way of summary, then, it may be said that the principle governing magic, the technique of the animistic mode of thinking, is the principle of the "omnipotence of thoughts".[33]

Thus, the accent has shifted from the omnipotence of desire to the omnipotence of thought. Homeopathy and telepathy are two modes of magical contact. The dominant mode of contact is founded on the claim of primacy of desire itself, which is desire for contact, whose magical nature seems to recede before two forms of association: similarity and contiguity. The final reference to taboo in this context is quite enlightening: at the start, desire is desire to touch, to take for one's own, to seize. The analysis of taboo identified the desire to touch, to eat, to kill.[34]

How are we to understand, then, Freud's statement that imitative magic is simpler and more important than contagious magic?

We take this to be an assertion of the paradoxical priority of figurative sense over the literal sense and an admission that the literal sense itself is only valid – meaningful – once the displacement, the separation, the transfer of thought has taken place: that is, once there has been the curious act of mimicking which separates desire from itself and seems to signal the birth of the subject. The thought involved here was hallucinatory at its inception: playful, dream-like, magical. A will to contact attached to desire. As a result, contiguity is also subjected to thinking, to omnipotent thought and its efficacy, as a magical "method"; it is subjected to the will of the thought that seems to be the initial psychic "processing" of desire: homeopathy. This is not without recalling the theory of the signifier: what is involved is the inherently metonymic nature of language.[35] Whereas Freud speaks of "thought", Lacan introduces the concept of a signifying chain.

Magic, hysteria and obsessional neurosis

But Freud continues to develop his theory of man's progress. At the first stages, there was the "child" hallucinating desire sensorially and then through play and "primitive man" hallucinating desire in thought and in the magical animistic technique. Now Freud introduces the new term *neurotic*. He places the words used in this series of texts on the work of interpretation in brackets to underscore the purely "theoretical" character of these interrelated terms.

The adult neurotic is governed by two types of thought: the first, unconscious, is the omnipotent thought of the child he once was and who can only survive in this lack of awareness of the other; the second is unsure, subject to judgment and repression, trying to submit to the harsh law of reality. The expression "omnipotence of thought" came from one of Freud's patients, the Rat Man.[36]

Although obsessional neurosis illustrates most clearly the omnipotence of thought, particularly through belief in the telepathic powers of hostile intentions, the fear that bad things will happen to loved ones and superstitious beliefs, omnipotence of thought should not be taken to be the distinguishing feature of obsessional neurosis because

> analytic investigation reveals the same thing in the other neuroses as well. In all of them what determines the formation of symptoms is the reality not of experience but of thought. Neurotics live in a world apart, where, as I have said elsewhere,[37] only "neurotic currency" is legal tender; that is to say, they are only affected by what is thought with intensity and pictured with emotion, whereas agreement with external reality is a matter of no importance.[38]

Thus, psychoanalysis uncovers in every neurosis a domain of magical thinking. In both neuroses, hysteria and obsession, we find the associative "paths" used by the two modes of magical action described here. It is as if the hysteric unconsciously has recourse to a homeopathic means to "cure" himself of his desire. Is it not the case that one of the major characteristics of the hysterical symptom, as we have so often pointed out, is the desire to be like someone – and that the means of choice for fulfilling this wish is usually identification? In a context of hysteria, the action, the enactment of a pretense, takes the place of the desire itself: a veritable triumph of imitative magic. As for the obsessive, most of his "obsessions" (fear of touching) can be understood as the unconscious expression of an omnipotent will to contact, associated with the overestimation of all psychic processes subjected to this will, as if all psychic activity suffered from contamination by the (metonymic) contagion of desire, telepathically crossing distances and time. In fact, animistic thought is at work in both neuroses by every means, be it imitative or contagious.

All forms of thought, even the highest, bear the traces of the magical origins. Religious man, who attributes omnipotence to the gods, and the man of science, who attributes it to a scientific spirit subject to the laws of reality, both recover what they claim to give up. Only the artist does not renounce his devotion to the omnipotence of thought:

> Only in art does it still happen that a man who is consumed by desires performs something resembling the accomplishment of those desires and that what he does in play produces emotional effects – thanks to artistic illusion – just as though it were something real. People speak with justice of the "magic of art" and compare artists to magicians. But the comparison is perhaps more significant than it claims to be. There can be no doubt that art did not begin as art for art's sake. It worked originally in the service of impulses which are for the most part extinct to-day. And among them we may suspect the presence of many magical purposes.[39]

The general structure that ties these very diverse psychic productions together is narcissism. It is the degree of importance of this narcissistic moment in the psychic economy of each element of the sequence that determines its role. Existence could be seen as being the process of doing something real with narcissism – that is, with the omnipotence of desires.

The theoretical sequence child-neurotic-primitive man now clarifies and elaborates Freud's description of a genealogy of libidinal tendencies, as given in *Three Essays*. Libidinal organisation takes place under the impetus of narcissism.

> Although we are not yet in a position to describe with sufficient accuracy the characteristics of this narcissistic stage, at which the hitherto dissociated sexual instincts come together into a single unity and cathect the ego as an object, we suspect already that this narcissistic organization is never wholly abandoned. A human being remains to some extent narcissistic even after he has found external objects for his libido. The cathexes of objects which the effects

are as it were emanations of the libido that still remains in his ego and can be drawn back into it once more. The state of being in love, which is psychologically so remarkable and is the normal prototype of the psychoses, shows these emanations at their maximum compared to the level of self-love.[40]

The omnipotence of thought is, in fact, its sexualisation – we may even say its narcissisation. In the beginning, sexuality becomes thought, desire appears as thought: an imitation of itself, magic. The neurotic displays this primitive sexualisation of psychic actions to a high degree, but in his case, repression occurs – in parallel with the development of the capacity for doubt, for judgment, for realistic assessment and logical reasoning. Repressed material comes to haunt this new form of thought and brings about a new sexualisation of mental processes, intellectual narcissism, the omnipotence of thought.

A note Freud added at the end of his discussion on narcissism reopens the question of magical identification. Alluding to the essence of animistic thought and to magic, as if in passing, he quotes an English author:

> It is almost an axiom with writers on this subject, that a sort of solipsism or Berkeleyanism (as Professor Sully terms it as he finds it in the Child) operates in the savage to make him refuse to recognise death as a fact.
>   (Marett, R. R., Pre-animistic Religion, *Folklore*, Vol. II, 1900, p. 178)

The preservation of narcissism (solipsism) and the refusal to recognise death: these are the difficult tasks incumbent upon magic, as if all that was required was to formulate the best possible description of this double imperative. The rest of *Totem and Taboo* seems to be an attempt to provide a conceptual explanation of the possible means available to one who starts out (the child/primitive man) to accomplish this difficult task.

Animism and paranoia: projective formations

Animism is a psychological theory. Magical techniques use the hypotheses of this theory whose basic premise is that, for the animist, things in the world correspond exactly to his inner reality. Primitive man transposes naturally the structural conditions of his own psyche into the outside world. All the psychoanalyst has to do is to reverse the process and relate to the soul what animist theory relates to the nature of things. At the start of his presentation of animism, Freud quoted David Hume, who wrote in *The Natural History of Religion*:

> There is a universal tendency amongst mankind to conceive all beings like themselves, and to transfer to every object those qualities with which they are familiarly acquainted, and of which they are intimately conscious.[41]

Primitive man sees reflected in the world the adventures of his psychology. Certain authors assert that magic, a technique intended to impose on things the laws of psychic life, predates the theory of animism itself. This theory, which attributes to spirits and demons the power formerly assigned by magic the omnipotence of thought, can be seen as being an initial renunciation. The process by which this renunciation is achieved is called projection. Renunciation is an attribution of power, a mandate, a procuration.

Freud wrote:

> Spirits and demons, as I have shown in the last essay,[42] are only projections of man's emotional impulses. He turns his emotional cathexes into persons, he peoples the world with them and meets his internal mental processes again outside himself – in just the same way as that intelligent paranoiac, Schreber, found a reflection of the attachments and detachments of his libido in the vicissitudes of his confabulated "rays of God".[43]

A new element is added to the sequence Freud is constructing. The paranoiac belongs to this structural domain of narcissism. Linking him to this chain widens even more the sphere of psychoanalytic understanding. *Totem and Taboo* is indeed a crossroads at which it becomes evident that the psychoanalytic explanation is now complete: all its components are interrelated. We must now elucidate the manner in which tying the paranoid process into the magical process transforms the question of identification.

We suppose projection and identification to be very closely related in the practice of magic and in animist theory. Each of them is a way of building a bridge between the inner and outer worlds; in other words, they are both ways of refusing this cruel separation. We have seen that identification presents itself as a means of appropriation, an incorporation: a renewal of the oral mode of relating to objects in general; a mimicking of the fulfilment of desire, self-transformation, auto-affection. As for projection, it appears from the start not as mimicking but as the path to a sort of expropriation, an exporting of desire which is lent to others, as it were. Things and people become proxies for desire. And the deciphering, the reappropriation of things created in this manner, is called thought (animistic). The world becomes livable because it has been peopled first: this also makes it identifiable, manipulable, differentiated.

Strangely, we might say that here, too, we are dealing with identification, in the sense of determination, of nomination. And since we are speaking from the perspective of magic, of a will to control as much through thought as through action, and since, in the final analysis, what we attempt to "control" is desire, we must conclude that projection and identification constitute a combined "methodology", a double path towards achieving this control: expulsion and reappropriation, renunciation and conservation.

Let us examine this process more closely based on the link Freud establishes between paranoia and animism.

The paranoid process and animistic thought can both be seen as attempts to resolve a conflict and thereby bring about psychic relief. Projection is their common strategy.

> [T]he tendency to project mental processes into the outside. . . will be intensified when projection promises to bring with it the advantage of mental relief. Such an advantage may be expected with certainty where a *conflict has arisen* between different impulses all of which are *striving towards omnipotence* – for they clearly cannot all become omnipotent. The pathological process in paranoia in fact makes use of the mechanism of projection in order to deal with mental conflicts of this kind. The typical case of such a conflict is one between the two members of a pair of opposites – the case of an *ambivalent attitude,* which we have examined in detail as it appears in someone mourning the death of a loved relative. This kind of case must seem particularly likely to provide a motive for the creation of projections. Here again we are in agreement with the writers who maintain that the first-born spirits were *evil* spirits, and who derive the idea of a soul from the impression made by death upon the survivors. The only difference is that *we* do not lay stress on the *intellectual* problem with which death confronts the living; in our view the force which gives the impetus to research is rather to be attributed to the *emotional* conflict into which the survivors are plunged.[44]

This text leads directly to the analysis of taboo, the subject of the second part of Freud's book. Earlier, we defined magic as the most primitive manner of fulfilling desire. But we must complete and clarify this definition by saying that the psychic work that produces magic, dreams, neurosis or paranoia is done on fragmentary material: there is no unified desire but only *Wünsche*: instinctual drives competing with each other, each one aspiring to omnipotence. The concept central to the analysis is certainly ambivalence.

The paradigmatic conflict illustrating the effects of ambivalence is the emotional conflict faced by every "survivor". The problem of death is not, initially, a theoretical problem of a purely intellectual nature. There is no "death" as such, since "the skeleton which we use to-day to picture the dead stands for the fact that *they themselves were slayers*".[45]

> But originally, says Kleinpaul, *all* of the dead were vampires, all of them had a grudge against the living and sought to injure them and rob them of their lives. It was from corpses that the concept of evil spirits first arose.[46]

Animist beliefs and the magical techniques they employ originated in these impressions death makes on the survivors. These impressions are contradictory, mixed – ambivalent. What ethnologists define as a taboo against the dead, psychoanalysts encounter in cases of pathological mourning and obsessional neurosis.

We find that in a certain sense these obsessive self-reproaches are justified, and that this is why they are proof against contradictions and protests. It is not that the mourner was really responsible for the death or was really guilty of neglect, as the self-reproaches declare to be the case. None the less there was something in her – a wish that was unconscious to herself – which would not have been dissatisfied by the occurrence of death and which might actually have brought it about if it had had the power. And after death has occurred, it is against this unconscious wish that the reproaches are a reaction.

In almost every case where there is an intense emotional attachment to a particular person we find that there is a concealed hostility in the unconscious. This is the classical example, the prototype, of the ambivalence of human emotions.[47]

Thus, ambivalence has existed from the earliest times. But the manner in which it serves the psychic process of the obsessional is quite different from the manner in which it serves primitive man. In primitive man, the feeling of hostility – so painful to experience – is not turned against himself but is exteriorised. The mechanism elaborated to defend against this feeling is a displacement onto the object of the hostility: that is, the deceased himself. "This defensive procedure, which is a common one both in normal and pathological mental life, is known as projection".[48]

When death occurs, opposing emotions – tenderness and hostility – emerge at the same time, in the form of mourning and satisfaction. These antagonistic emotions naturally result in conflict. Most often, this conflict is resolved not by conscious acceptance or forgiveness but by the intervention of a projection mechanism. The internal perception of a hostility that must remain unacknowledged is rejected outside oneself, separated from oneself and projected onto the other. And this other, who continues to be mourned, becomes an evil spirit. Internal oppression is replaced by external persecution.

Hostile feelings towards one's closest kin could remain latent as long as the latter were alive, but after their death, long-suppressed feelings burst through their dams. Painful mourning, born of an excess of tenderness, grows more and more intolerant of latent hostility and refuses to let it produce a feeling of satisfaction. Hostility is therefore repressed through projection, and this repression is associated with mourning rituals and taboo prohibitions against the dead.

In this instance, projection enables repression. It takes the form of a defence mechanism, serving to resolve an unbearable conflict. But projection is not always linked to the resolution of a conflict.

Projection is also the path to knowledge: the image of the world primitive man creates is the result of projection outwards of his internal perceptions. Psychology itself, the theory of souls, appears, when all is said and done, as the intellectual elaboration of projective formations.[49]

It is precisely when they function as systems that animist theory and paranoia reveal their kinship. According to Freud, systematicity is the response to a requirement of the psychic apparatus, which we have learned to recognise in the secondary elaboration of dreams. In other words, the systematic and the secondary go together. The secondary elaboration to which the material provided by dream thoughts is subjected after being "processed" by the dream-work itself intends to confer a "meaning" to that which otherwise appears incomprehensible to consciousness. The following is an excellent explanation of how a system comes into being, with its characteristics and its requirements.

> There is an intellectual function in us which demands unity, connection and intelligibility from any material, whether of perception or thought, that comes within its grasp, and if, as a result of special circumstances, it is unable to establish a true connection, it does not hesitate to fabricate a false one. Systems constructed in this way are known to us not only from dreams, but also from phobias, from obsessive thinking and from delusions. The construction of systems is seen most strikingly in delusional disorders (in paranoia), where it dominates the symptomatic picture; but its occurrence in other forms of neuropsychosis must not be overlooked. In all these cases it can be shown that a rearrangement of the psychical material has been made with a fresh aim in view; and the rearrangement may often have to be a drastic one if the outcome is to be made to appear intelligible from the point of view of the system. Thus a system is best characterized by the fact that at least *two reasons* can be discovered for each of its products: a reason based upon the premises of the system (a reason, then, which may be delusional) and a concealed reason, which we must judge to be the truly operative and the real one.[50]

The system is deceiving and arbitrary but seductive. Psychoanalytic investigation goes beyond the constructions that act like screens, like defensive shields: superstition, anxiety, dream and demons fall away in its path. They are all products that must not block the way to the productive forces themselves or to the paths they take to exert their action.

Identification and projection are two such paths – unconscious sources and means of elaboration of instinctual drives.

What animistic, infantile and neurotic "thoughts" have in common is that they dispense the psychic apparatus from carrying out to the very end (at great risk) the work required by the impulse: that is, from translating it into reality. Animistic thought maintains desire and its accomplishment in the sphere of the unconscious, of the imaginary, where everything is possible but fictional so that magical technique, the neurotic symptom or the child's play are substitutes for sexual activity. Here, the act is "thought". Unconscious thought is the space of "as though", the mimicking of satisfaction. The predominant field of magical-playful-neurotic identification is that of unconscious thought, in which there is no real impediment to the manifestation of any conceivable stand-ins and substitutions. Thus, in this context, identification "satisfies" desire by imitating it since (magical) mimicking is (metaphorical) contact. Projection, on the other hand, exerts another action on desire: it displaces its impetus from inside to outside; this unconscious transfer leads to a form of knowledge of the soul which is a lack of knowledge of the unconscious.

In summary, we could say that magical identification imitates the preservation of the object of desire, its assimilation; as for projection, it imitates the renouncing of desire, its repudiation. These are two different paths taken by desire to wear a mask and transform itself, by becoming either theatrical enactment or knowledge since both the enactment and the knowledge are illusory.

Totemism and the father complex

At times, the work of psychic derivation and elaboration serves not just as an illusion, such as the illusion in play, in magic or in the symptom, because the reality of death exists. This reality demands that this work modify not only internal psychic economy but also the economy of the relation to reality. *Totem and Taboo* explores the question of death and the technical elaboration it requires.

The fourth chapter of the book describes a new path of elaboration, that of identification with the totem, recognised by all authors as an essential support for totemism.

This totemic identification differs from the forms described previously because it creates a unique connection between desire and reality by means of a transformation of the social link. Simply put, it appears that the death of a loved one requires that the psyche employ a different system of elaboration than the system we have called "magical".

A theoretical clarification is needed as we embark on this discussion of totemism. Contemporary ethnologists and sociologists have pointed out the scarcity of information and even the errors in the conceptions used by Freud almost naively. There was a reference to ethnocentrism, primitivist myth and archaic illusion. We do not intend to prolong this debate since our focus is psychoanalysis, not ethnology. Our aim is to analyse the modes of functioning of the identification process. We must point out that Freud was not completely unaware of the difficulty associated with using the concept "primitive". Suffice it to quote Freud, who seems to have anticipated modern-day objectors:[51]

> The determination of the original state of things thus invariably remains a matter of construction. Finally, it is not easy to feel one's way into primitive modes of thinking. We misunderstand primitive men just as easily as we do children, and we are always apt to interpret their actions and feelings according to our own mental constellations.[52]

To analyse ethnological material or infantile phenomena (even fragmentary, biased or distorted) based on the psychic configuration of psychoanalysis can only result in misunderstanding them, but it remains the only way to say something about the subject.

Identification, the essence of totemism

A system both religious and social, totemism is founded on two principles whose more or less close association seems universal: the prohibition of cannibalism and the prohibition of incest.

The prohibition of cannibalism is a "religious" rule: it governs the relations of the members of the clan among themselves and with the totem. Relying on Frazer's descriptions, Freud writes:

> [T]he members of a totem clan call themselves by the name of their totem, and *commonly believe themselves to be actually descended from it.* It follows from this belief that they will not hunt the totem animal or kill or eat it and, if it is something other than an animal, they refrain from making use of it in other ways. The rules against killing or eating the totem are not the only taboos; sometimes they are forbidden to touch it, or even to look at it; in a number of cases the totem may not be spoken of by its proper name. Any violation of the taboos that protect the totem are automatically punished by severe illness or death.[53]

It is clear that the prohibition of cannibalism is founded on a series of symbolic equivalences creating a system: to name, to kill, to eat, to touch, to look. Respect for totemic relations appears as the negative of cannibalistic desire. Repression of cannibalism allows an individual to have an identity (that is, a genealogy), as well as kinship relations confirming this identity in the clan of his "kin". Individual transgression of the prohibition is punished by death, but in certain circumstances, its collectively organised transgression confers it a solemn ceremonial character:

> This identification with the totem is carried into effect in actions and words on the ceremonial occasions of birth, initiation and burial. Various magical and religious purposes are served by dances in which all the clansmen disguise themselves as their totem and imitate its behaviour. Lastly, there are ceremonies in which the totem animal is ceremoniously killed.[54]

Birth, initiation, death: all of them representations of a man's identity, passages from one mode of recognition to another, through which one acquires a place as a distinct individual in a body, belonging to a particular sex, to whom death grants permanent status as an ancestor. It is only in these circumstances that identification can be taken on, mimicked, acted out and utilised.

The prohibition of incest is a "social" rule: it governs the sexual relations of the members of the totemic clan and, more specifically, the possibilities regarding marriage, setting out strict rules concerning the manner in which a new generation of members is to be produced. Freud is of the opinion that exogamy, "the notorious and mysterious correlate to totemism",[55] is a result of incest phobia, analysed in the first chapter of *Totem and Taboo*.

We are aware that Freud's arguments are tenuous and are seen as too inclined to "psychologising" by today's sociologists and ethnologists. What remains of interest is his attempt to understand the enigma of totemism, which is the enigma of the relation between genealogy and exogamy. He refuses to simply acknowledge this enigmatic character since he believes he has the tools required to analyse the "psychic needs" underlying totemism. Although he may not have formulated the problem in the best way, it is clear that he understood what was at stake. In our view, this was the theory of identification. The difficulty comes from the fact that Freud discusses this essentially psychoanalytic question using outmoded ethnological concepts. But this should not deter us from following the development of his thinking.

His reflection is motivated by a desire to understand, which for him always meant finding new relations between observed phenomena – a desire to understand the connection at the roots of totemism, between prohibition of cannibalism (which concerns belonging to the totem, the clan's identity as such) and the prohibition of incest (which concerns totemic generation based on lineage). How are they linked; what is their secret connection (*Zusammenhang*)? As we shall see, Freud constructed this link by clustering seemingly heterogenous material, gathered together as he saw fit but coherent in his view.[56]

How did primitive men come to call themselves (and their clans) after animals, plants and inanimate objects? To this question, Freud can only give a number of different hypothetical answers. Unhampered by the vagueness of these hypotheses, he examines the question of exogamy, claiming that this practice is not related to a horror of incest but to the need for repression of desire. He seems to find confirmation of his views in Darwin's writings, on which he draws directly: the sexual jealousy seen in all mammals (including man) and the law of the fittest – that the strongest males take the females for themselves. This jumble of hypotheses on the origins of totemism does not disorient psychoanalysis completely. Experience gained in the psychoanalysis of children throws a "unique" but pertinent light on the question.

The child and his totem: zoophobic identification

The illumination provided by psychoanalysis consists of the clinical discovery of a sort of infantile totemism. Several analysts, including Abraham, Wulff, Ferenczi and Freud himself, observed that the attitude of the child to animals has much in common with that of primitive man.

> Children show no trace of the arrogance which urges adult civilized men to draw a hard-and-fast line between their own nature and that of all other animals. Children have no scruples over allowing animals to rank as their full equals. Uninhibited as they are in the avowal of their bodily needs, they no doubt feel themselves more akin to animals than their own elders, who may well be a puzzle to them.[57]

This perfect understanding can suddenly be broken. The child starts to be afraid of a certain species of animal, and most often, this animal is the one in which he previously showed the greatest interest. An animal phobia emerges: Freud maintains that, without exception, when the child is a boy, the fear is inspired by the father and displaced on the animal. Freud illustrates this play of substitution of the phobic object by using the example of Little Hans, treated by the boy's father with Freud's assistance, and the case of Arpad, treated by Ferenczi.

Freud sees Little Hans's phobia as a sort of negative totemism governed by fear. He considers Arpad's case to be a manifestation of positive totemism governed by admiration. But a closer look reveals that these two cases illustrate both commonly found forms of attachment to the totem animal: that is, ambivalence. It becomes clear that the phobic symptom gives concrete form to ambivalence through identification serving multiple aims. Identification appears as both the mechanism of symptom formation and the means of its resolution.

Let us examine Little Hans's horse phobia.[58] If we follow the series of statements expressing the child's questions and fears, we observe a series of attitudes towards the father and the mother, characterised by equivalences and reversals.

The analysis uses material drawn from dreams, phantasies and associations involving horses. The major symptom is fear of being bitten by a horse, associated with the fear of seeing one fall; gradually, this fear is extended to draft horses and even carriages or carts driving past, especially if they are carrying heavy loads.

The period preceding the onset of the phobia was marked by intense masturbatory activity, a great interest in his sexual organ, which he tried to compare to that of his father and which he tried to glimpse in little girls who were his playmates, as well as his mother and little sister. He was fascinated with horses' "widdlers", which he could observe at his leisure in the riding warehouse across from his house. One of his favourite games was to play "horsey" with his father or his playmates. He also takes great pleasure in going to the W.C. and accompanying his mother there. Whenever his father is absent, he sleeps in his mother's bed, with no objection on her part. During summer holidays at Gmunden, he became aware that his mother was pregnant. It was shortly after the baby was born – his sister Anna – that the fear of being bitten by a horse first appeared. He was particularly frightened by what horses wore in front of their eyes and by the black around their mouths. He was afraid a horse would come into his room to bite him. Freud wrote:

> Thus he was situated in the typical attitude of a male child towards his parents to which we have given the name of the "Oedipus complex" and which we regard in general as the nuclear complex of the neuroses. The new fact that we have learnt from the analysis of "little Hans" – a fact with an important bearing upon totemism – is that in such circumstances children displace some of their feelings from their father on to an animal.[59]

The mere displacement of hostility onto an animal cannot be considered neurosis. Its neurotic character results from the phobic reversal of hostility. Thus, it is fear as a particular instinctual transformation that opens the way to understanding totemism. Some of the feelings are displaced from the father onto an animal. Freud goes on to summarise his interpretation:

> Analysis is able to trace the associative path along which the displacement passes – both the fortuitous paths and those with a significant content. Analysis also enables us to discover the *motives* for the displacement. The hatred of his father that arises in a boy from rivalry for his mother is not able to achieve uninhibited sway over his mind; it has to contend with his old-established affection and admiration for the very same person. The child finds relief from the conflict arising out of this double-sided, this ambivalent emotional attitude towards his father by displacing his hostile and fearful feelings on to a *substitute* for his father. This displacement cannot, however, bring the conflict to an end, it cannot effect a clear-cut severance between the affectionate and the hostile feelings. On the contrary, the conflict is resumed in relation to the object on to which the displacement has been made: the ambivalence is extended to *it*. There could be no doubt that little Hans was not only *frightened* of horses; he also approached them with admiration and interest. As soon as his anxiety began to diminish, he identified himself with the dreaded creature: he began to jump about like a horse, and in his turn bit his father. At another stage in the resolution of his phobia he did not hesitate to identify his parents with some other large animals.[60]

A passage in the original text dedicated to little Hans can shed light on this transformation of the identificatory position. One day, Hans saw the horse drawing the omnibus fall; it was a very large and heavy horse. His father asked him, "When the horse fell down, did you think of your daddy?" Hans replied, "Perhaps. Yes. It's possible". This interpretation, or rather recognition by the little boy that there is, "perhaps", a relation between the scene of the horse falling and his father, had a freeing effect on his play activities. His father wrote to Freud:

> For some time now Hans has been playing horses in the house: he trots about, falls down, kicks about with his feet and neighs. Once he tied a small bag round his neck for a nosebag. He repeatedly runs up to me and bites me.

Freud sees this as confirmation that Hans has accepted the interpretation emerging from the conversation he had with his father.

> In this way he was accepting the last interpretations more decidedly than he could in words, but naturally with a change of parts, for the game was played in obedience to a wishful phantasy. Thus *he* was the horse, and bit his father, and in this way was identifying himself with his father.[61]

In fact, this identification with the horse is even more complicated. The game is overdetermined, we have reason to think, based on the rest of the analysis. The interpretation made by the boy's father and by Freud is accurate but partial since the horse also represents the pregnant mother (heavily laden horses), and the wish to see the horse fall is a wish to aggress the mother who carries a baby threatening Hans's libidinal possession of her. We should add that there is an intermediary association linking the fall of a horse with the fulfilment of a hostile wish. One of Hans's playmates, Fritzl, had fallen and struck a rock, hurting himself. Thus, the "totemic" choice of a horse carries multiple traces and representations of wishes.

But the indications provided by Freud are sufficient to shed light on the functioning of identification in its various forms.

First, it is striking that the phobia consists of a transitive identification, an identificatory position which transgresses, in the unconscious, distinctions of gender and species. The horse is the father (and the mother). The common trait needed for this identification, as we have seen in the dream, is the considerable size of their widdlers. There are also secondary traits: the black above the mouth (the father's moustache) and blinders (his monocle). These are "associative paths". It is the discovery of the "motives" that partly loosen the hold of the symptom: that is, the wish to eliminate the father and take revenge on the mother. In the game, which enacts recognition of unconscious wishes, Hans is the horse. He bites and he falls. He attacks and punishes himself. The game brings the impulse, repressed until then, closer to reality, through the use of masks and mime: an effective and therapeutic playful modality since it reduces the fear of horses (without eliminating it completely) and makes Hans clearly more defiant, in a high-spirited way, in his interactions with his father.

- The symptom: "the horse is the father" immobilises an unconscious position unbearable for little Hans, who loves and admires his father and also hates him and wants to see him "leave", "fall". The phobic behaviour is the avoidance of any situation in which this fascinating and dangerous horse might appear.
- The game: "Hans is the horse" activates the phantasy and symbolically fulfils the dangerous wish. The symbolisation concerns the other (the father); the game is addressed to the father. It celebrates, as it were, the active identification with the paternal totem: "Hans is the father" replaces "Hans hates the father".

It is interesting to learn everything this clinical "example" teaches since it is central to the reasoning Freud used to validate his hypothesis (his "sequence of components") concerning the origins of totemism. Indeed, the totemism of primitive men was never subjected to Freudian analysis. Freud's "evidence" comes from his own and his disciples' psychoanalytic experience. Infantile totemism, evident in zoophobia, is therefore the cornerstone of his construction, whose description and elaboration are centred around identification.

The formation of a phobic symptom comes about through condensation – that is, the identification of several objects and their representation by an image which masks their common significance, drawing attention away from the "actual" meaning. But the situation in which the horse is the "figure" or the metaphor for the father (the parents) only occurs when the affect tied to one is displaced on the other. The main defence mechanism against the anxiety produced by the emergence of hostile feelings consists of dissociating them from affectionate feelings which counter them and transfer them onto a substitute object. Divide ambivalence and conquer! But it seems that ambivalence is irreducible so that the conflict is transferred to the substitute. The zoophobic solution offers an advantage: it makes Hans agoraphobic, so he stays close to his mother, receiving her attention and affection. But the horse is ever present; the unresolved anxiety spreads. As long as the identification horse = father (= mother) remains unconscious, it haunts Hans's entire relation to reality.

The intervention of the father-analyst modifies the positions involved, and the boy's high-spirited defiance validates this intervention, as it were. Somewhat like the joke which, by producing a new expression – condensed, nonsensical and full of sense – transforms subjective positions: the one who rebels becomes the one who laughs. "I am a horse" functions like a witticism: Hans's play illustrates its structure. The exchange of unconscious meaning creates a circulation of positions, places, roles. Once the unconscious equivalence has been enacted, it loses some of its paralysing power of fascination: "I hate the father", "I want to be the father" becomes "I am a horse just like the father 'is' a horse".

In other words, the manner in which phobic neurosis is formed resembles that of magic: creating an illusory solution to a real conflict. A path to reality and to the resolution of ambivalence-related conflict only opens when the sphere of magical imagination is left behind, to be transformed into words or games addressed to a real other. This symbolic identification (taken on and avoided at once) with the phobic and totemic objects breaks the spell. If I play at being the horse, it means I am not the horse, but it is a figure of what I wish to be. The phobia was the metaphor (the substitute), literal and unrecognised, captive of the unspoken wish. Now the horse acquires the metaphoric depth of the ego ideal, of the symbolic totem.

Little Arpad's case is similar. Unfortunately, we do not have a detailed description of the analysis. Here, the totemic animal is not the horse, but a hen – more specifically, the chick, the hen and the rooster. This second example makes it possible to see more clearly that, in Hans's case, the Oedipus complex and the castration complex are related. Freud writes about Ferenczi's patient:

> [I]n the case of little Arpad his totemic interests did not arise in direct relation with his Oedipus complex but on the basis of its narcissistic precondition, the fear of castration. But any attentive reader of the story of little Hans will find abundant evidence that he, too, admired his father as possessing a big penis and feared him as threatening his own. The same part is played by the father alike in the Oedipus and the castration complexes – the part of a dreaded enemy to the sexual interests of childhood. The punishment which he threatens is castration, or its substitute, blinding.[62]

What Freud has called "positive totemism" is the passionate interest the child takes in his animal and the mimetism associated with it. But Arpad did more than spend hours in the barnyard crowing and clucking like the inhabitants of the chicken coop; one of his favourite games was to watch hen fights and then to dance wildly around the body of the victim.

> From time to time he translated his wishes from the totemic language into that of everyday life. "My father's the cock", he said on one occasion, and another time: "Now I'm small, now I'm a chicken. When I get bigger I'll be a fowl. When I'm bigger still I'll be a cock". On another occasion he suddenly said he would like to eat some "fricassee of mother". . . . He was very generous in threatening other people with castration, just as he himself has been threatened with it for his masturbating activities.[63]

The traits common to this case, Hans's case and Frazer's observations about totemism are complete identification with the totemic animal and an ambivalent affective attitude towards it. Arpad's game is to be a rooster or a hen (like his father is the rooster) but also to aggress others like a hen (the one that tried to bite his penis when he was urinating in the henhouse) and like his father, who threatens him with castration. Actively enacted identification "heals", as it were, both his sexual interest (to have a large penis) and his hate of those who threaten this narcissistic position.

For Hans and for Arpad, playful identification appears to offer a path more open to the expression of ambivalent desires than the phobic path.

In the case of little Hans, the formation of the phobic symptom allows no expression of the conflict between admiration and affection on the one hand and rivalry and hatred on the other. The wish for death, displaced onto the horse, is manifested in the fear that the horse will fall, but this is accompanied by a punishment expressed in the fear that the horse will bite. Phobia enacts Oedipal desire and the associated fear of castration; in other words, it enacts the "negative totemism" Freud referred to earlier. Transposition into play, by means of identification, "creates" a unified elaboration of ambivalent desires. Hans plays at love and at hate; transformed into a horse, he has the attributes of power (the phallic traits which give access to the mother), and he bites the rival who threatened him (through words spoken by the mother or through anger shown by the father directly). The horse becomes a metaphor of his Oedipal desires, a living metaphor and no longer a fascinating and magical reality.

Play is speech freed from the infernal and quasi-paranoid sphere of a phobic universe. Little Arpad's declaration "I will be a rooster", rather than "I will be the father", reveals a veritable totemic (symbolic) reflection. The loved and feared object becomes the ideal. The "object" relation becomes reflexive: "I unconsciously turn my father into a horse" becomes "I consciously turn myself into a horse". Through this procedure, totemic identification becomes the assimilation of a symbolic figure; it introduces a split in the ego: the metaphoric distance.

Phobic identification is like identification in dreams and hysteria: there is a lack of awareness of the interchangeable positions present, as well as a lack of awareness of the desire which secretly creates the substitutions. Phobic identification "changes nothing"; it remains a private phantasy. By contrast, playful identification (totemic, we might say) "enacts" this wishful phantasy, turns it into a "declared" desire addressed to someone. This identification is also more advantageous in terms of psychic economy because it maintains the ambivalence of desire; it prevents recourse to interminable and psychically costly displacement-identification.

These two observations make it possible to introduce the missing element into the formula of totemism if the series is to be comprehensive. This element is, for the male at least, the father.

But we have already learned this from primitive men, who called their totemic animals their ancestors and their archaic fathers. Thus, psychoanalysis hasn't discovered anything new by substituting the totemic animal for the father. Freud admits:

> All we have done is to take at its literal value an expression used by these people, of which the anthropologists have been able to make very little and which they have therefore been glad to keep in the background. Psycho-analysis, on the contrary, leads us to put special stress upon this same point and to take it as the starting-point of our attempt at explaining totemism.[64]

To take the expression *Ur-vater* literally is to effect an unprecedented connection. If the totemic animal is no other than the father, what psychoanalysis reveals about paternal functions sheds light at once on the functions of the totem and

> the two taboo prohibitions which constitute its core – not to kill the totem and not to have sexual relations with a woman of the same totem – coincide in their content with the two crimes of Oedipus, who killed his father and married his mother, as well as with the two primal wishes of children, the insufficient repression or the re-awakening of which forms the nucleus of perhaps every psychoneurosis.[65]

If this connection is not merely irrelevant play, the birth of totemism and even of humanity itself appears to be a product of the conditions imposed by the Oedipus complex, like the totemism of the two boys analysed here.

Totemic identification: mourning and celebration

In little Hans's play, there are accents of triumph, an atmosphere of celebration. He feels triumphant after slaying the unconscious beast, a triumph which, in the analytic process, signals that a certain oppression is nearing its end. There is joy in being free to enact the totemic metaphor instead of enduring the persecution of an unconscious projection. It is the joy of recognition/emergence of the ego ideal.

In a lighthearted tone, Freud continues on triumphantly to his conclusion. Prim-itive man, and *in principio* humanity in general, is like a child. Psychoanalytic experience provides the thread that will sew together the fragments strewn here and there by the "psychologists of peoples" – the anthropologists – and by histo-rians of culture and religion. The totemic games of the child are the equivalent of the totemic celebration of the primitives. Correspondences, analogies, identical structures, identical motives: to start with, there is the paternal complex.

There is no need to repeat here the details of the "sequence of events" used by Freud to make his demonstration of origins. But in the last pages of *Totem and Taboo*, there is a remarkable discussion of all that Freud was able to set in place, through his ethnologic and prehistoric explorations, to conceptual-ise the identification processes. In the course of the analysis of animism and totemism, the discussion focused specifically on the psychic elaboration of death, which will now make possible the theoretical formulation of the ques-tion of identification.

Freud is indebted to Robertson Smith, author of *The Religion of the Semites*, for the idea that the particular ceremony of the totem feast is an integral part of totemism. And more than this: the sacrifice and the meal shared by all the mem-bers of the clan constitute the acts which substantiate and create the group. They are demonstration, consecration and celebration of the totemic relation itself. For the clan to live, there must be mediation by one who dies. The animal killed in a solemn ceremony is not just any animal. The one killed, whose flesh is eaten and whose blood is drunk in this sacred communion, is the totemic animal itself. The social link, the community of the clan, is born out of its death and the ingestion of its substance. Eating together confirms the consubstantiality of clan members and their totemic deity.

> It was in fact the ancient totem animal, the primitive god himself, by the kill-ing and consuming of which the clansmen renewed and assured their likeness to the god.[66]
>
> Let us call up the spectacle of a totem meal. . . . The clan is celebrating the ceremonial occasion by the cruel slaughter of its totem animal and is devour-ing it raw – blood, flesh and bones. The clansmen are there, dressed in the likeness of the totem and imitating it in sound and movement, as though they were seeking to stress their identity with it. Each man is conscious that he is performing an act forbidden to the individual and justifiable only through the participation of the whole clan; nor may anyone absent himself from the killing and the meal.
>
> When the deed is done, the slaughtered animal is lamented and bewailed. The mourning is obligatory, imposed by dread of a threatened retribution. As Robertson Smith. . . remarks about an analogous occasion, its chief purpose is to disclaim responsibility for the killing.
>
> But the mourning is followed by demonstrations of festive rejoicing: every instinct is unfettered and there is licence for every kind of gratification.[67]

The festive rejoicing springs from this massive lifting of prohibitions. But why is there mourning? Why is the death of the totemic animal mourned?

We have learned that clansmen become sanctified when they incorporate the totem, reinforcing in this manner their identification with it and with each other. To eat and incorporate the sacred life embodied by the animal produces joy. But psychoanalysis teaches us that the totemic animal is, in fact, a father substitute and that the affective attitude characteristic of the father complex is ambivalence. The triumph felt as a result of taking into oneself the power of the totem/father is associated with guilt, due to the ambivalence characterising the relation to the father. There was a "first time: when the real father of the horde", "violent and jealous", who "keeps all the females for himself and drives away his sons as they grow up",[68] was killed and devoured by them. Darwinian theory about the origin of human society confirms the reality of this archaic father who had to be killed in order for totemic law to live.

> [T]he tumultuous mob of brothers were filled with the same contradictory feelings which we can see at work in the ambivalent father complex of our children and our neurotic patients. They hated their father, who presented such a formidable obstacle to their craving for power and their sexual desires; but they loved and admired him too. After they had got rid of him, *had satisfied their hatred and had put into effect their wish to identify themselves with him, the affection which had all this time been pushed under was bound to make itself felt*. It did so in the form of *remorse*. A sense of guilt made its appearance, which in this instance coincided with the remorse felt by the whole group. The dead father became stronger than the living one had been – for events took the course we so often see them follow in human affairs to this day.
>
> What had up to then been prevented by his actual existence was thenceforward prohibited by the sons themselves, in accordance with the psychological procedure so familiar to us in psycho-analysis under the name of "deferred obedience". They revoked their deed by forbidding the killing of the totem, the substitute for their father; and they renounced its fruits by resigning their claim to the women who had now been set free. They thus created out of *their filial sense of guilt* the two fundamental taboos of totemism, which for that very reason correspond to the two repressed wishes of the Oedipus complex. Whoever contravened those taboos became guilty of the only two crimes with which primitive society concerned itself.[69]

The psychic elaboration of death is the psychic elaboration of the death of the other, whether this death is desired or actually brought about. In both cases, the "deceased" is rendered more alive than ever. The rituals of sacrifice, mourning and celebration appear, from the psychoanalytic standpoint, to be a massive attempt to erase, forget and disavow the death wish, as well as the triumphant cry of this same wish.

Freud attempts to observe the becoming of Oedipal impulses in the institutional forms of totemism. Thus, what has been written about these archaic institutions must have an equivalent in the psychic life of "our children and our neurotic patients". The cannibalistic devouring of the totem/father, far from being the pure and simple fulfilment of this desire, has the effect of distancing it from its object (the father's phallus, the father's woman or women).

This is the paradox of totemic identification.

But no matter how many times clan members eat the flesh of the father, in how many ceremonies, the father will remain just as alive, just as powerful. This power manifests itself in deferred obedience, in the compulsion to repeat the ritual murder, in the mourning associated with triumphant joy. This is why the devouring remains magical, a phantasy of desire. In reality, mourning and celebration distance man from his desire. They are the ambiguous path to renunciation. Licentiousness, orgies, the lifting of prohibitions, excess and general indulgence are misleading because after the act comes the law.

This applies to the prohibition of incest and the prohibition of murder.

Once the obstacle to access to the women of the clan has been removed, they are more unattainable than ever. Once the protector and tyrant has been removed, he is more irreplaceable than ever. Even if there could be mastery of reality – the body and flesh of the father – still, his "being" could not be mastered. There is nothing left but to recreate the relation to the father, to nurture the desire to be the father. Resuscitating the relation to the dead father is the "religious" component of man.

Religion commemorates the totem feast. It is the collective attempt to reconcile with the offended father; it achieves this reconciliation for the group. To use the terms of Freud's analogy, the individual's religion develops in the relation with the Ideal, with this part of ourselves transformed into "father" (into a horse, a rooster. . .) by the play of totemic identification:

> There was one factor in the state of affairs produced by the elimination of the father which was bound in the course of time to cause an enormous increase in the longing felt for him [*Vatersehnsucht*: passionate longing, nostalgia]. Each single one of the brothers who had bonded together for the purpose of killing their father was inspired by a wish to become like him and had given expression to it by incorporating parts of their father's surrogate in the totem meal. But, in consequence of the pressure exercised upon each participant by the fraternal clan as a whole, that wish could not be fulfilled. For the future no one could or might ever again attain the father's supreme power, even though that was what all of them had striven for. Thus after a long lapse of time their bitterness against their father, which had driven them to their deed, grew less, and their longing for him increased; and it became possible for *an ideal* to emerge *which embodied the unlimited power of the primal father against whom they had once fought as well as their readiness to submit to him.*[70]

These are the forms taken by Oedipal impulses, existing in the collective cultural life of "primitives" and in the psychic structures of the child: through the act of incorporation, a fundamental psychic transformation takes place, from outright ambivalence to the desire to be the father's equal. Admiration and love for the actual father are transformed into the desire to be like the ideal father, more powerful than before; hate and resentment are transformed into guilt which, "in time", becomes submission. Freud sees this submission, and nostalgia, as means of elaboration, attempts to eliminate, to erase the criminal act.

> The memory of the first great act of sacrifice thus proved indestructible, in spite of every effort to forget it; and at the very point at which men sought to be at the farthest distance from the motives that led to it, its undistorted reproduction emerged in the form of the sacrifice of the god.[71]

Thus, the development of a religion corresponds to a kind of long mourning process: that is, an impossible attempt to disclaim responsibility for the death of the god. Freud agrees with Robertson Smith's interpretation of mourning:

> The mourning is not a spontaneous expression of sympathy with the divine tragedy, but obligatory and enforced by fear of supernatural anger. And a chief object of the mourners is to disclaim responsibility for the god's death – a point which has already come before us in connection with theanthropic sacrifices, such as the "ox-murder at Athens".[72]

We can see more clearly now the function of totemic identification. It commemorates the dead father; it repeats the scene of the fulfilment of desire by producing an ideal substitution of it; the incorporated father begins to exert again, with greater force, his power of fascination and intimidation over the son. Thus, this identification with the dead father is the reproduction of the ambivalent relation to the father, the paradoxical fulfilment of the desire to eliminate him and of love, but in a different context. The context of the sacred for religion, the context of the ideal for the individual. The chief role of identification is to conserve: it maintains desire by transposing it. After the "death of the father", there is still a father to love, to be equal to and to confront in a battle lost in advance since its aim is to erase an indestructible desire.

We see the identification process as the predominant mode of psychic work for maintaining the relation with the lost object. The success of this process depends on its ability to elaborate, to work through ambivalence; we have called this "totemic" identification because it leads to the psychic (or collective, to use Freud's ethnological explanations) construction of the "totem": that is, an "ideal".

However, constructing the ideal requires the death of the other. The work of formation of the ideal consisting of identification as psychic incorporation of the lost object requires this "death". Yet identification, by its very nature, eliminates this object; it substitutes itself for it, replacing it. Paradoxically, it also reanimates the object it eliminates, and the incorporated object is more powerful than ever.

It is not surprising that *Totem and Taboo* ends with an interpretation of the mythical production of the hero. This interpretation completes the conceptualisation process at the heart of our reading, which, despite its specificity, is illuminating thanks to its focus on the functions of identification. Creating the figure of the hero signifies giving oneself the narcissistic means to reconcile with the father. We might say that totemic identification is heroic – even tragic – identification, more effective than "magical" identification.

The hero is the double – the double of the choir, representing the horde of rebellious and guilty brothers – the one who embodies the crime and redeems, a grandiose representation of desire itself charged with the tension of its accomplishment. Identification makes it possible to displace desire to the hero – the ideal – who is the emblem, the symbol, the impossible example. The triumph engendered by this identificatory rejoicing, which is also mourning and endless work of substitution, is the triumph of narcissism. It is narcissism which succeeds in negating death through the economical strategy of the formation of the ideal.[73]

Identification theory and practice

Totem and Taboo is a truly pivotal text. It represents a crucial moment in the theoretical formulation of the concept of identification. This weave is gradually enriched by the addition of a thousand threads of "evidence" developed on the basis of clinical experience. In fact, this daring essay – perhaps the most daring of Freud's writings – owed its theoretical strength to this clinical foundation. *Totem and Taboo* was written during the period when Freud was conducting the analysis of the "famous cases" he later published. The problems related to these cases influenced his search for a theoretical language whose manner of expression was particularly complex and problematic in 1914 in *Narcissism: An Introduction*.

Essentially, Rank sheds light on narcissism and its relation to death. Freud used these mythological and literary investigations again in his 1919 article "The 'Uncanny'", S.E. 17.

In *Totem*, Freud referred to little Hans, to the Rat Man and to Schreber's "paranoid intelligence". The analysis of the Wolf Man, the most complex, which Freud was conducting at that time but only described later, after the (temporary) termination of the treatment, is a striking illustration of the lengthy process of conceptual formulation based on the broadening and the meanders of the therapeutic investigations.[74]

The obsessional identification of the Rat Man

A brief note indicates the path to follow in order to show the "presence" of patients in the elaboration of the identification theory exposed in *Totem and*

Taboo. Regarding the conflict in which the Rat Man's neurosis is rooted and frozen, Freud comments:

> It is worth emphasizing that his flight into illness was made possible by his identifying himself with his father. The identification enabled his affects to regress on to the residue of his childhood.[75]

This note summarises accurately the young man's dramatic "situation": he is prisoner in a scenario he did not write, which could justifiably be called a "family saga" or "myth".[76] Lacan perceives the singularity of this case as revealing a universal phenomenon on which Freud commented insightfully. He writes:

> We could say that the original constellation from which the subject's personality development proceeded – I use the term constellation in its astrological acceptance – the thing to which the personality owes its birth and its destiny, its prehistory, that is, the *fundamental family relations* that governed his parents' coming together, the circumstances leading to their union, is something that has a relation which we might say could be defined in terms of a certain transformation literally *mythical*, a very specific relation with what, with the thing that seems the most contingent, the most phantasmatical, the most paradoxically morbid: the last stage of development of the major obsessional anxiety of the subject, that is, the *imaginary scenario* he creates as being the one that will eliminate the anxiety triggered by the onset of his major breakdown.
> (See Freud, *Family Romances*, 1909; emphasis added)

The Rat Man's illness becomes the theatre of a substitute for life which requires the impossible of him: to cut an unconscious link with his parents' desire and particularly with the memory of his dead father – a dead father he refuses to "bury" and in relation to whom he acts like the parricidal sons of the primitive horde: he is in the paradoxical state of retroactive submission, of deferred obedience. But in his case, everything takes place in the unconscious: the patient doesn't know "who" is in charge. The following passage provides the broad outline of the story which repeats itself in this theatre of the unconscious:

> His mother was brought up in a wealthy family with which she was distantly connected. This family carried on a large industrial concern. His father, at the time of his marriage, had been taken into the business, and had thus by his marriage made himself a fairly comfortable position. The patient had learnt from some chaff exchanged between his parents. . . that his father, some time before making his mother's acquaintance, had made advances to a pretty but penniless girl of humble birth. So much by way of introduction. After his father's death the patient's mother told him one day that she had been discussing his future with her rich relations, and that one of her cousins had declared

himself ready to let him marry one of his daughters when his education was completed; a business connection with his firm would offer him a brilliant opening in his profession. *This family plan* stirred up in him a conflict as to whether he should remain faithful to the lady he loved in spite of her poverty, or whether he should follow in his father's footsteps and marry the lovely, rich, and well-connected girl who had been assigned to him. And he resolved this conflict, which was in fact *one between his love and the persisting influence of his father's wishes*, by falling ill; or to put it more correctly, by falling ill he avoided the task of resolving it in real life.[77]

His father's will opposes his present desire, just as it once opposed his infantile sexual activity. By means of transference, this "school of suffering",[78] he would come to discover his unconscious hatred of his father. This recognition allowed him to arrive at a solution ending his obsession with rats, the major symptom of his neurosis. Identification with the dead father who governs this neurosis seems to have been the "fate" of this hatred related to the father complex. Let us try to reconstitute the process that brings this neurotic identification into existence.

A whole series of typically obsessional symptoms are attached to this neurotic conflict; they can serve to illustrate concretely the particular psychology of obsessive individuals. But clearly, it is the "great obsessive anxiety" developed around the cruel story of the torment involving rats which constitutes the nuclear complex of the neurosis. When the analytic work connected this great anxiety (that is, the idea that such a torment could be inflicted on someone he loved) with the "father complex", this pivotal symptom disappeared.

In our opinion, these tormenting rats can be considered the neurotic "totem" of the patient. Of course, it is not by chance that this dread (desire mixed with fear) attached itself to the signifier "*Ratte*". The various associative currents of the patient show the repressed meanings in which it is rooted.[79] This signifier condenses the entire obsessive difficulty, which can be formulated in terms of identification, as if this obsession showed all its representations in this series of imaginary positions – positions the Rat Man refuses to hold in reality – a series compressed into one overdetermined representation which must be disassembled, taken apart, made inoperative. "It was almost as though Fate, when the captain told him his story, had been putting him through an association test; she had called out a 'complex-stimulus-word' and he had reacted to it with his obsessional idea".[80]

This incoherent series of associations can be summarised as follows: rats – anal erotism – linked to intestinal functions – infantile sexual theory; rats = child, himself, disgusting, dirty, furious, able to bite and receiving terrible punishments for it from his father; cruel father, like the captain who ordered him to repay a debt; father who has debts ("gambling rat"); rats = money, father's inheritance; father's questionable conduct in the military, carrier of syphilis; rat = the infected penis, resembling a worm; rat = dirty animal that eats excrement and lives in sewers; rats – florins = prostitution; sexual relations "per anum"; marriage (*heiraten*); Ibsen's rat-wife, context in which the rat signifies the child and, as a sinister and disturbing chthonian animal, symbolises the souls of the dead; rat glimpsed scampering over father's grave.

The analysis takes on the appearance of a veritable process of rat disinfestation: that is, the "detaching" of multiple masked figures introduced by these rats into the unconscious. The common traits bringing about the unification of these super-posed series are traits of the constellation of erogeneities linked to anal erotism: sadism, cruelty, anal sexual theory, the equivalence faeces – money – penis – child – dirt. The "totemic" choice of rats is not exactly sublime or ideal, and it leaves the patient immersed in a guilty and worthless childhood, only serving to make him take up sado-masochistic sexual positions, ambivalent, hateful and compulsive.

"I am a rat, like my father was a rat (and 'orders' me to be one), like the captain is one". This is a clear illustration of identification with the aggressor, described by Anna Freud.[81] It is the assimilation of a split, incomplete model: the rat is the figure representing the hateful side of the dead father, an oppressive figure laden with guilt. The repression of hate is accomplished through this unconscious and magical identification. The subject is the object of his own hate; he is the cruel will of the father blocking the expression of masturbatory and genital impulses. This is the fate of unrecognised ambivalence: the aggressor with whom the patient identifies is incorporated but functions like a foreign body which erodes him from within instead of reinforcing his male narcissism. In other words, here identification functions in the service of neurotic repression; it is not the means of creating an ideal through complete mutation of the paternal figure (loved and hated at the same time). The relation to the dead father is not really resolved as long as the "memory" retained excludes hate. This is why the Rat Man is experiencing inter-minable mourning and is subject to "pathological sorrow". The illness itself is the pathological expression of the impossible death of the father who never finishes dying, like a sinister ghost.

The ritual formula of this obsessional patient: "Kill yourself to punish yourself for having such desires" is the imperative, reversed form of Oedipal desire: "Die, so that I can have such desires". The "normal" formulation would be "You are dead, and, like you, I will allow myself to have such desires", since the iden-tification we have called totemic promises the fulfilment of desire ("I will be a rooster").

The Wolf Man: between masculine and feminine identification

The conflict in which the Wolf Man is caught[82] concerns the very roots of sexual-ity and leads us to examine the fundamental relation between identification and sexual orientation: that is, the psychic conditions underlying sexual choice. The new factor discussed here, as compared to the types of conflicts analysed in the cases of Little Hans and the Rat Man, is the question of bisexuality. The field of conflict is not predominantly the dramatic Oedipal conflict manifest in ambiva-lence towards the father, which fails to achieve definitive resolution, but rather the enactment of the "primitive scene".

In this very complicated analysis of a case of infantile neurosis, all types of questions emerge and acquire new depth: narcissism, love, identification, castration, to be a man, to be a woman. This patient, who prompted Freud and his followers to reflect on very complex and critical questions, had, as a result, an unusual destiny and surprising fame. We shall see that our discussion will be enriched if we venture to explore the depths and supporting structures of this enigmatic character. There is no need to summarise the story or recount it in detail.[83] We shall simply attempt to identify the indications, remarks and topics which we see as helping to elaborate the notion of identification, a notion coinciding with the conceptualisation of narcissism.

We see this elaboration taking place at the moments of the analysis when Freud tries to understand the transitions from one "phase" of the illness to another. Freud does not categorise these transitions because his attention is focused on several factors at once, but it is clear to see that they are attempts to "heal" an insistent, archaic conflict, endlessly reborn in renewed form, while each time the identificatory conflict becomes more serious. Freud divides the patient's childhood into four epochs:

> [F]irst, the earliest period up to the seduction when he was three and a quarter years old, during which the primal scene took place; secondly, the period of the alteration in his character up to the anxiety dream (four years old); thirdly, the period of the animal phobia up to his initiation into religion (four and a half years old); and from then onwards the period of the obsessional neurosis up to a time later than his tenth year. That there should be an instantaneous and clear-cut displacement of one phase by the next was not in the nature of things or of our patient; on the contrary, the preservation of all that had gone before and the co-existence of the most different sorts of currents were characteristic of him.[84]

Let us examine the whys and wherefores of these instances of transformation (instinctual restructuring) which consisted of 1) alteration in character, "naughtiness"; 2) the wolf dream, sign of zoophobia; 3) "blasphemous" thoughts and religious piety; and 4) symptoms at the "end" of analysis.

ALTERATION IN CHARACTER

First, in a memory that suddenly surfaced, there was a scene, repeated in various forms, in which his older sister, "when he was still very small, had seduced him into sexual practices" by proposing that they show each other their "bottoms" in the lavatory or by taking hold of his penis, saying that their Nanya used to do the same thing with other people.

The little boy reacted to these acts of seduction by a refusal, not of the thing, but of the person. He substituted Nânya for his sister and began to play with his penis in her presence, which can be interpreted as an active act of seduction. But the nanny disappointed him and told him, with a stern look, that what he was doing was bad. She said that children who did this "got a 'wound' in that place". Regretfully abandoning his choice of the beloved Nanya, he began to search secretly for another sexual object. His seduction by his sister had given him the passive sexual aim of being touched on his genitals. The threat proffered by Nanya prompted sexual researches, evident in his observing two little girls urinate, but these discoveries were quickly rejected. Thought about castration began to occupy his mind, but he did not believe in it or dread it.

After having been rejected and disdained by Nanya, yet intrigued by her threat, he gave up masturbation. "His sexual life, therefore, which was beginning to come under the sway of the genital zone, gave way before an external obstacle, and was thrown back by its influence into an earlier phase of pregenital organization".[85]

The change in his character can be traced back to this suppression of masturbation: he became sadistic-anal, tormenting Nanya out of a desire for revenge, "seducing" her in an anal mode; he also tortured insects while being cruel to horses in his imagination. These active sadistic phantasies were associated with passive masochistic phantasies: he imagined children being beaten on the penis; these phantasies also served to punish him for his onanistic activities.

Thus, active-sadistic aspirations existed side by side with passive-masochistic aspirations: to beat and be beaten. This ambivalence, apparent in the parallel development of two partial impulses, was extraordinarily intense and persistent. This double libidinal position remained present throughout the later stages of his history.

The new sexual object of his regressive aspirations was his father, absent at the time. This choice was not fortuitous because, in addition to associations involving a snake being cut to pieces by the father, it renewed

> his first and most primitive object-choice, which in conformity with a small child's narcissism, had taken place along the path of identification. We have heard already that his father had been his admired model, and that when he was asked what he wanted to be he used to reply: a 'gentleman' like his father. *This object of identification of his active current became the sexual object of a passive current in his present sadistic-anal phase.* It looks as though his seduction by his sister had forced him into a passive role, and had given him a passive sexual aim. Under the persisting influence of this experience he pursued a path from his sister via Nanya to his father – from a passive attitude towards women to the same attitude towards men – and had, nevertheless, by this means found a link with his earlier and spontaneous phase of development. His father was now his object once more; in conformity with his higher stage of development, identification was replaced by object-choice; while transformation of his active attitude into a passive one was the consequence and the record of the seduction which had occurred meanwhile. It would naturally not have been so easy to achieve an active attitude in the sadistic phase towards his all-powerful father. When his father came home in the late

summer or autumn the patient's fits of rage and scenes of fury were put to a new use.

They had served for active-sadistic ends in relation to his Nanya; in relation to his father their purpose was masochistic. By bringing his naughtiness forward he was trying to force punishments and beatings out of his father, and in that way to obtain from him the masochistic sexual satisfaction that he desired. His screaming fits were therefore simply attempts at seduction. In accordance, moreover, with the motives which underlie masochism, this beating would also have satisfied his sense of guilt.[86]

The sequence of sexual objects can be summarised as follows:

- Initial object-choice: the admired father, in active identification with him;
- Seduction by sister, passive attitude;
- Attempted active seduction of Nanya, but with a passive aim: fury, fits of rage;
- Attempt at seduction of father, transformed into a sexual object, with passive aim.

This series was established through reconstruction. What matters for our discussion is that Freud showed that the original form of attachment to the father is narcissistic; identification with the admired model is the path taken towards this primary object-choice. Here, the aim is active: to be like the father.

The father becomes his object again, after a period of time in which there was anal sexual development and transition to the genital phase in the masturbatory activity exhibited and in the attempts to be touched on the penis after the seduction by the sister. The rejection by Nanya and her threat make this emerging genital sexuality recede; the new object-choice now follows the path of anal sexuality: the re-found father is the object which satisfies masochistic impulses (to be beaten, to be punished). The sexual aim becomes passive: to be "loved" by the father.

But, as Freud points out a number of times, this patient's characteristic is a sort of libidinal conservatism: that is, the preservation of all infantile sexual choices. What followed illustrates the greater and greater conflict – increasingly "costly" – in identifying with the father: active, narcissistic identification (to be like him) and the search for passive satisfaction (to be loved/beaten), which represents a powerful and indestructible current. In our view, the variety of forms taken by the "illness" are, in reality, a series of efforts to cause one of the two competing libidinal currents to triumph.

THE WOLF DREAM

This anxiety dream is a dramatic reactivation of a very old fear of wolves or, rather, of the image built in his mind by superstition, the "collage" of multiple stories, legends and illustrated tales that haunted his imagination as a child.[87] We might expect a simple interpretation of his great fear of wolves, keeping in mind what we learned from Little Hans's analysis and seeing the wolf as a substitute for the father, the object of Oedipal ambivalence. But this patient appears to confront the Oedipal drama unarmed, haunted by unresolved archaic libidinal conflicts and fascinated by the traces of an unassimilated, unintelligible and anxiety-provoking scene: a "primal" scene that returns, as it were, in this dream. This scene locks him into the search for an impossible knowledge, the "knowledge" of castration. When the child observed, but did not understand, the copulation between his parents – concerning which Freud attempts to reconstruct the facts and interpret the phantasmatic reality – he effected a double identification. The frightening figure of the wolf is overdetermined, and the "totem", the ideal that the wolf could constitute, does not allow heroic identification capable of resolving the Oedipal dilemma because he is a she-wolf and a wolf: a wolf of both sexes. The impossible identification with the partners of the primal scene prevents the Wolf Man from being able to give up any one of the sexual aims or to assume them and choose a definitive sexual orientation.

Let us look at the conclusion of the interpretation of his dream:

> The dream ended in a state of anxiety, from which he did not recover until he had his Nanya with him. He fled, therefore, from his father to her. His anxiety was a repudiation of the wish for sexual satisfaction from his father – the trend which had put the dream into his head. The form taken by the anxiety, the fear of "being eaten by the wolf", was only the (as we shall hear, regressive) transposition of the wish to be copulated with by his father, that is, to be given sexual satisfaction in the same way as his mother. This last sexual aim, the passive attitude towards his father, succumbed to repression, and fear of his father appeared in its place in the shape of the wolf phobia.
>
> And the driving forces of this repression? The circumstances of the case show that it can only have been his *narcissistic genital libido*, which, in the form of concern for his male organ, was fighting against a satisfaction whose attainment seemed to involve the renunciation of that organ. And it was from his threatened narcissism that he derived the masculinity with which he defended himself against his passive attitude towards his father.
>
> We now observe that at this point in our narrative we must make an alteration in our terminology. During the dream he had reached a new phase in his sexual organization. Up to then the sexual opposites had been for him active and passive. Since his seduction, his sexual claim had been a passive one, of being touched on the genitals; it was then transformed, by regression to an earlier phase of the sadistic-anal organization, into the masochistic aim of being beaten or punished. It was a matter of indifference to him whether he reached this aim with a man or with a woman. He had travelled, without considering the difference of sex, from his Nanya to his father, he had longed to have his penis touched by his Nanya, and had tried to provoke a beating from his father. Here his genitals were left out of account; though the connection

with them which had been concealed by the regression was still expressed in his phantasy of being beaten on the penis. The activation of the primal scene in the dream now brought him back to the genital organization. He discovered the vagina and the biological significance of masculine and feminine. He understood now that active was the same as masculine, while passive was the same as feminine. His passive sexual aim should now have been transformed into a feminine one, and have expressed itself as 'being copulated with by the father' instead of 'being beaten by him on the genitals or on the bottom'. The feminine aim, however, underwent repression and was obliged to let itself be replaced by fear of the wolf. . . .

For the proper appreciation of the wolf phobia we will only add that both his father and mother became wolves. His mother took the part of the castrated wolf, which let the others climb upon it; his father took the part of the wolf that climbed. But his fear, as we have heard him assure us, related only to the standing wolf, that is, to his father. It must further strike us that the fear with which the dream ended had a model in his grandfather's story. For in this the castrated wolf, which had let the others climb upon it, was seized with fear as soon as it was reminded of the fact of its taillessness. It seems, therefore, as though *he had identified himself with his castrated mother during the dream, and was now fighting against the fact*. "If you want to be sexually satisfied by Father", we may perhaps represent him as saying to himself, "you must allow yourself to be castrated like Mother; but I won't have that". In short, a clear protest on the part of his masculinity! Let us, however, plainly understand that the sexual development of the case that we are now examining has a great disadvantage from the point of view of research, for it was by no means undisturbed. It was first decisively influenced by the seduction, and was then diverted by the scene of observation of the coitus, which in its deferred action operated like a second seduction.[88]

The dream functions as an attempt at healing, like a coded message carrying old unconscious knowledge – repressed – about castration. As Freud writes, this dream takes the child from the anal stage to the genital stage. The figure of wolves (and associations related to the loss of their tails) represents the combined conflicting desires awakened by the primal scene. It is also a disguised form of protest rooted in masculine narcissism against the desire to be, "like his mother", penetrated by the father's penis. "To be beaten by the father" becomes "to be copulated with by the father": a change in "terminology", a transition from an anal current to a genital current. It would be even more accurate to speak of an attempt at transformation because, although the dream is the event which takes the little boy from his phase of naughtiness to his neurotic phobic phase, he does not content himself with active/passive ambivalence but piles upon it punished/unpunished ambivalence. The dream enacts an anxiety-provoking conflict between incompatible identities.

THE "RELIGIOUS" PHASE: PIETY AND REVOLT AGAINST GOD THE FATHER

When his mother introduced him to the sacred story, the narrative distracted him from his anxiety and "elevated his soul". In fact, without renouncing any of his old conflictual desires, the unconscious kneaded this new pious material into a new type of symptomatology. Anxiety neurosis was replaced by obsessional neurosis.

This time, it was the suffering figure of Christ that filled his phantasies and focused the boy's still-unresolved antagonistic aspirations. He reacted to this religious instruction with ambivalent behaviour, betraying the unconscious persistence of the radical ambivalence of his sexual aims. He became pious and devout but also adopted a rationalist and critical attitude, questioning all the teachings and dogmas into which his mother and Nanya initiated him. Preoccupied with questions regarding Christ's physical/human reality (Did Christ have a behind too? Did he shit too?), the boy made the Son of God his spokesman, the substitute carrier of his conflicts. His outrage turned against God the Father, who was responsible for the evil acts of men, for all suffering, for all the torments in the world and for the passion of his own son.

Freud's observations provide a key to deciphering the meaning of this transformation in the development of the illness:

> We shall be in a better position to understand these ruminations if we return to a piece of his sexual development which we have already mentioned. We know that, after the rebuff from his Nanya and the consequent suppression of the beginnings of genital activity, his sexual life developed in the direction of sadism and masochism. . . . *In his sadism he maintained his ancient identification with his father; but in his masochism he chose him as a sexual object.* He was deep in a phase of pregenital organization which I regard as the predisposition to obsessional neurosis. The operation of the dream, which brought him under the influence of the primal scene, could have led him to make the advance to the genital organization, and to transform his masochism towards his father into a feminine attitude towards him – into *homosexuality.* But the dream did not bring about this advance; it ended in a state of anxiety. *His relation to his father* might have been expected to proceed from the sexual aim of being beaten by him to the next aim, namely, that of being copulated with by him like a woman; but in fact, *owing to the opposition of his narcissistic masculinity, this relation was thrown back to an even more primitive stage. It was displaced on to a father-surrogate, and at the same time split off in the shape of a fear of being eaten by the wolf. But this by no means disposed of it.*

Thus, narcissistic masculinity repressed homosexuality, into which anal passivity would otherwise have evolved. As a result of this repression, he regressed to an oral position.

It was as though, despite these surrogate "solutions" of naughtiness, the anxiety dream, the fear of wolves and the obsessional piety, it was impossible for him to be rid of the father: a sexually ubiquitous, unavoidable father. Throughout these instinctual meanderings, the relation to the father is subjected to all sorts of strategies, but each time, its hold is strengthened.

All possible means are deployed to preserve the passive sexual relation with the father. In effect, three sexual aims remain solidly attached to this irradicable object:

> From the time of the dream onwards, in his unconscious he was a homosexual, and in his neurosis he was at the level of cannibalism; while the earlier masochistic attitude remained the dominant one. All three currents had passive sexual aims; there was the same object, and the same sexual impulse, but that impulse had become split up along three different levels.[89]

An archaic attachment to the father was never abandoned but was redistributed during the extremely "conservative" upbringing of this child, thanks to a split (*Spaltung*) along the different sexual modes. This triple relation to the father can be formulated as follows: to be beaten, to be penetrated, to be devoured – in this order, based on the reconstruction in analysis, since the patient paid no attention to "normal" chronology.

For the theory, what presents an interest is that the attempted resolution by recourse to obsessional neurosis, – to "elevation of the soul" through religious initiation – achieves an advance towards sublimation of the indestructible impulse through a play of identification. Once again, a connection between identification and sublimation is made evident:

> His knowledge of the sacred story now gave him a chance of *sublimating his predominant masochistic attitude towards his father. He became Christ –* which was made specially easy for him on account of their having the same birthday. Thus he became *something great* and also (a fact upon which enough stress was not laid for the moment) a man.[90]

But this was another failed attempt. This ideal masculine identification was unable to repress the passive homosexual attitude towards his father because he could not stop himself from asking sacrilegious questions about this same Christ:

> We catch a glimpse of his repressed homosexual attitude in his doubting whether Christ could have a behind, for these ruminations can have had no other meaning but the question whether he himself could be used by his father like a woman – like his mother in the primal scene.[91]

These ruminations were also accompanied by a questioning of paternity: "Nanya had given him to believe that he was his father's child, while his sister was his mother's; and this closer connection with his father had been precious to him".[92] But Nanya's confusing explanations about Christ's father (Was it Joseph?

Was it God?) had planted doubt in his mind: if the relation between father and son could be questioned, it was clearly not as intimate as he had believed. This doubt was the prelude to a feeling of ambivalence towards the father and was quickly transformed into revolt, not against his father, but against God himself. He began to fear God.

> If he was Christ, then his father was God. But the God which religion forced upon him was not a true substitute for the father whom he had loved and whom he did not want to have stolen from him. His love for this father of his gave him his critical acuteness. He resisted God in order to be able to cling to his father; and in doing this he was really upholding the old father against the new. He was faced by a trying part of the process of detaching himself from his father.[93]

Here we have a reformulation of the question we examined in *Totem and Taboo*.

We can say that the Wolf Man chose God the Father, as He is described by religion, as a "totem", as the figure of the father. But reconciliation is impossible because this figure of God is only the support of one part of the ambivalent feelings of the son. He rejects this image and identifies with Christ, the object of the Father's harshness (a father whose paternity is brought into question). Onto this religious background, an unconscious struggle is transposed, which Freud resumes in the term *Ablösung*. The use of this term in this context serves to express precisely the aim of the Oedipal conflict, since *ablösen* means: 1) to detach, remove, unstick; 2) to transmit, take over from; 3) to pay back, buy back. But how was he to detach himself from his father and take over – that is, "be the father" – when one libidinal current was stubbornly opposed to this identification that would resolve the Oedipal conflict? Indeed:

> His old love of his father, which had been manifest in his earliest period, was therefore the source of his energy in struggling against God and of his acuteness in criticizing religion. But on the other hand this hostility to the new God was not an original reaction either; it had its prototype in a hostile impulse against his father, which had come into existence under the influence of the anxiety-dream, and it was at bottom only a revival of that impulse. The two opposing currents of feeling which were to rule the whole of his later life, met here in the ambivalent struggle over the question of religion. It followed, moreover, that this struggle produced in the shape of symptoms (the blasphemous ideas, the compulsion which came over him of thinking "God-shit", "God-swine") were genuine compromise-products, as we shall see from the analysis of these ideas in connection with his anal erotism.[94]

One of these compromise products took the form of a curious symptom: he felt compelled to exhale at the sight of beggars, cripples and ugly or old people. He also submitted to a pious ritual: each time he made the sign of the cross, he had to breathe in deeply or exhale forcibly. The rationale for this was that he was breathing in the power of the Holy Ghost and breathing out evil spirits.

The analysis was able to establish the relation between these symptoms: they are the expression of an old identification with the father, but one which was rejected: the breathing game is a concrete enactment of this identificatory conflict, whose ubiquitous nature is obvious. The father spent some time in a sanatorium, where the boy visited him with his mother. His father was now the prototype of the cripples in whose presence he was obliged to exhale, but not only the father who was ill but also the more archaic father of the primal scene. The exhaling represented compassion: compassion for the father, denied identification. Two fragments of Freud's text support this statement:

> Thus his determination not to become like cripples (which was the motive of his breathing out in their presence) was his old identification with his father transformed into the negative. But in so doing he was also copying his father in the positive sense, for the heavy breathing was an imitation of the noise which he had heard coming from his father during the intercourse.[95]

When he was still very small, there had been on the family estate a day-labourer whose tongue had been cut out and who was probably a deaf-mute. The little boy was very fond of him and pitied him deeply. This man had been the first cripple for whom he felt compassion – undoubtedly a father surrogate. In his recollections, this man was associated with other servants whom he had liked, who were Jews or were sickly. All these people belonged to the period before the father's stay in the sanatorium: that is, before the formation of the respiratory symptom.

Here is the second fragment, giving an interpretation of this pity:

> [T]he [respiratory symptom] must therefore rather have been intended to ward off (by means of the breathing out) any identification with the object of the patient's pity.

And Freud goes on to say:

> Then suddenly, in connection with a dream, the analysis plunged back into the prehistoric period, and led him to assert that during the copulation in the primal scene he had observed the penis disappear, that he had felt compassion for his father on that account, and had rejoiced at the reappearance of what he thought had been lost. So here was a fresh emotional impulse, starting once again from the primal scene. Moreover, the narcissistic origin of compassion (which is confirmed by the word itself) is here quite unmistakably revealed.[96]

Much is to be learned from these remarks on the nature of pity: they bring into question a whole set of ethical and metaphysical precepts regarding relations to others, sympathy and compassion which so many moral philosophers have tried to establish.[97]

It is noteworthy that, in the analysis of this case, pity is revealed to be a narcissistic defence: the emotional expression of a desire of the ego "not to be like", motivated by anxiety, dread, the threat of identification with the object of this pity. We are clearly dealing with repudiated identification. Here we find ourselves at the very heart of all discussions on the essence of the tragic effect defined by Aristotle, who asserted that, in the production of the cathartic effect, terror and pity are closely linked. Freud returned to this topic in a text titled "Our Attitude to Death".[98]

But to come back to the Wolf Man: in his case, the feeling of pity constituted a "counter-current": it masked a death wish manifest in his rebellion against God the Father. Although the first threats of castration had come from women (Nanya and then Grusha), the father became – in accordance with the "phylogenetic order" – the one from whom he feared castration.

> His identification of his father with the castrator became important as being the source of an intense unconscious hostility towards him (which reached the pitch of a death-wish) and of a sense of guilt which reacted against it.[99]

This is a typical Oedipal attitude, exhibited by all neurotics with a positive Oedipus complex.

And Freud adds:

> But the astonishing thing was that even against this there was a counter-current working in him, which, on the contrary, regarded his father as the one who had been castrated and as calling, therefore, for sympathy. . . . which denotes a negative Oedipus complex.

We could hazard this simple formulation to describe the Wolf Man's conflict: he wants to be the father and have the father at the same time. The two unconscious aims oppose each other and are enacted dramatically in the double series of morbid identifications, each one negating the other. This repetitive conflict is also apparent in the symptomatic formations we shall now examine, before concluding these "series".

WHEN THE INTESTINES "JOIN IN THE CONVERSATION": IDENTIFICATION WITH THE MOTHER

The sadistic-anal constitution provides the illness with its terrain and its language.[100] We have seen the transformations and remodelings of sadism in repeated attempts at neurotic solutions, acted out in contradictory identifications. The other instinctual aspect of the sadistic-anal phase, specifically anal erotism, contributed in large measure its modes of functioning and its symbolism to the formulation of the Wolf Man's crucial and crucifying experience.

In fact, a sort of monopoly exercised by anal language is what complicates, for the patient, the recognition – that is, the awareness, apperception, acknowledgement and acceptance – of the reality of castration.

Anal erotism and all the unconscious attitudes associated with it began to manifest themselves as the end of the treatment approached. As a consequence of his illness, the patient had developed intestinal troubles; to combat his chronic constipation, he took to having enemas administered by his manservant. Freud recognised the "functional" nature of these problems and decided to put them to use: the associative material emerging from the narrative regarding these symptoms played a major role in precipitating the end of the treatment. Freud writes:

> At last I recognized the importance of the intestinal trouble for my purposes; it represented the small trait of hysteria which is regularly to be found at the root of an obsessional neurosis. I promised the patient a complete recovery of his intestinal activity, and by means of this promise made his incredulity manifest. I then had the satisfaction of seeing his doubt dwindle away, as in the course of the work his bowel began, like a hysterically affected organ, to "join in the conversation", and in a few weeks' time recovered its normal functions after their long impairment.[101]

What unlocked the meaning of these intestinal troubles was a fragment of a sentence emerging from an old memory: at the age of four and a half, after a period of unrestrained pleasure connected with excrement (incontinence, anal jokes and exhibitions), he entered a period of anxiety. When he soiled himself, he was ashamed and would moan while he was being cleaned up, "I cannot go on living like this". This phrase turned out to be the exact reproduction of words previously spoken by his mother. The child had heard her describe abdominal pain and bleeding to her doctor and say emphatically, "I cannot go on living like this". He made this phrase his own and repeated it many times during his illness. Thus, this lament had the significance of an identification with his mother.[102]

During the same period, he became afraid of dying of dysentery and started to look for blood in his stool. Later, a successful attempt at identifying with the mother was made manifest in the symptom of an obsessive fear of death.

This relation to the ill/wounded mother, played out in a morbid, "hysterical" identification, revealed a whole other aspect of his desire and provided the key to the neurotic process deployed to repress his desire. This relation with the mother – chosen in the identificatory game as a "figure" of his desire – like the relation with the father, is irremediably ambivalent. Identification through the symptom expresses both the desire to be like the mother and the refusal, even horror, of being in her place, in her position as a woman. Once again, identification is impossible. But this symptom appears after the primal scene: the fact that it is constructed on an anal (intestinal) theme – initially experienced positively and afterwards with horror – also means that identification still plays the role of hiding a genital scenario behind an anal scenario.

This agrees with Freud's interpretation:

> Under the influence of the primal scene he came to the conclusion that his mother had been made ill by what his father had done to her; and his dread of having blood in his stool, of being as ill as his mother, was his repudiation of being identified with her in this sexual scene – the same repudiation with which he awoke from the dream. But the dread was also a proof that in his later elaboration of the primal scene he had put himself in his mother's place and had envied her this relation with his father. The organ by which his identification with women, his passive homosexual attitude to men, was able to express itself was the anal zone. The disorders in the function of this zone had acquired the significance of feminine impulses of tenderness, and they retained it during the later illness as well.[103]

> [D]uring the process of the dream he understood that women are castrated, that instead of a male organ they have a wound which serves for sexual intercourse, and that castration is the necessary condition of femininity; we have been driven to assume that the threat of this loss induced him to repress his feminine attitude towards men, and that he awoke from his homosexual enthusiasm in anxiety. Now how can this comprehension of sexual intercourse, this recognition of the vagina, be brought into harmony with the selection of the bowel for the purpose of identifying with women? Are not the intestinal symptoms based on what is probably an older notion, and one which in any case completely contradicts the dread of castration – the notion, namely, that sexual intercourse takes place at the anus?[104]

What clearly appears to be a logical contradiction – we might even say epistemological, since the two "knowings" are antithetical – is the unconscious coexistence of two competing sexual views, which the identification process "identifies" by means of representing one – threatening – by the other from an earlier stage. Identification with the woman and a decision in favour of the "intestine" allows the child to set aside the new explanation of the sexual roles of the man and the woman in intercourse. This identification by recourse to the anus lets him hold on to the earlier "cloacal theory" – which does not involve the question of having or not having a penis – and lets him keep at bay (*festhalten*) the "new theory": that is, "castration" of the woman. Identification saves everything, or almost!

Thanks to identification, the feminine attitude towards men – one of the major currents of the Wolf Man's desire – is preserved unconsciously by finding refuge, as Freud says, in the intestinal symptoms while remaining concealed thanks to its anal disguise. In other words, the desire to be a woman for the father is "fulfilled" in the possession of an organ common to both men and women: the anus. But there is a problem: this anus does not provide pleasure (or does not anymore); it is the site of something shameful and of the fear of death. Here, identification is hysterical in nature: it consists of a compromise formation involving both desire and the defence against it. In effect, the child is unconsciously a woman but a woman who "cannot go on living like this" – a woman who is ill.

At the time of the primal scene, it was also an anal "resolution" that the child found: we learn that he "interrupted" his parents' intercourse by passing a stool, which "gave him an excuse for screaming".[105] The unconscious equivalence fae-ces-gift-child allowed him to fulfill in a quasi-positive sense his desire to be in the place of his mother:

> In his identification with women (that is, with his mother) he was ready to give his father a baby, and was jealous of his mother, who had already done so and would perhaps do so again.[106]

Transposing all this to the anal sphere guarantees the preservation of the desire in the unconscious, thanks to this series of identifications. The phenomenon of *Verwerfurg*,[107] which seems to be a defence of a different type than repression, is closely related to the identification mechanism which converts the fear of cas-tration into anal symptomatology. To choose the intestine over the vagina or to choose the beloved father over the castrating God named "God-shit"[108] for the occasion is what this conversion accomplishes. The system of anal identifications set in place is a regressive attempt to relieve the anxiety created by the discovery of the difference between the sexes and, moreover, to overcome the homosexual desire, which Freud sums up in the following terms: "a readiness to give up one's masculinity if in exchange for it one can be loved like a woman".

Through his jealous, miserly and vengeful behaviour and through his offensive obsessional ideas about God (God-pig, God-shit), the Wolf Man was expressing in anal language what Judge Daniel Paul Schreber expressed very clearly in his delusional system. Before detailing the similarity of the father complex in these two cases, let us try to bring together the theoretical elements disseminated in the fragments of the Wolf Man's conflictual identificatory act.

On a fixed background of instinctual ambivalence, constituted by two equally developed partial instincts – one with a passive aim and the other with an active aim – two series of opposing identifications are constructed. As we pointed out, identification is an unconscious process designed to preserve the object. Freud insists on the very conservative nature of the Wolf Man's libido, which cannot give up an acquired libidinal position. Thus, identification appears to be the most suitable process for consolidating acquired positions.

First series of sexual objects: a single object, the father, but several forms of attachment. Narcissistic object-choice is made through identification, which pro-duces the imaginary fulfilment of the wish to be like the father. Anal sexual object-choice by means of seeking homosexual satisfaction: to be penetrated by the father. This instinctual occurrence signals a struggle: genital development, mas-turbatory activity and sexual investigation stimulate narcissistic genital libido, the narcissistic investment in the penis. This narcissistic virility seeks confirmation through identification with an ideal masculine figure: Christ. This identification betrays an ambiguous desire: to be Christ, who suffered at the hands of his father. In this series, attachment to the father triumphs over hostility towards him, produced by his roles as prohibitor of masturbation, castrator and enemy of budding virility. There are also father surrogates: the "castrated" servants (old, crippled, Jews, ill) and positive ones (his tutor, the Latin master called Mr. Wolf).

Second series of sexual objects: women. They include his mother, his sister, Nanya and other women chosen based on a particular "trait" (the repetition of the mother's posture in the primal scene). Jealousy felt towards his sister, a rival for the father's love but also a seductress who awakens passive sexual desire: to be touched, to be looked at. Nanya, more maternal than his mother, is both tender and strict and threatens him with a "wound" to induce him to give up masturbation and exhibitionism. His mother, who suffers from intestinal and gynecological troubles, is chosen for this trait of a sexual nature as an object of hysterical identification. The desire motivating this identification: having the same sexual relation with the father as she has. In this series of choices, what dominates is identification with the woman as the passive object of the father.

Here, the conflict between instinctual impulses is not love for the father as opposed to love for the woman but, rather, to be virile as opposed to being the female object of the father. But in order to fulfill the homosexual wish for the father, a price has to be paid: castration.

Identification with the woman, which replaces the passive and masochistic anal position, serves to fulfill – in the imaginary sphere of phantasy – the passive homosexual desire, and because this desire creates anxiety, it also serves the narcissistic masculine desire since it "rejects" homosexual desire by covering it over with anality. The unabated anxiety clearly shows that this regressive cover-up is a failed compromise: masculine narcissism rebels against passive homosexual desire. The ambivalent conflict continues on, in a variety of forms of illness, in this unabashed and stubbornly conservative anal patient.

Judge Schreber

In the Wolf Man, Freud recognised a conflict similar, in terms of its origin, to the conflict he thought he detected when he read *Memoirs of My Nervous Illness* in 1911. This conflict consisted of the protest of masculinity against homosexual desire. At the theoretical level, comparing these two cases reveals how the paranoid process in one case and the obsessional neurosis process in the other can be seen as two different attempts at "healing".

The similarity of the pathogenic conflict is evident in this summary of the initial phase of the illness in Schreber's case:

> During the incubation period of his illness, as we are aware (that is, between June 1893, when he was appointed to his new post, and the following October, when he took up his duties), he repeatedly dreamt that his old nervous

disorder had returned. Once, moreover, when he was half asleep, he had a feeling that after all it must be nice to be a woman submitting to the act of copulation. The dreams and the phantasy are reported by Schreber in immediate succession; and if we also bring together their subject-matter, we shall be able to infer that, at the same time as his recollection of his illness, a recollection of his doctor was also aroused in his mind, and that the feminine attitude which he assumed in the phantasy was from the first directed towards the doctor. Or it may be that the dream of his illness having returned simply expressed some such longing as "I wish I could see Flechsig again!" Our ignorance of the mental content of the first illness bards our way in this direction. Perhaps that illness had left behind in him a feeling of affectionate dependence upon his doctor, which had now, for some unknown reason, become intensified to the pitch of an erotic desire. This feminine phantasy, which was still kept impersonal, was met at once with indignant repudiation – a true "masculine protest", to use Adler's expression, but in a sense different from his. But in the severe psychosis which broke out soon afterwards the feminine phantasy carried everything before it; and it only requires a slight correction of the characteristic paranoiac indefiniteness of Schreber's mode of expression to enable us to divine the fact that the patient was in fear of sexual abuse at the hands of his doctor himself. The exciting cause of his illness, then, was an outburst of homosexual libido; the object of this libido was probably from the very first his doctor, Flechsig; and his struggle against the libidinal impulse produced the conflict which gave rise to the symptoms.[109]

A little further, we read:

The patient's friendly feeling towards his doctor may very well have been due to a process of "transference", by means of which an emotional cathexis became transposed from some person who was important to him on to the doctor who was in reality indifferent to him; so that the doctor will have been chosen as a deputy or surrogate for some one much closer to him. To put the matter in a more concrete form: the patient was reminded of his brother or father by the figure of the doctor, he rediscovered them in him; there will then be nothing to wonder at if, in certain circumstances, a longing for the surrogate figure reappeared in him and operated with a violence that is only to be explained in the light of its origin and primary significance.[110]

Now, the defensive struggle to resist this phantasy of feminine desire (passive homosexual attitude) began. At first, it took the form of a persecutory delusion and then underwent transformations. Indeed, it changed into a megalomaniacal delusion – a narcissistic solution in the face of intolerable persecution:

It was impossible for Schreber to become reconciled to playing the part of a female wanton towards his doctor; but the task of providing God

Himself with the voluptuous sensations that he required called up no such resistance on the part of his ego. Emasculation was now no longer a disgrace; it became consonant with the Order of Things, it took its place in a great cosmic chain of events, and was instrumental in the re-creation of humanity after its extinction. "A new race of men, born from the spirit of Schreber".[111]

Megalomania compensates the ego, making transformation into a woman at once apparent and acceptable.

The transformation of the persecutory delusion into a megalomaniacal delusion – which provides a solution of sorts to the conflict between instinctual impulses – is what interests us here. We shall see that the formation of the paranoid delusion follows in reverse a path abounding with identifications. Paranoid regression sheds light on the identification process because it breaks it up; this process is, as we have seen, a way to preserve loved objects that were lost.

The question Freud is trying to clarify is "What are the paths and processes through which Flechsig is raised to the status of God?"

In one of Schreber's phantasies, Flechsig is designated as God-Flechsig, but if we keep in mind the entire delusional formation – if, in other words, we make an effort to follow the writing as it transforms the text – we observe a series of divisions, splits, decompositions. This causes the signifier Flechsig to undergo a veritable disassembling of its overdetermination.

[T]he persecutor is divided into Flechsig and God; in just the same way Flechsig himself subsequently splits up into two personalities, the 'upper' and the "middle" Flechsig, and God into the "lower" and the "upper" God. In the later stages of the illness the decomposition of Flechsig goes further still. *A process of decomposition of this kind is very characteristic of paranoia. Paranoia decomposes just as hysteria condenses.* Or rather, *paranoia resolves once more into their elements the products of the condensations and identifications which are effected in the unconscious.* The frequent repetition of the decomposing process in Schreber's case would, according to Jung, be an expression of the importance which the person in question possessed for him. All of this dividing up of Flechsig and God into a number of persons thus had the same meaning as the splitting of the persecutor into Flechsig and God. They were all *duplications* of one and the same important relationship. (Otto Rank has found the same process at work in the formation of myths.) But in order to interpret all these details, we must further draw attention to our view of this decomposition of the persecutor into Flechsig and God as *a paranoid reaction to a previously established identification of the two figures or their belonging to the same class.* If the persecutor Flechsig was originally a person whom Schreber loved, then God must also simply be the reappearance of some one else whom he loved, and probably some one of greater importance.[112]

This figure who "returns" is Schreber's father, famous throughout Germany for his child-rearing theories – certainly far more dangerously mad and uncanny than the son's delusions![113] Based on what we know, this father was very strict, and his divine transfiguration in the memory of his son – from whom death separated him too early, as Freud points out – cannot be attributed solely to filial affection. The son's ambivalence is clear in the displaced conflict of Judge Schreber with his God.

Here we find ourselves on the familiar grounds of the father complex. Schreber's delusion is the transposition into the delusional sphere of Oedipal ambivalence.

> In the final stage of Schreber's delusion a magnificent victory was scored by the infantile sexual urge; for voluptuousness became God-fearing, and God himself (his father) never tired of demanding it from him. His father's most dreaded threat, castration, actually provided the material for his wishful phantasy (at first resisted but later accepted) of being transformed into a woman.[114]

We feel we should also mention an observation Freud made much earlier, in the correspondence with Fliess, discussed in Chapter I of the present work. Freud was already pointing out the difference between hysteria and paranoia, in terms of the processes and paths involved. He was also attempting to frame morbid regression into a theory – as yet inchoate – of psychosexual development. This letter to Fliess seems to prefigure the entire theoretical discussion of the Schreber case.

> The lowest of the sexual strata is autoerotism, which dispenses with any psychosexual aim and seeks only locally gratifying sensations. It is then succeeded by alloerotism (homo- or heteroerotism), but certainly continues to exist as an undercurrent. Hysteria (and its variant, obsessional neurosis) is alloerotic, since its main path is identification with the loved one. Paranoia again dissolves the identification, re-establishes all the loved ones of childhood. . . and dissolves the ego into extraneous persons.
>
> (Letter December 9, 1899)

These writings testify to the fact that, over the years, Freud never ceased investigating the psychic processes involved in morbid formation and trying to differentiate them by other means than those used by psychiatry, which "names symptoms" while he is searching for "means and motives".

What the passages quoted here teach us is that the concept of identification can serve to distinguish two modes of entering illness: the hysterical and obsessional model – two "allo-erotic" (homo- or heteroerotism – illustrated by Dora and the Wolf Man) being the neurotic mode of attachment to those one loves: through identification which preserves the relation in the unconscious; and paranoia – serving as a model to understand psychoses, as in Schreber's case – being the psychotic mode of fragmenting the ego, through dissolution of that with which the ego was constituted: those one loved. And these are precisely the people with whom the paranoid patient cannot identify; that is, he cannot let their imaginary substance augment his ego. He pushes them away; he detaches them and places them outside himself in series. As for the hysteric, he condenses in the symptom the sequences of this impossible love by taking himself for the other person (loved, envied) in unconscious identification; the paranoid divides himself, dispersing the sequence. Everything Freud builds thanks to the concept of projection shows, as the text continues, how, in a context of paranoia, the old reawakened homosexual love is transformed and must be repressed.[115]

But at the heart of the discussion is the concept of repression.

The "problem" the patient has to solve is always the same: how to repress the dangerous impulse; how to detach the libido from the object which is concealed. The symptoms testify to the fate of these "liberated" libidinal investments. Indeed, Freud clearly says:

> [T]he process of repression proper consists in a detachment of the libido from people – and things – that were previously loved.[116]

The "attempt to heal" involves suppressing the repression. But while liberating the libido is a silent process, efforts to bring it back force themselves noisily upon our attention.

The process of reattaching the libido to the people it had abandoned as a result of repression takes place in paranoia through projection and in hysteria and obsessional neurosis through identification. Thus, by means of projection, "what was abolished internally returns from without". Through identification, what was abolished outside (prohibited, refused, repressed) returns inside, through the metamorphosis of the ego on the model of the object. But both these strategies fail, in the end, to preserve the relation with the object because, in one case, the price paid is loss of reality, and in the other, it is guilt. This is why the attempt to re-establish the relation, in both cases, remains "pathological". Freud had already said in *Jokes* that man does not give up anything but creates substitutes. He uses the same idea to distinguish the normal process from neurotic and psychotic processes:

> But it is certain that in normal mental life (and not only in periods of mourning) we are constantly detaching our libido in this way from people or from other objects without falling ill. . . . The detachment of the libido, therefore, cannot in itself be the pathogenic factor in paranoia; there must be some special characteristic which distinguishes a paranoiac detachment of the libido from other kinds. It is not difficult to suggest that that characteristic may be. What use is made of the libido after it has been set free by the process of detachment? *A normal person will at once begin looking about for a substitute for the lost attachment*; and until that substitute has been found the liberated libido will be kept in suspension within his mind, and will there give rise to tensions and colour his mood. *In hysteria* the liberated libido becomes

transformed into somatic innervations or into anxiety. But *in paranoia* the clinical evidence goes to show that the libido, after it has been withdrawn from the object, is put to a special use. It will be remembered that the majority of cases of paranoia exhibit traces of megalomania, and that megalomania can by itself constitute paranoia. From this it may be concluded that in paranoia the liberated libido becomes attached to the ego, and is used for the aggrandizement of the ego. A return is thus made to the stage of narcissism (known to us from the development of the libido), in which a person's only sexual object is his own ego. On the basis of this clinical evidence we can suppose that paranoiacs have brought along with them a *fixation at the stage of narcissism*, and we can assert that the length of *the step back from sublimated homosexuality to narcissism* is a measure of the amount of *regression* characteristic of paranoia.[117]

In its work of reconstruction, the theory produces an evolutive sequence: auto-eroticism, narcissism, homosexuality, sublimation of homosexuality into social relations, heterosexuality. To this sequence of libidinal positions corresponds a series of objects. The normal fate of objects is to be abandoned and replaced; indestructible objects, objects the libido clings to, irreplaceable objects – they become the core of the illness, the worm in the fruit. Neurotic identification and psychotic projection emerge as two desperate means of preserving or restoring the series of lost objects. Impossible repression – detachment – is, in this case, the opposite of what we call renunciation or mourning, which for psychoanalysis always signals the successful finding of substitutes. In every case, a failure of substitution is related to an auto-erotic fixation (oral, anal) or a narcissistic fixation (masculine protest, homosexuality).

These remarks on the various fates of the libido "detached" from its initial objects allow us to conclude our discussion of what we have called, based on our reading of *Totem and Taboo*, totemic or symbolic identification (at the origin of the ideal).

"Totemic" identification brings about successful substitution, which hysterical, phobic, obsessional or magical identification cannot achieve. These identifications point to the neurotic's inability to "mourn" the irretrievably lost object.

The association of feasting and mourning in the totemic rite indicated the possibility for the survivors of completing the work necessary to find a substitute for the dead father. It was a collective – religious – solution to the conflict created by ambivalence. Little Hans's playful triumph indicated his personal ability to deal with ambivalence, thanks to an ideal identification making possible detachment from the father, a detachment seen in the identificatory play which adds a negation – "as if" – to the desire to be the father, symbolised by the horse.

This identification allows sublimation of both love and hate. For little Hans, this small indication of his "wellness" is the promise that "later", when he grew up, he would be like his father. This form of identification has a narcissistic function: it creates an ideal entity with whom a new rivalry is established. The creation of this ideal entity appears to be the only possible successful outcome of substitution: it is "oneself", but transformed, who is substituted for the object. This identification with the totem seen as ideal reassures the ego in its narcissism, without allowing the boy to avoid the demands of reality since it is on himself that he has to work in order to be his father's equal, and this work coincides with reconciliation. Neurotic solutions do not produce reconciliation with the object.

The different forms of neurotic identification are also narcissistic variations, but of a narcissism akin to that of the dream, rather than to the triumphant narcissism of play. This means that in the dream, like in magic or neurosis, the enactment of desire through multiple identifications remains strictly confined to the realm of the unconscious; the desire remains unknown to consciousness, and the ego cannot take ownership of it. Therefore, splitting between the conscious and unconscious representations of desire, the lack of communication between them, is what characterises identifications in the dream, hysteria, phobia and obsessional neurosis. Thus, an "aesthetic" model, albeit limited and partial, continues to predominate in the construction of a non-neurotic mode of identification: we have seen it in jokes, in artistic creation (Leonardo da Vinci), in the totemic feast (religion) and in play. Each time, this identification makes it possible to preserve something of the desire, in a form we have not yet fully elucidated but only named in passing: sublimation.

Narcissistic identification

The so-called metapsychological texts written during the war years followed in the wake of the theory of narcissism introduced in *Totem and Taboo*. The pivotal clinical texts which lent depth to Freud's essay on the origins of totemism were now reinforced by theoretical texts which provided confirmation and elaboration. We have seen that the question of death – in the cases presented, essentially the death of the father – constitutes the psychic material for which "totemic" identification offers "ideal" elaboration. We must remember that the question of the death of the father is problematic because this death is caught up in the instigations of the death wish. In psychoanalysis, the death of the object constitutes a problem only because death is in collusion with desire. The possibility that this covert collusion can lead to illness is illustrated by the sad examples of "pathological grief", "insurmountable mourning", the "nostalgia" of neurotics like the Rat Man and the Wolf Man or of paranoid individuals like Schreber.

The series of morbid elaborations of this question of death – of loss, of the Oedipal object, which includes phobia, obsession and paranoia – is missing an important element that would allow complete understanding of the differences between them. This clinical element is melancholia. Thus, we go from the death of the father to the death of the loved object in general and, specifically, the first object: the mother's breast. Focusing on the loss of the object, on the psychic work it imposes on the ego with the elaboration of irrevocable ambivalence, this reflection is the subject of several texts centred around *Mourning and Melancholia*.

We know that between 1914 and 1918, Freud wrote more metapsychological essays than those available to us. Thanks to his correspondence,[118] we have the titles of the manuscripts he destroyed. Our aim is to reconstitute the elements which would have composed this metapsychology of identification by gathering together the indications of its functioning in the psychic model, dynamics and economy.

The fate of the lost object: mourning or melancholia

It is to Karl Abraham that Freud owes the starting point for his *Mourning and Melancholia*, since Abraham wrote one of the few analytic studies on the subject produced up to that point.[119] In a 1912 article, he set forth the premises for the analytic investigation of "manic-depressive insanity and allied conditions". These "allied conditions" were, specifically, mourning on the one hand and the depression characteristic of obsessional neurosis on the other. Manic reversal and the similarity between mania and infantile excitability completed the picture.

This article provided, above all, clinical information that was precious to Freud, who did not have the wide-ranging experience of a psychiatrist, but Abraham did not provide any explanation regarding the processes involved. In fact, it was Freud's essay which prompted Abraham to pursue his research,[120] focusing on a detailed study of libidinal development. Therefore, let us read Freud more closely, in his *Papers on Metapsychology*, which set the stage for *Mourning and Melancholia*.

> We are able to learn in various ways how advantageous it is for our researches to institute comparisons with certain states and phenomena which may be conceived of as *normal prototypes* of morbid affections. Among these we may include such affective conditions as grief or mourning and the state of being loved, but also the state of sleep and the phenomenon of dreaming.[121]

While the dream served as the normal prototype of narcissistic disorders such as psychotic hallucinations, here, melancholia, a "narcissistic neurosis", is elucidated through comparison with the normal affective condition of mourning. The analogy seems justified by the general description of the two states. Without going into details, let us try to identify what it is in this comparative clinical picture that points to the enigma of melancholia, whose solution, as we shall see, must count on the unconscious work of identification.

> Mourning is regularly the reaction to the loss of a loved person, or to the loss of some abstraction which is taking the place of one, such as one's country, liberty, an ideal, and so on. In some people the same influences produce melancholia instead of mourning and we consequently suspect them of a pathological disposition.[122]

In the event of loss of a love object, one of two psychic alternatives are possible: mourning or, if a "morbid affection" is present, melancholia. Mourning inhibits the ego for a period of time until the work of mourning is completed. It would be ill advised and even harmful to disrupt this process. Mourning and melancholia have certain common characteristics:

1 Profoundly painful dejection;
2 Loss of interest in the outside world, unless it recalls the person who was loved;
3 Loss of the capacity to love: that is, to choose a new love object that could replace the lost object; and
4 Suspension of any activity not directly connected with the memory of the deceased.

Melancholia presents an additional particularity: diminished self-esteem, expressed in self-reproaches and self-reviling, going as far as the delusional expectation of punishment.

What is it that so deeply and painfully inhibits the person in mourning? What exactly constitutes the work of mourning?

This work is ordered by reality testing: the loved object no longer exists; therefore, the libido must be withdrawn from all attachment to this object. But something rebels against this demand – there is understandable opposition: a libidinal position is never willingly abandoned, not even when a substitute is within reach. This opposition can go so far as to cause a break with reality and preserve the object through hallucinatory wishful psychosis. Normally, respect for reality wins out, but its orders are not obeyed at once. Freud explained that

> [they] are carried out bit by bit, at great expense of time and cathectic energy, in the meantime the existence of the lost object is psychically prolonged. Each single one of the memories and expectations in which the libido is bound to the object is brought up and hyper-cathected, and detachment of the libido is accomplished in respect of it.[123]

When describing the carrying out of the command of reality, Freud speaks of a compromise solution. The fact that this compromise is so painful seems at once natural and inexplicable in terms of economics. This question of pain recurs and remains unanswered throughout the essay, which refrains from offering even a hypothetical explanation.[124] Indeed, the same question will arise, inversely, when the joyful triumph of mania will require explanation.

The ego, required to enact a compromise between reality and libidinal demands, becomes free and uninhibited again once the mourning process is completed.

Let us apply to melancholia what we have learned about mourning. What kind of psychic work does melancholia produce?

There is now a shift in comparable characteristics. The clinical picture is different: specifically, in terms of self-regard. Moreover, the difference is one of kind; it concerns the very status of the "event" produced by the loss of the love object. A man in mourning knows what he has lost at the death of the person he loved. The melancholiac, on the other hand, reacts to an unknown loss, an object loss withdrawn from consciousness. "[T]he patient knows *whom* he has lost but not *what* he has lost in him".[125] In mourning, the loss is real; in melancholia, loss seems to be of a "moral" nature, a more "ideal" nature.

The work of mourning can be understood since it is carried out in the open, as it were. But the work of melancholia is internal; like mourning, the impression is of an enigma since neither the melancholic nor the observer knows what is absorbing him so entirely. As a result, in mourning, it is the world, deprived of the presence of the beloved, which has become empty and poor while in melancholia, it is the ego itself which is subjected to unconscious deprivation.

To understand this puzzling response, one must listen to the complaints, self-accusations and self-vilification of the melancholic and take them seriously. Freud explains that:

> It would be equally fruitless from a scientific and therapeutic point of view to contradict a patient who brings these accusations against his ego. He must surely be right in some way. . . . Indeed, we must at once confirm some of his statements without reservation. He really is as lacking in interest and as incapable of love and achievement as he says. But that, as we know, is *secondary; it is the effect of the internal work which is consuming his ego – work which is unknown to us but which is comparable to the work of mourning*. He also seems to us justified in certain other self-accusations; it is merely that he has a keener eye for the truth than other people who are not melancholic. . . . [I]t may be, so far as we know, that he has come pretty near to understanding himself; we only wonder why a man has to be ill before he can be accessible to a truth of this kind.[126]

Yet the melancholic does not behave like someone who clearly recognises his shortcomings and is remorseful. He proclaims for all to hear that he is the most vile of men: he makes a spectacle of himself, insists on self-exposure and enjoys burdening others with his laments. He has no shame: quite the contrary.

He has lost his self-respect and must have a good reason for it. But in that case, contrary to what the analogy with mourning might suggest, what occurred is not a loss of object but – as is clear in his own statements – a loss involving his ego.

If one listens attentively and patiently to what he says, one might form the impression that the most severe reproaches he formulates often do not apply to him, but that, with "insignificant modifications", they can apply to another person: a person he loves, has loved or should love. This analytic listening provides the key to the melancholic process. The enigma is resolved if we recognise that the self-accusations are addressed to a love object and are accusations addressed to the latter in the guise of self-blame.

If the melancholiac's complaints are made against someone ("*ihre Klagen sind Anklagen*"[127]), it becomes clear why he has so little shame, discretion and submissiveness towards those around him. He makes a great nuisance of himself, as though he felt slighted and had been treated with great injustice. He behaves like someone who is outraged.

Freud writes:

> All this is possible only because the reactions expressed in [his] behaviour still proceed from a mental constellation of revolt, which has then, by a certain process, passed over into the crushed state of melancholia.[128]

Here we come to the heart of the matter. After presenting a comparative clinical picture, Freud looks for the differential factor, seeking to identify the process which produces the melancholic profile.

He reconstructs the process and asks himself what conditions make it possible. The process is unconscious identification; the study of its conditions requires a radical conception of the ego's relation to the object. Melancholic identification is seen as retroactively revealing not only the object-choice of the melancholiac but also the very fabric constituting his ego and the human "ego" in general. Let us look closely at this theoretical development, crucial to our enquiry.

> An object-choice, an attachment of the libido to a particular person, had at one time existed; then, owing to a *real slight or disappointment* coming from this loved person, the object-relationship was shattered. The result was not the normal one of a withdrawal of the libido from this object and a displacement of it on to a new one, but something different, for whose coming-about various conditions seem to be necessary. The object-cathexis proved to have little power of resistance and was brought to an end. But the free libido was not displaced on to another object; it was withdrawn into the ego. There, however, it was not employed in any unspecified way, but served to establish an *identification of the ego with the abandoned object.* Thus the shadow of the object fell upon the ego, and the latter could henceforth be judged by a special agency, as though it were an object, the forsaken object. In this way an object-loss was transformed into an ego-loss and the conflict between the ego and the loved person into a cleavage between the critical activity of the ego and the ego as altered by identification.[129]

These concepts resemble those outlined earlier in *On Narcissism: An Introduction:* the question of object-choice, the withdrawal of the libido into the ego, the splitting of the ego into a critical agency and a judged object. This time, the concept of identification is added to the other considerations.

Thus, the enigmatic process of melancholia is an identification, defined in this case as a mode of transformation of the investment of an object having "little power of resistance". But when such an investment falls back onto the ego, it reveals its original narcissistic nature. This regression takes us back to the theory of a double object-choice (anaclitic and narcissistic) described in the 1914 essay. The advantage of this narcissistic operation is that the relation with the object is not abandoned.[130] Thus, the primary condition needed by the melancholic process (identification) consists of this low resistance of the investment in the object: that is, a narcissistic object-choice. In contrast, the second condition is a strong attachment to the love object: indeed, identification is not cessation of the relation to the object but its preservation; through identification, the object – or, rather, the relation to it – is preserved, provided a part of the ego is altered.

Paradoxically, the melancholic is at once very dependent on its object, on the unconscious aspect of the object (whose loss produces rebellion and dejection), and highly narcissistic. As Freud writes, when the "narcissistic identification with the object. . . becomes a substitute for the erotic cathexis",[131] it is because the object was originally a narcissistic double of the ego. But the trait which motivated its selection as a love object remained unconscious.

The term *narcissistic identification* is new. Its inscription in the theory produces a conceptual rearrangement and leads to an explicit explanation of certain distinctions made in the essays we examined, without being clearly classified. Initially, the concept of identification was used in the analysis of the hysterical process, the model for neurotic identification. But our concept of "totemic" identification hinted at a level of functioning more radical than the level of hysteria. The bits and fragments of theory developed so far come together and are clearly articulated in this text. Let us read the two passages which set forth this synthesis.

> The narcissistic identification with the object then becomes a substitute for the erotic cathexis, the result of which is that in spite of the conflict with the loved person the love-relation need not be given up. This substitution of identification for object-love is an important mechanism in the narcissistic affections; Karl Landauer (1914) has lately been able to point to it in the process of recovery in a case of schizophrenia.[132]

It represents, of course, a regression from one type of object-choice to original narcissism. "We have elsewhere[133] shown that identification is a preliminary stage of object-choice, that it is the first way – and one that is expressed in an ambivalent fashion – in which the ego picks out an object. The ego wants to incorporate this object into itself, and, in accordance with the oral or cannibalistic phase of libidinal development in which it is, it wants to do so by devouring it. Abraham is undoubtedly right in attributing to this connection the refusal of nourishment met with in severe forms of melancholia".[134]

Mourning and Melancholia goes on to say:

The conclusion which our theory would require – namely, that the disposition to fall ill of melancholia. . . lies in the predominance of the narcissistic
type of object-choice – has unfortunately not yet been confirmed by observation. . . . If we could assume an agreement between the results of observation
and what we have inferred, we should not hesitate to include this regression from object-cathexis to the still narcissistic oral phase of the libido in
our characterization of melancholia. Identifications with the object are by
no means rare in the transference neuroses either; indeed, they are a well-
known mechanism of symptom-formation, especially in hysteria. The difference, however, between narcissistic and hysterical identification may be seen
in this: that, whereas in the former the object-cathexis is abandoned, in the
latter it persists and manifests its influence, though this is usually confined
to certain isolated actions and innervations. In any case, in the transference
neuroses, too, identification is the expression of there being something in
common, which may signify love. *Narcissistic identification is the older of
the two and it paves the way to an understanding of hysterical identification,*
which has been less thoroughly studied.[135]

This passage brings to mind Freud's much earlier remarks, mentioned at the
start of the present work. In Draft N, included with his May 31, 1897, letter to
Wilhelm Fliess, Freud discusses impulses towards parents (wishing their death),
which he considers an integral part of neuroses.

"[It] is a manifestation of mourning to reproach oneself for their death or to
punish oneself in a hysterical fashion with the same states that they have had",
as a way of making amends. In this case, identification is only a perspective, not
a cause. Freud had already sensed at the time that identification, which can be
applied to both mourning and hysteria, is only a position one takes (a perspective). Now, 20 years later, only causes could make it possible to differentiate the
processes at work in these two affections.

Defining causes required a revision of libidinal theory and the radicalisation of
the concept of "ego". We learned that hysterical identification ("less thoroughly
studied") manifests in a condensed fashion the hysteric's desire (unconscious
desire for sexual identity) and the defence against this desire (refusal, self-punishment). In hysteria, the object-relation is maintained, but it is a forbidden relation,
and only the symptom and the dream bear the traces of the hysteric's unconscious
demands. In any case, hysterical identification does not radically alter the "ego"
but, on the contrary, protects it from the anxiety associated with the manifestation
of desire. Hysterical identification safeguards and preserves the ego.

In melancholia, the process is entirely different. There is a puzzling exultation
of the ego, internally devoured (and no longer externally fascinated) by the object.
Melancholic identification transforms the ego by absorbing the lost relation, with

its conflict, into itself, thereby creating a painful split and setting up an internal tribunal (critical agency), which pronounces a part of the ego guilty of an unpardonable crime. Narcissistic identification alters the ego by preserving the object the latter – regrettably – does not give up.

What makes us say that melancholic identification has been studied more thoroughly than hysterical identification?

Returning to the long passage we quoted earlier, we believe Freud based this statement on his theory of object-choice combined with that of the development of libidinal organisation. The decisive element is, of course, the positing of an "original" state. Freud makes frequent use of the concept of the original (*ursprunglich*): original narcissism, identification as a "preliminary" stage of object-choice, oral or cannibalistic phase of libidinal development. To be fair, the use of this language is accompanied by warnings and incitements to caution. Freud advises against "any over-estimation of our conclusions" and speaks of inferences. In their remarkable essay *Fantasme originaire, fantasmes des origines, origine du fantasme*, Laplanche and Pontalis discuss this question and its implications in very clear terms.[136]

In this passage from *Mourning and Melancholia*, as well as in the passage added to *Three Essays* in 1915, obviously influenced by Abraham's perspective, Freud tries to link the "choice of illness" with a stage of libidinal development. The stage associated with melancholia is the oral or cannibalistic phase, which, Freud points out, is a narcissistic phase.

Indeed, identification is the preliminary stage (*Vorstufe*) of object-choice or, as Freud writes elsewhere, its prototype (*Vorbild*); it is the first ambivalent manner in which the ego chooses the object. Thus, it is the work of constituted narcissism because there is an "ego" which chooses its "object". At this stage, to love the object means to devour it, to incorporate it, to take it into the ego or, if we may use the term, to "narcissise" it, to transform it into ego. But such a (phantasmatic) incorporation does not produce melancholia in the newborn – at most, as Melanie Klein says, a depressive state[137] – so, in the melancholic's narcissistic, incorporative relation with the object, there must be an added factor. Another condition must be present, in addition to the narcissistic object-choice with possible regression to narcissism.

This second condition in the melancholic process, beyond narcissistic identification, is the intensity of the ambivalence.

The loss of the love object is a very revealing event. It can affect the survivor in a normal way, though mourning; the duration and pain of this mourning are manifestations of the intensity of the attachment the mourner felt for the deceased. A pathological reaction to the loss reveals, in hindsight, the unconsciously problematic character of the relationship the loss has brought to an end. This is the case for what Freud called "pathological mourning" in obsessional neurosis. It takes the form of melancholia.

Depression in obsessional neurosis is well known to psychoanalysts. It allows us to understand a new component of melancholia, which appears to be the most serious depressive disorder. The pathological mourning of the obsessional patient is characterised by self-accusations and guilt for being responsible for the death of the object and blame for having wished it. This is an intermediary state between mourning and melancholia.

Freud wrote: "These obsessional states of depression following upon the death of a loved person show us what the conflict due to ambivalence can achieve by itself when there is no regressive drawing-in of the libido as well".[138]

Obsessional self-accusations are the result of a turning back of sadistic and hate-filled impulses upon the ego. This turning back is carried out, of course, through identification with the object, but in a hysterical mode: that is, without involving the ego. We will come back later to this particular functioning of the impulses when they turn back upon the subject and to the connection of this functioning with identification.

In melancholia, the process is triggered by causes beyond a clear case of loss due to the death of the object. These causes include every situation in which the ego suffers an injury, humiliation or disillusionment which introduces a conflict between love and hate in the relationship or reinforces already existing ambivalence. But the turning back of the hate upon oneself has catastrophic, suicidal effects destructive of the ego. The "constitutional" anal factor, present here as it is in obsessional neurosis,[139] is tied to narcissistic regression in melancholia. This association is what lends this condition its dangerously excessive quality.

Freud provides the following explanation:

> If the love for the object – a love which cannot be given up though the object itself is given up – takes refuge in narcissistic identification, then the hate comes into operation on this substitutive object, abusing it, debasing it, making it suffer and deriving sadistic satisfaction from its suffering. The self-tormenting in melancholia, which is without doubt enjoyable, signifies, just like the corresponding phenomenon in obsessional neurosis, a satisfaction of trends of sadism and hate which have been turned round upon the subject's own self. . . . The melancholiac's erotic cathexis in regard to his object has thus undergone a double vicissitude; part of it has regressed to identification, but the other part, under the influence of the conflict due to ambivalence, has been carried back to the stage of sadism which is nearer to that conflict.[140]

This displacement of sadism provides an answer to the enigma of suicidal tendencies:

> [T]he ego can kill itself only if, owing to the return of the object-cathexis, it can treat itself as an object – if it is able to direct against itself the hostility which relates to an object and which represents the ego's original reaction to objects in the external world.[141]

While forms of neurotic depression are a way of conserving the object, through magical identification, in the ego, melancholia, a narcissistic neurosis, tries to maintain the mode of relation to the lost object in the ego, thereby destroying both the ego and the object. In transference neurosis, the failure of the narcissistic conservatism of the ego is not so radical.

The melancholic manifestation of narcissism, evident in the devastating effects of narcissistic identification, forces us to revise the very concept of primary narcissism. Indeed, it would seem that the usual representation of narcissism is that of a self-sufficient monad, a closed libidinal solipsism, an undifferentiated cell impervious to any external incursion.[142] But if we give serious consideration to the implications and effects of narcissistic identification, we are forced to admit that this perception may not be accurate and that, from the start, narcissism is a mode of relation. If ambivalent cannibalistic identification is the first mode of loving an object – if, in other words, "in pricipio" love and identification coincide – we must consider narcissism a relation of the ego with itself as a "cannibalised" object, with "itself" being, in the same way, the cannibalised object narcissistically claimed. Freud places the oral relation in the sphere of narcissism. We must draw the conclusion that primary narcissism can only be seen as cannibalism and that, after all, narcissism is simply the functioning of narcissistic identification.[143]

This question of the status of primary narcissism – of primal identification – calls for clarification of the theory. It is left to us to accomplish this work since, as early as *Mourning and Melancholia*, the central question in ego theory becomes indissociable from the question of identification as the primary relation of the ego with the "object". There is no ego without object-cathexis. The work of psychoanalysis shows that it is only possible to speak of the structure and modes of functioning of the ego by taking as a starting point the vicissitudes of its libidinal investments. The possibility that the ego may be subject to a pathological condition is intimately tied to these libidinal vicissitudes. The question of the "object" arises from the beginning, from the stage of narcissism. Thus, *Mourning and Melancholia* introduces the need to re-evaluate the concepts of ego and object, suggesting a specific conclusion: the possibility that, at a certain point, what we call "object" and what we call "ego" may be the same thing. This text takes the question of identification beyond the understanding of processes of symptom formation, opening a deeper enquiry into the origin of the "ego" and its agencies.[144]

Supplemental note to Mourning and Melancholia: Karl Abraham

To complete our discussion on melancholia while remaining methodologically rooted in Freudian texts, it would not be out of place to make some remarks on the work of Karl Abraham, already mentioned several times.

Abraham strove to explore certain research paths identified by Freud, particularly early object-relations, by "fine tuning"[145] – to borrow Jean Laplanche's expression – the libidinal development theory. Our discussion will only deal with the ideas related to our own topic of investigation. Abraham expands or qualifies Freud's views on the following points:

- Melancholia is the archaic form of mourning. In normal mourning, there is always an introjective, cannibalistic phase. This is made evident by the funeral rites of "primitive" peoples. Contemporary anthropological studies and psychoanalytic studies on depression[146] also confirm this fact. We could say that in every instance of normal mourning, there is something like the introjection of the deceased, a partial identification ensuring the preservation of the deceased in the ego; the loved object survives, incorporated in the ego. Structurally, the ego only has this narcissistic resource to survive: it is constituted of a series of "dead" or relinquished objects, of which it integrates only what is good. Due to "normal" ambivalence, that which was hateful in the subject is destined to be forgotten. As we shall see, Freud himself considered the melancholic process a model of the normal process of relinquishing an object-relation. Thus, the distinction between mourning and (/or) melancholia is not as clear as he claims.
- At first sight, what strikes us about the melancholic are his self-accusations; Freud recognized the significance of this prominent "delusion of inferiority". But in the melancholic, there is also considerable overestimation of the ego: the part of the ego which hates is monstrous; the hate is unfathomable, gigantic, terrifying. The melancholic's demonic, negative excess reveals his persistent narcissism. Indeed, identification with the Devil is not infrequent in cases of melancholic delusion. Freud himself drew attention to it masterfully in his 1923 essay "A Seventeenth-Century Demonological Neurosis".[147] We shall come back to this.
- Repetition compulsion is particularly characteristic of the melancholic. He tends to repeat, in the unconscious choice of his objects, the condition leading to the failure of his relations with love objects and, consequently, with his melancholia: narcissistic identification, unconscious and ambivalent, with the other, who possesses the unique trait which makes him "the same". When the object is revealed to "lack" the element sustaining this identification and, therefore, his narcissistic love, rebellion and melancholic tragedy surface. Freud would need a number of years to uncover the complicity between the "death drive" and repetition. But it is already clear that the basis of the repetition is narcissism and that, for the melancholic, the compulsion to repeat the trauma is enacted in his choice of sexual object: that is, in narcissistic identification.
- According to Abraham, ambivalence towards the object and, as a result of inversion, towards the ego is the necessary condition for melancholia to be transformed into mania. Our discussion will not extend to the question of mania, developed by Freud in *Group Psychology and the Analysis of the Ego* (1920).

Finally, Abraham made a systematic list of the specific factors causing the onset of melancholia, in the place of normal mourning.

1   Oral eroticism: considered a constitutional factor;
2   Fixation of the libido on the oral level, where there was excessive pleasure in sucking, biting, chewing, eating: an insatiable demand for oral expressions of love;
3   Severe injury to infantile narcissism through disappointments in love, feeling of paternal and maternal abandonment;
4   Experience of first major disappointment in love before overcoming Oedipal wishes; that is, at a time when the libido has not advanced beyond the narcissistic stage, the overcoming (repression) of incestuous desires and the revolt against the father are effected in an "incorporative" mode. There is a permanent association between the Oedipus complex and libidinal cannibalism (oral-sadistic impulses); and
5   Repetition of primary disappointment in later life causes the onset of melancholic depression and hostility towards those who so inconsiderately thwarted the subject's narcissistic desire for love. According to August Stärcke,[148] the original disappointment is the experience of weaning, which can be considered a primal castration (*Urkastration*), generating an unquenchable thirst for revenge by biting (the mother's breasts or her imaginary penis).

In conclusion, let us quote Abraham's summary of his concepts on introjection and its consequences:

When melancholic persons suffer an unbearable disappointment from their love-object, they tend to expel that object as though it were feces and to destroy it. They thereupon accomplish the act of introjecting and devouring it – an act which is a specifically melancholic form of narcissistic identification. Their sadistic thirst for vengeance now finds its satisfaction in tormenting the ego – an activity which is in part pleasurable. We have reason to suppose that this period of self-torment lasts until lapse of time and the gradual appeasement of sadistic desires have removed the love-object from the danger of being destroyed. When this has happened the object can, as it were, come out of his hiding-place in the ego. The melancholic can restore it to its place in the outer world.

It seems to me to be of no little psychological interest to be able to establish the fact that in his unconscious the melancholic regards this liberation from his object as once more an act of evacuation. During the time when his depression was clearly beginning to diminish, one of my cases had a dream in which he expelled with the greatest sensation of relief a stopper that was sticking in his anus. This act of expulsion concludes the process of that archaic form of mourning which we must consider melancholia to be. We may truly say that during the course of an attack of melancholia the love-object goes through a process of psychological metabolism within the patient.[149]

Identification and metapsychology

In the interval between *Totem and Taboo* and the metapsychological writings culminating, for the moment, in *Introductory Lectures on Psycho-Analysis*, the clinical and theoretical material needed to construct the concept of identification has increased significantly. Now, identification is part of a series of interconnected topics, and it is discussed in all subsequent writings. Before ending this second chapter of the present work, it might be useful to provide a brief review of the various questions that arose along the way. Several directions for research emerged, all of them rooted in the theory of narcissism, which is the pivotal concept in the enquiry undertaken; these research paths made it possible to outline a "metapsychology" of identification.

1   Identification is fundamentally a narcissistic process in terms of its origin and aim. It is the work of incorporation carried out by the ego, the transformer of libidinal object investments into ego investments: precisely the aim of narcissistic regression. Identification serves primarily the libidinal interests of the ego; it is narcissism at work. It is the very process of *Selbsterhaltung* of the ego: incorporate to survive.

2   Thus, it ensures this self-preservation[150] of the ego but, paradoxically, by extending to impulses. As an essential process of ego preservation, it serves fundamentally to preserve the object: this "object" is originally some part of the ego, a fundamental "incorporated" portion, a prototype of the ego, the original figure of the object. Identification is an "egotisation" of the object. The problem this object poses for the ego is its evanescence, its "loss". Thus, the ego is, originally, the secondary object, the aftermath, what is left of something irretrievably lost, the obliterated and unnamable object of self-eroticism, the grandiose and mythical object of infantile narcissism, the object of romantic passion.[151]

3   Melancholic identification has served as an indicator in this sphere of the original relation of the ego with the object. The object proves to be narcissistic, appears as a "double" of the archaic ego, and is involved in the ambivalent instinctual functioning of orality, of cannibalism.

The analysis of melancholia, in conjunction with that of paranoia, that of megalomania in paraphrenia[152] and delusions of being observed in schizophrenia[153] demonstrate the combined character of the so-called normal ego and reveals its plural origin. The ego, made up of identifications masked by current love objects, can, following the (real or imaginary) loss of the object, lose itself, become decomposed, split, fragment, deconstruct, destroy itself. Psychoses provide clinical illustrations of the possible fragmentation of the ego, inverted figures of its construction, of its organisation, of its "institutions": ego ideal, censor, moral conscience, self-consciousness. The figure of the "double" in literary fiction also illustrates these processes.[154]

4   Although melancholia is a negative and sometimes suicidal processing of the (impossible) loss of the object, it demonstrates the working through of any renouncing of an object. An archaic form of mourning, narcissistic identification reveals the non-pathological process of ego preservation: that is, ideal formation. The identification we call "totemic" does not seem radically different from melancholic identification – it once was, positively, the means of resolving conflict arising from Oedipal ambivalence.

Ideal formation is no doubt the constitutive process of the ego itself, given its original divided state. We have already observed that this strategy of "adopting an ideal" constitutes a possible means of resolution for the ego, when confronting guilt-related conflict after the death of the father; thus, the son's identification with the father in the totemic feast ritual ends mourning and guilt by establishing the prohibiting and exemplary power of the father in the ego of the survivors. The examples of infantile totemism (Hans, the Rat Man, the Wolf Man, Arpad) also show that identification with the deceased father (or relinquished as a libidinal object) produces the ideal. What remains to be done is to describe this ideal formation process by placing it in the context of related concepts such as identification, idealisation, sublimation, ideal ego, ego ideal, superego.

5   To put into words the unfolding of the identification process, the middle-reflexive voice of the verb must be used. Preceding the division into active and passive, identification as narcissistic play centres on the self-love of the "subject" – ambivalent self-love, well-meaning or destructive. Identification is sustained and amplified self-love.

Without commenting in detail on the first text of the *Metapsychology: Instincts and Their Vicissitudes*, we shall turn to Freud's text to support what we assert in our conclusions. Freud's discussion concerns the transformations of impulses (especially of partial impulses: sadistic, masochistic, voyeuristic, exhibitionistic). The possible transformations considered are of two types:

• Reversal into the opposite; and
• Turning around upon the subject's own self.

The two other major forms of transformation or vicissitude which instincts undergo are sublimation (already examined in *Three Essays*) and repression, which requires a separate study. But for our present purposes, what attracted our attention was this comment in Freud's text on repression:

[R]epression is not a defensive mechanism which is present from the very beginning, and. . . it cannot arise until a sharp cleavage has occurred between conscious and unconscious mental activity. . . . *[T]he essence of repression lies simply in turning something away, and keeping it at a distance, from the conscious*. This view of repression would be made more complete by assuming that, before the mental organization reaches this stage, the task of fending off instinctual impulses is dealt with by the other vicissitudes which instincts may undergo – e.g. reversal into the opposite or turning round upon the subject's own self.[155]

The psychic cleavage effected by original repression, which introduces the mental organisation making possible the operation of "repression as such" – retrospective repression – appears then to be second in relation to an organisation in which protection against instinctual dangers is provided by early defence mechanisms. We see these associated processes, indistinguishable at times, as being intimately related to the identification process itself. As primary narcissistic defence processes, these two vicissitudes of the impulses – reversal into the opposite (from active to passive) and turning around upon the subject's own self (the object of the active impulse becomes the ego itself, which finds itself divided into the subject of this activity and its object) – bear a very close resemblance to identification.

Indeed, these processes seem to be closely related to the stage of auto-erotism, which they contribute to maintaining. In truth, their effect, which is to transform the ego into a masochistic or exhibitionistic object, is an exact reproduction of the original auto-erotic state. Passivity is, in fact, the preservation of the original instinctual narcissistic object. These transformations lead to a change of subject and the preservation of the auto-erotic object.

Auto-erotism, which precedes the cleavage active subject/passive object, is, as Freud says, the equivalent of the middle voice, in relation to the opposition between active and passive which result from it. Advent of the active impulse requires leaving narcissism behind; the passive impulse preserves narcissism.

Indeed, identification can be said to be a reproduction of an auto-erotic relation in which the instinctual subject and object merge. At the level of phantasy, identification reproduces an original sado-masochistic relation or an original voyeuristic-exhibitionistic relation. Instinctual ambivalence is primary; in fact, Freud defines *instinct* as an eruption of waves: not as a single wave, a succession of waves. He writes:

> We can then perhaps picture the first, original eruption of the instinct as proceeding in an unchanged form and undergoing no development at all. The next wave would be modified from the outset – being turned, for instance, from active to passive – and would then, with this new characteristic, be added to the earlier wave, and so on. . . . The fact that, at this later period of development of an instinctual impulse, its (passive) opposite may be observed alongside of it deserves to be marked by the very apt term introduced by Bleuler – "ambivalence".[156]

And he adds, a little further:

> We have become accustomed to call the early phase of development of the
> ego, during which its sexual instincts find auto-erotic satisfaction, "narcis-
> sism", without at once entering on any discussion of the relation between
> auto-erotism and narcissism. It follows that the preliminary stage of the
> scopophilic instinct, in which the subject's own body is the object of the
> scopophilia, must be classed under narcissism, and that we must describe
> it as a narcissistic formation. The active scopophilic instinct develops from
> this, by leaving narcissism behind. The passive scopophilic instinct, on the
> contrary, holds fast to the narcissistic object. Similarly the transformation of
> sadism into masochism implies a *return to the narcissistic object*. And in both
> these cases. . . *the narcissistic subject is, through identification, replaced* by
> another extraneous ego.[157]

This principle of an original ambivalent auto-erotic position now makes it necessary to postulate original masochism, which Freud refuses to do for the moment,
as if rejecting original "passivity" since he conceives impulses as "active". What
is really at stake here is jouissance. Freud says, in fact, that identification with
the suffering subject is what produces one's jouissance in sadism. This means
that, according to the regressive logic of identification, original masochism makes
sadistic jouissance possible.

This discussion, merely suggested in this text, would be reopened in 1919 in
Freud's essay *A Child Is Being Beaten*, in *Beyond the Pleasure Principle* in 1920
and then in 1924 in the metaphysical essay *The Economic Problem of Masochism*.
These texts make it even easier to understand that identification is of use to narcissism because, through the relation to an object (chosen for its narcissistic "trait"
as an unconscious double of the ego), it restores primal auto-erotic jouissance,
in which the budding, transient ego is its own ambivalent love object. Any "perverse" sexual organisation tends to reproduce this narcissistic mode of jouissance
in which the other has no intrinsic value but is considered a partial double of the
ego, the representation of an external object.[158]

To conclude these remarks, we must point out that the subject of instinct is not
to be considered a subjectivity, any more than the subject of identification. We
see this subjectivity as correlative to ideal formation dependent on this enigmatic
"new psychic action" which is added to auto-erotism "in order to bring about narcissism": that is, an action added to an ego that can be opposed to external stimuli
and thus to other egos. "[W]e are bound to suppose that a unity comparable to the
ego cannot exist in the individual from the start".[159] It is safe to say that this psychic action which brings about (*Gestalten*) a new auto-erotism to create the ego is
grounded in an "ideal" identification which must be related to original repression.

6   Knowing that narcissism motivates all repression, we must provide an
    explicit explanation of the relation between identification and repression

mechanisms. Identification seems to be an archaic form of ego "defence", anteceding repression. We see it as the enactment of joint processes of "turning round upon the subject's own self" and "reversal into its opposite", described by Freud as the earliest impulses.[160] In the analysis of the Schreber case, Freud gives the following definition of repression: "[t]he process of repression proper consists in a detachment of the libido from people – and things – that were previously loved": that is, an *Ablösung* which is a taking back, an attempted detachment of the libido. We know that this attempt fails in transference neurosis, which preserves the phantasmatic relation with the object. The psychoses which carry out this detachment successfully bring about, with the relinquishing of the object, the decomposition of the ego. Neurotic and narcissistic identification, for which melancholia is the best illustration, are the paths taken by this *Ablösung*, and they both lead to impasse. Subsequent Freudian texts which expand on the repression concept place greater emphasis on the aim of instinctual representations – representation and affect[161] – and set aside the narcissistic dimension of the question. Yet it is this narcissistic aspect of the question which renders the process of repression understandable: Freud's discussion in *A Case of Paranoia* and in *On Narcissism: An Introduction* makes this very clear.[162]

These considerations regarding the relation between repression-identification-narcissism raise many questions connected with subjects of enquiry encountered earlier in our discussion:

1   The composition of the ego, its differentiation into agencies or institution;
2   The primary object-relation and its renouncing (primary identification, primary repression); and
3   Success or failure criteria to be applied to repression and, in conjunction with this, the question of pathogenic or "structuring" identifications (neuroses, perversions, psychoses, personality formation).

Notes

1   This change from Freud I to Freud II came about for various reasons which converged at a certain point: Adler's dissent (1911), then Stekel's (1913), then Jung's (1913) forced Freud to clarify and reaffirm the importance of the theory of sexuality, of the sexual etiology of neuroses, of the Oedipus complex, of the reality of the unconscious. New perspectives brought by disciples with experience acquired in psychiatric hospitals (Bleuler, Abraham, Jung, Ferenczi, etc.) required a revision of the theory of the libido and an analysis of the genesis and differentiated structure of the Self to arrive at an understanding of "narcissistic" disorders: that is, of psychosis. Freud's 1914 text on narcissism is the theoretical turning point in this rearrangement of the doctrine initiated a long time earlier, in 1910, when Freud first used the term *narcissism* in his essay on Leonardo da Vinci. See Ernest Jones, *The Life and Work of Sigmund Freud*, London: Hogarth, 1956.

2 Freud, S., *Three Essays on the Theory of Sexuality*, S.E. 7: 198, London: Hogarth, 1915.

3 Ibid.

4 Ibid., pp. 197–198.

5 Jean Laplanche's work *Life and Death in Psychoanalysis*, Baltimore, MD: Johns Hopkins University Press, 1985, develops an in-depth interpretation of this question of layering and search for the object. Chapter 1 is of special interest to us since it deals with orality. See also: Nouvelle Revue de psychanalyse, No. 6, "Destins du cannibalisme", *Gallimard*, Autumn 1972.

6 Freud, S., *Three Essays on the Theory of Sexuality*, op. cit., p. 222.

7 Ibid., p. 234. Freud continued his explanation of the two stages of human love life in *Contributions to the Psychology of Love*; the second article, titled "On the Universal Tendency to Debasement in the Sphere of Love" (1912, S.E. 11), specifies two currents (the tender and the sensual) which should normally come together in puberty.

8 This idea of an object found initially and then rediscovered is not to be taken literally: obviously, the breast is never found again. But this idea is at the basis of a certain conception of desire defined as a movement of nostalgic return to the lost object. See Jean Laplanche, op. cit., Chapter 1: "The object to be found is not the lost object, but its substitute through displacement. The lost object is the object of self-preservation, of hunger, while the object sought in sexuality is the object displaced in relation to this first object. Hence the obvious impossibility of ever finding the object again, since the lost object *is not the same* as the one which must be found: this is the nature of the essential 'lure' which initiates the sexual search".

9 Freud, S., *Three Essays on the Theory of Sexuality*, op. cit., pp. 225–226.

10 Ibid., p. 222.

11 Freud, S., *On Narcissism: An Introduction*, S.E. 14, London: Hogarth, 1914, p. 90.

12 Freud, S., *Leonardo da Vinci and a Memory of His Childhood*, S.E. 11, London: Hogarth, 1910, p. 99.

13 Freud, S., *Three Essays on the Theory of Sexuality*, op. cit.

14 Freud points out the traces of this two-level process of choosing a sexual object in Leonardo. Quoting biographer Giorgio Vasari, he writes: "In his youth he made some heads of laughing women out of clay, which are reproduced in plaster, and some children's heads which were as beautiful as if they had been modelled by the hand of a master". Freud goes on to say: "Thus we learn that he began his artistic career by portraying two kinds of objects; and these cannot fail to remind us of the two kinds of sexual objects that we have inferred from the analysis of his vulture-phantasy. If the beautiful children's heads were reproductions of his own person as it was in his childhood, then the smiling women are nothing other than repetitions of his mother Caterina, and we begin to suspect the possibility that it was his mother who possessed the mysterious smile – the smile that he had lost and that fascinated him so much when he found it again in the Florentine lady".

15 Freud, S., *Leonardo da Vinci and a Memory of His Childhood*, op. cit., pp. 99–100.

16 Ibid., pp. 120–121.

17 His father's later concern could change nothing in this compulsion; for the compulsion derived from "the impressions of the first years of childhood, and what has been repressed and has remained unconscious cannot be corrected by later experiences" (Ibid., p. 121).

18 Ibid., p. 122.

19 This formulation is used by Freud in the following passage of *Three Essays on the Theory of Sexuality*: "*The Sexual Object During Early Infancy*: But even after sexual activity has become detached from the taking of nourishment, an important part of this first and most significant of all sexual relations is left over, which help to prepare

for the choice of an object and thus to restore the happiness that has been lost. . . .
A child's intercourse with anyone responsible for his care affords him an unending
source of sexual excitation and satisfaction from his erotogenic zones. This is especially so since the person in charge of him, who, after all, is as a rule his mother, herself regards him with feelings that are derived from her own sexual life: she strokes
him, kisses him, rocks him and quite clearly treats him *as a substitute for a complete
sexual object*" (S.E. 7: 222–223).
20 The formulation of the complete Oedipus complex would not be provided by Freud
   until 1923, when he wrote *The Ego and the Id*.
21 Jones, E., *The Life and Work of Sigmund Freud*, Vol. 2, New York: Basic Books,
   1981.
22 Freud, S., *Totem and Taboo*, S.E. 13, London: Hogarth, 1913, p. 77.
23 Ibid., p. 76.
24 "[M]en mistook the order of their ideas for the order of nature, and hence imagined
   that the control which they have, or seem to have, over their thoughts, permitted them
   to exercise a corresponding control over things" (Frazer, J. G., *The Golden Bough*,
   Oxford: Oxford University Press, 1998; quoted by Freud in S.E. 13).
25 Freud, S., *Formulations on the Two Principles of Mental Functioning*, S.E. 12: 218–
   226, London: Hogarth, 1911.
26 Freud, S., *Totem and Taboo*, op. cit., p. 81.
27 Ibid., p. 80.
28 Ibid., pp. 81–82.
29 Ibid., p. 83.
30 Ibid., pp. 83–84.
31 Ibid., pp. 84–85.
32 Ibid, p. 86.
33 See Chapter 2 of *Totem and Taboo*: "Taboo and Emotional Ambivalence".
34 Freud, S., *Totem and Taboo*, op. cit., p. 85.
35 "Touching is the first step towards obtaining any sort of control over. . . a person or
   object" (in *Totem and Taboo*, op. cit., chapter 2, pp. 33–34).
36 We are referring to Lacan's work and A. Zenoni's description of it: "Metaphor and
   Metonymy in Lacanian Theory", Enclictic, V, no. 1 (Spring 1981), pp. 5–18.
37 Freud, S., *Notes Upon a Case of Obsessional Neurosis*, S.E. 10, London: Hogarth,
   1909. By studying the characteristics of obsessional thought and the attitude of the
   obsessed patient towards reality, superstition and death, Freud connected the "omnipotence which he ascribed to his thoughts and feelings, and to his wishes, whether
   good or bad", with infantile megalomania (*Five Lectures on Psycho-Analysis*, S.E.
   11, London: Hogarth, 1910).
38 Freud, S., *Formulations on the Two Principles of Mental Functioning*, op. cit., p. 225.
   In this article, Freud describes neurotic thinking as follows: "The strangest characteristic of unconscious (repressed) processes, to which no investigator can become
   accustomed without the exercise of great self-discipline, is due to their entire disregard
   of reality-testing; they equate reality of thought with external actuality, and wishes with
   fulfillment – with the event – just as happens automatically under the dominance of
   the ancient pleasure principle. Hence also the difficulty of distinguishing unconscious
   phantasies from memories which have become unconscious. But one must never allow
   oneself to be misled into applying the standards of reality to repressed psychical structures, and on that account, perhaps, into undervaluing the importance of phantasies in
   the formation of symptoms on the ground that they are not actualities, or into tracing a
   neurotic sense of guilt back to some other source because there is no evidence that any
   actual crime has been committed. One is bound to employ the currency that is in use in
   the country one is exploring – in our case a neurotic currency" (emphasis added).

39 Freud, S., *Totem and Taboo*, op. cit., p. 86.

40 Ibid., p. 90.

41 Ibid., p. 89.

42 Ibid., p. 77.

43 "Neither fear nor demons can be regarded by psychology as 'earliest' things, impervious to any attempt at discussing their antecedents. It would be another matter if demons really existed. But we know that, like gods, they are creations of the human mind: they were made by something and out of something" (Freud, S., *Totem and Taboo*, op. cit., p. 24).

44 Ibid., p. 92.

45 Ibid., pp. 92–93.

46 Ibid., p. 59.

47 Ibid.

48 Ibid., p. 60.

49 Ibid., p. 61.

50 "[I]n the last analysis the 'spirit' [der Geist] of persons or things comes down to their capacity to be remembered and imagined after perception of them has ceased" (*Totem and Taboo*, op. cit., p. 94).

51 Ibid., pp. 95–96.

52 Claude Lévi-Strauss objected vigorously to the "archaic illusion" preponderant in Freud's discussion in Totem and Taboo. He commented on the psychoanalytic hypotheses concerned with the origins of totemism and exogamy in the following works: *Elementary Structures of Kinship* (1949; see particularly the Introduction) and *Totemism* (1963). See also Yvan Simonis, *Claude Lévi-Strauss ou La Passion de l'inceste*, 1968; Roger Bastide, *Sociology and Psychoanalysis*, 1968; Ortigues, M.-C., and Ortigues, E., *L'Œdipe africain*, 2005; Edmond Ortigues, "Les quiproquos du désir", in Problèmes de psychanalyse, 1973; Sami Ali, M., *De la projection*, 1970.

53 Freud, S., *Totem and Taboo*, op. cit., p. 103, Note.

54 Ibid., p. 104.

55 Ibid., p. 105.

56 Ibid.

57 In *An Autobiographical Study*, written in 1925, Freud explains the reasoning underlying Totem and Taboo. He says that he was looking for the "central core" of totemism, consisting of the killing of the father; the reaction of the son to this murder leads to the establishment of the rules of totemism. In this text, written just before the publication of the third edition of the book, he does not claim, as he had perhaps believed when he first fell upon these ideas, that he has provided a "hypothesis" serving as an explanation, but only a "vision" of a sequence of components: that is, the vision of a logically constructed account. In the last pages of *Moses and Monotheism*, he reiterates his belief that he has shown an illuminating sequence of events.

58 Freud, S., *Totem and Taboo*, op. cit., pp. 126–127.

59 Freud, S., *Analysis of a Phobia in a Five-year-old Boy*, S.E. 10, London: Hogarth, 1909. Michel De Wolf presents a detailed discussion of this case in his 1973 doctoral thesis La Castration dans l'oeuvre et l'expérience freudienne, Louvain University, Department of Psychology. Freud referred to this case of phobia several times to illustrate his theory of anxiety repression: see Repression (1915), The Unconscious (1915) and Inhibitions, Symptoms and Anxiety (1926), particularly Chapters 4 and 7.

60 Freud, S., Totem and Taboo, op. cit., p. 129.

61 Ibid.

62 Freud, S., *Analysis of a Phobia in a Five-year-old Boy*, op. cit., p. 52.

63 Freud, S., *Totem and Taboo*, op. cit., p. 130.

64 Ibid., pp. 130–131.

65 Ibid., p. 131.

66 Ibid., p. 132.
67 Ibid., p. 138.
68 Ibid., p. 140.
69 Ibid., p. 141.
70 Ibid., p. 143.
71 Ibid., p. 148.
72 Ibid., pp. 151–152.
73 Ibid., p. 152.
74 The mythological creation of the hero and of the double in literary works was a subject studied by Otto Rank, whose research interests were known to Freud. See Otto Rank, *The Myth of the Birth of the Hero* and *The Double: A Psychoanalytic Study.*
75 Freud, S., *Totem and Taboo*, op. cit.
76 Freud, S., *Notes Upon a Case of Obsessional Neurosis*, op. cit., p. 199.
77 The pertinence of such a "myth" in the Rat Man's neurotic process was described by Jacques Lacan in 1953 in a paper (unpublished) titled "The Neurotic's Individual Myth". Lacan saw in the singularity of this case a universal phenomenon Freud was able to decipher and describe. Lacan writes: "The constellation. . . . in the sense astrologers use it – the original constellation that presided over the birth of the subject, over his destiny, and I would almost say his prehistory, specifically the fundamental family relationships which structured his parents' union, happens to have a very precise relation, perhaps definable by a transformational formula [literally mythical], with what appears to be the most contingent, the most phantasmatical, the most paradoxically morbid in his case, that is, the last state of development of his great obsessive fear, the imaginary scenario he arrives at as a resolution of the anxiety associated with the precipitation of the outbreak" (emphasis added). See Freud's 1909 article "Family Romances".
78 Freud, S., *Notes Upon a Case of Obsessional Neurosis*, op. cit., pp. 198–199.
79 Ibid., p. 209.
80 A few pages devoted to a multitude of associations list the series of symbolic meanings this obsessive representation of rats had acquired. See S.E. II, pp. 210–218.
81 Ibid., p. 216.
82 Freud, A., *The Ego and the Mechanisms of Defence*, London: Routledge, 1992.
83 Freud, S., *From the History of an Infantile Neurosis*, S.E. 17, London: Hogarth, 1918.
84 The fate of this patient, who contributed to the advancement of the theory through the questions he prompted Freud to explore, has been studied in detail. An exhaustive investigation of the case was presented in 1972 by Michel de Wolf in his doctoral thesis "La castration dans l'œuvre et l'expérience freudienne" ("Castration in the Freudian Oeuvre and Practice"), Faculty of Psychology, Catholic University of Louvain. See also the special issue of Revue française de psychanalyse, January 1971: "About the Wolf Man". Freud summarises the originality of this case in Chapter 9 of his study in these terms: "It would seem palpably obvious that the repression and the formation of the neurosis must have originated out of the conflict between masculine and feminine tendencies, that is, out of bisexuality. This view of the situation, however, is incomplete. Of the two conflicting sexual impulses one was ego-syntonic, while the other offended the boy's narcissistic interest; it was on that account that the latter underwent repression. . . . Indeed, conflicts between sexuality and the moral ego trends are far more common than such as take place within the sphere of sexuality; but a moral conflict of this kind is lacking in our present case. To insist that bisexuality is the motive force leading to repression is to take too narrow a view; whereas if we assert the same of the conflict between the ego and the sexual tendencies (that is, the libido) we shall have covered all possible cases" (Ibid., p. 110).
85 Ibid., p. 61.
86 Ibid., pp. 27–28.

87 The reference is to the picture book with wolf stories that frightened him, which his sister made him look at as a way to taunt him – "Little Red Riding Hood", "The Wolf and the Seven Little Goats – and the story told by his grandfather, in which a tailor, startled by a wolf jumping through his window, grabs him by the tail and rips it off.

88 Freud, S., *From the History of an Infantile Neurosis*, op. cit., pp. 46–47.

89 Ibid., pp. 63–64.

90 Ibid., p. 64.

91 Ibid.

92 Ibid.

93 Ibid., p. 65.

94 Ibid., p. 66.

95 Ibid., p. 67.

96 Ibid., p. 88.

97 Among these: Max Scheler (*Phenomenology and Theory of the Feeling of Sympathy and of Love and Hate*), Pierre Kaufmann (*Emotional Experience of Space*), Emmanuel Levinas (*Totality and Infinity*), Maxime Chastaing (*L'Existence d'autrui*).

98 Freud, S., "Our Attitude to Death", in *Why War*, S.E. 22, London: Hogarth, 1918.

99 Ibid., p. 87.

100 "The obsessional neurosis. . . grew up. . . on the basis of a sadistic-anal constitution" (Ibid., p. 72). The relation between anal instinctual organisation and obsessional neurosis had already been pointed out in *Three Essays on the Theory of Sexuality* (1905) and was the subject of a separate study, Character of Anal Erotism (1908). The topic was discussed again in 1913, in *The Disposition to Obsessional Neurosis*, and once more in 1917, in On *Transformations of Instinct as Exemplified in Anal Erotism*, S.E. 17, London: Hogarth.

101 Freud, S., *From the History of an Infantile Neurosis*, op. cit., pp. 75–76.

102 Ibid., p. 77.

103 Ibid., p. 78.

104 Ibid.

105 Ibid., p. 80.

106 Ibid.

107 The translation and comprehension of the Freudian term *Verwerfurg* raises some difficulties. In the text we are examining, it is difficult to know whether Freud intended to present it as a theoretical concept distinct from the concept of repression since it is used at times as a synonym of repression and at other times as different from it. Lacan saw it as designating a specific mechanism capable of producing psychosis and named it foreclosure, to underscore its difference from neurotic repression.

108 Ibid., p. 66.

109 Freud, S., *On an Autobiographical Account of a Case of Paranoia*, S.E. 12, London: Hogarth, 1911, pp. 42–43.

110 Ibid., p. 47.

111 Ibid., p. 48.

112 Ibid., pp. 49–50. In Note 1, p. 50, Freud refers to the function of duplication detected by Jung in *Contributions to Analytical Psychology*. Freud writes: "Jung is probably right when he goes on to say that this decomposition follows the general lines taken by schizophrenia in that it uses a process of analysis in order to produce a watering-down effect, and is thus designed to prevent the occurrence of unduly powerful impressions". Freud referred to duplication again in 1919 in The Uncanny, where he alludes to Otto Rank's research on "the double" in literature.

113 Ibid., p. 50. Certain works available to us today provide facts which shed light on Judge Schreber's real relationship with his father. Maud Mannoni, in *Education Impossible*, Paris: Editions du Seuil, 1973, summarises Dr. Schreber's childrearing

theories and examines recent studies on Judge Schreber, particularly those of W. C. Niederland, Franz Baumeyer, Maurits Katan, Philip Kitay and Morton Schatzman.

114 Ibid., pp. 55–56.

115 Ibid., "On the Mechanisms of Paranoia", p. 59. The proposition to be denied, to be contradicted, is "I (a man) love him". The different modes of contradicting this give rise to the different forms of paranoid delusions, which can be classified into four types of defensive formulations: 1 Persecutory delusion: "I don't love him; I hate him", transformed through projection into "He hates me (or persecutes me)". 2 Erotomanic delusion: "It is not him I love; it's her", transformed through projection into "She loves me". 3 Jealous delusion: "It is not I who love the man – she loves him" (form of jealous delusion in alcoholic man) or in a woman "It is not I who love women – he loves them". 4 Delusion of grandeur: "I don't love at all – I love no one", turning the libido back to oneself: "I love myself". Freud extended his analysis of the relations between these various defence mechanisms in *Some Neurotic Mechanisms in Jealousy, Paranoia and Homosexuality*, S.E. 18, London: Hogarth, pp. 221–224.

116 Ibid., p. 71.

117 Ibid., p. 72.

118 Jones, E., *The Life and Work of Sigmund Freud*, Vol. 2, op. cit.

119 Abraham, K., "Notes on the Psychoanalytic Investigation and Treatment of Manic-Depressive Insanity and Allied Conditions", Lecture presented at the Third International Psychoanalytic Congress, September 21, 1911; published in *Selected Papers of Karl Abraham*, M.D., London: Routledge, 1989, p. 137.

120 Abraham, K., "Manic-Depressive States and the Pre-Genital Levels of the Libido", in Selected Papers of Karl Abraham, M.D., op. cit., p. 418. The path set by Abraham was pursued and developed in an original way by Melanie Klein, *The Writings of Melanie Klein*, Vol. I, Glencoe, IL: The Free Press, 1975; "A Contribution to the Psychogenesis of Manic-Depressive States" (1935); and "Mourning and Its Relation to Manic-Depressive States" (1940).

121 Freud, S., *Metapsychological Supplement to the Theory of Dreams*, S.E. 14, London: Hogarth, 1916.

122 Freud, S., *Mourning and Melancholia*, op. cit., p. 243. Emphasis added.
    Mourning is regularly the reaction to the loss of a loved person, or to the loss of some abstraction which is taking the place of one, such as *one's country, liberty, an ideal, and so on. In some people the same influences produce melancholia* instead of mourning *and we consequently suspect them of a pathological disposition.*

123 Ibid., pp. 244–245.

124 The enigma of pain, both psychic and physical, now takes its place alongside Freud's ongoing reflection on pleasure. He has always relied on an economic approach to this double enigma. He reformulated the question after 1920 but proposed no definitive answer.

125 Freud, S., *Mourning and Melancholia*, op. cit., p. 245.

126 Ibid., p. 246.

127 *Anklage* is a German legal term meaning indictment or accusation brought against someone.

128 Freud, S., *Mourning and Melancholia*, op. cit., p. 248.

129 Ibid., pp. 248–249; emphasis added.

130 Ibid., p. 249.

131 Ibid.

132 In the *Internationale Zeitschrift für artzliche Psychoanalyse*, II, 1914, Freud refers to Landauer's clinical contribution in a footnote.

133 "Elsewhere" refers to *Three Essays on the Theory of Sexuality* (II, Chapter 6, added in 1915). We have commented earlier on this term (narcissistic identification), which

will often recur in subsequent definitions of identification, particularly in *Group Psychology and the Analysis of the Ego* (1920) and in The Ego and the Id (1923).

134 See Karl Abraham, *Selected Papers of Karl Abraham*, M.D., Jones, E. (Ed.), London: Hogarth, 1942, p. 274. Abraham says: "Among the most important and striking manifestations of depressive mental disturbances are found two symptoms which have an immediate relation to the taking of food. These are the refusal to take food and the fear of dying of starvation".

135 *Mourning and Melancholia*, op. cit., p. 250; emphasis added. Freud returns to this comparison between hysterical and narcissistic (melancholic) identification in a text written during the same period, Lecture XXVI of the *Introductory Lectures on Psycho-Analysis: The Libido Theory and Narcissism*, S.E. 16: 412. Comparing hysteria (in transference neuroses) to melancholia (in narcissistic neuroses) would make possible, in subsequent theoretical texts, a very clear explanation of the identification concept.

136 Laplanche, J., and Pontalis, J.-B., "Fantasy and the Origins of Sexuality", International Journal of Psychoanalysis, 49 (1968), pp. 1–18.

137 It would be more accurate to say "depressive position", as Melanie Klein herself explains: "In my former work I have described the psychotic anxieties and mechanisms of the child in terms of phases of development. The genetic connection between them, it is true, is given full justice by this description, and so is the fluctuation which goes on between them under the pressure of anxiety until more stability is reached; but since in normal development the psychotic anxieties and mechanisms never solely predominate (a fact which, of course, I have emphasized) the term psychotic phases is not really satisfactory. I am now using the term 'position' in relation to the child's early developmental psychotic anxieties and defences. It seems to me easier to associate with this term, than with the words 'mechanisms' or 'phases', the differences between the developmental psychotic anxieties of the child and the psychoses of the adult: e.g. the quick change-over that occurs from a persecution-anxiety or depressed feeling to a normal attitude – a change-over that is so characteristic for the child" (1935). The International Journal of Psychoanalysis, "A Contribution to the Psychogenesis of Manic-Depressive States", p. 159.

138 *Mourning and Melancholia*, op. cit., p. 251. This intermediary form of mourning was the subject of an interesting study in a clinical setting: "Deuil pathologique", in La Psychanalyse, No. 2, Presses Universitaires de France, 1956, pp. 45–74.

139 Freud, S., *The Disposition to Obsessional Neurosis*, S.E. 12; *Character and Anal Erotism*, S.E. 9; *Notes Upon a Case of Obsessional Neurosis*, S.E. 10. See our discussion on the Rat Man, infra Chapter 2.

140 Freud, S., *Mourning and Melancholia*, op. cit., pp. 251–252.

141 Ibid., p. 252. In *Instincts and Their Vicissitudes*, this original hostility of the ego against objects in the external world is the source of hate while partial sexual impulses are the source of love. See the *Metapsychology*. Suicide was the topic of a discussion of the Vienna Psychoanalytic Society in 1910 (April 20 and April 27). Freud delivered a concluding address which outlined the premises for *Mourning and Melancholia*. "On Suicide" in The International Journal of Psychoanalysis, no. 49, pp. 741–742. See also Jones, E., *Life and Work of Sigmund Freud*, Vol. 2, 1956, London: Hogarth.

142 We read, in *On Narcissism: An Introduction*, "This leads us to look upon the narcissism which arises through the drawing in of object-cathexes as a secondary one, superimposed upon a primary narcissism that is obscured by a number of different influences. . . . Thus we form the idea of there being an original libidinal cathexis of the ego, from which some is later given off to objects, but which fundamentally persists and is related to the object-cathexes much as the body of an amoeba is related

to the pseudopodia which it puts out" (p. 75). In *Instincts and Their Vicissitudes*, Freud writes, "The three polarities of the mind are connected with one another in various highly significant ways. There is a primal psychical situation in which two of them coincide. Originally, at the very beginning of mental life, the ego is cathected with instincts and is to some extent capable of satisfying them on itself. We call this condition 'narcissism' and this way of obtaining satisfaction 'auto-erotic'. . . . If for the moment we define loving as the relation of the ego to its sources of pleasure, the situation in which the ego loves itself only and is indifferent to the external world illustrates the first of the opposites which we found to 'loving'" (S.E. 14: 132–133). Note 2, p. 132, adds: "Some of the sexual instincts are, as we know, capable of this auto-erotic satisfaction, and so are adapted to being the vehicle for the development under the dominance of the pleasure principle. . . . Those sexual instincts, which are never capable of auto-erotic satisfaction, naturally disturb this state. . . and so pave the way for an advance from it. Indeed, the primal narcissistic state would not be able to follow the development. . . if it were not for the fact that every individual passes through a period during which he is helpless and has to be looked after and during which his pressing needs are satisfied by an external agency and are thus prevented from becoming greater".

143 Laplanche, J., "Les normes morales et sociales", Bulletin de Psychologies, (1973), p. 884.

144 Freud considers the main agencies governing the ego to be conscience, censorship of consciousness and reality testing. He would come back to this question in 1933, in *New Introductory Lectures*.

145 Laplanche, J., art. cit., 1973, p. 884.

146 The topic of cannibalism and its relation to mourning and melancholia has been described very artfully in a series of ethnological and clinical articles in No. 6 of *Nouvelle Revue de Psychanalyse: Destins du cannibalisme*, Paris: Gallimard, fall 1972. Of particular interest to us are the articles by André Green, Nicolas Abraham and Maria Torok and Pierre Fedida.

147 It is the story of an Austrian painter, Christophe Haitzmann, miraculously delivered from a pact with the devil. The manuscript originating from his pilgrimage to Mariazell was brought to Freud's attention by one of his friends, the director of the former "royal and imperial family Fidei commis Library" in Vienna. We will describe this case of demonic possession in Chapter 3 of the present work, when discussing the general question of the resolution of the Oedipus complex and its representations.

148 Stärcke, A., quoted by Freud in "Intern", *Zeitschrift für Psychoanalyse*, III (1919). A more extensive discussion of this concept of an oral prototype of castration can be found in the work of Michel De Wolf, op. cit., pp. 319–330.

149 Abraham, K., Selected Papers of Karl Abraham M.D., Bryan, D., and Strachey, A. (Trans.), London: Hogarth, 1965, pp. 463–464.

150 Self-preservation does not fully convey the connotations of the German term *"Selbsterhaltung"*, containing the radical "halt", indicating an act of holding.

151 The development of the concept of object in psychoanalysis raises numerous difficulties. Throughout our discussion, it is clear that this concept is intimately linked with the equally problematic concept of "Ego". Moreover, it must be noted that Freud does not speak of "subject" in the modern philosophical sense of subjectivity, but rather the as-yet poorly defined object of an amalgamation of drives (poorly delimited and poorly differentiated) which constituted the ego in his new theory of the libido. We might add that all the concepts we have examined here when commenting on the texts written between 1912 and 1917 related to narcissism are not foreign to Lacan's research on the status to be attributed to "object (little) a".

152 Freud, S., *On Narcissism: An Introduction*, op. cit.

153 Our term "delusions of being observed" corresponds to the German *Beachtungswahn* or *Beobachtungswahn*.
154 This is the general nature of psychoanalytic enquiry: real knowledge of "normal" psychology can only be gained by first examining the pathological phenomena that are exaggerated versions, distortions or amplifications of it. Freud writes: "Just as transference neuroses have enabled us to trace the libidinal instinctual impulses, so dementia praecox and paranoia will give us an insight into the psychology of the ego. Once more, in order to arrive at an understanding of what seems so simple in normal phenomena, we shall have to turn to the field of pathology with its distortions and exaggerations" (*On Narcissism*, p. 82). And again: "we are familiar with the notion that pathology, by making things larger and coarser, can draw our attention to normal conditions which would otherwise have escaped us. Where it points to a breach or a rent, there may normally be an articulation present. If we throw a crystal to the floor, it breaks, but not into haphazard pieces. It comes apart along its lines of cleavage into fragments whose boundaries, though they were invisible, were predetermined by the crystal's structure" (*New Introductory Lecture*, S.E. 22: 58–59). Psychotic dissociations of the ego are often accompanied by a distressing experience of doubling, the hallucination of a double. Paranoia, whose inherent process destroys identifications and restores former love objects (see our earlier analysis of *Schreber*) provides a model for understanding these doubling phenomena. Paranoia projection expels the objects that were once incorporated, in an attempt to resolve the ambivalent relation with the object. The conception of the double (or of several doubles) as an "accomplishment" of these conflicting psychic currents constitutes a persistent theme in literature (novels, stories, myths). The power of these fictional works, which often arouse an uncanny feeling and which doubtless constitute the paradigm of all literary fiction, clearly lies in the fact that they play upon a terrifying possibility for the ego, a possibility enacted by the psychotic. The theme of the double deserves a separate study, to examine its connection with the question of instinctual narcissism. See Freud, S., *The Uncanny*, S.E. 17, London: Hogarth, 1919; Otto Rank, *The Double: A Psychoanalytic Study*, Chapel Hill, NC: University of North Carolina Press, 2011; Todorov, T., *The Fantastic: A Structural Approach to a Literary Genre*, Ithaca, NY: Cornell University Press, 1975. For a systematic study of this theme in literature, see Rogers, R., *A Psychoanalytical Study of the Double in Literature*, Detroit, MI: Wayne State University Press, 1970.
155 Freud, S., *Repression*, S.E. 14, London: Hogarth, 1915, p. 147.
156 Freud, S., *Instincts and Their Vicissitudes*, S.E. 14, London: Hogarth, 1915, p. 128.
157 Ibid., p. 129.
158 A discussion of the Freudian concept of masochistic perversion can be found in Gilles Deleuze's literary-philosophical work *Masochism: Coldness and Cruelty*, New York: Zone Books, 1991. Jean Laplanche rightly sets limits to Deleuze's criticism, which concerns the clinical description (entomological!), which never really interested Freud, pointing out that Freud's intent was to highlight a phantasmatic structure in which libidinal "positions" are interchangeable. See also *The Seminar of Jacques Lacan: Four Fundamental Concepts of Psychoanalysis*, Book XI, New York: W.W. Norton, 1998.
159 Freud, S., *On Narcissism: An Introduction*, op. cit., pp. 76–77.
160 Freud, S., *Instincts and Their Vicissitudes*, op. cit., p. 123.
161 Freud, S., *Repression*, op. cit.; *The Unconscious*, op. cit. Starting in his earliest writings, Freud identified representation and affect as instinctual elements. André Green made an in-depth study of this question in *The Fabric of Affect in Psychoanalytic Discourse*, London: Routledge, 1999. Michel Tort's 1966 article "Le concept Freudien de 'Représentant'" ("The Freudian Concept of 'Representative'"), focusing on

the analysis of Freud's term *Vorstellungs-Reprasentanz* (ideational representative), provided the basis for a theoretical discussion of drives from a Lacanian perspective.

162 "Repression. . . proceeds from the ego; we might say with greater precision that it proceeds from the self-respect of the ego. . . . For the ego the formation of an ideal would be the conditioning factor of repression" (*On Narcissism: An Introduction*, op. cit., pp. 93–94).

III

The Oedipus complex and the "institutions" of the ego

The introduction of the death drive, observed in repetition compulsion, is the start of the third period of the elaboration of Freudian theory. It results in the third reformulation of drive theory and of the metapsychology as a whole.

Ernest Jones, the loyal biographer, describes the circumstances surrounding this profound transformation in Freud's thinking and its surprising fecundity.[1] The major question which overturns the whole theoretical edifice, previously centred on narcissism, is the enigma of masochism. Masochism was first encountered in its clinical manifestation as perversion and infantile phantasm in the 1919 essay *A Child Is Being Beaten*,[2] which pursues the question raised in *Instincts and Their Vicissitudes*, in *Mourning and Melancholia* and soon afterwards again in the first pages of *Origin of Sexual Perversions*.[3] Once again, it was clinical experience that created the urgent need to go beyond the solidly established concepts associated with the pleasure principle. Indeed, *Beyond the Pleasure Principle* introduces a radical question concerning the enigma of the strange longing for death present in all living beings, which Freud never stopped investigating.[4]

Our task now is to show how shifting the theoretical focus brings into question the metapsychological foundations of the identification process. The involvement of this process in masochistic enjoyment, previously presented as a suggestion, will lead us to the most decisive related developments of the concept. The third topography starts as early as 1920, with the insertion of the question of identification in the general topic of the death instinct. The question of the status and function of the ideal, correlated with that of the genesis of the structure of the ego, will be examined from this new perspective.

Identification and repetition compulsion

Analysis of dreams and symptoms has made us aware of the primordial rule of the pleasure principle. But clinical experience requires the interpretation of facts to which the usual metapsychological model does not apply: dreams of patients with traumatic neuroses and certain children's games. These dreams and games show a sort of attachment to the traumatic event. Patients with traumatic neurosis can be compared to hysterics, about whom Freud said, in *Studies on Hysteria*, "Hysterics suffer for the most part from reminiscence".[5] But just as pathogenic reminiscences remain unconscious in hysteria, patients with traumatic neuroses are not perturbed in their waking life by the memory of the disaster. Or, more accurately, they try not to think about it. It is the dream which repeatedly takes them back to the traumatic situation which always has the same terrifying effect. In this case, the function of the dream, to be the guardian of sleep and provide wish fulfilment, fails. As a result, the choice is between recognising that the dream function, as presented in dream theory, has undergone important changes or admitting that, concurrent with the wish-fulfilment tendency, there are very enigmatic masochistic tendencies of the ego.[6] Freud does not analyse this question directly, taking instead an indirect approach:

> At this point I propose to leave the dark and dismal subject of the traumatic neurosis and pass on to examine the method of working employed by the mental apparatus in one of its earliest normal activities – I mean in children's play.[7]

Memory and mastery: the double game of Fort-Da

The game of the child with the bobbin has become famous in analytic circles and beyond. Lacan[8] was the one who connected its role as a paradigm and its propaedeutic function to the understanding of the symbolisation process. Philosophers like Alphonse De Waelhens have described the *Fort-Da* game as the primordial myth of an anthropology.[9] The author points out the overdetermination of the *Fort-Da* game, which signals for the child (and for human beings in general): 1) the renunciation of the immediate, 2) access to negativity and 3) the acquisition and establishment of a certain mastery over the real. Therefore, De Waelhens connects the emergence of subjectivity with accession to language and hence to "reality"; this accessing by the subject of the symbolic realm is identical to what Freud calls "original repression" (*Urverdrängung*) – whose failure characterises the psychotic structure.

What we would like is to propose an interpretation which does not see this game as the illustration of a doctrine but views it as part of the reasoning which includes the observation of the game.

Shortly after Freud abandoned his enquiry into traumatic neurosis and the enigma of masochistic tendencies, he encountered, through analysis of the original mode of psychic work reflected in children's play, the enigma of repetition. In fact, there are clear similarities with the mysterious dreams of these neurotics, discussed earlier. We have seen that dreams and play are related psychic activities since their aim is to enact, through transposition, a wish fulfilment phantasy[10] – an instinctual act. The enigmatic failure of the pleasure principle which governs wish fulfilment forces us to examine desire itself more closely and, at a more basic level, the status of what has been called an impulse.

Children's games had been studied by many psychologists;[11] Freud took a different perspective by focusing on what he called the "economic" standpoint: that is, taking into consideration the benefits of pleasure. What, then, can be said about the game of this 18-month-old child?

A closer look reveals that the game has variations; Freud's careful observation shows its increasing complexity. Based on his description of the many occasions of play he observed, we can identify three structurally distinct moments of the game. In Freud's words:

1   This good little boy. . . had an occasional disturbing habit of taking any small objects he could get hold of and throwing them away from him into a corner, under the bed and so on, so that hunting for his toys and picking them up was often quite a business. As he did this he gave vent to a loud, long-drawn-out "o-o-o-o", accompanied by an expression of interest and satisfaction. His mother and the writer of the present account agreed in thinking that this was not a mere interjection but represented the German word "*fort*" [gone]. I eventually realized that it was a game and that the only use he made of any of his toys was to play "gone" with them.

2   One day I made an observation which confirmed my view. The child had a wooden reel with a piece of string tied round it. It never occurred to him to pull it along the floor behind him, for instance, and play at its being a carriage. What he did was to hold the reel by the string and very skillfully throw it over the edge of his curtained cot, so that it disappeared into it, at the same time uttering his expression "o-o-o-o". He then pulled the reel out of the cot again by the string and hailed its reappearance with a joyful "*da*" [there]. This then, was the complete game – disappearance and return. As a rule one only witnessed its first act, which was repeated untiringly as a game in itself, though there is no doubt that the greater pleasure was attached to the second act.

A footnote reveals a third modality of play:

3   A further observation subsequently confirmed this interpretation fully. One day the child's mother had been away for several hours and on her return was met with the words "Baby o-o-o-o!" which was at first incomprehensible. It soon turned out, however that during this long period of solitude the child had found a method of making himself disappear. He had discovered his reflection in a full-length mirror which did not quite reach to the ground, so that by crouching down he could make his mirror-image "gone".[12]

The bobbin episode, the only one which depicts what Freud calls the complete game, is preceded and followed by play episodes consisting of the first act only: that is, of the repetition of a *fort-sein* (being gone), accompanied by the vocalisation "o-o-o-o".

Freud's interpretation is not simple. He analyses, by turns, the complete game and then the game divided into two distinct acts. He writes:

The interpretation of the game then became obvious. It was related to the child's great cultural achievement – the instinctual renunciation (that is, renunciation of instinctual satisfaction) which he had made in allowing his mother to go away without protesting. He compensated himself for this, as it were, by himself staging the disappearance and return of the objects within his reach. . . . The child cannot possibly have felt his mother's departure as something agreeable or even indifferent. How then does the repetition of this distressing experience as a game fit in with the pleasure principle? It may perhaps be said in reply that her departure had to be enacted as necessary preliminary to her joyful return, and that it was in the latter that lay the true purpose of the game. But against this must be counted the observed fact that the first act, that of departure, was staged as a game in itself and far more frequently than the episode in its entirety, with its pleasurable ending.

No certain decision can be reached from the analysis of a single case like this. On an unprejudiced view one gets an impression that the child turned his experience into a game from another motive. At the outset he was in a *passive* situation – he was overpowered by the experience; but, by repeating it. . . he took on an *active* part.

These efforts might be put down to an instinct for mastery that was act-ing independently of whether the memory was in itself pleasurable or not. But still another interpretation may be attempted. Throwing away the object so that it was 'gone' might satisfy an impulse of the child's which was sup-pressed in his actual life, to revenge himself on his mother for going away from him. In that case it would have a defiant meaning: "All right, then, go away! I don't need you. I'm sending you away myself.[13]

We know of other children who like to express similar hostile impulses by throwing away objects instead of persons.[14] We are therefore left in doubt as to whether the impulse to work over in the mind some overpowering experi-ence so as to make oneself master of it can find expression as a primary event, and independently of the pleasure principle. For, in the case we have been discussing, the child may, after all, only have been able to repeat his unpleas-ant experience in play because the repetition carried along with it a yield of pleasure of another sort but nonetheless a direct one.[15]

Freud draws no definite conclusion. Is the *fort-sein* game motivated by a search for pleasure or not? Can the repetition of a painful event through a new psychic scenario – that is, a structured enactment – be explained by the pleasure principle, or must it spring from a different source?

We are speaking of a series of enactments. Indeed, the playful transposition of a notable event displays perceptible variations. We have specified them in our description of Freud's observation. The first version of the child's enactment con-sists of throwing away from him all the objects within reach and accompanying this riotous action by a loud exclamation whose meaning only comes to light later. A second enactment, which provides the other half of the theme (and thus the meaning) and the opposing gestures (throwing away and bringing back the bob-bin), enables us to decipher the enigma of the first game.

This second enactment, which Freud calls the "complete game", is the one most often interpreted, due to its completeness and apparent conclusiveness.[16] But in his added footnote, Freud observes a third playful enactment of the painful event – the most complex in our opinion – the one which retroactively confers meaning to the entire game.

The third enactment involves the acting out of an identification. Indeed, the child has found a way to make himself disappear – more precisely and more accurately speaking, he has found a way to play at *fort-sein* (being gone) by using his image in the mirror. Thus, it would appear that Lacan's mirror stage, in which the child greets his image with joyful gestures and sounds, also comprises a complementary, "negative" double, just as essential for the advent of the "I".[17] The "Here I am!" of the mirror stage is accompanied by an "I'm gone". In Heideggerian terms, the *"Da-sein"* of the specular phase is accompanied by the *"Fort-sein"* of the death game.

Thus, an identificatory enactment highlights an instinctual construction between life and death. But the identification played out here raises questions about our previous interpretation. Based on the hypothesis presented in this passage of *Beyond the Pleasure Principle* in which the game not only fulfills a wish but also works over in the mind a painful impression close to death (the absence of the mother as such), the identification enacted in the game can no longer be said to aim merely at wish fulfilment. In fact, it seems to be the very passage, the necessary means, of reconciling the death instinct and the life instinct.

The mirror image which disappears from the child's sight replaces "indifferent" objects, which carry the primal projection of rage and vengeance. The first game was a total enigma, painful to watch because of its suggestion of imminent death, its wild compulsivity and its repeated irresolution. The introduction of the bobbin is a relief: finally, there is mastery and, therefore, meaning; finally, we are in the joyful sphere of the pleasure principle. The third game comprises an aspect similar to one of the first game: the exclamation "o-o-o-o" addressed to the returning mother, now endowed with a "subject": "Baby o-o-o-o". Indeed, the child does not cry out, "Baby d-a-a-a!" But in the bobbin game, there is also a latent aspect at first: the invisible thread linking the child to his double in the mirror. This double prolongs the series of projective doubles (literally) consisting of the objects compulsively ejected from his space and the lost and found bobbin. The bobbin is, in fact, an "intermediary" object – Winnicott speaks of a "transitional" object[18] – symbol of the loved and hated mother and, as a symbol, the place of emerging ability to be like her, sometimes near, sometimes far, sometimes living and sometimes dead. The director of the bobbin game is certainly not the "ego" of the child: admirable model of mastery, indeed, of the Logos itself! The director, the "subject" of the entire enactment, is a strange intrication taking place between repetition compulsion, the draw of the death instinct and the psychic inscription of an experience of death, an inscription acting as a link and representation of the drive.[19]

Love and identification: the function of the ideal

At this stage of our explorations, we come to a text we consider symptomatic: *Group Psychology and the Analysis of the Ego*,[20] published in 1921.

We see it as symptomatic because, although it follows *Beyond the Pleasure Principle*, which marked a break with the metapsychological system, it pursues the train of thought initiated in 1913, making no attempt to re-establish continuity yet unimpeded by the theoretical reorientation prompted by the introduction of the death instinct. Thus, this text is located between two perspectives which remain independent: the first, that of Freud II, centred on narcissism and the conflictual relations between ego-libido and object-libido and on the splitting of the ego into bodily ego and ideal ego, and the second, still uncertain and formulated in the "speculative" language of Freud III, whom we have seen emerge for the first time.

But this text is symptomatic for another reason as well. This is the first time Freud discusses directly and specifically the question of identification, with the intention of locating it in the theory of the libido and defining its clinical and theoretical role. The seventh chapter of his essay, titled "Identification", is an attempt at a summary or synthesis of the text. But it is a failed, incomplete synthesis, which leaves Freud dissatisfied. He has not been able to develop a "metapsychology" of identification, to integrate it into the conceptual field created by *Beyond the Pleasure Principle*. A kind of theoretical latency period would prove necessary before Freud would take the risk of associating the two questions, to create what we know as the "second structural model", presented in the seminal work *The Ego and the Id* in 1923. From that point on, it became possible to link the question of the life-and-death impulses with that of the concept and structure of the ego.

Therefore, *Group Psychology and Analysis of the Ego* might be seen as a sort of supplement to *On Narcissism: An Introduction*.[21] The same questions are discussed and developed in a similar manner. They relate essentially to love and to its "perverse" instinctual elements, to the normal and pathological manifestations of narcissism and to the origin and function of the ideal.[22]

The singular and the plural

Freud states his thesis strongly from the start of his essay. Our intention is not to summarise the essay but to examine how he develops the concept of identification. A short passage from the introduction is sufficient to provide a clear understanding of the objectives of "social psychoanalysis":[23]

> The contrast between individual psychology and social or group psychology, which at a first glance may seem to be full of significance, loses a great deal of its sharpness when it is examined more closely. It is true that individual psychology is concerned with the individual man and explores the paths by which he seeks to find satisfaction for his instinctual impulses; but only rarely

and under certain exceptional conditions is individual psychology in a position to disregard the relations of this individual to others. In the individual's mental life someone else is invariably involved, as a model, as an object, as a helper, as an opponent; and so from the very first individual psychology, in this extended but entirely justifiable sense of the words, is at the same time social psychology as well. . . . Now in speaking of social or group psychology it has become usual to leave these relations on one side and to isolate as the subject of enquiry the influencing of an individual by a large number of people simultaneously. . . .

Group psychology is therefore concerned with the individual man as a member of a race, of a nation, of a caste, of a profession, of an institution, or as a component part of a crowd of people who have been organized into a group at some particular time for some definite purpose. . . . Our expectation is therefore directed towards two. . . possibilities: that the social instinct may not be a primitive one and insusceptible of dissection, and that is may be possible to discover the beginnings of its development in a narrow circle, such as that of the family.[24]

The developments predicted by this introduction draw our attention to a fundamental characteristic of Freud's thinking. Where a superficial view of things sees separation, closed off areas and breaks, psychoanalysis recognises "natural continuity" that intellectual and affective resistances conceal, such as between normal and pathological, between individual and social, between sexual activity and love.

Therefore, in Freud's view, what happens initially in the narrow circle of the family is of the same nature as what happens in a group. It is not necessary to invoke "special instincts", concepts invented specially for this purpose, such as "herd instinct",[25] group mind, et cetera.

It bears repeating that the object of psychoanalysis is not an individual but the totality of instinctual relations connecting him to other individuals – this predominance of relationships, of the network, outweighing the concept of the individual to such an extent as to render it insignificant. From this point of view, Freud's essay is a rigorous response to Alfred Adler's doctrine, not unintentionally called "individual psychology".[26] This shift in perspective, this change of emphasis, had significant consequences. There can be no doubt that, after Freud, the insistence on what phenomenology called intersubjectivity and Lacan called the symbolic makes it clear that psychoanalysis broke with this "psychology". In this context, "psychology" divides, separates, classifies – whether it calls itself individual or social.

The subject of Freud's study becomes apparent through reference to a series of figures representing the social psychology of the times (Le Bon, Tarde, MacDougall, Trotter). In their work, Freud identifies an enigmatic central concept for which each author contributes a new name but not an explanation. These names include "suggestibility" or "suggestion", "mental contagion", "racial unconscious", "imitation" and "herd instinct". Freud replaced these concepts designating a partial

reality with that of a libidinal differentiation process. The surprising metamorphosis of an individual when he is in a group or a crowd is essentially a "love
relationship" phenomenon – although, on the surface, it appears quite different.
Social psychologists have described perfectly this individual transformation and
the specific characteristics of group behaviour.[27] But they overlooked the close
libidinal ties between individual and collective functioning.[28] Freud concludes his
review of psychologies by emphasising this kinship:

> We will try our fortune, then, with the supposition that love relationships (or,
> to use a more neutral expression, emotionalities) also constitute the essence
> of group mind. Let us remember that the authorities make no mention of any
> such relations. What would correspond to them is evidently concealed behind
> the shelter, the screen, of suggestion. Our hypothesis finds support in the first
> instance from two passing thoughts. First, that a group is clearly held together
> by a power of some kind: and to what power could this feat be better ascribed
> than to Eros, which holds together everything in the world? Secondly, if an
> individual gives up this distinctiveness in a group and lets its other mem-
> bers influence him by suggestion, it gives one the impression that he does
> it because he feels the need of being in harmony with them rather than in
> opposition to them – so that perhaps after all he does it for love of them.[29]

Thus, the analytic perspective is still that which we saw in *On Narcissism: An
Introduction*; only the mention of Eros, "which holds together everything in the
world", refers to the second theory of drives. The task becomes to describe libidinal economy as it takes place in the individual who constitutes its sphere of action.

Freud's description of this economy takes a different road than those of the
authorities quoted in his essay. He begins by discussing groups, with their well-
defined characteristics: permanence, conventional structure, organisation. These
groups are protected against the danger of dissolution and provide the advantage
of bringing to light processes which remain hidden in the groups described by
Gustave Le Bon (on whom Prussian militarism in the First World War left a strong
impression); these groups are the Catholic Church and the army.

These two conventional groups clearly have a libidinal structure: explicit in
the case of the Church, founded on a doctrine of love with Christ as its source;
implicit in the case of the army, made up of a series of groups united by "libidinal" ties, from the commander in chief to the non-commissioned officer. Freud's
essential idea is that in the Church, like in the army, despite their differences,
there exists the same illusion: that of the presence, visible or invisible, of a leader
who loves all the individuals in the group with an equal love. Freud adds: "Everything depends upon this illusion".[30] But he does not hesitate to call this illusion
"untrue" and a "phantasy", albeit necessary for the cohesion and organisation of
the group.

In these two organised groups, each member has libidinal ties to the leader on
the one hand and to all the other members on the other.

The well-known phenomenon of panic, in which each individual becomes concerned only with himself, experiencing paralysing fear so great that it bears no relation to the real danger, testifies to the fact that the emotional ties which have hitherto made the danger seem smaller have ceased to exist. This panic fear presupposes a relaxation in the libidinal structure of the group, which has been weakened; it can only occur in the wake of such libidinal cathexes.[31]

Now, let us look more closely at the nature of the double emotional connection which provides a group with cohesion, in order to prove the libidinal nature of these connections. The key to solving this problem can be found in a parable inspired by Schopenhauer. Freud presents this famous simile of the porcupines in abbreviated form:

> A company of porcupines crowded themselves very close together one cold winter's day so as to profit by one another's warmth and so save themselves from being frozen to death. But soon they felt one another's quills, which induced them to separate again. And now, when the need for warmth brought them nearer together again, the second evil arose once more. So that they were driven backwards and forwards from one trouble to the other, until they had discovered a mean distance at which they could most tolerably exist.[32]

Psychoanalysis sheds a mercilessly clear light on this parable:

> [E]very intimate emotional relation between two people which lasts for some time – marriage, friendship, the relation between parents and children – contains a sediment of feelings of aversion and hostility, which only escapes perception as a result of repression. . . . When this hostility is directed against people who are otherwise loved we describe it as ambivalence of feeling; and we explain the fact, in what is probably too rational a manner, by means of numerous occasions for conflicts of interest which arise precisely in such intimate relations. In the undisguised antipathies and aversions which people feel towards strangers with whom they have to do we may recognize the expression of self-love – of narcissism. This self-love works for the preservation of the individual, and behaves as though the occurrence of any divergence from his own particular lines of development involved a criticism of them and a demand for their alteration.[33]

Butin a group, all this intolerance, all this sensitivity to the details of individual differences disappears in a more or less lasting fashion. Such a restriction of narcissistic demands can only be produced by one factor – the same factor which motivates early development of the child, bringing him out of original narcissism – specifically, libidinal attachment to another person. "Love for oneself knows only one barrier – love for others, love for objects",[34] from which, in truth, it benefits. This had already been the central hypothesis of *On Narcissism: An Introduction*.

Psychoanalysis recognises in the group formation process the process of libido development. The libido finds support in the satisfaction of the major vital needs and chooses as its objects the people who contribute to this satisfaction (anaclitic attachment type). Similarly, the development of the human community relies mainly on love as a civilising factor, which effects a change from egoism to altruism. But while, in the case of the child, sexual instincts invest their objects while pursuing directly sexual aims, in groups, although ties are of a libidinal nature and sexual drives retain all their energy, they are diverted from their original aims.

It must be noted, however, that even the sexual relationships existing between a man and a woman present a diversion of the sex drive from its sexual aim. This degree of being in love, described elsewhere,[35] clearly produces a certain limitation of narcissism and an encroachment upon the ego. These phenomena of being in love proved to the very valuable to Freud's subsequent enquiry: they provided the key to certain processes at work in groups, where they are more difficult to observe. In this context, it is important to know whether sexual investment in the object is the only type of emotional tie with another person or whether other mechanisms of the same sort must be taken into account. Indeed, such similar mechanisms have often constituted objects of study for psychoanalysis.

> As a matter of fact we learn from psycho-analysis that there do exist other mechanisms for emotional ties, the so-called *identifications*, insufficiently – known processes and hard to describe, the investigation of which will for some time keep us way from the subject of group psychology.[36]

We now come to the heart of our discussion, Chapter VII of *Group Psychology and the Analysis of the Ego*, considered by many hasty commentators to be the text par excellence outlining the Freudian theory of identification. In our opinion, this theory is present throughout Freud's work, and the rapid synthesis given here is more akin to a summary of the ideas presented at different stages of his development than to a definitive theory.

Identifications

The structure of this chapter seems strange, at least to someone who has followed the detours, hesitations and apparent contradictions in the elaboration of the concept of identification. Given the exhaustive nature of the development, Freud might have been expected to gather together in a coherent cluster fragments of the theory dispersed throughout the chronology of his experiences with patients. But, instead of doing that, he presents, in random order, facts about identification taken from clinical material. Moreover, surprisingly, he begins this inventory, which remains incomplete, by describing a type of identification he never discussed previously, although our reading of his texts detected it on numerous occasions: the earliest identification of the child (the little boy) with his father, which precedes the Oedipal conflict. This primary identification is described in this summary as the only one not associated with any pathology.

This novelty is very enlightening; the apparent disorder of Freud's presentation elucidates our discussion. Let us examine Freud's presentation, pointing out the crucial connections in his development, in which we can distinguish five interpsychic configurations:

I Identification in the "early history of the Oedipus complex"

> Identification is known to psycho-analysis as the earliest expression of an emotional tie with another person. It plays a part in the early history of the Oedipus complex. A little boy will exhibit a special interest in his father; he would like to grow like him and be like him, and to take his place everywhere. We may say simply that he takes his father as his ideal. This behaviour has nothing to do with a passive or feminine attitude towards his father (and towards males in general); it is on the contrary typically masculine. It fits in very well with the Oedipus complex, for which it helps to prepare the way.[37]

The specifically, electively masculine character in this identification distinguishes it at once from identification with the father as seen in the Wolf Man and the Rat Man, which served as the symptomatic manifestation of the repression of passive homosexual tendencies. What is described here is clearly of a different nature than identification with the woman. This non-neurotic identification is a relation of being, not of having. In the cases mentioned here, the homosexual investment of the father takes place in a relation to having (where the father functions as the sexual object of masochistic-anal impulses).

But let us return to Freud's text. What will be the fate of this identification which places the father in the position of an ideal, at the stage of the Oedipus complex, which it helps to prepare?

> At the same time as this identification with his father, or a little later, the boy has begun to develop a true object-cathexis towards his mother according to the [anaclitic] attachment type. He then exhibits, therefore, two psychologically distinct ties: a straightforward sexual object-cathexis towards his mother and identification with his father which takes him as his model. The two subsist side by side for a time without any mutual influence or interference. In consequence of the irresistible advance towards a unification of mental life, they come together at last; and the normal Oedipus complex originates from this confluence.[38]

The two types of emotional ties previously distinct now come together, organise and tend to integrate. This process of integration, which applies to the ego as well as to sexual instincts,[39] brings the child into the Oedipal conflict stage.

The increased genital investment of the mother undermines the tie to the father and reveals the hostility previously hidden but structurally present in the primal urge to replace the father "everywhere". The primary ambivalence of primordial identification to the model is revealed in retrospect through sexual access to the mother. For the boy: "[his] identification with his father then takes on a hostile colouring and becomes identical with the wish to replace his father in regard to his mother as well".[40] The desire to be ideal is the desire to be what the ideal father is for the mother. To be the father means to have the mother.

The origin of the overtly ambivalent Oedipus complex, which expresses both tenderness and a desire to remove the other, is quite obvious: it can be found in the first, oral phase of organisation of the libido, when the loved object was at once assimilated and removed by being devoured. The "ideal" identification to the father is the result of oral investment of the father. This adds to the complexity of the problem. The "devoured" father was only devoured metaphorically. This is not the case for mother's milk, the metonymic support of cannibalistic assimilation. To take the father for one's ideal, originally, means to take him in orally. To "take in" the father (devour him with the gaze, drink in his words, etc.) signifies having him (choosing him as the ambivalent object of oral impulses) and being him (desire to become him, to be him).

This tie to the father as that which the little boy wants to be, as his ideal, can undergo a displacement at the level of "having". This is what happens in cases of "inverted" Oedipus: the father is taken as the object of a feminine attitude, an object from which the directly sexual drives look for satisfaction (by becoming the object of the father's sexual activity). Identification with the father becomes the precursor of an object-relation with him. Let us keep in mind that Freud related this sexual objectivation of the father to the intensity of anal impulses.

At the primary level – and this can only be orally – the father is what one wants to be; secondarily, after an inversion, a reversal of Oedipus, the father is what one wants to have. Freud concludes his reference to this primitive tie to the father with a statement that serves as a springboard for the development of these concepts:

> [The] distinction between an identification with the father and the choice of the father as an object. . . depends upon whether the tie attaches to the subject or to the object of the ego. The former kind of tie is therefore already possible before any sexual object-choice has been made. It is much more difficult to give a clear metapsychological representation of the distinction. We can only see that identification endeavors to mould a person's own ego after the fashion of the one that has been taken as a model.[41]

Thus, at the primary level, the ideal is the "ego ideal". This terminology is new, and we will find it useful later, when this idea will have been more fully developed. Indeed, at this point, Freud's formulation is particularly elliptical, as if he only just glimpsed the function of a primordial tie to the father, which is not an outright "sexual" tie. This suggests the need to re-examine the theory of libidinal developments, which might have been too simple. The oral stage, cannibalistic – which Freud in his *Three Essays* had described as a prototype of sexual attachment and of identification[42] – turns out to be very complex, notwithstanding its archaic nature. In fact, this discussion brings to mind segments of *Totem and Taboo* in which the totemic meal illustrates the archaic devouring of the father. When we discussed this topic, we suggested using the term *totemic identification* to designate the desire articulated in the phantasy leading to this cannibalistic feast. At that stage, we could discern the "ideal formation" function characteristic of this identification serving to resolve guilt and mourning for the sons. But these are still only bits and pieces, and a more detailed explanation of the function and genesis of the ideal remains to the given.

2 Identification in the formation of neurotic symptoms

The second type of identification is based on the hysterical identification model. Here, we go back to the beginnings of identification theory, which combined dream analysis and the analysis of hysterical symptoms. The beautiful butcher's wife and Dora have been the eminent and impassioned figures of these beginnings.

Freud pointed out frequently that identification constitutes the most common mode of hysterical symptom formation. Here, he gives a rapid summary of his previous conclusions. The clinical example is no longer the little boy, but the little girl. She develops the same painful cough as her mother, but in Dora's case, it is also a symptom of her father's. Double identification to sexually distinct people – an overdetermination of the symptom indicating a tangle of contradictory desires.

Identification with the mother, in this case, comes from the Oedipus complex; it signifies the girl's hostile desire to take her mother's place, as well as her object-love towards her father. But this imaginary substitution, expressed in a painful symptom, produces suffering. Thus, in addition to the satisfaction of desires (being the mother, having the father), identification also expresses a counter-desire coming from the ego, which reveals feelings of guilt. Freud summarises the whole process in a condensed formula:

> You wanted to be your mother, and now you are – anyhow so far as your sufferings are concerned.[43]

Identification with the father, through the same symptom – painful cough – is not identification with the Oedipal rival this time but with the person who is loved. Here, identification takes the place of a prohibited sexual investment; it comes about through the transformation of this investment and regression from object-choice to identification. Encountering the obstacle to repression, the libido, subjected to the primary process of the unconscious, modifies the ego to fit the characteristic which symbolises its relation to the denied object. Object-choice is turned back into identification, the most primitive and most narcissistic form of attachment, in which the ego "assumes the characteristics of the object".

It must also be noted that in this regression from object-love to identification, the transformation of the ego is only partial. Whether identification imitates, "copies", the person who is not loved or the person who is loved, in both cases, it only modifies a part of the ego to conform to the single trait serving as the metaphorical support (condensation) or metonymic support (displacement) of the emotional tie (be it love or hate).

Hysterical identification, and neurotic identification in general, are limited, partial, since they only borrow a single trait from the object. This is what distinguishes them from "primary" identification, involved in the creation of the ideal and having a totalitarian objective: to equal or even replace the model. Thus, it seems that the ego must have a certain capacity to repress, in order to limit its libidinal identification with the object. At the initial stages of ego development, this identification is all-devouring and omnipotent. Consequently, neurotic identifications can justifiably be called secondary. They presuppose a primary oral prototype, and, in addition, they serve to replace an object-tie, a relationship of having. Therefore, they are secondary in a second sense: secondary to an object-choice that could not be maintained due to repression.

In other words, primary identification rules the emergence of the ideal to which the ego is subjected. Secondary identifications imitate abandoned or impossible emotional ties with object-choices, based on the narcissistic model of assimilation or cannibalistic incorporation, but in any case limited, condensed, attached to a single trait, to a symptomatic and overdetermined signifier. Neurotic identifications, therefore, maintain the object-tie because the object is only partially incorporated. We have seen that the opposite is true of totemic and melancholic identifications, characterised by the extreme narcissistic regression encountered in psychosis.

To conclude the second point, we could say that what is new in presenting identification as a mode of symptom formation is the highlighting – crucial, in our opinion – of its partial nature (the singular trait, unique or "unary", to use Lacan's term[44]) on the one hand and, on the other hand, the connection made between the neurotic process and its archaic oral prototype, a connection not yet glimpsed by the Freud of the 1900–1905 period, when he was writing *The Interpretation of Dreams* and *Dora: An Analysis of a Case of Hysteria*.

A negative remark might be made as well. Freud does not address at all the question of homosexuality underlying the symptomatology of hysteria or, rather, that of bisexuality. Dora's identification with her father (loved object) is ambivalent; this father is hated because he holds in Frau K.'s life and in the mother's life (the lost "good mother", since Dora is indifferent to her actual mother) a place that Dora unconsciously desires. This more "complete" aspect of the situation – of the Oedipal imbroglio – and of the system of adaptive identifications at the instinctual level is left out of the discussion. It will only be considered explicitly in *The Ego and the Id*.

3 "Boarding school" identification: mental infection and empathy

Freud points out a third type of identification in his overview of clinical observations. He calls it a "particularly frequent and important" mode of symptom formation – neurotic as well but with a remarkable particularity: this identification leaves out entirely any object-relation with the person being copied. It is not, therefore, a substitute expression of a libidinal tie. Freud's example of a typical case remains in the sphere of hysteria.

> Supposing, for instance, that one of the girls in a boarding school has had a letter from someone with whom she is secretly in love which arouses her jealousy, and that she reacts to it with a fit of hysterics; then some of her friends who know about it will contract the fit, as we say, by means of mental infection. The mechanism is that of identification based upon the possibility or desire of putting oneself in the same situation. The other girls would like to have a secret love affair too, and under the influence of sense of guilt they also accept the pain involved in it. It would be wrong to suppose that they take on the symptom out of sympathy. On the contrary, the sympathy only arises out of identification, and this is proved by the fact that infection or imitation of this kind takes place in circumstances where even less pre-existing sympathy is to be assumed than usually exists between friends in a girls' school.[45]

Freud had already described this form of identification through empathy in *The Interpretation of Dreams*, in reference to the mental infection sometimes seen in psychiatric hospital wards. The patients, Freud wrote, know more about each other than the doctor knows about each of them.[46] He described the identification of several of these patients with one patient having an attack of hysteria as the effect of an unconscious "syllogism". This reasoning can be summed up as follows: "If it is a possible to have this kind of attack from such causes, I, too, may have this kind of attack, for I have the same reasons". The "conclusion" of this reasoning is the attack itself, the appropriation of the symptom. Freud's earlier description (1900) is very similar to the one he gives here, in 1921:

> One ego has perceived a significant analogy with another upon one point – in our example upon openness to a similar emotion; an identification is thereupon constructed on this point, and, under the influence of the pathogenic situation, is displaced on to the symptom which the one ego has produced. The identification by means of the symptom has thus become the mark of a point of coincidence between the two egos which has to be kept repressed.[47]

As in the previous case, this identification is made based on a point of significant (sexual) analogy. Identification is, in truth, a capturing, an unconscious apperception of the same sexual desire, only repressed. This identification, this recognition of a libidinal resemblance, is the basis for imitation. Mimetic behaviour is secondary to this identification. Contrary to identification described earlier as partial narcissistic regression, this "boarding school" identification results from the unconscious perception of a significant similarity, in which two egos coincide on a specific point (a sexual claim). The identification involved in hysterical symptom formation (a symptom borrowed from another ego) is, therefore, not necessarily a regressive substitute for an object-choice. The highly valued "empathy" of the phenomenology of other relatedness is therefore not at all altruism but constitutes a purely narcissistic appropriation through an unconscious sign of communality. Empathy is not originally love: it springs from identificatory fascination. Indeed, love, pity, altruism and simple imitation are rooted in this type of identification "based upon the same etiological claim".[48]

Let us resume these initial facts taken from different empirical sources. First, identification is the original form of an emotional tie with an object; second, through a regressive path, it becomes the substitute for a libidinal object-choice, a sort of introjection of the object into the ego; third, it can occur upon the perception of each new common point with another person who is not the object of a libidinal impulse. The more significant the communality, the greater the effects of this partial identification, which constitutes the beginning of a new attachment. This attachment must be analogous to that existing between the members of a group or collectivity. This form of attachment replaces indifference and primitive hostility with the feeling of a shared emotional bond. Here, sympathy is rooted in unconscious identification based on one common trait. In the case of the young girls in the boarding school and the patients in the hospital ward, all of them bordering on hysteria, this trait is sexual in nature. The pathological nature of their "sympathy" is related to the repression of a sexual claim. Thus, identification is an unconscious process, at work in a psychological configuration where feelings and even "the most lofty sentiments" only play a secondary role. This process is not accessible to introspection, unlike "social" sentiments; the mimetic symptom only expresses a "me, too" attitude, indicating that one puts oneself "in the other's place", the sign of an unconscious claim that one is in a similar situation.

Thus, psychoanalysis delimits a psychic space for identification, which is neither "subjective" (emotions) nor "social" (roles, imitation of behaviour). It is, rather, an unconscious structure which, in retrospect, "produces" social ties.

What creates sympathy or, in the language of group psychology, social cohesion, is a common libidinal claim. In a group, as we have seen, the common trait, the specific point on which the bond is founded, is each member's claim to the love of the leader, each one's illusion that the leader loves all of them equally.

4 Identification in the genesis of homosexuality

The essay on *Leonardo da Vinci*, the additions to the *Three Essays* and the Schreber case focused on fixation in the sense of the Oedipus complex. Homosexuality comes into play at puberty, when Oedipal reviviscence occurs and when the choice of a sexual object – and therefore, the choice of one's sexuality – must be made. Fixation prevents the possibility of renouncing the object. Conserving the object (or rather, the libidinal tie with the Oedipal object) is achieved through identification with this object.

In this text, Freud only looks at male homosexuality. But this discussion is also pertinent to the clinical observations presented in *A Case of Homosexuality in a Woman*, written in 1920.[49]

> [T]he young man does not abandon his mother but identifies himself with her; he transforms himself into her, and now looks about for objects which can replace his ego for him, and on which he can bestow such love and care as he has experienced from his mother. . . . A striking thing about this identifica-tion is its ample scale; it remoulds the ego in one of its important features – its sexual character – upon the model of what has hitherto been the object. In this process the object itself is renounced – whether entirely or in the sense of being preserved only in the unconscious is a question outside the present dis-cussion. Identification with an object that is renounced or lost, as a substitute for that object – introjection of it into the ego – is indeed no longer a novelty to us. A process of this kind may sometimes be directly observed is small children. A short time ago an observation of this sort was published in the *Internationale Zeitschrift für Psychanalyse*.[50] A child who was unhappy over the loss of a kitten declared straight out that now he himself was the kitten, and accordingly crawled on all fours, would not eat at table, etc.[51]

The identification which generates homosexuality, preserves the tie with the "lost" Oedipal object and modifies the sexual character of the adolescent is lik-ened to identification as mourning in a child. The ego is the forsaken or lost object. Freud says that the remarkable thing about this identification is its scope. This is no longer a partial identification, based on "a single trait", as seen in hysteria, but an identification of the entire ego. Here, narcissistic regression takes the entire ego as its object. This is what Freud had called narcissistic identification in *Mourning and Melancholia* – an identification following upon narcissistic object-choice.

5 Melancholic identification

We will remember that the major trait of the melancholic profile is self-abasement combined with merciless self-accusations and severe self-blame. Analysis reveals that this blame and criticism are really addressed to the object and express the vindication of the ego against this object which disappointed, betrayed and aban-doned it. As Freud wrote, "the shadow of the object fell upon the ego".[52] Here, the introjection of the object is remarkably clear.

Thus, the process is similar to that described in Chapter 4 earlier. It is intro-jection of the object into the ego, through narcissistic regression from libidinal investment in an object-choice.

But, unlike the homosexual, the melancholic is not simply transformed into a loving object. His ego is deeply divided, "split off (*geteilt*)", fallen apart into two pieces, one of which rages against the other. The second piece is the one which was altered by the introjection of the lost object. The part which is so cruel to the other is an agency well known to psychoanalysis: conscience, the ego ideal.

> On previous occasions we have been driven to the hypothesis that some such agency develops in our ego which may cut itself off from the rest of the ego and come into conflict with it. We have called it the "ego ideal", and by way of functions we have ascribed to it self-observation, the moral conscience, the censorship of dreams, and the chief influence in repression. We have said that *it is the heir to original narcissism in which the childish ego enjoyed self-sufficiency*; it gradually gathers up from the environment the demands which that environment makes upon the ego and which the ego cannot always rise to; so that a man, when he cannot be satisfied with his ego itself, may nevertheless be able to find satisfaction in the ego ideal which has been differentiated out of the ego. In delusions of observation, we have further shown, the disintegration of this agency has become patent, and has thus revealed *its origin in the influence of superior powers, and above all of parents*. But we have not forgotten to add that the amount of distance between this ego ideal and the real ego is very variable from one individual to another, and that with many people this differentiation within the ego does not go further than with children.[53]

Thus, what distinguishes melancholia is this troublesome, tormenting cleavage of the ego. The tearing apart of the ego is greatest in melancholia and nonexistent in mania[54]. But these pathological entities reveal the structure, the "constitution" of the human ego, made up of parts, fragments that are what is left of forsaken or lost objects. As we have seen, melancholic torment is rooted in enormous ambivalence.

Melancholic identification drives the hated object into the ego, which introjects it and thereby becomes loathsome to the other aspect of the ego: the ego ideal. This second part of the ego appears to be stronger and more stable than the other part, which undergoes the fluctuations, the ups and downs of libidinal investments and their desirable and undesirable substitutes. Once the object is abandoned, it becomes introjected into the ego, reproducing the lost relation at the narcissistic level.

In the case of homosexuality, the object-choice is the ego loved by the mother, and the ego is transformed, through identification, into the loving mother. . . searching for substitutes for the initial love object. Identification changes sexual position and type of object-choice; it causes the altered ego to search for new objects consistent with the "ego". By contrast, melancholic identification puts an end to any search for an object; it restricts the ambivalent libidinal relation to the ego itself; it encloses the ego within the narrow confines of a sado-masochistic relation which cuts it off from reality. Here, narcissistic regression is radical and deadly; in truth, it is psychotic.

For the homosexual, there is coherence between the ego and the ego ideal transformed, through identification, to fit the model of the lost mother, unconsciously preserved by this transformation, which perpetuates her. In melancholia, the whole scenario is internalised; the ego ideal turns against the ego transformed by identification and perpetrates on it the unconscious destruction of the object. What is the status of this ego ideal?

Freud refers to his 1913 discovery: the ego ideal is the heir to original narcissism. But he also refers to the influence of coercive authorities, especially parental. The "institutions of the ego", already set forth in *Mourning and Melancholia*–conscience, censorship of consciousness and reality testing, to which are added self-scrutiny and repression – are said to result from the influence of these "authorities". But how can we reconcile these two origins of the ego ideal (original narcissistic self-sufficiency and parental authority)? It could be that the parents were characterised by "original" narcissism from the start, in which infantile "self-sufficiency" contrasts with a devastating inability to survive without external objects.

The question which arises here is that of the origin of the ideal and its function within the ego, as well as in its relations with ego-objects, which have become the other aspect of the ego. This makes it possible to imagine a sequence, a series of egos, generated by identifications within the "ego".

Freud's essay, which classifies identification into the five categories we have just examined, raises a number of questions. But let us start by making use of the summary presented in this section of the essay.

Identification with the father, identification resulting in hysterical symptom formation, identification leading to empathy, identification with the Oedipal libidinal object and melancholic identification: these five types of identification constitute a complex and diverse domain – that of the normal and the pathological. Thus, identification is a psychic process whose function can be both "normalising" and pathogenic.

1   Two of the forms described are not paths to regression: identification with the father, which creates the ego ideal, and the identification involved in empathy. They are motivated by the desire to be; the desire to be like the model becomes the desire to be, in an absolute sense: the desire to take the other's place. The aggressiveness inherent to this desire to be the other is obvious. But in the case of identification with the father of the prehistory of the Oedipus complex, this aggressiveness remains latent; it is love for another object, the mother, which turns the relation to the model into rivalry. This taking as a model, "exemplary" identification – typically masculine, "ideal" and "primary", as long as the tie stays away from any desire to have – replaces and does away with aggressiveness. The case of Little Hans has already shown us that identification can protect from aggressiveness or provide a means of

sublimating Oedipal hostility. In a note at the end of Chapter VII, called *Iden-tification*, Freud observes:

> [T]he manifestations of identifications. . . result among other things in a person limiting his aggressiveness towards those with whom he has identified himself, and in his sparing them and giving them help.

The same is true in the case of empathy. Freud identifies the origin of the mechanism that allows us, as a general rule, to take up an attitude towards another psyche (what he calls "mental life"). This mechanism originates in unconscious identification and produces empathy, after taking the form of imitation and contagion.

2   Identification can be partial, based on a single trait which symbolises the unconscious element in common with the other ego. This is what happens in hysterical symptom formation and in empathy. But some identifications exert a much greater effect, transforming the ego itself entirely. This is what takes place in the altering of the homosexual's sexual position, in the "totemic" identification of the child, in the primary identification which makes the father the ideal model for the little boy and in melancholia.

3   The process of identification is always narcissistic. It supports the ego in its fundamental tendency to maintain itself. Therefore, when the ego introjects a model, it fulfills its desire for omnipotence. Or, in other cases, regressive transformation of an object-choice into identification ensures continuity of the object while appearing to renounce it. The melancholic process is the par-adigm best illustrating this regressive process. Cannibalistic introjection has proven to be the dominant metaphor for all these forms of attachment consti-tuted by identification. To love is to devour; to love is to be and, secondarily, to have. Oral narcissism is present in all forms of identification, with all its inevitable ambivalence. Melancholic identification or "narcissistic" (but this is a pleonasm, of course) holds a strategic position at the level of theory: it provides the key to all secondary identifications and, probably, to primary identification itself. Our reading of *Mourning and Melancholia* seems to indi-cate that regression from object-choice to identification retroactively reveals that the original choice of object was narcissistic.[55] In *On Narcissism: An Introduction*, Freud gives the following "formulas" for choosing the object: "A person may love. . . what he himself is, what he himself was, what he himself would like to be [identification with the father as ego ideal], [or] someone who was once a part of himself".[56] Clearly, the relation to the father in the period before the Oedipus complex is narcissistic, and we have reason to ask ourselves whether a "narcissistic object-choice" is not an "ideal" type of identification.

Freud's essay *Group Psychology and Analysis of the Ego* can provide some answers.

The ego and the ego ideal

This internal differentiation in the ego constituted a crucial step in Freud's conceptualisation in 1913–1914. The fact that the ego could divide, as is the case when there are feelings of guilt or melancholia, revealed its layered structure. Behaviours commonly observed when people are in love, hypnosis and phenomena linked to group psychology confirm the existence of such a split structure of the ego and allow us to better understand its economy and vicissitudes.

A striking characteristic of the state of being in love is overvaluation: the blind adoration shown to the object. This, of course, is a narcissistic phenomenon, since "the object is being treated in the same way as our own ego, so that. . . a considerable amount of narcissistic libido overflows on to the object".[57]

The more highly the object is valued, the more the ego, in comparison, will perceive itself as humble and insignificant. The ego becomes more and more unassuming; its own narcissism becomes limited and is transferred instead to the loved object. At the same time, the ego gradually loses its usual functions: critical faculty, conscience and reality-testing. The object literally hypnotises the ego of the lover.[58] This situation can be summed up in the formula: "*the object has been put in the place of the ego-ideal*".[59] This transfer of the ideal is precisely what constitutes idealisation of the object.

Idealisation can be said to be a kind of transitive identification: the object becomes the ego ideal. In simple terms, the ego is impoverished and the object enriched, gaining the narcissistic libido normally invested in the ego's own ideal – an ideal which is itself rooted in original narcissism. The "idealising" identification characteristic of the state of being in love makes the object synonymous with the ideal. Thus, this identification does not eliminate the object, which is retained, and there is idealising libidinal investment of it. This can easily be seen in the sexual attachment of the ego to the loved object. But it must be noted that direct sexual satisfaction reduces the degree of idealisation of the object. "Spiritual" or "platonic" love is the purest form of idealisation: the most sublime, we might say, but the most desexualised, the most narcissistic – the "maddest" – form of love.

This is why hypnosis, in which all sexual (sensual) impulses are inhibited, illustrates, at the experimental level, the process of idealisation. For there is no doubt that the hypnotist takes the place of the ego ideal.[60]

The attitude of the subject undergoing hypnosis can be likened to that of a man in the electrified atmosphere of a group with a leader. The hypnotic relation, which holds this position of ego ideal, could be said to be a collective construction made up of two people. This relation provides the key to the individual's relation to the leader. Freud considered that this is the essential element of group psychology since, among group members, the other type of attachment – their mutual identification with each other (all of them are equal, brothers, "the same") – is rooted in this relation which each of them enjoys, in phantasy, with the leader.

We can therefore state that a primary group – that is, one with a leader and at an inchoative level of organisation, *in statu nascendi* – is a collection of individuals who have replaced their ego ideal with the same object and who, after making this collective substitution, have identified with each other. A suitable formulation would be as follows: the ideal (aggrandised in phantasy by all these forsaken narcissisms) has become the subject of their ego at the very moment when their ego became the object of this idealised object.

In view of these summary considerations, the ego ideal appears to be the subject of the ego, with which it maintains a love relation like that of the ego with its objects. Thus, the intrapsychic constellation has the structure of an interpsychic constellation.

These last remarks about groups confirm what we have glimpsed when looking at "boarding school" identification. The illusion of being loved equally by the leader generates empathy, creates cohesion and allows each member to set aside his personal claims and envy-related aggressiveness. Identification of the ego ideal is primary; collective identification is secondary. In light of these considerations, human beings appear not as "gregarious" animals, as M. W. Trotter maintained,[61] but as herd animals. In German, man is not a *Herdentier* but a *Hordentier*. Freud has now gone back to the founding myth in his *Totem and Taboo*. From this perspective, suggestion, hypnosis and psychic contagion all have their origins in the primitive history of the human family, headed by the omnipotent hypnotist-father, embodiment of the ideal and founder of the primal horde.

Let us try to resume the discussion of *Group Psychology and the Analysis of the Ego* by focusing on two concepts Freud put forth in his essay.

> [W]hat we have been able to contribute towards the explanation of the libidinal structure of groups leads back to *the distinction between the ego and the ego ideal* and to the double kind of tie which this makes possible – *identification and putting the object in the place of the ego ideal*. The assumption of this kind of differentiating grade in the ego as a first step in an analysis of the ego must gradually establish its justification in the most various regions of psychology.[62]

This essay completes *On Narcissism: An Introduction* (1914) in a remarkable manner.

The major theoretical contribution concerns these "degrees", "stages", "layers" or "grades" in the Ego: all of them translations of the German *Stufeim Ich*. What remains to be explored are the implications of this internal differentiation in the ego for identification theory because identification is involved in the formation of the ego ideal and, as if in reverse, in the idealisation of the object and the replacement of the ego ideal with the idealised object, as well as in the formation of the ego, made up of previous object-cathexes. Therefore, this differentiated – we might say hierarchical – structure of the ego raises the question of genesis, which is indicated in *Group Psychology*, but not resolved.

Still, we can appreciate the scope of this structural development, of this endeavour to analyse the ego, which opens the way to an original differential psychopathology.

The psychoses, a preferred field for the analysis of pathologies of the ego, highlight the internal relations of this ego which reproduces, in its various relations with the ego ideal, actions and mutual reactions reminiscent of what analysis of the neuroses has shown regarding the possible relations of the ego as a whole (*Gesamt-Ich*) with the external object.

Thus, any pathology brings into play substitute relations and conflicts within the ego itself, divided and divisible, or within a collection of "egos".

Each psychic differentiation we have identified constitutes a new difficulty in psychic functioning and can be the origin of a failed function, of an illness. Human life is therefore punctuated by three problematic events, three moments of differentiation and separation, responsible for the structural fragility of the ego.

1   *Birth* brings to an end an initial state of original narcissism, of self-sufficiency of the prenatal being, propelling him into a world subjected to the alternation of night and day. For a while, sleep will palliate this disruption.
2   *Repression*, which creates the ego by driving out the unconscious, exposes the ego to repeated attempts at a return of the repressed. Neuroses, dreams, wit and humour all testify – each in accordance with its own structure – to this pressure exerted by the unconscious at the threshold of the conscious.
3   *Separation between the ego ideal and the ego* cannot always be endured and must, from time to time, undergo regression. Ancient celebrations, accompanied by the systematic violation of prohibitions, testify to this tension in human communities. Mania and melancholia testify to it at the individual level.

Manic-depressive alternation illustrates the periodicity of the rebellion of the ego against the ego ideal. In the manic phase, the ego and the ego ideal are fused; the person thus reconciled celebrates this victory over division and his freedom from obstacles, remorse and criticism. Conversely, the depressive phase expresses the suffering of the tearing apart, of the painful separation between the ego and ego ideal. The ego ideal treats the ego in the manner in which the ego unconsciously wishes to treat its object, unworthy of love. Identification serves to displace the conflictual scene from the outside to the inside.

What is left is to connect these characteristics of structure with the antagonistic play between the life and death instincts (an opposition not discussed in the text we just examined) and with the question of the origin of the ideal and the determination of its functions.

Genesis and structure of formations of the ego: ego and ego ideal – the superego

In 1923, in *The Ego and the Id*, Freud described the structure of the second topography in an attempt to integrate the analysis of ego structure in his new theory of drives. Identification theory is given its final formulation, which includes the elucidation of the Oedipus complex and of the conditions of its "destruction". The dispersed fragments of a doctrine of identification are assembled around the Oedipus. The question of identification becomes a question of the Oedipus.[63]

This is the topic of the last stage of our journey. The texts Freud wrote after 1923 did no more than rely on the theoretical concepts presented in the fundamental work *The Ego and the Id*.[64]

In the Preface, Freud outlines his intentions: to continue to explore the hypotheses presented in *Beyond the Pleasure Principle* by linking them to facts gleaned from psychoanalytic observation, without borrowing any further from biology. This new work, Freud says, "is more in the nature of a synthesis than of a speculation and seems to have. . . an ambitious aim in view".[65] Moreover, he specifies that the questions discussed "have not yet been the subject of psycho-analytic consideration". These questions are, in fact, those raised by Adler and Jung, the first two major dissenters whose theories focusing on the "ego" and on the "transformations of the libido" marked a radical departure from the established orientation of psychoanalytic theory.

These disagreements underlying the developments Freud outlines in this essay are apparent in the organisation of the text itself: reaffirmation of the unconscious, the link between the first topography and ego theory, which leads to the elaboration of the second topography, through recourse to Georg Groddeck's concept of the *It*[66] and, finally, the radicalisation of the question of the ideal, which makes it possible to redefine the overall instinctual economy of psychic life. We shall focus on the effects of this new metapsychological theory on the identification concept and on the associated concepts of idealisation, desexualisation and sublimation.

Oedipal identifications

The third chapter of *The Ego and the Id* is titled "The Ego and the Super-Ego (Ego Ideal)". This extremely condensed text brings together all the questions regarding the origin and differentiations of the ego; it is here that Freud introduces the notion of the superego, which, in this essay, is used as an equivalent to the ego ideal. But a new term is never introduced without a reason. A purely semantic synonymy would make no contribution to the theoretical construction. From the start, the signifying overtones of these two concepts seem to be directed towards two poles: a pole which assembles the notions of model, example, ideality, ideal and a pole bringing together the notions of hierarchy, layering and domination. Thus, this semantic play introduces a subtle complexity in what had been termed since 1914 a self-observing agency in the ego. The "last" identification theory develops around this complex nucleus whose status would remain unclear in subsequent Freudian texts. Later, the reasons for this lack of theoretical clarity, which troubled many analysts, remained to be found. Talented commentators, rigorous theoreticians and adventurous clinicians were faced with sorting out this formidable but crucial entanglement. We shall have to compare our own reading with the best-known interpretations without becoming bogged down in details. Such bibliographical elements can be found in many reports on scientific psychoanalytic colloquia.[67]

Let us go back to Freud's text, to this important Chapter III of *The Ego and the Id*:

The nucleus of the ego

At the end of Chapter II, Freud proposed a simple definition of the ego, articulated in statements such as these:

> [T]he ego is that part of the id which has been modified by the direct influence of the external world through the medium of the *perception-consciousness*. . . . For the ego, perception plays the part which in the id falls to instinct.[68]
>
> The functional importance of the ego is manifested in the fact that, normally, control over the approaches to motility devolves upon it.[69]
>
> The ego is first and foremost a bodily ego; it is not merely a surface entity, but is itself the projection of a surface. . . . [W]e can best identify it with the "cortical homunculus" of the anatomists.[70]
>
> The conscious ego. . . is first and foremost a body-ego.[71]

Yet if the ego was only a biological apparatus intended to perceive, to sort and to collect perceptions, to submit to the "reality principle" the instincts of the id governed only by the "pleasure principle", things would be very simple. But for psychoanalysis, the ego is more than this.

On Narcissism: An Introduction and *Group Psychology* presented a very different aspect of the ego. These texts recognised the need to acknowledge an internal differentiation in the ego, a split, a layering (*Stufe*). A differentiation is made between the ego and the ego ideal or superego. The reasons for introducing this kind of layering in the ego remain valid, despite Freud's earlier descriptions of the ego.

This double discourse on the ego deserves separate examination.[72] However, a correction must be made concerning what was said earlier about the functions attributed to the ego ideal. Freud makes this correction in a footnote – and we have seen how important these remarks in his footnotes can be:

> I seem to have been mistaken in ascribing the function of "reality-testing" to this super-ego – a point which needs correction. It would fit in perfectly with the relations of the ego to the world of perception if reality-testing

remained a task of the ego itself. Some earlier suggestions about a "nucleus of the ego", never very definitely formulated, also require to be put right, since the system Perception-consciousness alone can be regarded as the nucleus of the ego.[73]

This corrective note is congruent with classical biology-centred psychology. Commenting on this text, Jean Laplanche justifiably wonders if Freud's initial attribution of a "reality-testing" function to the ego ideal was merely an error, a slip-up. Laplanche disagrees with Freud's correction, asserting that this notion of a relation between the superego and the question of reality is a very fruitful concept. He writes:

> As for me, I think that this suggestion Freud later revised could be interpreted in the context of the law (that is, the legality introduced by the super-ego, both a moral and a logical legality, that of the sharp logical opposition introduced by the prohibition of castration).[74]

Once these "corrections" were made, the new concept held that the part of the ego called ego ideal or superego has a more tenuous and less intimate relation with consciousness than the part of the ego governed by perception. The new topographical model – the first – of mental life has now been established. The "superior" portion of the ego is not the most conscious. The scene of the ideal is unconscious; morality and prohibition are located in large part in the unconscious sphere.[75]

This radical notion brings into question simplistic dualist or "centauric" traditional representations of the soul. On the one hand, Freud seems to hold on to them for the time being, saying that the nucleus of the ego – if there is a nucleus, and only one – is subject to perception and governs motility. On the other hand, he destabilises the ego or, more precisely, points out another centre which is, in truth, an interval, a concavity, a grade (*Stufe*): that is, the differentiation introduced by the firmly established discovery of the ego ideal or superego. In fact, this part of the ego originates in the replacement of object-cathexes by identifications. This transformation process, based on the theoretical model of melancholia, leads to the building of the ego into what is called character. Freud reiterates the description of this process, which contributes in great measure to the shaping of the ego.

> At the very beginning, in the individual's primitive oral phase, object-cathexis and identification are no doubt indistinguishable from each other. We can only suppose that later on object-cathexes proceed from the id, which feels erotic trends as needs. The ego, which to begin with is still feeble, becomes aware of the object-cathexes, and either acquiesces in them or tries to fend them off by the process of repression.[76]

In a footnote, Freud reminds the reader of the concepts presented earlier in *Totem and Taboo*:

> An interesting parallel to the replacement of object-choice by identification is to be found in the belief of primitive peoples, and in the prohibitions based upon it, that the attributes of animals which are incorporated as nourishment persist as part of the character of those who eat them. As is well known, this belief is one of the roots of cannibalism and its effects have continued through the series of usages of the totem meal down to Holy Communion. The consequences ascribed by this belief to oral mastery of the object do in fact follow in the case of the later sexual-object choice.[77]

The text continues:

> When it happens that a person has to give up a sexual object, there quite often ensues an alteration of his ego which can only be described as a setting up of the object inside the ego, as it occurs in melancholia; the exact nature of this substitution is as yet unknown to us. It may be that by this introjection. . . the ego makes it easier for the object to be given up or renders that process possible. It may be that this identification is the sole condition under which the id can give up its objects. At any rate the process. . . makes it possible to suppose that the character of the ego is a precipitate of abandoned object-cathexes and that it contains the history of those object-choices.[78]

Thus, Freud raises the question of the origin of the character of the ego immediately after discussing the status of the nucleus of the ego. Fundamental character "traits" are precipitates of former object-cathexes, incorporated remnants of loved objects the id had to renounce. In a manner of speaking, character is a substitute for infantile totemism. But totemism introduces the question of the ideal. Determining the origin of the ideal is the aim of the questioning on this aspect of the ego called "character", which, in a certain psychology, represents the nucleus of the ego.

Identification appears as the most universal means employed by the psychic economy to retain that which, in light of reality, should be renounced. Replacing an erotic object-choice by a transformation of the ego is a strategy allowing the ego to acquire mastery over the id and establish closer relations with it, provided it remains very responsive to the id. When the ego takes on the traits of the object, it presents itself to the id as a substitute object, in an attempt to compensate for the loss. The ego's recourse is summed up clearly in the statement: "Look, you can love me too – I am so like the object".[79]

This manoeuvre of the ego constitutes narcissistic regression, in accordance with the oral prototype. By transforming object-libido into narcissistic libido, identification leads not only to renouncing the object-choice but also to abandoning the sexual aims inherent to it. Thus, identification is a desexualisation process and, consequently, a sort of sublimation. It is not unreasonable to wonder whether all sublimation might not have been achieved by this intermediary means of identification. The narcissistic transformation of the libido subjects it to the aims of the ego. Here, we can see once again the close ties between identification and repression. In this context, sublimation appears to be successful repression, which precludes the risk of return of the repressed. Indeed, we will remember that one of the definitions of *repression* is "withdrawal of libidinal cathexis hitherto directed on to them, from people [and things] in [the] environment".[80] This confirms the desire to preserve ascribed to repression: a human being never consents to give up satisfaction; he only finds substitutes for it. The best substitute for an object is another object. If a satisfactory substitute is not found, the best substitute for the lost object is the ego, which is malleable and amenable to countless uses.

These revised formulations of the relation between the ego and the id lead to the reconsideration, or at least a more precise definition, of an idea dating back to the introduction of narcissism in libidinal theory. Now that the ego and the id have been differentiated, it has to be made clear that the "great reservoir"[81] of libido is not the ego but the id. The libido stored in the ego, through identifications which form character, introduces the secondary narcissism of the ego. As for primary narcissism, it is seen as the libidinal state existing before the separation between the ego and the id. Clearly, the process bringing about this separation which defines an ego possessing a "character" can only be an identification – a truly structuring identification, since it "establishes" an ego. As discussed earlier, when the question of character focuses on the superposition of a "characterised" ego, the need arises to examine primary identification, constitutive of the ego ideal nucleus. We shall do this by making an incursion into the sphere of ego pathology.

When the ego's object identifications are too intense, too numerous and incompatible with each other, the result can be a splitting of the ego. The different identifications pull apart, opposing each other; this is what explains the enigma of cases of "multiple personality",[82] discussed in the context of hysteria. Each of these identifications, in turn, strives to be acknowledged by consciousness. An ego torn between such identifications does not always disintegrate but can be subjected to serious conflict. The case of the Wolf Man presents such an identificatory conflict (identification with the woman, identification with the man) in the subject's fascination with the primal scene.[83] Character, formed through early identifications with abandoned objects, does not change as a result of new object-cathexes the id must renounce. After a time, the character resists renewed transformations. We might speak of a nucleus of resistance that protects the ego from the discomfort created by the ups and downs associated with the random libidinal attachments and adventures of the id. What constitutes this hard and resistant nucleus?

But, whatever the character's later capacity for resisting the influences of abandoned object-cathexes may turn out to be, the effects of the first identifications made in earliest childhood will be general and lasting. This leads us back to the origin of the ego ideal; for behind it there lies hidden an individual's first and most important identification, *his identification with the father in his own personal prehistory.*

(We shall return to the Note which follows this passage.)
Freud goes on:

> [T]his is apparently not... the consequences or outcome of an object-cathexis; *it is a direct and immediate identification and takes place earlier than any object-cathexis.* But the object-choices belonging to the first sexual period and relating to the father and mother seem normally to find their outcome in an identification of this kind, and would thus reinforce *the primary one.*[84]

This sums up succinctly the major points of the discussion: the relation of character to early identifications, the status of the first of these identifications: one that is not, like those which follow, the result of a libidinal transformation originating in the ideal represented by the father figure hiding behind it – a father belonging to "personal prehistory" – bringing to mind the "prehistory of the Oedipus complex": a father, then, whose traits, as soon as they are described, are erased at once by the curious remarks in this footnote:

> Perhaps it would be safer to say "with the parents"; for before a child has arrived at definite knowledge of the difference between the sexes, the lack of a penis, it does not distinguish in value between its father and its mother. I recently came across the instance of a young married woman whose story showed that, after noticing the lack of a penis in herself, she had supposed it to be absent not in all women, but only in those whom she regarded as inferior, and had still supposed that her mother possessed one. In order to simplify my presentation I shall discuss only identification with the father.[85]

Indeed, these strange remarks amount to a veritable denial, as Jean Laplanche rightly observes.[86]

For although Freud started by saying "identification with the father", he must have known what he was leading up to. As for us, we recognise the identification he described at the start of Chapter VII of *Groups Psychology and Analysis of the Ego*. Let us note that the term *primary identification* appears for the first time in *The Ego and the Id*.

When Freud writes "the father of personal prehistory", we are reminded of his daring *Totem and Taboo* and the prehistoric dimensions of the individual and of humanity itself. The father of this prehistory is certainly not the equivalent of the asexual pair called the parents, the first reliable objects sustaining the newborn's life. Therefore, the problem raised by this symptomatic note is sexual in nature: it involves sexual difference, the lack of a penis and castration. Freud tells us that personal prehistory precedes definite knowledge about the difference between the sexes. There is no definite knowledge but some knowledge nevertheless; otherwise, why describe the clinical case in which the major problem concerns the value of the penis, the worthiness of those who possess one and the inferiority of those who don't? And why end the note by specifying that only identification with the father will be discussed – a remark which nullifies the whole content of the note?

Given the manner in which the concept of identification developed, it is difficult to define it with precision. Let us try to summarise what we know about it.

- It is hidden behind the ego ideal, which it generates;
- Its object is the "father of personal prehistory" or "the parents";
- It is direct, immediate and anterior to object-cathexes; in other words, it seems to avoid following the melancholic model of narcissistic regression. It occurs very early during the oral phase of development, but its object is not the breast, the first sexual object-cathexis;
- Identifications originating in the earliest object-cathexes are the ones which find their *Ablauf* (meaning: outlet, accomplishment, final expression) in primary identification; and
- These early identifications reinforce primary identification: they are secondary identifications; it may be said that primary identification exerts a kind of attraction on them – captivates them, as it were.

Explaining the relations between primary and secondary identifications requires a more detailed description which locates this prehistory in its inevitable relation to the story which renders it understandable in retrospect. The story serving to reconstruct prehistory is that of the Oedipus complex.

The Oedipal relations complex

What complicates the relations between primary identification and secondary identifications – in other words, what creates the complexity of the ego – is the combined effect of two factors, one social and the other biological: specifically, the triangular constellation composed of the Oedipus and the subject's constitutional bisexuality.

We have been given the simplified formula describing Oedipal relations, at least for boys. Freud presented their structure in Chapter VII of *Group Psychology*.[87] We can summarise it as follows:

- Before the development of the Oedipus as such, we can describe its prehistory: coexistence of identification with the father – a way of taking hold of him – and object cathexis with the mother, particularly the breast, illustrating typical diphasic object-choice. After a time, the sexual instincts intensify, and so does libidinal investment in the mother; now, the father is perceived as an obstacle to the child's desire. This intersection of the relationship with the father and the relationship with the mother produces the Oedipus complex. In this situation, the ambivalence present in the previous identification with the father becomes obvious.

- The Oedipus complex, in its simple, "positive" form, consists of this ambivalence towards the father and tenderness towards the mother.
- The destruction of the complex – and this expression indicates that Freud considers this complex a phase, a situation which must be "destroyed"[88] – comes about by coercion, when the boy is forced (Freud does not say by what agency) to renounce his libidinal investment in the mother. He does this by recourse to identification.

Libidinal investment in the mother can be replaced by one of two means: identification with her or reinforcement of the identification with the father. The second solution is generally considered the normal resolution of the complex, which disappears but has served to consolidate masculinity in the boy's character.

As for the girl, the process is similar in her case: the complex disappears through reinforcement of identification with the mother,[89] which consolidates feminine character. But, surprisingly, these identifications replacing the complex do not fulfill our expectations since they do not give the abandoned object back to the ego. The theoretical model provided by the melancholic process does not seem to apply in this case. Still, there is a partial fit since Freud notes that with girls, analysis often reveals a masculine ideal: that is, identification with the father, their lost libidinal object; this process of introjection of the father is consistent with the doctrine. But Freud adds that for this process to take place, it must be supposed that there has been a certain degree of development of masculine characteristics of one type or another. This means that a constitutional factor must be taken into account.

These oedipal identifications fall short of our expectations due to the relative intensity of the sexual – bisexual – inclinations of the boy and the girl. This is the first way in which bisexuality plays a role in the vicissitudes of the Oedipus complex. But they also present another aspect, one that is much more important and significant. The simplified schematisation given earlier, that of the "positive" complex, rarely resembles what is observed in most cases. Closer study reveals a more complex situation which would have to be called the "complete" Oedipus complex, in which the constituents of the Oedipal triangle take on positive and negative manifestations, due to the child's original bisexuality. Let us look at how Freud's reasoning proceeds:

[A] boy has not merely an ambivalent attitude towards his father and an affectionate object-choice towards his mother, but at the same time he also behaves like a girl and displays an affectionate feminine attitude to his father and a corresponding jealousy and hostility towards his mother. It is this complicating element introduced by bisexuality that makes it so difficult to obtain a clear view of the facts in connection to the earliest object-choices and identifications, and still more difficult to describe them intelligibly. It may even be that the ambivalence displayed in the relations to the parents should be attributed entirely to bisexuality and that it is not, as I have represented above, developed out of identification in consequence of rivalry.[90]

This more complete description allows a clearer understanding of neuroses and of sexual inversion. Thus, based on this complex structure, we can posit a series of possibilities with, at one end, the normal, positive form of the complex and, at the other, its negative, inverted form; the intermediary members exhibit the complete form, with a preponderance of one of its two components.

After the dissolution of the Oedipus complex, these four trends will group together to produce identification with the mother and identification with the father. This process can be supposed to unfold as follows: identification with the father maintains the maternal object of the positive complex and, at the same time, replaces (takes) the inverted object-relation to the father (complex). The same will be true, *mutatis mutandis*, of identification with the mother. The relative intensity of each of these identifications in an individual will reflect the dominance of one or the other of the original sexual dispositions.

At this point, Freud formulates the conclusion to be drawn from this in-depth analysis of this complicated Oedipal configuration:

> The broad general outcome of the sexual phase dominated by the Oedipus complex may, therefore, be taken to be the forming of a precipitate in the ego, consisting of these two identifications in some way united with each other. This modification of the ego retains its special positions; it confronts the other contents of the ego as an ego ideal or super-ego.[91]

This conclusion makes a significant contribution to what we knew about the origin and content of the ego ideal (superego). The ego ideal was defined as a particular type of relation with the father: the prehistoric father, the one preceding the Oedipus. This ego ideal, as a narcissistic introjection, has also been described as an outcome of the original narcissism lost once and for all due to the newborn's complete helplessness.

Yet when Freud completes the notion of ego ideal by adding that of superego, which in the texts we examined is often affixed to the ego ideal concept, he displaces the origin of the ideal, locating it in a historical, multipolar, "triangular" space: the Oedipal constellation. As if the Oedipus complex is needed to establish definitively the complex of identifications producing the ideal coupling ego/superego. These multiple identifications occur with object-cathexes. They consolidate character, which must be supposed to exist before the Oedipal phase, and to be either masculine or feminine since we are told that identifications replacing Oedipal relations reinforce masculinity or femininity already present in the character.

What is the origin of the character, always already sexual gendered, and what is the origin of the ego ideal or superego which establishes definitively the child's sexual disposition?

The superego seems to spring from a transformation of the first bisexual investments of the id, which developed independently in the course of a certain prehistory and were subsequently intricated, combined and intensified by the Oedipus complex and ultimately "destroyed" by identifications which take their place. Thus, it appears that the ego ideal, which Freud attempts to affix to the superego, was present before any object-cathexis.

As a result, we are faced with a serious difficulty when searching for a clear and reassuring solution to the problem of the origin of the ego, the origin of character, the origin of the ego ideal and the origin of the superego – this last being a concept which emerged later, although Freud tried to connect it with the ego ideal. As for identifications, we might summarise their role as follows: the ego ideal originates in primary identification with the "father of personal prehistory"; the superego emerges from the reinforcement of this primary identification by secondary identifications springing from the narcissistic transformation of Oedipal object-cathexes.

Unfortunately, we have no definition of the "father of personal prehistory" for girls. It is tempting to suppose a counter-figure to this "father", a "mother of personal prehistory". We have seen that Freud tried to solve the problem by using the general formulation identification with the parents, which precedes the definite and certain knowledge of sexual difference. Of course, the father "endowed with" a penis and the mother "deprived" of a penis are not interchangeable in the combinatory process. Thus, we are given no answer concerning the question of what differentiates the feminine from the masculine Oedipus, since the "prevalence's" constituting bisexuality does not explain the primary identification which establishes "character". But let us continue to examine Chapter III of Freud's text.

The superego as residue and reaction formation: heir of the Oedipus

Leaving aside, for the time being, questions concerning the origin, Freud turns his attention to the specific role of identifications generating the superego.

The superego is not merely a precipitate, a sedimentation or a residue of the id's primitive object-choices that have become ego formations or representatives. The superego is also a powerful reaction-formation against these old choices. Its relation to the ego cannot be summed up by the precept: "You ought to be like this (like your father)"; it also includes the prohibition: "You may not be like this (like your father)", meaning: "You may not do all that he does; some things are his prerogative".[92]

This double aspect of the ego ideal derives from the fact that its primary mission is to repress the Oedipus complex and that it owes its advent solely to this revolution. For it is a veritable libidinal revolution – Freud uses the term *Umschwung*,

meaning sudden reversal, sudden change, overturning – which creates the superego and defines it both as a model (be like the father) and as a prohibitor (don't be
like him). The assertion confirms, once again, the repressive function of identification, the "ideal" solution of libidinal conservatism, despite the demands of reality, which imposes losses, abandonment and renunciation. The very first objects
are never lost. But retaining them in the ego as agencies produces an ineffable
constitutive contradiction in the ego: to be and not to be.

But where does the infantile ego, so defenceless, so dependent on its libidinal
objects for support and consolidation, find the strength to renounce them?

Surprisingly, the infantile ego borrows the strength needed for repressing its
Oedipal wishes from the obstacle to their realisation. In the case of the boy –
although Freud could be speaking of children in general – this strength is borrowed, so to speak, from the father, and this loan (*Anleike*) has momentous
consequences. Indeed, the superego retains the character of the father. The more
powerful the Oedipal impulses and the more forceful the paternal prohibition, the
more quickly repression is achieved, under the influence of religious teaching,
authority, schooling and reading. The superego's domination is proportional to
the intensity of the material to be repressed. Pangs of conscience and unconscious
guilt feelings will emerge in the wake of this impulse inhibition.

It must be noted that the superego's strictness is not a direct reflection of the
father's strictness, but rather of the intensity of Oedipal impulses. In certain
other texts, Freud focused on the figure of the father himself to establish this
strictness of the superego. In all probability, this is what led Melanie Klein to
formulate her particular views. We shall examine this disagreement later since
our discussion will require a reading of other texts (namely, *Civilisation and Its
Discontents*). Without wanting to bias the outcome of the debate, we can turn to
what Freud asserts in the present text to support the idea that source at which the
"still feeble" ego draws the strength to repress object-cathexes and constitute an
implacable superego is also instinctive in nature, in addition to being the reflection of an external constraint. Still, there is reason to be surprised that Freud never
once specifies the motive for the constraint to repress the Oedipus, to destroy it,
although in *Totem and Taboo*, he indirectly pointed to the threat of castration.

To come back to the discussion on the manner in which the superego is constituted, its emergence is attributed to two very important factors: the lengthy
duration in man of childhood helplessness, and the Oedipus complex, whose
repression is connected with a period of sexual latency and, therefore, with the
diphasic onset of sexual life. The first factor is biological in nature, consisting
of what certain authors have called prematurity of birth, a specifically human
characteristic. Freud goes on to say that the second factor[93] is historical, cultural:
a heritage of the development made necessary by the glacial epoch. Thus, the
separation, in the ego, between the ego and a portion of itself constituting the ego
ideal (superego) is not an accidental event but the outcome of the development of
the individual and the species. Once again, we encounter Freud's relentless obsession with heritage, an obsession evident in his definition of the superego: "*the heir*

of the Oedipus complex". This is not the place to undertake a systematic study of the insistence with which Freud pursued the question throughout his self-analytic inquiry: the question of heritage, inheritance and heirs. But this fact is nevertheless noteworthy.[94]

The chapter ends with a discussion whose contentious character impels Freud to leave the strictly theoretical framework of metapsychological considerations and venture into the field of general anthropology.

By doing so, he intends to provide a resolute answer to those who reproach psychoanalysis with a lack of interest in the higher, more noble, supra-personal side of human nature.

It was when psychoanalytic research moved on to discuss abnormalities of the ego and no longer only the repressed elements in mental life that Freud focused his attention on the "higher nature" of man, apparent in the form and functions of the ego ideal, the superego. From the start, psychoanalysis recognised in the superego the outcome of a concrete relation: the Oedipal relation inherent to mankind. This higher nature can be attributed to the influence of our parents. As Freud puts it:

> When we were little children we knew these higher natures, we admired them and feared them; and later we took them into ourselves.
>
> The ego ideal is therefore the heir of the Oedipus complex, and thus it is also the expression of the most powerful impulses and most important libidinal vicissitudes of the id. By setting up this ego ideal, the ego has mastered the Oedipus complex and at the same time placed itself in subjection to the id. Whereas the ego is essentially the representative of the external world, of reality, the super-ego stands in contrast to it as the representative of the internal world, of the id. Conflicts between the ego and the ideal will, as we are now prepared to find, ultimately reflect the contrast between what is real and what is psychical, between the external world and the internal world.[95]

But this internal world represented by the ego ideal within the ego is the expression of the libidinal vicissitudes of the human species, re-experienced by the individual ego. The lowest part of the individual psychic history becomes what is highest in the human psyche thanks to the formation of the ego ideal. The ancestral roots of the ideal, its far-reaching genealogy, make it abundantly clear that the ego ideal cannot be localised in the psychic apparatus in the sense in which the ego or its relation with the id were localised.

Freud completes his demonstration by pointing out to the detractors of psychoanalysis the similarity of this ego ideal with the higher nature of man. These fundamental elements of man's higher nature are represented by religion, morality, a social sense, the sciences and art. Leaving aside the last two cultural forms, Freud tries to show the common origin of the first three. Once again, the predominant place in his thought of the hypotheses in *Totem and Taboo* is eminently clear.

In that work, Freud showed that it was thanks to the father-complex that these three elements of civilisation were acquired in the course of phylogenic evolution. Religion, morality and a social sense all originate in a victory won over the father-complex (understood here as the equivalent of the Oedipus complex). Indeed, religion is the "substitute for a longing for the father"; morality is the internalisation of his authority; and social feelings (sympathy, pity, solidarity) are substitutes for the hostility born of rivalry between brothers who all aspire to the father's prerogatives. Identification transforms this rivalry by means of the totemic feast when the same object is internalised by each individual ego as its libidinal goal. The original hostility is converted into a shared feeling of sympathy, solidarity and equality.

Remarks on the ideal agency

The extraordinary complexity of libidinal relations (object-cathexes and identifications) characteristic of the Oedipal constellation requires clarification. Now that we understand the complete structure of the Oedipus complex, rendered doubly triangular by bisexuality, we can elucidate certain hitherto obscure points. At the same time, this Oedipal complexity raises new questions and brings certain others into sharper focus. To clarify these questions, we must turn to the commentators we see as having most successfully laid the groundwork.

Possible or impossible distinction between ideal ego and ego ideal (superego)

Freud's readers are inevitably struck by the multitude of concepts he proposed to designate the agency of the ideal within the ego. In truth, this profusion leads to confusion.

In *On Narcissism: An Introduction*, Freud introduced the coupled terms *ideal ego (Ichideal)* and *ego ideal (Idealich)*, with a clear preference for the first. In fact, Freud often speaks simply of the ideal, or of formation of an ego ideal (*Idealbildung*). But the term *Idealich* no longer appears in the texts that follow. What matters is to note in the construction of these two German words the change of accent, which in one case is placed on *Ich* and in the other on *Ideal*. In the text we are discussing, Freud starts off by connecting repression to the ego, to the ego's self-esteem function; repression is the consequence of an ideal against which the subject measures his present ego. "For the ego, the formation of an ideal would be the conditioning factor of repression". And he adds: "This ideal ego is now the target of the self-love which was enjoyed in childhood by the actual ego. The subject's narcissism makes its appearance displaced on this new ideal ego".[96]

Thus, it is reasonable to say that the expression of the ideal ego emphasises this narcissistic dimension that the ideal inherited from original narcissism. The term *ego ideal* is introduced in particular following the conceptual formulation of the relation between formation of the ideal and sublimation. In idealisation, which concerns the libidinal object, the latter is magnified and psychically exalted without changing its nature. Idealisation is possible both in the sphere of ego libido and in that of object libido. Now the discussion shifts to the first libidinal objects, the parents.

> For what prompted the subject to form an ego ideal, on whose behalf his conscience acts as watchman, arose from the critical influence of his parents (conveyed to him by the medium of the voice), to whom were added, as time went on, those who trained and taught him and the innumerable and indefinable host of all the other people in his environment – his fellow men – and public opinion". Freud goes on to specify: "In this way large amounts of libido of an essentially homosexual kind are drawn into the formation of the narcissistic ego ideal.[97]

This last statement foreshadows the publication of *Mourning and Melancholia* and *On Metapsychology*.[98]

What is provided here is only a summary. Other analysts have studied these concepts in depth, always insisting on their differences, on the specificity of their use, on the particularity of each field involved. It must be kept in mind that Freud seemed to consider the confusion deliberate, or at least unproblematic. In his view, the major and decisive theoretical novelty was the formulation of an ideal agency, which explains the main forms of pathology (failed repression in the neuroses, injury to the ego and to the narcissistic ideal in the psychoses). Thus, Freud's successors undertook to comb through the texts mainly in view of systematising the concepts, for didactic or academic purposes.

But these efforts, whose aim was to clarify and classify, brought to light the problems raised by the psychoanalytic construction of the concept of the ideal. Our focus concerns these problems, rather than the different systems themselves. We rely on the definitions given by Jean Laplanche and J. B. Pontalis in *Vocabulaire de la psychanalyse* to summarise these different contributions.

Herman Nunberg was the first to attempt to use the paired concepts ideal ego/ego ideal as the foundation of two distinct psychic formations. He asserts that the ideal ego is chronologically and genetically anterior to the superego.

> The still unorganised ego, existing as if united to the id, corresponds to an ideal condition; this is why it is called *ideal ego*. The ego itself is probably the ideal of the small child, until it encounters the first opposition to the satisfaction of its needs.[99]

Nunberg compares this concept of ideal ego to the Freudian notion "purified-pleasure-ego" he describes as an "ideal condition in which the ego grants itself everything it desires and rejects everything that displeases it". This condition seems to coincide with original narcissism, a narcissism of omnipotence or "narcissism of the id".[100] The author goes on to say that in the course of development, an individual outgrows "this narcissistic ideal", but in truth, he always aspires to return to it. This is what happens most often in the psychoses but also in the neuroses. Thus, "each symptom contains the satisfaction of a positive or negative desire, which the patient uses to achieve omnipotence".[101]

We conclude from these observations that Nunberg considers the ideal ego to be an unconscious archaic formation, entirely narcissistic, not to be confused with the superego, which originates in identification – in other words, an external relation with something other than the self-sufficient id/ego. Thus, Nunberg posits an ego anterior to any identification. In *The Psychoanalytic Theory of Neurosis*, Otto Fenichel[102] agrees with Nunberg's view.

No doubt, Daniel Lagache formulated the most systematic theory of the internal differentiation of the ego. His presentation at the 1958 Royaumont colloquium, subsequently published in the article "Psychoanalysis and Personality Structure", offers a detailed and carefully structured explanation of this differentiation.[103] His objection to Nunberg's view is that the latter does not take into account the intersubjective context, particularly that of the mother-child relationship. Lagache maintains that there is primary identification with the mother through syncretic participation in her omnipotence. This identification is the source of all subsequent megalomaniacal dreams and "heroic identification". Similarly, the ideal ego, seen as a narcissistic ideal of omnipotence, is not merely fusion with the id, as Nunberg claims, but involves primary identification with another all-powerful being: in this case, the mother. Lagache argues that the primary conflict occasioned by the mother's opposition to persistent interference prefigures identification with the ideal ego or the superego.

This alternative corresponds to the essential distinction Lagache wants to introduce: the concept of two systems, that of the ideal superego and that of the ideal ego.

In parallel with primary identification with the mother, there is primary identification with the father, which opposes the subject to the father and not only in terms of rivalry for the possession of the mother. This identification with the father must be relinquished (this is where Lagache differs from Freud, who never speaks of renouncing this primary identification), causing a fundamental narcissistic wound, in order for secondary identification with the father to take place – an identification establishing the ideal superego of the Oedipal phase ego.

In Lagache's "personological model", the superego corresponds to authority and the ego ideal to the way in which the subject must behave in order to satisfy that authority's expectations. The ego must obey the superego by conforming to the ego ideal. In short, the ego ideal corresponds to the way in which the subject must behave so that the subject-ego identified with parental authority can approve of the object-ego.[104] As for the ideal ego, it is presented as an autonomous formation in relation to the superego/ego ideal system. Lagache considers this autonomy to be based on the clinical distinction between inferiority feelings and guilt feelings. Inferiority feelings denote the subject's dissatisfaction at failing to achieve his own ideal of narcissistic omnipotence; guilt feelings correspond to his unhappiness at not achieving his ego ideal, which, initially, reflected the expectations of others: namely, the parents and, specifically, the father. It is as if we were dealing with two codes or two value systems whose difference from each other depends on the person: the narcissistic code of the ideal ego (heroic) and the moral and social code of the superego/ego ideal.

Thus, Lagache considers that the most archaic forms of the ego originate in identification. The ideal ego is "intersubjective" from the start, and so are the subsequent formations of the superego/ego ideal. The ego bound to the id is, in reality, a mythical projection, nothingness. There is no ego, not even purely narcissistic, outside a primary relation to the other.

Jacques Lacan, whose earliest theories focused on the status of the *imago*, the imaginary and narcissism,[105] recognised from the first the originally imaginary – and therefore ideal – nature of the ego. Agreeing on this point with Lagache, on whose systematisation he commented directly, Lacan assigns a separate status to the ideal ego. Let us look at this paraphrase from *Remarks on Daniel Lagache*:

> By means of the ego-ideal, the subject wants to gain appreciation by the Other, who is the authority. The ideal ego, at the risk of displeasing the Other, only triumphs by feeling himself satisfactory.[106]

But for Lacan, the essential aspect of the distinction between the ego ideal and the ideal ego, beyond Lagache's didactic considerations, is the split of the symbolic and the imaginary. The relation to the Other, unavoidable even in a theory of narcissism, as Lagache emphasises, has two aspects: it is characterised by the double presence of narcissistic illusion, the radical misconstruction that *The Mirror Stage*[107] associates with the ego formation principle and with the desire of the Other, in the sphere of signifiers. The fundamental difference between Lacan and Lagache lies in their view of the function of intersubjectivity:

> For Lagache, intersubjectivity is defined in a relation to the other "like me", a symmetrical relation by definition, as shown by the fact that Daniel Lagache states that through the other the subject learns to treat himself like an object. For us [Lacan], the subject has to emerge from the trove of signifiers which represent him in an Other who is their transcendental place, in which the subject establishes himself in an existence which can include the primordial vector of the Freudian field of experience: that which is called desire.[108]

In this formation of a "subject" – a broader concept than "ego" – a distinction remains to be made between an identification which founds the ideal ego – a specular, imaginary or narcissistic identification – and a non-specular, symbolic identification founded not on a projection of omnipotence but on the introjection of a signifier. This symbolic identification, contrary to the first, does not create an imaginary wholeness, an unassailable space for the ego; instead, it establishes, through its relation to the signifier, the impossibility of a complete ego, the lack of an "ideal" representation of the self – in other words, castration and therefore a "subject of desire" (a lacking subject).[109]

In the wake of Lacan's thought, Piera Aulagnier's work on the question of identification also establishes a separation between the ideal ego and the superego, a separation corresponding to Lacan's distinction between imaginary and symbolic identification. She designates as ideal model, present throughout life, the image the ego presents of itself, which she considers to be both the cause and the effect of secondary narcissism: the narcissism of the ego distinct from the id. This ideal model looks in two directions, as it were: to the time when, as Freud says, it "conforms with its own narcissism" and to the ever-anticipated time of the projected return, always yet to come, of the original narcissism forever gone. Aulagnier insists on this essential trait pointed out by Freud in 1914, in his attempt to identify the origin of the ideal. This founding trait of the ideal is constituted of parental voice – therefore acoustic traces, words. Thus, the identification which renders the superego heir to the Oedipus complex is identification to signifiers, to statements about and addressed to the child "subject". We think it worthwhile to paraphrase here a portion of the seminar given by Piera Aulagnier on the theme of identification at the Sainte-Anne Hospital in Paris in 1967. In this presentation, the distinction between the ideal ego and the superego is illustrated through a highly revealing observation:

> Anyone who has been in the company of a small child, 2 or 3 years old, has had occasion to see self-reproach at work, and to observe how easily the child makes two opposing statements, with equal satisfaction: "me nice" and "me bad". This indicates that each time the child tries to define himself, he apparently does one of two things – either he projects himself in a narcissistic image (which brings us back to the specular ego) presented to the Other and then taken back from him to become his image of himself; – or he identifies with words he heard spoken about him, which throw doubt on the narcissistic image – "bad" constituting from the start a moral judgement – splitting the ego that judges the ego which is judged (subject-ego, object-ego).
>
> In the second case, the speaking subject recognises that he is divided off from the subject being spoken of. The "bad" self is not the subject who speaks, but the subject spoken of. The satisfaction derived from the second statement seems related to two different mechanisms. The first concerns the function of "no-saying", negativism as self-affirmation, as autonomy of the ego (the bad ego is the one which refuses to conform to the will of the other). In the second case, the subject offers himself up as pure echo of the Other's discourse, at the expense of a portion of his ego on which he makes a negative judgement. But although the source of satisfaction is different in each case, they are based on the same acquiescence to the will of the Other. For the subject to take pleasure in being bad, he first has to accept as "badness" the fact of being different from the image valued by the parents. Similarly,

the other statement, "me nice", illustrates what Freud described as an equivalence between the self-image narcissistically invested by the subject, and the image he supposes the Other to desire. But when we use this to illustrate the primordial specular image, we are also shedding light on the very nature of imaginary alienation and of splitting: – on the one hand, the specular ego only satisfies or fascinates the subject as a symbol emerging from the narcissistic field of the Other (desubjectivating); – on the other hand, when the image succeeds in creating libidinal desire, it is not because it takes over the already existing relation of the subject to the problem of the desire of the Other. Before the specular encounter, there was an initial introjection of a signifier of desire (as the original signifier of the encounter) on which the subject projects a "signified" that will serve as the imaginary corresponding element, to make sense of what the discovery of the object might have represented: omnipotence, negation of lack, found object, etc.

Thus, from the first, identification must take into account the primacy of the discourse of the Other, and of the irrefutable fact that the subject is above all a projection screen: that is, for the parents, the "heir" to their reborn narcissism which, despite its transformation into object-love, clearly displays its former nature.[110]

It seems that the ideal ego is to the eye what the ego ideal (superego) is to the voice. The visual and auditive fields comprising the ego seen as a perceptive apparatus are originally invested by narcissism: that of the child and, secondarily, that of the parents. These considerations allow us to grasp the inadequacy of a discourse on the ego which limits itself to a purely empirico-sensualist definition (perceptual-conscious ego) since the corporeal ego is indissociably perceptive and erogenous – "real" body representing the *Aussenwelt* (external world) in the psyche, and imaginary and symbolic body – a sphere of narcissistic investment and a nexus of meanings.

In Lacan's work, the prevailing structural concept is signifying identification: identification to the desire of the Other. Specular identification, which is identification to an image, is an illusory narcissistic formation, alienating and deceptive, which transforms the ego into a defence mechanism against the anxiety arising from the lack in the Other.[111]

To support this view, we turn to Moustapha Safouan and quote from an article which presents the fundamental hypotheses of Lacan's theory of the subject and, therefore, of identification:

What the analyst discovers – and what makes Freudian desire so much more open to mediation than Hegelian desire – is that all specular identifications with the ideal ego, when the subject captures one image after another, are dependent on another identification, repressed, symbolic and non specular, which constitutes the ego-ideal and which, in the process of interpretation, appear in the unconscious as a thought, a wish, ready to be expressed in common language, so much so that it might be said that in that instance desire *is* its interpretation.[112]

Safouan adds this remark in a footnote, to elucidate the ego ideal: "We consider specular identification (ideal ego) and symbolic identification (ego-ideal) to correspond respectively to projection and introjection in analytic doctrine".

Or, as Piera Aulagnier put it: "The imaginary is projected, the symbolic is introjected".[113]

Of course, such concise statements do not amount to an explanation. Our discussion on the ideal agency, at this point in our work, is aimed at defining "families" of concepts. Lacan's theory of the subject involves the formulation of concepts related to the symbolic, such as symbolic castration, the instituting of the symbolic order or the lack of this order.

In the present exploration of Freud's work, our intention is not to reconstruct the genesis of Lacan's identification theory. But we are not adverse to Lacan's views, on which we hope to shed light by determining their points of origin in Freud's work.

Questions of origin

Among the difficulties connected with Freud's concept of an ideal agency, one in particular confronted us on numerous occasions: what is the origin of the ego, and what is the place and the function of the ideal in its genesis?

We know that Freud indicated the origin of the ego to be a "psychic action" he left unspecified, which we can presume to be a primary form of repression. This passage in *On Narcissism: An Introduction* arouses our curiosity:

> I may point out that we are bound to suppose that a unity comparable to the ego cannot exist in the individual from the start; the ego has to be developed. The auto-erotic instincts, however, are there from the very first; so there must be something added to auto-erotism – a new psychic action – in order to bring about narcissism.[114]

While Freud later called "primary narcissism" (of the id) the original auto-erotic stage of instinctual functioning, it is clear that when he seeks the origin of narcissism, the latter is an attribute of the ego – what is involved is secondary narcissism. The emergence of this unity comparable to the ego marks the end of the auto-erotic stage and of primary narcissism, in which the ego functions like the id. In the German statement "*das Ich muß entwickelt werden*" ("the ego must undergo development"), the word *entwickelt* must be viewed etymologically, with special attention paid to the prefix *ent*, which indicates a violent separation. The ego as part of the id, as Freud describes it in the initial chapters of *The Ego and the Id*, must undergo the action that will produce a disconnection, a differentiation, a pulling apart separating the ego – which immediately constitutes a "unity" – from the id, where anarchic impulses arise in disorderly fashion.

The process introducing narcissism must also, subsequently, ensure its permanence, protect its domain and guarantee its unity against attacks of the id and its fragmenting influence. This process must have its source outside the id, which will be subjected to its operation; the process in question is one of primary repression, which separates and promotes an entity with its own libido: the narcissism of the ego.

The still-fragile ego, as long as it remains governed by the id while it tries to establish its initial hold on "reality" through its perceptual and motor apparatus, cannot form a unity on its own. The psychic action which creates it, although exterior to the primitive id-ego, must develop a degree of complicity with it. Primary repression must have "inside accomplices", as it were. Thus, the agent of repression is the ego, assisted by an ally "real" and "libidinal" at the same time. The only such decisive ally we can think of is "the father of personal prehistory". (This is where Lacan introduces his name-of-the-father concept.) This is a father taken from the start as the ideal that the little boy wants to become. Freud specifies that this father is taken hold of directly, through the identification process. Let us remember the exact phrasing: "A direct and immediate identification [which] takes place earlier than any object-cathexis" (primary identification), as well as "At the very beginning, in the individual's primitive oral stage, object-cathexis and identification are no doubt indistinguishable from each other". The second formulation makes it clear that there is no time when there is no object, by describing an originary mode of functioning in which the distinction between what one is and what one has does not exist. A distinction between object-cathexis and identification only starts to exist at the point, brought about by the theoretical need for a psychic founding myth – through an "original fantasy"[115] – where an "ego" whose major libidinal mechanism serves to preserve the objects of the id is identification (secondary, in this case), where an "ego" functions like an ego. Primary repression is a primary mode of relinquishing the auto-erotic mode of cathexis; it is identification of the ego, which presents it from the start as "being" the captive of another: the ideal father. (Freud's theory does not allow a distinction between the symbolic part and the imaginary part of this founding identificatory relationship.)

As we have seen, Freud states that the ego ideal, the superego, emerges in the wake of primary identification reinforced by secondary identifications. The latter are secondary to object-cathexes (towards the father and the mother) forced by the Oedipal conflict to change into identifications.

In order to be effective, the frequent secondary acts of repression that the ego will be forced to carry out, often for internal narcissistic reasons (not only for external "censoring", social or political reasons)[116] will demand the abandonment of the object (substitution for the object), either as object-libido or as ego-libido, thanks to identification with the "abandoned" object.

The question of the origin of repression – more precisely, of its "cause" or motivation – coincides to some extent with the question of the origin – instinctual and/or "real" – of the superego. Freud first examined this question very early, and soon after the publication of *The Ego and the Id*, he was prompted by Melanie Klein's work to rethink it.

Conceptually, "primary" repression and identification refer to two aspects of this process of releasing the ego from its collusion with the id. These two concepts designate this coming into being: repression underscores its energetic or dynamic aspect while identification stresses the personological aspect of the shaping of an identity, of an ego.[117]

Primary identification as appropriation of the ideal object, the father, acts to oppose auto-erotism while using its libidinal energy to create an ego. What ensures the unity of this ego is also what originally divides it: an ideal part responsible for primary repression and for all subsequent acts of repression – an auto-erotic, instinctual part. This is a desexualised part of the ego, subject to repression, governed by partial sexual impulses. The ego ideal, emerging from primary identification, is cathexed by ego libido; it is the heir to original narcissism. Keeping in mind that at the end of this passage on identification with the father of personal prehistory, Freud adds that, at the same time, the child develops an anaclitic attachment to the mother, we must conclude that the child originally forms, in one and the same process – since at this stage cathexis and identification are indistinguishable one from the other – a double psychic bond. Thus, the father and the mother are present from the start. If this is the case for the father as well, in what form can he be present – metaphorically – if not as the object of the mother's desire while being absent as a libidinal object? The enigmatic content of this primary identification, which constitutes the actual content of primary repression, of original repression, is the child's personal prehistory, beyond which there is "no one". If, during the oral phase, the father is taken possession of simultaneously with breast incorporation, we can imagine the significance and mystery of these parents between whom the being is constructed: the narcissism, the ego before it becomes an outright ego. Freud does not conduct a thematic examination of the status of this primordial repressed material. Because it constitutes what makes an auto-erotic being an individual, "one" – coherent, in other words, that which constitutes his difference – Lacanians regard this primary repressed material as a signifier, referring to the libidinal object of the mother: the phallus.[118] More traditional interpretations of Freud's texts have been unable, in our view, to elucidate in as rigorous a manner the status of identification and of primary repression.

The work of the ego, between life instinct and death instinct

Identification, sublimation, desexualisation

Let us finish reading *The Ego and the Id*. On the one hand, the text connects the new topographical organisation of the psyche (id, ego, superego) to Freud's dualistic conception of drives; on the other hand, it shows how, in the realm of psychodynamics, identification functions like a kind of "transformer" and constitutes the major psychic process located in the ego, performing its work under the triple domination of the id, the superego and reality.

We remember that in *The Ego and the Id*, Freud had stated:

> On the basis of theoretical considerations, supported by biology, we put forward the hypothesis of a death instinct, the task of which is to lead organic life back into the inanimate state; on the other hand, we supposed that Eros, by bringing about a more and more far-reaching combination of the particles into which living substance is dispersed, aims at complicating life and at the same time, of course, at preserving it. Acting in this way, both the instincts would be conservative in the strictest sense of the word, since both would be endeavouring to re-establish a state of things that was disturbed by the emergence of life. The emergence of life would thus be the cause of the continuance of life and also at the same time of the striving towards death; and life itself would be a conflict and compromise between these two trends.[119]

Construction and destruction: this double instinctual process appears to be at work in all the parts of living matter. Both instincts are active in the process, but they are unevenly mixed (*in ungleicher Mischung*).

Once we have established the possibility of an instinctual mixing, it becomes possible to imagine that there can also be more or less complete dissociation of the mixture (*Entmischung*).

A useful classical example of instinctual mixing is provided by the sadistic component of the sexual instinct. By contrast, sadism, as an independent perversion, would exemplify a very advanced instinctual dissociation. From this point of view, it is possible to observe varying degrees of instincts in different psychic disorders. For instance, severe types of obsessional neurosis, libidinal regression from the genital to the sadistic-anal stage, as well as the ambivalence so frequently seen in neurotics could be illustrations of more or less pronounced dissociation of mixed impulses or, when the ambivalence is constitutional, could indicate incomplete integration of the impulses.

A very common phenomenon can serve to connect the process of identification with this play of instinctual association-dissociation.

This phenomenon is the coexistence of love and hate. It is often the case that, surprisingly, hate accompanies love (this is ambivalence) or that hate precedes and announces love in human relations. In some circumstances, hate changes into love and love into hate. Freud foresaw these possibilities when building his metapsychological framework around 1915, when he wrote *Instincts and Their Vicissitudes*. At that time, his interpretation was not based on the duality of instincts we are examining now but, rather, on the theory of narcissism. Now, Freud is bringing into question the difficult-to-understand concept of direct impulse transformation, in order to propose the economic hypothesis of energy displacement.

His research in *Group Psychology and the Analysis of the Ego* revealed that the emergence of homosexuality and of desexualised social emotions is accompanied by highly aggressive feelings of rivalry which must disappear. This aggressiveness can be overcome if the hated object becomes an object of identification. Is this a direct transformation of hate into love, although the object's behaviour has not changed in any way? In truth, the transformation must be rooted in an internal change. The mechanism of paranoia might provide an explanation. We know that delusions of persecution are a defence against strong homosexual attachment to a person who is passionately loved, a person the paranoid process transforms into a persecutor showing dangerous aggressiveness. In such a case, we must suppose the existence of original ambiguity. Here, the ego represses homosexual love not through identification with this person but through the use of its opposite, a process of dis-identification of sorts: projection onto destructive components, through displacement of the energy previously connected, above all, with the erotic components of the "mixture". This would mean that hostile tendencies increase in intensity to the extent to which the intensity of erotic tendencies decreases.[120]

In the equivalent case of the transformation of rivalry into affection, into homosexual feelings, the same displacement of energy occurs but in the opposite direction with respect to the paranoid process. The impossibility of satisfying hostile tendencies due to group restraint promotes the emergence of feelings of love that can find actual satisfaction. The reasons for the transformation are presented as purely economic. The hypothesis of a displaced investment eliminates the need for direct transformation – whose means of occurring had not been explained – and also preserves the qualitative difference between the two types of impulses.

Therefore, it must be supposed that within the psychic apparatus, there is energy that can be displaced, which, exerting no effect on its own, can attach itself to the erotic or the destructive tendency and augment its effect.

Freud hypothesises that this energy which animates the ego and the id comes from a reservoir of narcissistic libido, a sort of desexualised Eros. Why Eros? Because clinical experience has shown the incredible plasticity of sexual drives ruled by the primary process, which allows all derivations and displacements obeying the pleasure principle, allowing the energy to be discharged. Destructive impulses do not seem to possess the same plasticity.[121]

The paths chosen to discharge energy matter little: erotic transference can be made onto any object, without any particular preference. Freud notes that this is obvious in the course of an analysis, where transferences take place no matter what, regardless of the person who becomes their object. The ego seems to be in charge of choosing the suitable objects and paths of discharge for this free-floating energy. The main objective of the ego is unity; for this reason, it adopts the aims of Eros, which serve to unify, to create ties. But the work of the ego, the work of unification, the fight against the fragmentation and stagnation caused by the death drive, is carried out essentially through the transformation of drives into desexualised, sublimated libido. The intellectual processes of the ego, reinforced by this sublimated energy, acquire the extraordinary unifying plasticity of the libido transferred to them. These considerations bring us back to the original definition of the concepts of identification, sublimation and desexualisation.

There is no doubt that they constitute the essential aspects of the work of the ego. Freud wrote:

> Here we arrive again at the possibility which has already been discussed that sublimation may take place regularly through the mediation of the ego. The other case will be recollected, in which the ego deals with the first object-cathexes of the id (and certainly with later ones too) by taking over the libido from them into itself and binding it to the alteration of the ego produced by means of identification. The transformation (of erotic libido) into ego-libido of course involves an abandonment of sexual aims, a desexualisation. . . . By thus getting hold of the libido from the object-cathexes, setting itself up as sole love-object, and desexualizing or sublimating the libido of the id, the ego is working in opposition to the purposes of Eros and placing itself at the service of the opposing instinctual impulses. It has to acquiesce in some of the other object-cathexes of the id; it has, so to speak, to participate in them.[122]

In this sphere fraught with contradictions, identification is the most compelling, urgent and vital activity of the ego. It maintains the paradoxical instinctual assumption consisting of safeguarding Eros while working against it. This task binds the ego irretrievably to the id. And we shall see that this great dependence is not the only one. But first, let us point out a consequence of this elucidation of the relations between the ego and the id for the theory of narcissism, a consequence which confirms our interpretations regarding the origins of the ego:

> At the very beginning, all the libido is accumulated in the id, while the ego is still in process of formation or is still feeble. The id sends part of this libido out into erotic object-cathexes, whereupon the ego, now grown stronger, tries to get hold of this object-libido and to force itself on the id as a love-object. *The narcissism of the ego is thus a secondary one, which has been withdrawn from object.*[123]

The subjections of the ego

The last chapter of this essay, which Freud intended as a synthesis closely based on clinical observations made in psychoanalysis, achieved its aim. In regard to identification theory, this chapter constitutes its completion. Questions previously raised in different contexts are brought together here. Those left in suspense are named, and the conceptual frameworks in which they can be formulated are defined. As a result, this chapter, bearing the apt title "The Ego's Dependent Relations", allows us to complete our own discussion. We shall show, when the time comes, how the theory of identification in *The Ego and the Id* serves as a model, in a manner of speaking, for the formulation of the last important questions dealt with in Freud's work.

In order to remain true to the synthetic perspective suggested by Freud, we shall summarise what the present research has been leading to. We believe that focusing on the concepts of guilt, anxiety and the difference between the sexes will allow us to define the essential points constituting the culmination of Freud's work.

THE EFFECTS OF AN UNCONSCIOUS SENSE OF GUILT

Reconnecting with the practice of analysis, Freud connected certain phenomena which had long been awaiting theoretical elaboration. These were the various and more or less serious manifestations of a puzzling unconscious sense of guilt.

The first of these manifestations occurred in the analysis of certain patients who, as the work progressed, and with it the hope of being cured, started to criticise the therapist and to offer growing resistance to the progress of the treatment. This "negative therapeutic reaction" indicated the action of a force opposing recovery, whose imminent arrival was perceived as a threat, as if the overt will to recover was unconsciously accompanied by a strong need, in the person involved, to remain attached to the symptom. The analytic work could only discern this element after breaking through the provocative attitude towards the therapist and overcoming narcissistic inaccessibility. What is at work here is a "moral" factor, as it were: a sense of guilt. This feeling finds fulfilment in the illness and causes refusal to give up suffering as a punishment. This feeling is not experienced consciously; the patient simply feels ill, and his resistance takes the form of the idea that the treatment does not suit him. The technical possibility of reversing such an obstacle is relatively slight. Analysis has no means of combatting it, particularly since it is not susceptible to any hypnotic influence or "soul-saving" attitude (*Seelenretter*). Freud observes that there is a chance to succeed in cases in which this unconscious feeling is borrowed: that is, results from identification with a person who was once the object of a forsaken love-relation. In such a case, this feeling is the only remnant – albeit barely recognisable – of the abandoned love-relation. The process is similar to what we see in melancholia, and the therapeutic work consists of bringing to light this old ambivalent erotic attachment. But the silent action of such a sense of guilt is no doubt at work in every neurosis.

"In fact, it may be precisely this element in the situation, the attitude of the ego ideal, that determines the severity of a neurotic illness".[124]

This hypothesis is confirmed in practice. The tension between the ego ideal and the ego produces normal guilt feelings (pangs of conscience). The torments which obsessional neurotics and melancholic patients with inferiority feelings inflict on themselves demonstrate the power, severity and cruelty of the ego ideal. But the difference between obsessional neurosis and melancholic psychosis is that in the first, the ego rebels against the sense of guilt, whose origin and purpose are unknown (as if the superego knew more than the ego about the intensity of repressed drives), and in the second, the ego accepts its own guilt and submits to punishment. In neurosis, the ego remains intact; in psychosis, the ego gives up, becomes dissociated and allows itself to be devoured by guilt. We have seen that this melancholic dissociation is the result of an identification that equates the ego with the primitive object of hostile and destructive impulses.

Guilt feelings originate in the drives that generate the Oedipus complex. Therefore, repression of the Oedipus complex is responsible for the unconscious nature of these feelings. Their intensity can be so great that they can turn a man into a criminal. One can be driven to crime out of a sense of guilt – when what we generally expect is that a sense of guilt will follow the crime. The role of the crime is to transfer unbearable, unconscious guilt feelings onto something real and immediate.[125]

All these phenomena demonstrate the autonomy of the superego in relation to the conscious ego, as well as the close ties of the superego to the unconscious id. These two traits of the ideal agency force us to ask what the origin (or origins) of the superego are. They seem to have two facets: one consisting of their differentiation from the ego and another consisting of their close proximity to the id.

> Having regard, now, to the importance we have ascribed to preconscious verbal residues in the ego, the question arises whether it can be the case that the super-ego, in so far as it is unconscious, consists in such word-presentations and, if it does not, what else it consists in. Our tentative answer will be that it is as impossible for the super-ego as for the ego to disclaim its origin from things heard; for it is part of the ego and remains accessible to consciousness by way of these word-presentations (concepts, abstractions). But the *cathectic energy* does not reach these contents of the super-ego from auditory perceptions (instruction or reading) but from sources in the id.[126]

Once again, we are brought back to questions of origin. Freud's answer here is relatively cautious, but his surprising insistence on the id is clear, when he says, for example, that the superego "is the heir to the Oedipus complex" or that the superego (ego ideal) cannot "disclaim its origin from things heard (from the parents)". Originating in the interiorisation of a parental power, in the powerful prohibitions whose severity is bolstered by the threat of castration, the superego also draws its cathectic power from the id. Its origin is therefore double: exterior and interior.

As we have glimpsed earlier in our discussion, the question of the double origin of the superego leads us to Melanie Klein's work. Relying on clinical observations of very young children, she was impelled to disagree with Freud's invariably Oedipus-centred concept of the superego. (Freud never ceased seeing the paternal agency as predominant in the construction of the superego.) Klein defended the hypothesis of an early-stage, pre-Oedipal superego, taking the mother as its object.[127]

Perhaps this debate about topographical definitions served to usher in further discussions among psychoanalytic theorists. The quote to which we referred earlier defines the superego either by emphasising the "things heard" (words, orders, prohibitions expressed verbally by the parents), a notion we feel corresponds to the "words presentation" concept put forth by Lacan and his disciples or by placing the accent on the effects of the instinctual, affective facet of cathectic or libidinal energy, as Melanie Klein did, and later André Green.[128]

Controversies often serve to reveal a theoretical indecision or tension. But as far as our own research topic is concerned, these unresolved contentious questions point to the complexity of the identification process itself, which is clearly the mechanism producing the superego. This is an intermediary process between the external world (parental agency, voices, society) and the internal world (instinctual investment, life drives, death drives, masochism, sadism); it is a process which transforms not only affect (therefore preventing or provoking the emergence of anxiety) but also representations (signifiers of parental prohibition which become conscience, self-criticism, self-blame). In its role as an agent of instinctual transformation, this process is a major mechanism of repression, desexualisation and sublimation. These multiple traits of identification make it difficult to formulate a coherent theoretical synthesis.

To remain close to the letter of Freud's text as he was elaborating the theory, we shall turn to the question of the severity of the sadism of the superego, which concludes *The Ego and the Id*, in order to reconcile the various theoretical disagreements to which we referred earlier.

SADISM OF THE SUPEREGO AND MASOCHISM OF THE EGO

Freud asks the following question:

> How is it that the super-ego manifests itself essentially as a sense of guilt (or rather, as criticism – for the sense of guilt is the perception in the ego answering to this criticism) and moreover develops such extraordinary harshness and severity towards the ego?[129]

The two illnesses involving the sense of guilt provide the material needed to answer this question. In melancholia, an extremely powerful and violent superego opposes a very vulnerable and fragile ego. This superego makes the conscience its ally, to attack the ego with incredible violence, as if making use of all the sadism available in the person concerned. Indeed, Freud recognised sadism to be the most obvious representative of the death drive. He can therefore conclude that what dominates in the melancholic's superego is this destructive component. He writes:

> What is now holding sway in the super-ego is, as it were, a pure culture of the death instinct, and in fact it often enough succeeds in driving the ego into death, if the latter does not fend off its tyrant in time by the change round into mania.[130]

Here, Freud says no more about the tyranny of the death instinct. He completes his explanation in a text dedicated to *The Economic Problem of Masochism*,[131] published a year later in 1924. Freud calls "morbid masochism" all morbid forms of invasion of the ego by an unconscious sense of guilt. He makes use of a significant detail to complete the explanation left in suspense: the fact that the super-ego's sadism is most often quite conscious, while the masochistic tendency is something of which the person remains unaware and must be inferred from his behaviour. The fact that moral masochism is unconscious gives rise to an obvious hypothesis:

> We are able to translate the expression 'unconscious sense of guilt' as meaning a need for punishment at the hands of a parental power. We now know that the wish, which so frequently appears in phantasies, to be beaten by the father stands very close to the other wish, to have a passive (feminine) sexual relation to him and is only a regressive distortion of it. If we insert this explanation into the content of moral masochism, its hidden meaning becomes clear to us. Conscience and morality have arisen through the overcoming, the desexualisation, of the Oedipus complex; but through moral masochism, morality becomes sexualised once more, the Oedipus complex is revived and the way is opened for a regression from morality to the Oedipus complex. . . .
>
> The turning back of sadism against the self regularly occurs where a cultural suppression of the instincts holds back a large part of the subject's destructive instinctual components from being exercised in life. We may suppose that this portion of the destruction instinct which has retreated appears in the ego as an intensification of masochism. The phenomena of conscience, however, leads us to infer that the destructiveness which returns from the external world is also taken up by the super-ego, without any such transformation, and increases its sadism against the ego. The sadism of the super-ego and the masochism of the ego supplement each other and unite to produce the same effects. It is only in this way, I think, that we can understand how the suppression of an instinct can – frequently or quite generally – result in a sense of guilt and how a person's conscience becomes more severe and more sensitive the more he refrains from aggression against others. . . .
>
> Thus moral masochism becomes a classic piece of evidence for the existence of fusion and instinct. Its danger lies in the fact that it originates from the death instinct and corresponds to the part of that instinct which has escaped being turned outwards as an instinct of destruction. But since, on the other hand, it has the significance of an erotic component, even the subject's destruction of himself cannot take place without libidinal satisfaction.[132]

What becomes even clearer in this 1924 article is the importance of the Oedipus, which propels the parental agency into the ego – the two parents, with their power, their severity, their tendency to supervise and to punish. The desexualisation of Oedipal instincts, brought about by the creation of the superego, has a dangerous consequence: the division of the instincts. This division causes increased severity and cruelty of these agencies which are no longer libidinal objects of the id or, to be more exact, which have stopped being objects of direct sexual drives – after the Oedipus phase, these drives are partly sublimated and partly inhibited in their aims, now transformed into "attachments of affection". But these persons also belong to the real, external world, from which they were drawn. They are bolstered by all past influences and by tradition, and their power illustrates reality – destiny – in the most tangible fashion.[133]

As for the other illness provoked by a sense of guilt, the illness of "morality" we call obsessional neurosis, it also includes the torments of melancholia. We have said that the difference consists of the fact that in obsessional neurosis, the ego is not destroyed by the cruelty of the superego because it fights against it as if it were something foreign (in truth, unconscious). Now, Freud points out another difference: the obsessional neurotic never goes as far as suicide; he is even more protected from it than the hysteric. What ensures this safety of the ego, as we have already seen, is the maintenance of object-cathexis. In other words, regression of ambivalence is not achieved through an identification that modifies the ego, as is the case in melancholia, but rather through reaction formations. It is regression to a sadistic-anal organisation that transforms libidinal impulses into aggressive impulses, unconscious and unknown to the ego. The ego does not take into itself the destructive impulses freed by repression: it resists them by means of defences, protective measures and reaction formations. As a result, the obsessional neurotic's ego finds itself trapped, caught in the middle, between a killer id and an accusatory and punitive superego. Since it can only prevent the most drastic effects of each, the ego ends up torturing itself indefinitely or, if possible, systematically torturing the object. This characteristic also differentiates the obsessional neurotic from the melancholic, in whom the entire intensity of the death drive focuses on the ego.

Let us come back again to the main consequence of the fact that the superego is constructed based on identification with a paternal model.[134]

Given that identification implies desexualisation or even sublimation, it must be associated with a dissociation of the instincts, with a break in the association of the instinctual drives of the id. Erotic elements, transformed by the identification process into narcissistic investments – ego libido – can no longer inactivate the destructive elements to which they were originally linked.

It appears that the duplicity of the superego – this ferocious and obscene agency which issues the commands "be like him" and "don't be like him" at the same time – is founded on this dissociation of Eros and on the destruction inherent in primordial investment in the father (in the parents). Kant's categorical imperative carries its entire charge of aggression in his transcendental "you ought".[135]

The following statement illustrates clearly Freud's position at this point:

Clearly the repression of the Oedipus complex was no easy task. The child's parents, and especially his father, was perceived as the obstacle to a realization of his Oedipus wishes; so his infantile ego fortified itself for the carrying out of the repression by erecting this same obstacle within itself. It borrowed strength to do this, so to speak, from the father, and this loan was an extraordinarily momentous act. *The super-ego retains the character of the father,* while the more powerful the Oedipus complex was and the more rapidly it succumbed to repression (under the influence of authority, religious teaching, schooling and reading), the stricter will be the domination of the super-ego over the ego later on – in the form of conscience or perhaps of an unconscious sense of guilt.[136]

Here, the severity of the superego seems to originate from the severity of the "real" father. Although there is reference to a "powerful" Oedipus complex, – and therefore to its strong instinctual investment – Freud stresses the link between the character of the superego and the character of the father.

It is to this link that Melanie Klein would object. As early as 1919, her theoretical work, which defines the principles of her analytic interactions with children,[137] clearly reveals the themes that were to be her major focus, those related to the earliest conflicts and the anxiety they create. At the 1924 Salzburg conference on the analysis of young children, her views on early childhood anxieties openly opposed those of Anna Freud. But it was her 1928 essay *Early Stages of the Oedipus Conflict* which contradicted Freud's ideas on the origin of the superego and, specifically, on its severity. Later contributions reinforced her position; among them were *The Early Development of Conscience in the Child* (1933), *A Contribution to the Psychogenesis of Manic-Depressive States* (1934) and *Mourning and Its Relation to Manic-Depressive States* (1940), which show her work to be in keeping with that of her teacher, Karl Abraham, as well as *The Oedipus Complex in the Light of Early Anxieties* (1945).

Let us illustrate by quoting a revealing passage from the insightful 1928 essay *Early Stages of the Oedipus Conflict*:

The analysis of little children reveals the *structure of the super-ego as built up of identifications dating from very different periods and strata in the mental life.* These identifications are surprisingly contradictory in character, over-indulgence and excessive severity existing side by side. We find in them, too, an explanation of the severity of the super-ego, which comes out specially plainly in these infant analyses. It does not seem clear why a child of, say, four years old should set up in his mind an unreal, phantastic image of parents who devour, cut and bite. But it is clear why in a child of about one year old the anxiety caused by the beginning of the Oedipus conflict takes the form of a dread of being devoured and destroyed. The child himself desires to destroy the libidinal object by biting, devouring and cutting it, which leads to anxiety, since awakening of the Oedipus tendencies is followed by introjection of the object, which then becomes one from which punishment is to be expected. This child then dreads a punishment corresponding to the offence: the super-ego becomes something which bites, devours and cuts. *The connection between the formation of the super-ego and pregenital phases of development* is very important from two points of view. On the one hand, the sense of guilt attaches itself to the oral and anal-sadistic phases, which as yet predominate; and on the other, the super-ego comes into being while these phases are in the ascent, which accounts for its sadistic severity. . . . Since the Oedipus tendencies are at first chiefly expressed in the form of oral and anal impulses, the question of which fixations will predominate in the Oedipus development will be mainly determined by the degree of repression which takes place at this early stage. Another reason why the direct connection between the pregenital phase of development and the sense of guilt is so important is that the oral and anal frustrations, which are the prototypes of all later frustrations in life, at the same time signify punishment and give rise to anxiety. This circumstance makes the frustration more acutely felt, and this bitterness contributes largely to the hardships of all subsequent frustrations.[138]

This essay condenses a number of original hypotheses that the author was going to develop continually and in greater and greater detail in her work. But we know, just by reading this first essay, that Melanie Klein's aim was to get a firm hold on a question Freud left unclarified, at the mercy of hypothetical fluctuations: the content of the first identifications. In her brilliant contributions, Melanie Klein undertook the meticulous analysis and careful critique of these different "layers" of early identification, so surprisingly contradictory. She is undoubtedly one of the few authors who stayed as close as possible to the question of the death drive strongly defended by Freud and who pursued, even more consistently than he did, the implications of this strange and disquieting discovery.

As far as the severity of the superego is concerned, Melanie Klein relates it essentially to the severity of the child's sadistic oral and anal impulses. The introjected object keeps the whole destructive charge it contains and works constantly at mounting ruthless criticism of the ego. Contrary to Freud, in Klein's view, the severity of the superego does not directly reflect that of the "frustrating" parents or of the father but, rather, the literally unbelievable power of the death drive characteristic of all very young children. Thus, a sense of guilt is produced through a mechanism more complex than the mere interiorisation of the aggressor – which reflects Anna Freud's position, attacked by Melanie Klein at the Symposium on Child Analysis, held in London in 1927.[139] Klein's reference to Little Hansin her presentation at the symposium showed clearly that the horse was a figure serving as a forerunner of an ideal agency: namely, the superego. The meanness and dangerousness of this horse and the great anxiety it arouses in the child are not related to his parents; they, and particularly the father, show surprising good will and a touching and unshakable – even naïve – understanding, based on Freud's ideas. Melanie Klein contributes other analytic material, especially cases much more serious than that of Little Hans; she shows that the father the child internalises is not the real father, who forbids and who deprives him of the mother, but rather a

phantasmatic "father-imago"[140] on which the child's destructive instincts are projected. Thus, Oedipal figures are narcissistic doubles, the personifications of the
little Oedipus's own very early instincts.[141]

Despite the outlandish fact that Melanie Klein was opposing his own daughter,
Freud could not help paying attention to the ideas of this analyst who appeared
more "loyal" to the fundamental doctrine of psychoanalysis than her rival, the
daughter he had trained himself. A brief note in *Civilisation and Its Discontents*
attests to the fact that Freud took into account Klein's objections and to the quan-
dary they created for this staunch defender of the "father complex".

This comment is part of Freud's discussion, in Chapters VII and VIII of this text
written in 1929, regarding his concept of unconscious sense of guilt and human
guilt in general as a dominant factor in the "discontent" produced by civilisation.
Freud's discussion is full of detours, advances and retreats, as if he was trying
to reconcile his "paternal" hypothesis with Melanie Klein's instinctual theory of
guilt. To illustrate, we refer the reader to these passages:

> [C]onscience (or more correctly, the anxiety which later becomes con-
> science) is indeed the cause of instinctual renunciation to begin with, but. . .
> later the relationship is reversed. Every renunciation of instinct now becomes
> a dynamic source of conscience and every fresh renunciation increases the
> latter's severity and intolerance. . . . [C]onscience is the result of instinctual
> renunciation, or. . . instinctual renunciation (imposed on us from without)
> creates conscience, which then demands further instinctual renunciation.[142]

Freud then takes the aggressive instinct and its renunciation as an example:

> The effect of instinctual renunciation on the conscience then is that every
> piece of aggression whose satisfaction the subject gives up is taken over by
> the super-ego and increases the latter's aggressiveness (against the ego). . . .
> A considerable amount of aggressiveness must be developed in the child
> against the authority which prevents him from having his first, but none the
> less his most important, satisfactions, whatever the kind of instinctual dep-
> rivation that is demanded of him may be; but he is obliged to renounce the
> satisfaction of this revengeful aggressiveness. He finds his way out of this
> economically difficult situation with the help of familiar mechanisms. By
> means of identification he takes the unattackable authority into himself. The
> authority now turns into his super-ego.[143]

Instinctual renunciation is primarily motivated by anxiety in the face of aggression coming from the external authority; this anxiety is founded essentially on the
fear of losing love, because love protects against the aggression which translates
into punishment. Anxiety in relation to authority, caused not only by the severity of the latter but also, above all, by the intensity of the aggressive impulses, is
transformed through identification into anxiety in relation to an internal authority,

into moral anxiety. Thus, the relationship between the ego and the superego duplicates an original relation and aggressive tension.

But, this being so, which view should prevail? Or how should the two views be reconciled? Freud continues his questioning:

> Which of these two views is correct? The earlier one, which genetically seemed so unassailable, or the newer one, which rounds off the theory in such a welcome fashion? Clearly, and by the evidence, too, of direct observations, both are justified. They do not contradict each other, and they even coincide at one point, for the child's revengeful aggressiveness will be in part determined by the amount of punitive aggression which he expects from his father. Experience shows, however, that the severity of the super-ego which a child develops in no way corresponds to the severity of treatment which he has himself met with.[144]

Freud adds a brief comment: "as has rightly been emphasized by Melanie Klein and by other English writers".

Still, he does not abandon the hypothesis he proposed in *Totem and Taboo*. The sense of guilt originates in the Oedipus complex, the murder of the father by the brothers united against him. This aggression was not suppressed but actually enacted. Yet the same aggressiveness, not acted out in reality but only wished for, produces the same sense of guilt in the child.

Remorse, which follows the murder, originates in the primitive ambivalence of feelings towards the father. It is the love component of this instinctual "mixture" which changes, through identification, into an ego ideal, but identification results in the division, the dissociation of the original ambivalence. The aggressiveness, the sadism, now turns against the ego. In a manner of speaking, indestructible love for the father grants the superego the right and the power previously held by him to punish the act of aggression carried out against him; this love creates the obstacle intended to prevent the aggression from being repeated. In each generation, the sense of guilt persists and is reinforced by being transferred to the superego of the energy inherent to each new, suppressed aggression.

These developments lead Freud to the following conclusion:

> Now, I think, we can at least grasp two things perfectly clearly: the part played by love in the origin of conscience and the fatal inevitability of the sense of guilt. Whether one has killed one's father or has abstained from doing so is not really the decisive thing. One is bound to feel guilty in either case, for the sense of guilt is an expression of the conflict due to ambivalence, of the eternal struggle between Eros and the instinct of destruction or death.[145]

These lines show the extent to which Freud is willing to take Melanie Klein's views into consideration. But we can also see that he does not abandon his Oedipus theory, with its key concept of the father. In his subsequent writings, he never ceased to go back and forth between the two theories, until the end of his life.[146]

But what Freud strangely does not take into account in Klein's theories based on clinical experience is the importance of the central relation to the mother, whose "castrating", frustrating and prohibiting function must arouse strong vengeful feelings – and consequently, the extent to which maternal identifications contribute to the creation of the pre-Oedipal superego of the child. We believe that this peculiar oversight explains Freud's failure to advance a precise formulation of feminine sexuality.

Let us now set aside the disagreements between Freud and Melanie Klein and consider once again Freud's conclusions regarding the opposition between the ego and the superego in *The Ego and the Id*. The discussion centres around the sadism shown by the superego towards the ego, suggested by the melancholic's suicidal tendencies. Freud undertakes a kind of comparison of the probabilities of suicide in melancholia, obsessional neurosis and hysteria. This question of the death of the ego, real or symbolic, was to find another form of expression a few years later, when Freud would focus his attention on epilepsy.

In his 1928 article *Dostoevsky and Parricide*, which was to serve as a preface to the German edition of the complete works of the Russian writer, Freud reiterates and develops the idea that the need for punishment reproduces an Oedipal scene transposed in the ego into a sado-masochistic scenario. For our purposes, we intend to look at the portions of this text which contribute directly to the perspective we opened in this last chapter on the relation of identification with the superego's sadism and the ego's masochism.

Freud interprets Dostoevsky's epileptic or epileptiform seizures as a young man[147] as "*death-like attacks*". Their meaning and intention are those of an identification with a death, of a person already deceased or whose death is intensely wished for. The attack serves as a punishment. One has wished for the death of another – who, psychoanalytically, is in principle the father, at least for the boy – but now one is this other person who was the target of the death wish and is dead oneself. Thus, the epileptic seizure is the equivalent of a hysterical attack. This uniquely Freudian conception brings epilepsy out of the isolation in which neuropsychiatry[148] had enclosed it. The seizure serves as self-punishment for the death wish targeting the hated father. Biographical evidence Freud takes to be reliable[149] testifies to young Fiodor's hatred of his father and to the exceptional cruelty of the latter. All this fits in perfectly with the hypothesis that the superego's cruelty reflects that of the father. This is how Freud sums up this aspect of the Dostoevsky "case":

His early symptoms of death-like attacks can thus be understood as a father-identification on the part of his ego, which is permitted by his super-ego as a punishment. "You wanted to kill your father in order to be your father yourself. Now you *are* your father, but a dead father" – the regular mechanism of hysterical symptoms. And further: "Now your father is killing *you*." For the ego the death symptom is a satisfaction in phantasy of the masculine wish and at the same time a masochistic satisfaction; for the super-ego it is a punitive satisfaction – that is, a sadistic satisfaction. Both of them, the ego and the super-ego, carry on the role of father.

To sum up, the relation between the subject and his father-object, while retaining its content, has been transformed into a relation between the ego and the super-ego – a new setting on a fresh stage.[150]

An old scene, set in reality (like the murder of the father by the primitive horde) has been transferred into the psychic setting, with the punitive superego playing the role of the threatening father and the masochistic ego that of the threatened father. Of all the dependencies of the ego, the most striking, clinically, is the ego's dependency on the superego. The possibility of suicide clearly shows the extreme intensity of the tension that can oppose the ego to the superego. The suffering inflicted on the ego by the aggression of the superego can lead to death: real death in melancholic suicide or psychic death, "absence", in the epileptic seizure.

CASTRATION ANXIETY AND SUPEREGO FORMATION

Anxiety: between ego and superego

The question left in suspense, or barely mentioned, in the development of the discussion of an ideal agency and its "primary" and "secondary" origins is the determination of what actually brings about the repression of the Oedipus complex.

Of course, the nature of this imperative started to become clear to us long ago: since the analysis of Little Hans and the Wolf Man, the Schreber case and the "totemism" present in every neurosis. The threat of castration causes the rebellion of "narcissistic virility" and represses threatening desires (masturbation, passive desire and feminine attitude in relation to the father, desire to be transformed into a woman, desire to possess the mother). These desires are met with real or imagined threats of castration, proffered mainly by the father buy also by the mother or the governess. The last paragraphs of *The Ego and the Id* set out these clinical observations and the theoretical framework developed in Freud's third topographical model. The theory strives to articulate the threat – and the anxiety – of castration, the means of repression, the differentiated structure of the ego, the dualism of Eros and of the death drive. The work of describing this detailed elaboration has been accomplished in large part by Michel de Wolf in *La castration dans l'œuvre et l'expérience freudiennes* and by Jean Laplanche in *La castration, ses précurseurs et son destin*.[151]

Our present purpose is not to describe the path Freud followed in his research on anxiety and castration but only to show how identification theory is connected to these concepts.

In our view, Freud never developed the concept of identification beyond what was discussed in *The Ego and the Id*. However, this text enumerates the difficulties and aporias to which this concept gives rise. We have seen that Oedipal identifications provide the child with a means of repressing the Oedipus complex. If this repression were completely successful, we could imagine that there would be no further manifestation of the Oedipus complex in ensuing years. But neuroses, psychoses and perversions, each in their own way, reveal the relative or complete failure of the work of identification undertaken by the child in order to free himself from the Oedipus complex. It appears that identification must be associated not only with economic advantages but also with disadvantages. Oedipal identifications do not bring anything to an end but start a personal history in which hang suspended all the reminiscences of a very problematic "prehistory". Moreover, these identifications do not replace attachment to the parents, whose love and protection the child continues to seek. Our task, then, is to elucidate the fate of these identifications.

To that purpose, let us look at the end of Freud's essay. In it, he refers to the ego as a "poor creature" subjected to triple servitude: to the external world, to the libido of the id and to the superego. This triple servitude corresponds to a triple threat and, consequently, to three types of danger that it must confront as best it can. If anxiety can be defined roughly as the expression of a retreat (*Rückzug*) from danger, the ego, the creature that senses such danger, can rightfully be called the frontier of anxiety.[152]

As for its relation to the id and the external world, the task of the ego is to mediate between them, to adjust the id to the world and the world to the id. To accomplish this, it offers itself, with its experience of the external world, as a libidinal object to the id and tries to attach the id's libido to itself. The identification process is the main method used by the ego in this "fraudulent" operation. But the ego's behaviour towards the two classes of instincts is not impartial:

> Through its work of identification and sublimation it gives the death instincts in the id assistance in gaining control over the libido, but in so doing it runs the risk of becoming the object of the death instincts and of itself perishing. In order to be able to help in this way it has had itself to become filled with libido; it thus itself becomes the representative of Eros and henceforward desires to live and to be loved.
>
> But since the ego's work of sublimation results in a defusion of the instincts and a liberation of the aggressive instincts in the super-ego, its struggle against the libido exposes it to the danger of maltreatment and death.[153]

This is the most harmful effect of the dependence on the id that the ego must fight against while preserving its libido. Strangely, the struggle against the id provokes violent attacks from the superego. Why make all this effort? What need is there to fight the id? What is the even greater threat that the ego is trying to avoid?

The dreaded danger from the external world or the id is servitude or annihilation, to which the pleasure principle governing the ego is violently opposed. As for the danger hiding behind the ego's dread of the superego, psychoanalysis provides a more precise answer: because the superego has replaced the superior being who once threatened castration, all forms of anxiety in relation to the superego can be traced back to castration anxiety, whose by-products they are; this applies to conscience, moral qualms, guilt feelings.

The fear of death, particularly evident in melancholia, can also be seen as springing from castration anxiety. Here, the ego relinquishes a large part of its libidinal cathexis; it sacrifices itself because it feels hated or persecuted, instead of being loved by the superego. Indeed, it must be kept in mind that the superego has taken over not only the prohibitive and rule-making authority of the father but also his protective, providential function. A particularly serious real danger which the ego cannot surmount alone provokes a reaction similar to the melancholic's fear of death: the ego gives in and lets itself die, feeling abandoned by all protective forces (parents, providence or destiny). It is possible that the first great anxiety is that felt by the infant at birth: Otto Rank considered birth trauma the prototype of all subsequent forms of anxiety.[154] Freud's conclusion is that in infancy, there is anxiety of longing (*Sehnsucht-Angst*) due to separation from the mother.

Thus, the fear of death, the fear of conscience and neurotic libidinal anxiety can all be located in the relation between the ego and the superego.

The Ego and the Id ends with this discussion of anxiety. Freud continued to develop this concept, despite the hesitations, uncertainties and detours which persisted in his work until the end. Establishing a metaphysical theory of anxiety proved to be an almost unsurmountable task.

But what interests us here is castration anxiety. This is the son's fear of the father, fear in the face of a terrible narcissistic threat. It triggers the ego's "work of identification and sublimation", which transforms multiple Oedipal object cathexes into a substitute, functioning like a powerful reaction formation: the superego. This mechanism, which put an end to the Oedipus complex, required further explanation. Freud began this work in 1923, shortly after *The Ego and the Id* was published, in an article placing the phallus, and therefore castration, at the centre of Oedipal organisation: "The Infantile Genital Organization".[155] Then, in 1924, he discussed "The Dissolution of the Oedipus Complex", in which he raised the question of the difference of this complex in the boy and in the girl.[156]

Castration and sexual identity (difference)

We shall limit ourselves to discussing some passages in these two essays which take psychoanalysis into the most problematic – and most delicate – segment of its journey: the development of a theory of sexual differentiation.

The first essay, "The Infantile Genital Organization", must be placed in the context of the theory of sexuality. It contributes a decisive element to the theory of identification. Since the arguments presented in *The Ego and the Id*, the term *identification* must be understood in its strongest, most etymological sense. Identification, a highly important drive-development process, is the name given by psychoanalysis to what present-day anthropology and "philosophy" call the "constitution of the subject". Indeed, it is primary identification governing the formation and shaping of the ego; at the same time, it is secondary identification which creates a fold in the weave of the ego – we might even say a tear – constituted by the ego ideal or superego. As we have suspected for some time, for Freud, the formation of an "identity" refers almost exclusively to the sexual identity of a sexual "character" – the Oedipus complex – or, better yet, its repression, which reinforces the sexual position of the child. The question we have been trying to answer from the start is to whom, to what, the child identifies to become "identifiable", to become "himself": is it to the father, to the mother, to their relationship, to a "trait"? The text that introduces the concept of a phallic stage into the general theory of sexuality provides an important element to the development of this theory. What the child seeks, through his persistent "researches", through his insatiable curiosity about his body, his origin, his future and his desire, is his identity.

> [T]he main characteristic of this "infantile genital organization" is its difference from the genital organization of the adult. This consists in the fact that, for both sexes, only one genital, namely the male one, comes into account. What is present, therefore, is not a primary of the genital, but a primary of the phallus.[157]

The little boy perceives this difference between men and women, but he does not yet connect it with a difference between their genitals. He naturally supposes the male organ to be present in every living being and even looks for something resembling his own penis in inanimate objects. This part of the body, which is so exciting, so changeable and so full of sensations interests him greatly and constantly assigns new tasks to his urge to investigate. Freud goes so far as to say that this pressing need to investigate, this overwhelming sexual curiosity, is what brings to light the importance of the male organ at that stage. The boy's initial reaction to the lack of a penis in little girls is denial; he continues to believe he still sees one, despite everything. The little boy covers over this contradiction between his perception and his "belief" and draws a conclusion charged with enormous affective consequences: there was a penis there before, and it's not there now because it was removed. Thus, he sees the lack of a penis as the result of castration; henceforth, the child must face the relationship to castration as it concerns his own person.

And Freud concludes:

> But it seems to me that the significance of the castration complex can only be rightly appreciated if its origin in the phase of phallic primary is also take into account.[158]

Castration is seen as the result of punishment for blameworthy desires and practices. But, Freud points out, respectable women like the girl's mother "retain a penis for a long time". We believe that the note Freud added here refers to a case he mentioned in a note in *The Ego and the Id*, the well-known note in which he speaks of identification "with the parents" rather than with "the father of personal prehistory". The two notes in question are quoted here:

> I learned from the analysis of a young married woman who had no father but several aunts that she clung, until quite far on in the latency period, to the belief that her mother and her aunts had a penis. One of her aunts, however, was feeble-minded; and she regarded this aunt as castrated, as she felt herself to be.[159]

This note brings to mind a previous one, as we have said:

> I recently came across the instance of a young married woman whose story showed that, after noticing the lack of a penis in herself, she had supposed it to be absent not in all women, but only in those whom she regarded as inferior, and had still supposed that her mother possessed one.[160]

It is only at puberty, when sexual development is complete, that this initial opposition, "phallic or castrated", is replaced with another, in which the sexual polarity becomes "male and female". But here, too, the primacy of the phallus is maintained:

> Maleness combines [the factors of] subject, activity and possession of the penis; femaleness takes over [those of] object and passivity. The vagina is now valued as a place of shelter for the penis; it enters into the heritage of the womb.[161]

The second essay ties this discovery of the primacy of the phallus to castration as the foundation of sexual identity, as well as to repression, to the dissolution of the Oedipus complex. Freud starts by reminding the reader that this infantile genital organisation does not continue its development in this infantile form until a definitive genital organisation is reached at puberty; instead, it is buried and abandoned during a latency period. But what finally causes the abandonment of the phallic stage and, with it, the abolition of the Oedipus complex? What provokes this destruction? Freud comes to the following conclusion: "These connections justify the statement that the destruction of the Oedipus complex is brought about by the threat of castration".[162]

This threat only acquires all its force after a series of experiences, observations and repeated reasoning, all very trying because, although the child has noticed the absence of a penis, he did not at first believe it. The discovery of the female sexual organ has given real form to threats he might have received as a result of his masturbatory practices. Thus, the effect of these threats is deferred. But the threat of castration does more than put an end to such practices since the child's sexual life at this stage consists of an Oedipal attitude towards his parents. Masturbation serves to discharge the sexual excitement produced by these Oedipal relations. The "complete" Oedipus complex provides the child with two possibilities of satisfaction: one active and one passive. He can, in a masculine mode, put himself in the place of the father and, like him, desire a relationship with the mother; in this scenario, the father becomes an obstacle. Or the child can replace the mother in order to be loved by the father, as she is. In this scenario, the mother becomes superfluous. But the little boy has only a very vague idea of what such a relationship might be, although he suspects that the penis must play a role in it.

It is the recognition and acceptance of the possibility of castration, which destroys the phallic illusion, that renders this double possibility of Oedipal satisfaction unattainable.

> If the satisfaction of love in the field of the Oedipus complex is to cost the child his penis, a conflict is bound to arise between his narcissistic interest in that part of his body and the libidinal cathexis of his parental objects.[163]

If the narcissistic interest wins out, the child turns away from the Oedipus complex. This is the "normal" course of events. The question is, however, to what extent the child really turns "away" from this complex. If we give total credence to the theory developed in *The Ego and the Id*, crossed identification with the parents enables the child to abandon his object-cathexes by reinforcing sexual character. Freud writes:

> The authority of the father or the parents is introjected into the ego, and there it forms the nucleus of the super-ego, which takes over the severity of the father and perpetuates his prohibition against incest, and so secures the ego from the return of the libidinal object-cathexis. The libidinal trends belonging to the Oedipus complex are in part desexualized and sublimated (a thing which probably happens with every transformation into an identification) and in part inhibited in their aim and changed into impulses of affection. The whole process has, on the one hand, preserved the genital organ – has averted the danger of its loss – and, on the other, has paralysed it – has removed its function.[164]

Paralysis and removal of function: the phallus is "relieved" of its organising function in the instinctual Oedipal field. It has been replaced by a system of identifications, thereby saving the narcissism attached to this organ and increasing the narcissistic capital of the ego, which acquires an additional, ideal organ, an internal symbolic phallus, the core of the superego. Henceforth, the superego will become as indispensable as the penis he did not want to lose, for the same narcissistic reasons. The phallic organ, the place of masturbation and the organiser of Oedipal seduction phantasies, becomes the object of an identification serving to reinforce narcissism: a psychic phallus.

The question that arises is the following: is this process one of repression – taking place without the help of the superego since the latter is only just being formed – while all subsequent repression will occur with its assistance? Or is this a different process? Freud answers:

> But the process we have described is more than a repression. It is equivalent if it is ideally carried out, to a destruction and an abolition of the complex. We may plausibly assume that we have here come upon the borderline – never a very sharply drawn one – between the normal and the pathological. If the ego has in fact not achieved much more than a repression of the complex, the latter persists in an unconscious state in the id and will later manifest its pathogenic effect.[165]

These considerations lead to a whole series of speculations as to whether a psychic process can really "dissolve" instinctual demands. This surprising idea clashes directly with another very early precept of psychoanalysis: namely, that infantile wishes are indestructible.

Whatever we may make of this astonishing idea of Freud's, he was forced to return to the question of what brings about the repression of the Oedipus complex, a process only described thus far in reference to the male child. But how does this process take place in the little girl?

Freud goes on to say that the female sex, too, develops an Oedipus complex, a superego and a latency period, and – despite the feminists' objections – even a phallic organisation and a castration complex. And castration anxiety is what brings about the formation of the superego and the dismantling of infantile sexual organisation. If we cast doubt on the existence of this anxiety in the girl – with reason, since she no longer has to fear castration, which she supposes to have occurred in the past – how can we explain the formation of her superego? These questions do not require a revision of the identification concept, the process which transforms Oedipal-stage object-choice seen in all children, but require us to define a special motive, different from that of the boy, explaining the repression of the Oedipus complex.

The solution presented in this essay is not really satisfactory:

> Once has an impression that the Oedipus complex is then gradually given up because this wish [to receive a baby from her father as a gift] is never fulfilled.

The important 1925 essay *Some Psychical Consequences of the Anatomical Distinction Between the Sexes* discusses this question directly, placing it in the overall context of developmental differences between boys and girls. The central idea of the essay is expressed by borrowing a saying by Napoleon: "Anatomy is destiny".[166] What is beginning to take shape here, and will be more and more clearly defined later, particularly in *Female Sexuality* (1931) and in the 33rd lecture of *New Introductory Lectures on Psycho-Analysis*, entitled "Femininity" (1933), is an examination of the primordial relation of the girl with her mother and of the conditions for relinquishing this object-cathexis. In this economy, castration is situated before the Oedipus complex: recognition of the mother's, and her own, castration produces this complex in the girl. Her father becomes the sexual object; she develops a feminine attitude towards him and wishes to receive a child from him. When this attitude towards the father is abandoned, given the need to turn away from the Oedipus, it is possible that identification with the father reawakens the old phallic demand and produces a masculinity complex[167] or the springboard of homosexuality.[168]

What remains very mysterious is the following comment made by Freud in *Some Psychical Consequences of the Anatomical Distinction Between the Sexes*:

> I cannot evade the notion (though I hesitate to give it expression) that for women the level of what is ethically normal is different from what it is in men. Their super-ego is never so inexorable, so impersonal, so independent of its emotional origins as we require it to be in men.[169]

We might think that in Freud's logic, as we have seen it at work until now, the lesser severity of the feminine superego is to be attributed to the fact that the little girl is not subjected to the terrifying threat the castrating father represents for the boy. Of course, the mother is also "castrating", but what she takes away from her daughter is imaginary phallic omnipotence, not a real organ to which a boy is particularly attached. This difference in register between the two types of threats must create a different relation to the real and to the body, as well as a different narcissistic economy, in the boy and in the girl. Indeed, keeping in mind the essays to which we just referred, the child identifies with the imaginary phallus, and it is this identification that the castration complex shatters, before the Oedipus in one case and after it in the other.

But such considerations take us beyond the concepts Freud has formulated and would need a more appropriate framework.

We believe, along with a number of psychoanalysts of both sexes who have tried to rethink this fundamental question of sexual difference, that Freud's statements and hypotheses should be reconsidered, at least in part, and should, in any case, be developed further. Melanie Klein seems to have most convincingly laid out an initial research path: both the boy and the girl experience destructive impulses from the beginning; they build an internal armor very early – the pre-Oedipal superego – to inhibit their own destructive impulses.

But the perspective introduced by Lacan seems to us to suggest a more accurate analysis of this question of the difference between the sexes. The key factor here, as we see it, is the role attributed to the strictly analytic meaning of the concept of "phallus".

The famous aphorism "Anatomy is destiny" also merits serious examination. It focuses attention on the body and on the subject of erogenous zones, different in men and women. It leads to questioning what decides an individual's sexual identification within a given cultural group; this takes the analyst into a field shared with sociologists and ethnologists. Finally, to explore the whole scope of this aphorism and its limits, the Freudian notion of bisexuality[170] would have to be reexamined.

Thus, the last contributions Freud makes to his identification theory concern the enigma of sexual identity – that is, the enigma of the singularity of the subject's desire. The theory itself, unfinished and no doubt interminable, was one that he firmly intended to establish – therein lies the productivity of the thinker and of his unconscious – on the solid foundation of his discovery: the Oedipus complex which, for him, was equivalent to the "father complex".

Notes

1 Jones, E., *The Life and Work of Sigmund Freud*, Vol. 3, London: Hogarth, 1957. Freud's study of masochism starts with this 1919 essay (*A Child Is Being Beaten*); the masochistic phantasy he reconstructs in the psychology of an Oedipal-aged child is secondary masochistic perversion. In *Beyond the Pleasure Principle*, the originally masochistic form of the ego is suggested, as yet cautiously.

2 See infra, Chapter II, § 3, A.

3 Freud, S., *A Child Is Being Beaten: A Contribution to the Study of the Origin of Sexual Perversions*, S.E. 17, London: Hogarth, 1919, p. 175.

4 The theme of masochism is examined specifically in *Beyond the Pleasure Principle* in 1920 (S.E. 18), in *The Ego and the Id* in 1923 (S.E. 19) and in *The Economic Problem of Masochism* in 1924 (S.E. 19).

5 Freud, S., *Studies on Hysteria* (with Breuer, J.), S.E. 2, London: Hogarth, 1895.

6 Freud, S., *Beyond the Pleasure Principle*, S.E. 18, London: Hogarth, 1920.

7 Ibid.

8 Lacan, J., "Family Complexes: 'The Complex, a Concrete Factor in Familial Psychology'", in *Autres Écrits: 2001*, Paris: Editions du Seuil, 1938.

9 De Waelhens, A., "Figures of the Unconscious", in *Phenomenology and Lacan on Schizophrenia*, Ver Eecke, W., and De Waelhens, A. (Eds.), Leuven: Leuven University Press, 2001.

10 Freud, S., *The Interpretation of Dreams*, S.E. 4-5, London: Hogarth, 1900, Chapter VII.

11 Freud refers to the work of Sigmund Pfeifer on this subject: "Ausserungen infantile-erotischer Triebeim Spiele", *Imago*, V, no. 4 (1919).

12 Freud, S., *Beyond the Pleasure Principle*, op. cit., pp. 8–9.

13 Ibid., pp. 9–10. Freud describes another episode in the life of the same child, to complete his explanation: "A year later, the same boy. . . used to take a toy, if he was angry with it, and throw it on the floor exclaiming: 'Go to the fwont!' He had heard at that time that his absent father was 'at the front', and was far from regretting his absence; on the contrary, he made it quite clear that he had no desire to be disturbed in his sole possession of his mother". Freud adds, in a note: "When this child was five and three-quarters, his mother died. Now that she was really 'gone' ('o-o-o-o'), the little boy showed no signs of grief. It is true that in the interval a second child had been born and had roused him to violent jealousy" (p. 10).

14 The child's strategy of displacement onto objects is reminiscent of certain remarks in *Totem and Taboo* about magical power and its transmission. See previous chapter infra.

15 Freud, S., *Beyond the Pleasure Principle*, op. cit., p. 16.

16 Jacques Lacan built his own concept of the symbolic on this complete game. Indeed, in "The Function and the Field of Speech and Language", he gives this interpretation, which no longer relies on the primary masochism Freud associates with the death drive: "Thus there is no further need to resort to the outdated notion of primary masochism to explain repetitive games in which subjectivity simultaneously masters its dereliction and gives birth to the symbol.

These are the occultation games which Freud, in a flash of genius, presented to us so that we might see in them that the moment at which desire is humanized is also that at which the child is born into language.

We can now see that the subject here does not simply master his deprivation by assuming it – he raises his desire to a second power. For his action destroys the object that it causes to appear and disappear by *bring about* its absence and presence in advance. His action thus negativizes the force field of desire in order to become its own object to itself. And this object, being immediately embodied in the symbolic pair of two elementary exclamations, announces the subject's diachronic integration of the dichotomy of phonemes, whose synchronic structure the existing language offers up for him to assimilate; the child thus begins to become engaged in the system of the concrete discourse of those around him by reproducing more or less approximately in his *Fort!* and *Da!* the terms he receives from them.

Fort! Da! It is already when quite alone that the desire of the human child becomes the desire of another, of an alter ego who dominates him and whose object of desire is henceforth his own affliction. Should the child now address an imaginary or real partner, he will see that this partner too obeys the negativity of his discourse, and since his call has the effect of making the partner slip away, he will seek to bring about the reversal that brings the partner back to his desire through a banishing summons" (*Écrits*, Fink, B. (Trans.), New York: W.W. Norton, 1996, p. 262).

17 We are referring to Lacan's well-known text "The Mirror Stage as Formative of the Function of the I as Revealed in Psychoanalytic Experience", in *Écrits: A Selection*, London: Tavistock, 1977.

18 Winnicott, D.W., "Transitional Objects and Transitional Phenomena", *International Journal of Psychoanalysis*, 34 (1953), pp. 89–97.

19 The fifth chapter of *Beyond the Pleasure Principle* discusses the *psychic function* of repetition compulsion. The mission of the psychic apparatus is to achieve mastery of instinctual stimuli by effecting a binding (*Bindung*) of the energy liberated by the primary process. This binding function is not carried out in opposition to the pleasure principle but independently of it.

20 Freud, S., *Group Psychology and the Analysis of the Ego*, S.E. 18: 67–143, London: Hogarth, 1921.

21 Freud, S., *On Narcissism: An Introduction*, S.E. 14: 67–102, London: Hogarth, 1914.

22 See last paragraph of *On Narcissism: An Introduction*, which starts: "The ego ideal opens up an important avenue for the understanding of group psychology" (S.E. 14: 82).

23 This "social" tendency of psychoanalysis has developed to a great extent in the USA since the Second World War, particularly thanks to the work of Kurt Lewin, as well as the Adlerians. In France, a remarkable example of this tendency is exemplified by Dr. Angelo Hesnard's book *Psychanalyse du lien interhumain*, Paris: Presses Universitaires de France, 1957. The author's discussion includes phenomenological concerns, particularly those of Merleau-Ponty.

24 Freud, S., *Group Psychology and the Analysis of the Ego*, op. cit., pp. 69–70.

25 The term *herd instinct* was introduced by Wilfred Trotter, *Instincts of the Herd in Peace and War*, London: Ernest Benn, 1930. This kind of psychology, which classifies tendencies and posits, for each behaviour, the existence of a corresponding "instinct" is severely criticized by Jacques Lacan: "If. . . one uses 'instincts' to mean atavistic behaviors whose violence might have been necessitated by the law of the primitive jungle, which some physiopathologic lapse supposedly releases, like morbid impulses, from the lower level in which they are bottled up, one can wonder why impulses to shovel, plant, cook, and even bury the dead have not surfaced since man has been man" (Lacan, J., *Écrits*, Fink, B. (Trans.), New York: W.W. Norton, 1996, pp. 120–121).

26 Adler not only wrote *Individual Psychology* but also founded the society of *Individual Psychology*, as well as a journal of same name, in 1914. He did the same thing in 1935 in the USA, where he founded the *Journal of Individual Psychology*. See *Theory and Practice of Individual Psychology*, New York: Humanities Press, 1951.

27 See Gustave Le Bon, *The Crowd: A Study of the Popular Mind*, New York: Dover Publications, 2002; and Mannoni, O., *Conditions psychologiques d'action sur les foules*, Nancy: Publications du Centre Européen Universitaire, 1952.

28 Freud, S., *Group Psychology and the Analysis of the Ego*, op. cit., p. 95.

29 Ibid., pp. 90–91.

30 "Groups demand illusions and cannot do without them" (S.E. 18: 80). The function of the ideal, the importance of the leader, the need to nurture illusion (omnipotence of desire) – these are the elements Freud wants to bring together from the start, as an argument against Le Bon's view.

31 Freud, S., *Group Psychology and the Analysis of the Ego*, op. cit., p. 97.

32 Ibid., pp. 100–101.

33 Ibid., p. 101.

34 Ibid.

35 As early as *Three Essays on the Theory of Sexuality*, Freud held that a love relationship had two constituent aspects: tenderness and sensuality. Often, these aspects coexist in a sexual relationship, but in some cases, they develop separately. The vicissitudes of this sexual development are analysed in *Contributions to the Psychology of Love* (1910, 1912, 1918) and in *On Narcissism: An Introduction* (1914).

36 Freud, S., *Group Psychology and the Analysis of the Ego*, op. cit., p. 104.

37 Ibid., p. 105.

38 Ibid.

39 This concept of integration serves to describe the (theoretical) aim of libido development – partial instincts, initially distinct, come together and merge at the genital stage – and ego development. In a note, Freud observes: "In the process of a child's development into a mature adult there is a more and more extensive integration of his personality, a co-ordination of the separate instinctual impulses and purposive trends which have grown up in him independently of one another. The analogous process in the domain of sexual life has long been known to us as the co-ordination of all the sexual instincts into a definitive genital organization. . . . Moreover, that the unification of the ego is liable to the same interferences as that of the libido is shown by numerous familiar instances, such as that of men of science who have preserved their faith in the Bible, and other similar cases" (S.E. 18: 79).

40 Freud, S., *Group Psychology and the Analysis of the Ego*, op. cit., p. 79.

41 Ibid., p. 106.

42 See *Three Essays on the Theory of Sexuality* for the description of the oral phase. (See infra, Chapter II).

43 Freud, S., *Group Psychology and the Analysis of the Ego*, op. cit., p. 106.

44 In his identification theory, Lacan gave a primordial place to this description of hysterical identification (based on the assimilation of a single trait). In fact, he designated this relation to the single trait as the foundation of the identification of the subject as such, based on the relation to the signifier (Lacan, J., *The Seminar of Jacques Lacan, Book IX: Identification*, unedited, 1961–1962).

45 Freud, S., *Group Psychology and the Analysis of the Ego*, op. cit., p. 107.

46 Freud, S., *The Interpretation of Dreams*, S.E. 5, op. cit.

47 Freud, S., *Group Psychology and the Analysis of the Ego*, op. cit., p. 107.

48 Freud, S., *The Interpretation of Dreams*, S.E. 4: 127, op. cit.

49 See *The Psychoanalysis of a Case of Homosexuality in a Woman*, S.E. 18: 147–172, London: Hogarth, 1920.

50 Freud quotes Markuszewicz: *Beitrag Zumautistischen Denken bei Kindern*, IZP VI, 1920.

51 Freud, S., *Group Psychology and the Analysis of the Ego*, op. cit., pp. 108–109.

52 Freud, S., *Mourning and Melancholia*, S.E. 14, London: Hogarth, 1917, p. 249.

53 Freud, S., *Group Psychology and Analysis of the Ego*, op. cit., pp. 109–110.

54 See the end of Chapter XI in *Group Psychology and the Analysis of the Ego*. There is an exercise in the application of this discovery of the split of the ego in the 1927 text *Humour* (S.E. 21), where Freud gives a new interpretation of the particular pleasure provided by humour, defined as a victory of narcissism over unpleasant reality, as the triumph of the superego over the ego frightened by danger.

55 Freud, S., *Mourning and Melancholia*, op. cit., pp. 237–258.

56 Freud, S., *On Narcissism: An Introduction*, op. cit., p. 90.

57 Freud, S., *Group Psychology and Analysis of the Ego*, op. cit., p. 112.

58 Ibid., p. 113.

59 Ibid.

60 Ibid., p. 114. "From being in love to hypnosis is evidently only a short step. The respects in which the two agree are obvious. There is the same humble subjection, the same compliance, the same absence of criticism, towards the hypnotist as towards the loved object. There is the same sapping of the subject's own initiative; no one can doubt that the hypnotist has stepped into the place of the *ego ideal*. . . . The hypnotic relation is the unlimited devotion of someone in love, but with sexual satisfaction excluded; whereas in the actual case of being in love this kind of satisfaction is only temporarily kept back, and remains in the background as a possible aim at some later time".

61 Trotter, M.W., *Instincts of the Herd in Peace and War*, op. cit.

62 Freud, S., *Group Psychology and Analysis of the Ego*, op. cit., p. 130.

63 G. Deleuze and F. Guattari equate the psychoanalytic representation of the subject with capitalist ideology based on private property, limits, territories, delimited individuality: a figuration of the despot. The destruction of this representation corresponds to the collapse of this idea of the "subject" unified by the Oedipus; the model is no longer integral but rather molecular, burst open, "schizophrenic". See *Anti-Oedipus: Capitalism and Schizophrenia*, London: Penguin Classics, 2009.

64 These subsequent texts we might call applications of the conceptual apparatus described in *The Ego and the Id* are: "A Seventeenth-Century Demonological Neurosis", S.E. 19, 1923; "Dostoevsky and Parricide", S.E. 21, 1928; *Moses and Monotheism*, S.E. 23, 1939.

65 Freud, S., *The Ego and the Id*, S.E. 19, London: Hogarth, 1923, p. 12.

66 Groddeck, G., *The Book of the It*, New York: Vintage Books, 1949. Freud comments that Groddeck followed the example of Nietzsche when using this impersonal grammatical form to designate that which is subject to natural law in us (*The Ego and the Id*, op. cit., p. 23).

67 Janine Chasseguet-Smirgel reviews this question and provides her own views in her presentation at the 33rd Congress of Romance Language Psychoanalysts, titled "Some Thoughts on the Ego Ideal: A Contribution to the Study of the 'Illness of Reality'", in *The Psychoanalytic Quarterly*, 45, no. 3 (1976).

68 Freud, S., *The Ego and the Id*, op. cit., p. 25.

69 Ibid.

70 Ibid., p. 26.

71 Ibid., p. 27.

72 See Zenoni, A., *"Analyse du moi et langage: Essai d'articulation des théories analytiques du moi"* ("Analysis of Ego and Language: An Attempt at Linking the Analytic Theories on Ego"), particularly Chapter 1. Dissertation, Université Saint-Louis Library, 1973. Unpublished manuscript.

73 Freud, S., *The Ego and the Id.*, op. cit., p. 28.

74 Laplanche, J., "Les normes morales et sociales", *Bulletin de Psychologie*, (1973), p. 888.

75 Freud, S., *The Ego and the Id*, op. cit., p. 26.

76 Ibid., p. 29.

77 Ibid., p. 19, Note 2.

78 Ibid.

79 Ibid., p. 30.

80 Freud, S., *Notes on a Case of Paranoia*, S.E. 12, London: Hogarth, p. 70; see infra, Chapter II.

81 Freud, S., *The Ego and the Id*, op. cit., pp. 63–66: Appendix B, "The Great Reservoir of Libido".

82 The term *multiple personality* is used in many texts related to hysteria. For instance: *Some General Remarks on Hysterical Attacks*, S.E. 9, London: Hogarth, p. 227. The overdetermined hysterical attack is clearly shown to originate in multiple identification.

83 Freud, S., *From the History of an Infantile Neurosis*, S.E. 17, London: Hogarth, 1918; see infra, Chapter II.

84 Freud, S., *The Ego and the Id*, S.E. 14: 31.

85 Ibid.

86 Regarding this odd passage, Jean Laplanche writes: "Negatively stated, Freud's 'primary identification' is certainly not the same thing as the primary relation to the mother and to the breast; nor does it resemble what Lacan described as the primary identification of the mirror stage (identification structuring the ego, not the ideal – identification with a form: the form of the other as a totality).

  Positively stated, the conclusion is even more delicate. I consider this singular passage in Freud's texts to be incompatible: it cannot be attached to other texts, either for the sake of diversity or synthesis. As is often the case when a text reveals the unconscious, and is often the case with Freud, I think this passage should be taken as a symptom, if any interpretation is to be attempted. It has the typical contradictions and shows the typical remorse; its rationalisations display contradictions (first, we are told identification with the father is essential, then, that identification can be with both parents, and finally that, to simplify, only identification with the father will be discussed" (Laplanche, J., art. cit., 1973, p. 890).

87 See references to this text in *The Ego and the Id*, op. cit., pp. 29, 32, 37.

88 For an enlightening discussion of this concept of "destruction", see Moustapha Safouan, "Is the Oedipus Complex Universal", in *Power/Knowledge*, Foucault, M. (Ed.), Sussex: Harvester Press, 1980.

89 Freud, S., *The Ego and the Id*, op. cit., p. 33.

90 Ibid.

91 Ibid., p. 34.

92 Ibid.

93 Ibid., p. 35. This is an insertion added by Freud in the second English translation (1927).

94 The question of heritage refers to everything psychoanalysis, from Freud to Lacan, has elaborated around the notion of debt. The analysis of the Rat Man provided Freud with the foundations for his own development of the concept and, notably, for the ideas developed by Lacan: relation of the ego ideal with the dead father, symbolic father (name-of-the-father, the law, symbolic debt, structure of the subject). See special issue of journal *L'Inconscient*, on "Paternity", Paris: Presses Universitaires de France, 1968, No. 5; as well as Wladimir Granoff, *Filiations: L'Avenir du complexe d'Oedipe*, Paris: Les Éditions de Minuit, 1975.

95 Freud, S., *The Ego and the Id*, op. cit., p. 36.

96 Freud, S., *On Narcissism: An Introduction*, op. cit., p. 94.

97 Ibid., p. 96.

98 This classification of Freud's texts into philological and theoretical categories is one of the major clarifications provided by J. Laplanche and J.-B. Pontalis in their *Vocabulaire de la psychanalyse* and their commentary on Freud's texts. See entries on Ego Ideal and Ideal Ego (p. 184 and p. 255).

99 Nunberg, H., *Principles of Psychoanalysis*, New York: International Universities Press, 1955.

100 See Laplanche, J., and Pontalis, J.-B., *Vocabulaire de la psychanalyse*, Paris: Presses Universitaires de France, 1997, pp. 261–265, on the concept of primary narcissism (prior to the distinction between ego and id).

101 Quoted by Lagache, D., "La psychanalyse et la structure de la personnalité", *La psychanalyse*, no. 6 (1961), p. 38, Presses Universitaires de France.

102 Fenichel, O., *The Psychoanalytic Theory of Neurosis*, New York: W.W. Norton, 1945.

103 Lagache, D., "La psychanalyse et la structure de la personnalité", op. cit. Lagache had also presented a theory of his own in the chapter "La vie sexuelle de l'homme", *L'Encyclopédie Française*, VIII (1938). He didn't make a distinction between primary identification, based on love for the all-powerful father; secondary identification, based on fear, resulting from the Oedipal situation dominated by an ambivalent attitude towards the father; and "tertiary" identification, based on neutralised aggressivity. According to Lagache, the superego is the result of this triple identification with the father.

104 Lagache, D., "La psychanalyse et la structure de la personnalité", op. cit., which describes the opposition between object-ego and subject-ego.

105 All those who ventured to comment on Lacan's work have pointed out this early stage, in which the concept of the imaginary is introduced, before the second stage, in which the concept of the symbolic is formulated. It would be worthwhile to examine more closely the importance of this opposition in the chronological development of Lacan's work. In our opinion, the symbolic dimension is present in the "mirror stage".

106 Hook, D., Neill, C., and Vanheule, S. (eds.), *Reading Lacan's Écrits: From 'The Freudian Thing' to 'Remarks on Daniel Lagache'*, London: Routledge, 2019.

107 Lacan, J., *Écrits*, Sheridan, A. (Trans.), New York: W.W. Norton, 1977. From the start, there is "form", which "situates the ego in a fictional direction, which will always remain irreducible for the individual alone" (p. 2). From this follows the discussion of "mirage", "exteriority", et cetera.

108 Hook, D., Neill, C., and Vanheule, S., *Reading Lacan's Écrits: From 'The Freudian Thing' to 'Remarks on Daniel Lagache'*, op. cit.

109 Lacan, J., *The Seminar of Jacques Lacan, Book IX: Identification*, 1961–1962, translated by C. Gallagher, from unpublished French transcripts. Following in Lacan's

footsteps, the following authors have shed much light on the Lacanian theory of identification: J. Clavreul, "Identification et complexe de castration", in *L'inconscient*,
no. 7 (July 1968), pp. 67–98; Castoriadis-Aulagnier, P., "Demande et identification",
ibidem, pp. 23–66; Safouan, M., "De la structure en psychanalyse", in *Qu'est-ce que
le structuralisme?*, Paris: Editions du Seuil, 1968, pp. 239–298; Anonymous, "Le
Clivage du sujet et son identification", in *Silicet*, nos. 2-3 (1970), pp. 103–136; Fedida, P., *L'inceste et le meurtre dans la généalogie, in Szondiana*, VIII, Paris: Nauwelaerts, 1971; Ortigues, E., *Problèmes psychologiques et conventions sociales*, ibidem.

110   Aulagnier, P., "Le concept d'identification", lecture at Sainte-Anne, Paris, Winter
1967. Unpublished notes. Later developments of this reflection are included in her
book *The Violence of Interpretation*, London: Routledge, 2001.

111   "Based on the principle of real resistances discussed in Ego theory in psychoanalysis,
there is a refusal to admit that the Ego has the right to be what experience shows it
to be: a function of misconstruction" (Hook, D., Neill, C., and Vanheule, S., *Reading
Lacan's Écrits: From 'The Freudian Thing' to 'Remarks on Daniel Lagache'*, op.
cit.).

112   Safouan, M., *De la structure en psychanalyse*, art. cit. infra, Note 47.
The dissymmetry between projection and introjection processes, evident in the formula "The imaginary is projected, the symbolic is introjected", is forcefully underscored by Lacan. For instance, in the following: "When the subject is connected
to language, he experiences his lack of being; this is when the psychoanalyst must
define certain moments, because the psychologist's questionnaires or recordings do
not easily reveal them – not before a film shows the structure of the error to be part
of the game of chess. An image that counters this moment of lack emerges to bear the
cost of desire: *projection, a function of the imaginary*. Conversely, at the centre of the
being, to mark the lack, an indicator emerges: introjection, relation to the symbolic"
(*Reading Lacan's Écrits: From 'The Freudian Thing' to Remarks on Daniel Lagache*,
op. cit.).

113   Aulagnier, P., Unpublished 1967 lecture, op. cit.

114   Freud, S., *On Narcissism: An Introduction*, op. cit., pp. 76–77.

115   Laplanche, J., and Pontalis, J.-B., "Fantasy and the Origins of Sexuality", *The International Journal of Psychoanalysis*, 49, no. 1 (1968).

116   Popularised notions of psychoanalysis and Freudo-Marxism mistakenly reduce the
process to socio-economic repression. This misunderstanding is due in part to the
ambiguity of the English word *repression*, which translates the Freudian term *Ver-
drängung*, leaving out that term's meaning of "displacement".

117   Lacan's contribution consists of having differentiated the Freudian concept of the
ego from the concept of "subject". The subject as such is an effect of the signifier (of
unary trait identification).

118   See Jacques Lacan, "The Signification of the Phallus" (1958), in *Écrits: A Selection*,
London: Routledge, 1977; see Moustapha Safouan, *De la structure en psychanalyse*,
art. cit. infra, Note 47; "Is the Oedipus Complex Universal", nos. 5–6 (1981); and
"Questions Concerning Feminine Sexuality", *The Centre for Freudian Analysis and
Research Web Journal*, (2004).

119   Freud, S., *The Ego and the Id*, op. cit., pp. 40–41.

120   Freud, S., *On Narcissism: An Introduction*, op. cit. We know that in melancholia
the process is the opposite of that seen in paranoia: unconscious hostility is not
turned outward (towards people formerly loved or their transferential substitutes) but
towards the ego, which has been transformed into the object-cathexis of ambivalent
attachment.

121   Freud, S., *The Ego and the Id*, op. cit.

122   Ibid., pp. 45–46.

123 Ibid., p. 46.
124 Ibid., p. 50.
125 As early as 1906, Freud saw certain phenomena in psychoanalysis as shedding light on criminology: *Psycho-Analysis and the Establishment of the Facts in Legal Proceedings*, S.E. 9, London: Hogarth, 1906; *Some Character-Types Met With in Psycho-Analytic Work*, S.E. 14, London: Hogarth, 1916 (discussion of guilt feelings leading to crime). See: Lacan, J., "A Theoretical Introduction to the Functions of Psychoanalysis in Criminology", in *Écrits: A Selection*, London: Tavistock, 1977. For one of the first important psychoanalytic contributions to criminology, see Alexander, F., and Staub, H., *The Criminal, the Judge and the Public*, Glencoe, IL: The Free Press, 1956.
126 Freud, S., *The Ego and the Id*, op. cit., pp. 52–53. The superego is composed of signifiers: that is, internalized parental "do's" and "don'ts". What is scandalous, according to Lacan, is that "the unconscious is structured like a language". See his Preface to Anika Rifflet-Lemaire's book *Jacques Lacan*, London: Routledge and Kegan Paul, 1982.
127 Klein, M., "Early Stages of Oedipus Complex", *International Journal of Psychoanalysis*, 9 (1928), pp. 169–180.
128 Green, A., *The Fabric of Affects in the Psychoanalytic Discourse*, London: Routledge, 1999.
129 Freud, S., *The Ego and the Id*, op. cit., p. 53.
130 Ibid.
131 Freud, S., *The Economic Problem of Masochism*, S.E. 19: 159–170, London: Hogarth.
132 Ibid., pp. 168–170.
133 Ibid., p. 168.
134 Freud, S., *The Ego and the Id*, op. cit. "The super-ego arises. . . from an identification with the father taken as a model".
135 "Kant's Categorical Imperative Is Thus the Direct Heir of the Oedipus Complex", Freud, S., *The Economic Problems of Masochism*, op. cit., p. 167. See also Lacan, J., *The Ethics of Psychoanalysis: The Seminar of Jacques Lacan*, Book VIII, London: Routledge, 2015; and *Kant with Sade*, Swenson, J. B. (Trans.), Cambridge, MA: Massachusetts Institute of Technology Press, October 1989.
136 Freud, S., *The Ego and the Id*, op. cit.
137 In 1919, Melanie Klein presented a paper on child development to the Hungarian Psychoanalytic Society at the prompting of Ferenczi, her first analyst. The paper was published in 1921 in Berlin.
138 Klein, M., "Early Stages of the Oedipus Conflict", *International Journal of Psychoanalysis*, 9 (1928), pp. 168–169.
139 Ibid.
140 "Imago" and "imagic introjection" were key concepts in the work of Pierre Luquet, author of *Les Identifications*, Paris: Presses Universitaires de France, 2003.
141 See Safouan, M., "Note sur le père idéal". *Lettres de l'École freudienne de Paris*, no. 5 (1968).
142 Freud, S., *Civilization and Its Discontents*, S.E. 21: 59–145, London: Hogarth.
143 Ibid., p. 129.
144 Ibid.
145 Ibid.
146 Freud's texts before and after *Civilisation and Its Discontents* testify to this hesitation; for instance: *Introductory Lectures on Psycho-Analysis* (1916–17); *Inhibitions, Symptoms and Anxiety* (1926); and later *New Introductory Lectures on Psycho-Analysis* (1933) and *An Outline of Psycho-Analysis* and *Moses and Monotheism* (1940).
147 For an excellent biographical treatment of the "great Russian", see Dominique Arban's works *Dostoievski par Lui-Même, Écrivains de Toujours*, Paris: Editions du Seuil, 1962; and *Dostoievski le Coupable*, Paris: Julliard, 1968.

148 It is only recently that analysts became interested in epilepsy from a clinical and theoretical point of view, in order to extricate it from a strictly neurological or psychiatric context. We refer the reader to Grasset, A., *L'Enfant épileptique*, Paris: Presses Universitaires de France, 1968; Mélèse, L., *La psychanalyse au risque de l'épilepsie*, Toulouse: érès, 2001; Mélèse, L., "Critical Transference in a Case of Severe Epilepsy", *American Journal of Psychoanalysis*, 72, no. 3 (August 31, 2012), pp. 223–241. For a more detailed analysis of this larger perspective, see Poncelet, C., *Les questions de l'épilepsie à travers la psychanalyse et la Schicksanalyse*, Licentiate Dissertation in psychology, University of Louvain, 1974. Unpublished.

149 See Pontalis, J.-B., preface to his French translation of "Les Frères Karamazov", *Gallimard*, 1973.

150 Freud, S., *Dostoievski and Parricide*, S.E. 21, London: Hogarth, pp. 185–186.

151 De Wolf, M., *La castration dans l'œuvre et l'expérience freudiennes*, Ph.D. Dissertation, Louvain, 1972; Laplanche, J., "La castration, ses précurseurs et son destin", *Bulletin de Psychologie*, XXVI (1973–4). See also Lacan, J., "L'Étourdit", *Scilicet*, no. 4 (1973).

152 Freud, S., *The Ego and the Id*, op. cit., S.E. 19: 1–66.

153 Ibid.

154 Rank, O., *The Trauma of Birth*, New York: Harper Collins, 1973.

155 Freud, S., *The Infantile Genital Organization*, S.E. 19, London: Hogarth, 1923.

156 Freud, S., *The Dissolution of the Oedipus Complex*, S.E. 19, London: Hogarth, 1924.

157 Freud, S., *The Infantile Genital Organization*, op. cit., p 142.

158 Ibid., p. 144. In Note 1 appearing on the same page, Freud adds an interesting remark drawing attention to some points we often highlighted in our interpretation of the "intermediary" status of the ego's "objects" (which are at once the ego and the portion of the other which is a part of this narcissistic ego). In Freud's words: "It has been quite correctly pointed out that a child gets the idea of a narcissistic injury through a bodily loss from the experience of losing his mother's breast after suckling, from the daily surrender of his faeces and, indeed, even from his separation from the womb at birth. Nevertheless, one ought not to speak of a castration complex until this idea of a loss has become connected with the male genitals". We have seen that, despite this recommendation, an analyst like Françoise Dolto does not hesitate to call such early separation experiences "castration". She is no doubt relying on the function of Lacan's notion of the symbolic, which makes it possible to form a structural conception of castration, beyond the simply genetic conception. See Dolto, F., *Au jeu du désir – Essais cliniques*, Points, 1988.

159 Ibid., p. 145.

160 Freud, S., *The Ego and the Id*, op. cit.

161 Freud, S., *The Infantile Genital Organization*, op. cit., p. 145.

162 Freud, S., *The Dissolution of the Oedipus Complex*, op. cit., p. 177.

163 Ibid., p. 176.

164 Ibid., pp. 176–177.

165 Ibid., p. 177.

166 Ibid., p. 178. This Napoleonic aphorism is also found in the 1912 essay *Sexuality and the Psychology of Love*.

167 Freud. S., *Some Psychical Consequences of the Anatomical Distinction Between the Sexes*, S.E. 19: 243–258, London: Hogarth, 1925. Freud had already attempted to show the origin of a "masculinity complex" in *Dissolution of the Oedipus Complex*.

168 Freud, S., *Psychogenesis of a Case of Homosexuality in a Woman*, S.E. 18, London: Hogarth, 1925.

169 S. Freud, *Some Psychical Consequences of the Anatomical Distinction Between the Sexes*, op. cit.

170 Freud's text "Femininity", the 23rd (undelivered) lecture in his *New Introductory Lectures on Psycho-Analysis*, written in 1932, gives us an idea of the debate on feminine sexuality as it unfolded at that time. In more recent times, this debate has been renewed by women psychoanalysts who, in agreement or disagreement with their male colleagues who discuss sexuality abundantly, question the accepted Freudian hypotheses on sexual differentiation, on bisexuality and on masculinity and femininity. See Lasch, C., "Freud and Women", *The New York Review of Books*, XXI, no. 15 (October 3, 1974).

For a discussion on the historical evolution of the concept of feminine sexuality and the theoretical perspectives of analysts since Freud, see De Wolf, M., *La castration dans l'œuvre et l'expérience freudienne*, op. cit.

In conclusion

"Having" and "being" in children.
Children like expressing an object-relation
by an identification: "I am the object".
"Having" is the later of the two; after the
loss of the object it relapses into "being".
Example: the breast. "The breast is
part of me, I am the breast". Only later:
"I have it" – that is, "I am not it".[1]

Putting an end to the slow progress of time for understanding, ushered in by the logic of subjective assertion, despite the doubt that suspends certainty for an instant, the time to conclude has arrived.[2]

The pressing and inevitable presumption of concluding, with the breaking off that it produces, reveals nothing of the truth that demands it. But it foresees it. We therefore ask the reader to interpret our haste to conclude as the indefinite anticipation of a truth we have not finished understanding.

We have attempted to follow as closely as possible, in Freud's texts, the construction of a psychoanalytic concept: the concept of identification.

Freud did not start out with a thematised presentation of this concept. His early discussions of it are simply descriptive – not theoretical – and use what could be considered ordinary language. The term is graduallyv inscribed in the theoretical framework of psychoanalysis as Freud's writing becomes more explicit. Once it is inserted in this construction, the concept becomes more and more complex and branches out.

Recognising the decisive moments of the concept's genealogy encounters the difficulty, inherent to the reading of a work of such magnitude, of respecting chronology without eradicating the anticipatory and feedback effects of the contexture. Every "thesis", based as it is on a theoretical obsession, implies an arbitrary act of selection in its searching through the compact material of an unfinished and impossible-to-finish text, focusing on an idea or, worse, a "theme". We do not claim to have avoided this pitfall of commentary or the violence of cutting up the text and rummaging through it.

A rapid overview, in free-association style, of the meanings language attributes to the word *identification* itself eliminated from the start any illusion of being able to delimit and circumscribe this concept. The semantic variations, the multiple etymologies and the philosophical connotations of the term clearly reveal the unlimited nature and wide scope of this concept. Indeed, its exploration requires solving such daunting problems as finding a psychological and metaphysical definition of the ego, of subjectivity, of the "other", of empathy, of identity and difference, of being and having, of the individual and the collective. . .

By submitting this term to his own purposes, Freud turned to the subversion – still hard to conceive – of this question of the same and the other. The topic is, in fact, enormous. To find our way in this vast territory, we followed Freud's own path closely.

As is the case with every psychoanalytic concept, the careful pursuit of the development of the identification concept in its entirety and its connection to the other concepts provides a solid thread to follow in the work of unravelling the knot of Freudian concerns.

Thus, between Freud's first topographical model (Freud I) and his third, between 1895 and 1939, a journey marked by anticipation, forgetting and systematisation gives rise to a conceptualisation whose development is worth going over.

Concluding an itinerary

An analysis requires the analysand to carry out a labour which, relying on the unforeseeable wanderings of memory, repetition and working through, reconstitutes, from disconnected words, a fragmented story. Our "conclusion" is constructed in the same way.[3]

It is not possible to recount how a psychoanalytic concept is born and how it develops. When examining it, one is unavoidably confronted oneself (and this "self" is never identical) with the differences separating the "subject" from what he stated, when he has to reproduce, recall and repossess the text he composed.

So let us not be misled by the notion of development, which does not endeavour to reproduce an exact or linear chronology. Development comes by taking many paths so many times that the before and after are exhausted by overuse and become a mere pretext.

Let us then tie together all the identifications specified throughout this development. Given that they are multiple versions in a dialectic of the same and of the other, the ego and its objects, how can Freud's identifications, variously described depending on Freud's clinical experiences, be concluded? Which should be included in the discussion? Which should be left out?

Freud I: dream, hysteria and jokes

The letters between Freud and Wilhelm Fliess, which can rightfully be considered the origins of psychoanalysis – or, more precisely, the origins of its questions and its language – outline the premises of Freud's major discoveries, sometimes introducing early considerations of ideas to which he would only return much later. His constant aim, in all his theoretical texts clearly concerned with intellectual honesty, was to shed light on the differential characteristics of the defences (or attempts at healing) in the psychic disorders so variously described and classified in psychiatric nosographies. He was looking, under the highly diversified appearance of symptoms, for an underlying principle of intelligibility and articulation.

The concept of identification appears very early, associated with hysterical symptoms. From the start, it refers to a path chosen by unconscious motives and intolerable desires as a means of arriving at expression and discharge. The repeated use of this term to designate the most frequent mode of hysterical symptom formation leads Freud to draw the structural conclusions ensuing from this: to say that a hysteric identifies at times with one person, at other times with another, or even with several people at once, condensing a series of fascinating figures, means that the "ego", subjected to these unconscious events, is everyone and no one: that he is, literally, a plurality of psychic persons. But these multiple identifications which follow each other come into conflict and are sometimes incompatible, causing the splitting of the ego, which becomes a puppet in a comedy whose meaning is unknown to it. Identifications enact impossible, contradictory desires: they illustrate the impasse in which the hysteric is caught.

As a means of symptom formation, identification provides a compromise: it functions as a "wish fulfiller" and, at the same time, as a punishment since the enactment of unconscious desires through the screen figures it imitates causes the ego to become alienated and fall ill. A process closely resembling that of condensation, a primary process responsible for all shortcuts, all metaphors and all ellipses through which the unconscious transforms representations, identification is, in a manner of speaking, a figurative, acted out condensation. A single symptom can, in fact, indicate the unconscious desire to be or to have several people at once, when it is built on a trait they have in common.

The analyst's task is to discern this common unconscious trait, which so despairingly links an ego to other egos.

Identification, whose function was already being described in this correspondence with Fliess, was discussed even then as having several morbid forms, connected and differentiated based on the type of defence or repression at their source: hysteria and obsessional neurosis, where identifications do not eliminate attachment (real or fantasised) to objects; the contrasting of these two neuroses to paranoia, which erases identifications, breaks attachments to objects and splits the ego; the linking of guilt, shame and neurotic remorse with states of depression, mourning and melancholia. Thus, Freud's entire scientific project finds its tone and style in this discussion.[4]

The Interpretation of Dreams (1900) takes up and discusses in greater detail the role of identification as wish fulfilment in distorted form. The analysis of the dream of a hysterical patient – the "beautiful butcher's wife"[5] – elucidates the discussion: hysterical identification expresses a sort of unconscious logical process; it produces dream figures or, in reality, creates symptomatic attitudes which mask a desire while representing it. This desire, projected unto other people (love object, rival), is of a sexual nature: it is the pretence of being like or being the other, a desire for comm-union. To be sure, this wish to be like is not limited to a desire to imitate. In the unconscious, to be like is to be the other person, to take his place. As Freud would write much later, in 1932: "This 'like' dropped out, of course, so far as the unconscious was concerned".[6]

The desire for communion (comm-union), which is a desire for appropriation – whose scope is not yet clear to Freud – is the unconscious aspect of any imitation that takes place, in general, at the preconscious or conscious level. The need to distinguish between identification and imitation topographically is also apparent in the analysis presented in *Jokes and Their Relation to the Unconscious* (1905), in which a distinction is made between the intrapsychic structure of the joke (*Witz*) and other forms of humour. The joke requires three people to function, and the pleasure it produces relies on the unconscious identification of the listener with the joke teller; humour, on the other hand, results from a comparison of the ego to itself or to another person.[7] The two processes, imitation – a pivotal mechanism of group psychology – and identification – a process underlying any form of sympathy, pity, need for equality – are coherently connected in *Group Psychology and the Analysis of the Ego* (1921).[8]

The analysis of the Dora case[9] shows even more clearly the effects of identification in hysteria. The well-known "nervous cough" of the young girl condenses multiple ambivalent relations with all the "objects" in her milieu (her parents and their "doubles", Frau K and Herr K), so much so that Freud loses track and only succeeds in solving the enigma of her desire in the aftermath, when he is writing up the case. The sexual position is at the heart of the matter, with its interconnected identifications involving mysterious dream figures and real events: Dora's identifications take place in several superimposed incompatible scenarios, whose unknown secret source is psychic bisexuality.

Thus, the symptom emerges to replace the choice of a sexual positioning, of "identification" with one of the sexes – a choice the hysteric and, no doubt, any neurotic has difficulty making. To be of one gender or the other is to accept castration, in any case: that is, the definitive disjunction between being and having. The case of the Wolf Man[10] and the analysis of Schreber's autobiographical account[11] confirm the harrowing existence of this refusal of castration (of the law governing sexual difference) in neurotics. This refusal involves an exceptionally strong fixation on primary relationships, on "archaic" objects that cannot be relinquished.

Identifications create within the ego – whose structural complexity is becoming apparent and whose substance seems to be composed of images – a plurality of relations whose contradictory character escapes the logic of the secondary process. Indeed, identifications constitute the repetition, on a different stage, of wish-related scenarios. Given that object-relations spill over into the realm of phantasy, we can conclude that the term *identification with someone* is a shortcut because, in truth, the only identification is with scenes (phantasies), connections or relationships that are dreamed of, longed for, desired but impossible. The identification process revealed by the analysis of neuroses leads to these conclusions, calling for unambiguous theoretical definition.

Also worthy of discussion, and akin to hysterical identification, are the identifications associated with "esthetic" pleasure, in which, regardless of the type of artistic production, the "spectator" is in contact with the workings of a desire which unconsciously motivates him.

Ideational identifications, "comic", "tragic", "extravagant" et cetera function somewhat like hysterical identification: they express displaced and mimetic pleasure connected to repressed desires, but they maintain the repression, instead of weakening it, as is the case in hysteria, in which suffering is also present. We can venture to say that the small difference between them is that esthetic identification produces sublimation since desire is transformed into collectively recognised symbols and can circulate through this common language subject to "rules". Still, these identifications are defensive in nature since they make the illusion last. But only because the illusion is immediately denied, controlled, assigned to a place: that of the waking dream, of the imaginary. It is a victory of repression that a distinct place in the psyche can be reserved for certain phenomena.

These considerations underscore the relation between identification and repression. They also raise the question of the strange nature of the ego, an agency of repression, an organ of perception and motility connected to the outside world and a scene with multiple registers and levels for the circulation of images, dreams and symbols.

Freud II: narcissism

The introduction of narcissism in the doctrine radicalised identification theory.[12] That is, it gave access to its roots, to its foundations, to the depths of the process.

As early as *Three Essays on the Theory of Sexuality* with its many revisions[13] and, above all, *Totem and Taboo*,[14] Freud's primary aim seems to have been to elucidate the genesis of psychic processes, differentiate between them and go back to their origins, be they those of the ego and the ideal, of conscience, of sexual choice or of mechanisms like repression or the various transformations of instinct.

Clearly influenced by some of his pupils (Rank, Abraham, Ferenczi, Jung), Freud investigates these origins and focuses on problems of ontogenesis and phylogenesis, history and prehistory. As far as identification is concerned, this new perspective grants the oral phase of libidinal development major importance. The layering that builds the sexual on the physiological creates the specifically human redoubling of life: psychic reality, desire. This makes it possible to think of the intake of food as a key metaphor for all sexual relations with the object. Henceforth, the identification concept is associated with object-choice. Original narcissism, auto-eroticism, the discovery of the ego as the domain of narcissistic splitting, the balanced play of the libidinal economy between the ego and chosen objects – all this opens into the question of identification.

The 1910 analysis in *Leonardo da Vinci and a Memory of His Childhood*[15] had already allowed Freud to clarify this radical transformation brought about by the definition of narcissism as a primary relation. In this text, the genesis of masculine homosexuality is presented as the product of an identification bearing all the traits of narcissistic regression. The homosexual's identification is the phantasmatic incorporation of a timeless relation which the child, faced with the task of selection imposed by puberty, refuses to renounce. This identification reproduces, in the sphere of the ego, a very early relationship with the mother; it prolongs incest in phantasy, permanently influencing character and sexual orientation.

By keeping the mother with whom he identifies, Leonardo is preserving his own infantile ego in his love objects.

The preservative function of this major mechanism of the ego now becomes obvious: identification is the narcissistic operation par excellence.

The theoretical construction of the archaic series child-neurotic-psychotic-primitive, presented in *Totem and Taboo*, describes this complicity invoked in identification, which is gradually revealed to be more than simply a defence mechanism but, rather, the very process of *Selbsterhaltung* (self-preservation, self-constitution) of the ego. The archaic relation to the world is cannibalistic, or identificatory, which amounts to the same thing. Magical processes, animistic and infantile modes of thinking and totemistic rituals testify to this dominance of an oral model in the genesis of love, as well as that of thought. Totemic identification is the means by which the ego processes the death of the object: a death resulting from an actual primal murder (of the ancestor, the father), a death desired in an atmosphere of fear and trembling (the father-horse, the object of little Hans's phobia,[16] the dead father, object of the Rat Man's obsession,[17] the wolf father [mother?] of the Wolf Man[18]).

Identification, as revealed through these mythical stories and clinical accounts, displays the complex structure of all love relations; it is an attempt to process an unbearable ambivalence.

The ideal, which we see emerge in little Hans through the use of play and which we sense to be at work in Arpad's words, is formed in the same way as the institutions of the first human communities: by the psychic incorporation – or ritual – of the love object or the object of hate. But this identification, serving to transform and teach, functions at the cost of a painful splitting of the ego. It is within the ego that love (regression of the libido to narcissism) and hate (guilt, remorse, moral conscience) are re-established.

It is essential to emphasise the importance of *Totem and Taboo*, a work which constitutes a turning point in Freud's thinking. This work owes its analytic power to clinical material, much more than to material borrowed from the ethnological sciences. Identification is given a theoretical status whose effect is decisive; it is defined as an operation producing an ego originally divided, separated from the ideal. This operation explains the "layered", stratified and multifold structure of the ego.

Invoking a "totemism" that is infantile, neurotic and primitive inscribes the identification concept in the context of guilt, mourning and death. So-called totemic identification constitutes the detour – we might even say the narcissistic stratagem – that protects the ego from the anxiety caused by the absence of the object and by the terrifying proximity brought about by its death.

In *Mourning and Melancholia*,[19] an extremely dense text discussing the functioning of identification in great depth, Freud begins an analysis of the ego, akin to a chemical analysis, because the process of incorporation of the object of unconscious ambivalence produces, depending on the extent and strength of hostile feelings, unhappiness, dissociation or the death of the ego. The key to the enigma of melancholia, with its catastrophic self-depreciation, resides in revealing a deadly identification. This regressive identification is the means by which an extremely ambivalent relation is created in the ego. The content of *Totem and Taboo* and of the essay on Leonardo have provided the foundation: Freud can now build an identification model, distinct from the model of hysteria and certainly more important than the latter. Melancholic identification, supremely narcissistic, transforms libidinal attachment to an object that reality forces one to lose into a transformation of the ego. This regression from an object-choice to an identification presupposes narcissistic object-choice; the tragic nature of melancholic identification resides in the unsuspected strength of the constitutional ambivalence of the person predisposed to melancholia. But the melancholic process resembles that of the normal phenomenon of mourning, in which there is also partial identification with the lost object. However, here the identification is limited to certain traits of the object, of which the ego takes possession. Moreover, once the ego has accomplished the "precision" work consisting of disinvesting everything that brings to mind the lost object, it can find love and take an interest in reality once again. Filled with the positive attributes of the deceased, the subject comes back to the world from which mourning had exiled him.

The suicidal aspect of melancholia raises an immensely worrisome question: what is the source of the melancholic's terrifying power of self-destruction? We cannot help but think that the melancholic subject is a plaything in a sado-masochistic drama that shatters him, a drama which repeats the trauma of previously experienced cataclysmic destruction and loss.

From that point on, Freud never stops probing the enigma of suicide, the possibility of an unfathomable primary masochism, of an original auto-affection of the ego.

Freud III: the death instinct and the second topographical model

The discovery of repetition compulsion[20] follows the investigation of sadism and masochism, which are present in melancholia. Traumatic neurosis and, extraordinarily, the marvelous playful discovery of an 18-month-old child confronted, in his own way, with the trauma of the alternating proximity and absence of the object, cause Freud to postulate the existence of a death drive silently at work – an entity entirely independent of the pleasure principle.

The identification which produced the Fortsein game[21] – another version of the well-known *Dasein* – allies itself with this death drive. It enacts the memory of a loss, bringing back the fear of death and simultaneously producing its symbolic, compulsive repetition.

We have to insist upon the fundamentally evanescent nature of the present/ absent object: it is "something" missing, which returns in the lapse of intermittent presence. It is not simply the mother. It is a part of the ego which becomes absent in her absence. We pointed out how instructive the last version of this game, commonly called the *Fort-Da* game, is. The image in the mirror is the object of the disappearing game; it is the imaginary support of the declaration to the mother in which the "subject" designates himself as absent: "Baby o-o-o-o!" The object of symbolisation, playful or linguistic (where phonetic opposition indicates the emergence of language) is not an individual, nor is it the subject. Identification produces a game creating a "there was" which shall be "never again". In other words, what is produced is an original, narcissistic relationship now lost. This unknown early element, which puts an end to and simultaneously (re)produces the game, is not explicitly connected by Freud to the question of identification or repression. Yet this remarkable game involves primary identification and/or repression. It was Lacan who later elucidated this original subjective foundation.

In 1921 Freud wrote another essay in curious contrast with his major achievement of the previous year, *Beyond the Pleasure Principle*. The 1921 essay, *Group Psychology and the Analysis of the Ego*, which pursued the line of thought begun in *On Narcissism*, came to be considered a major contribution to the "second model". Its main contribution is the attempt to put in order the various forms of identification encountered in clinical practice. Freud was driven to this attempt at synthesis by the need to specify the types of relations required to create human groups on any scale. The major factor he identified in his discussion is the theoretical impossibility of separating the analysis of the affective processes at work in large groups from the analysis of the structure and genesis of the ego. In both collective and individual psychology, what is needed is to shed light on the transformations and functions of libidinal relations. The choices in one's love life, the alarming manifestations of the metamorphoses undergone by individuals in crowds, hypnosis can be analysed, each in its own context, as structural transformations of the ego, likely to substitute the loved object, the chief or the hypnotist for one's own ideal. But we shall keep in mind the work of putting in order mentioned earlier when we make these comparisons. The function of the ideal explains various types of human relations. In addition to erotic attachments, human beings can be united by identifications. Freud listed the following identifications: primary identification with the father, which introduces the ideal; hysterical identification, based on the unconscious appropriation of a trait of a loved or envied person; empathetic identification, the foundation of collective ties (along with each individual's identification with the ideal); the narcissistic identification of the homosexual; and, finally, the narcissistic identification of the melancholic.

Freud orients all the elements of his discussion towards a single focus: the Oedipal constellation. All the identifications he describes can be understood when placed in the general context of the prehistory and history of the Oedipus complex. The agencies of the ego – specifically censure, repression, reality testing, the ideal and moral conscience – must be reconsidered in the context of the Oedipus complex. The interaction of Oedipal relations, made more complex by instinctual ambivalence and bisexuality, allows Freud to come to a coherent understanding of the interplay of identifications.

In this classification proposed by Freud, two important elements related to identification are missing. First, an explanation for the instinctual economic foundation of the different levels of identification and second, a description of the structural effects this plurality of levels (layers) and modes of functioning (primary and secondary) produce in the ego. In addition, questions of anxiety and regression have to be considered.

The Ego and the Id (1923) laid out the complex connections constituting the foundations of an analysis of the genesis of the ego and its internal agencies.

Identifications enable the child to free himself from Oedipal conflict; he is driven to do this by the imminence of an inescapable anxiety: the fear of castration. The double relation with the mother (active and passive) and the double relation with the father (object of admiration and passive libidinal cathexis) intersect in concurrent libidinal cathexes and in bilateral hostile currents. It is a narcissistic reaction to this contradictory influx of impulses, a reaction prompted by the threat of castration in the boy and disappointment in the girl, which transforms these instinctual drives into identifications. The ego identifies with Oedipal partners, based on a specific economy in which the dominance of a sexual position is determined not only by the strength of the libidinal investment in one or the other of the parents but also by everything that occurred in the subject's prehistory, before the Oedipus. This is how the superego comes into being.

In 1932, Freud said:

> I myself am far from satisfied with these remarks on identification, but it will be enough if you can grant me that the installation of the super-ego can be described as a successful instance of identification with the parental agency.[22]

Thus, it is clear that the superego is heir to the Oedipus complex. This means, literally, that it takes the place of the "lost" or "deceased" parents. Ideally, identification is sublimated, desexualised interiorisation of the great Oedipal drama. The identifications constituting the superego "liquidate" a situation made unbearable by the prohibition of incest and castration. As a result, the superego reproduces on the stage of the ego, in the narcissistic space, a fateful relational entanglement.

The various forms of recurrent guilt are all ways of repeating Oedipal anxieties: fear of losing love, narcissistic fear of castration. The layered, stratified nature of the ego, further underscored by this last version of identification theory, is therefore not to be imagined merely as a superposition of characters, but, rather, as a multipolar setting where the voices of several "subjects" can make themselves heard better, depending on the circumstances. The severity of the superego introduces a rather difficult question concerning its origin: does it simply reflect the severity of the "castrating" external agency, the "father", or, on a deeper level, is this severity rooted in the strength of erotic and destructive impulses that the installation of the superego has "converted"?

Guilt in all its forms, from the light forms like remorse and self-criticism to its more detrimental obsessional forms and melancholia, reveals the splitable nature of the ego. As Freud had written to Fliess, the term *identification* literally designates a multitude of psychic characters. Severe states of ego destruction designate acute identification-related conflict.

But there is more to say. Identification, which transforms the ego by modifying the investments of the id, brings about a dissociation of mixed instincts. Because it desexualises instinctual energy, it separates life instincts from death instincts, freeing the latter, which, until then, were neutralised by being combined with Eros. This is what occurs when the death drive is freed in melancholia, when the ego ideal subjects the masochistic ego (transformed by the object) to merciless sadism.

These remarks reveal the double character of identification: on the positive side, it places itself in the service of narcissism, supports the ego by enriching it with traits borrowed from the object and preserves it by preserving its objects, but on the negative side, it separates the life instinct from the death instinct and threatens to kill the ego.

These are the crucial principles presented in *The Ego and the Id*. Two types of questions remain in suspense: establishing the status of primary identification (to the father, to the parents, to the mother?) and the details of the Oedipus complex's prehistory for the boy and especially for the girl. This double question can perhaps be combined into a single quest: determining the origin (origins?) of the superego and its status as the originator of a law, the law of the difference between the sexes: that is, the law governing castration. If, as Freud says, the superego reinforces the sexual nature of the child and assigns his sexual orientation – until puberty, which repeats the Oedipus and connects his psychic heritage with the transformations of the body, enabling the choice of a genital object – it must be accepted that even before the Oedipal stage, there existed a sexual ideal, a sexual identification and, therefore, a sort of "pre-Oedipal superego". This is the hypothesis advanced by Melanie Klein.[23]

The concept of identification poses a double problem: it calls for a discussion of origins, of its genesis, and it calls for a discussion of structure, of ego differentiation. This ego is something very different than the "ego" of psychology. Indeed, the theory of identification formulated in psychoanalysis moves away from the image of the ego elaborated by a metaphysical tradition influenced by transcendental idealism. Freud, in any case, stayed away from any such tradition;

he has been blamed by some for having adopted a positivist materialism described as restrictive and dehumanising. This is, in fact, a very interesting misunderstanding, insidiously kept alive by philosophers "open" to psychoanalysis.[24] The misunderstanding consists of saying, "Yes, Freud's discovery brings into question the cogito, the idealistic ego, the locus of thinking and will, and Freud was right to dispel the subjective illusions associated with this representation of an ego, a place of freedom and to condemn archeological determinations, but, by doing this, he purified the ego, ridding it of its lies and its deceptions, to set the ground for an authentic subject, an 'I'".

Indeed, Freud's originality consisted of insisting on connecting the most seemingly unrelated human psychic formations with each other. This perspective, which deliberately overlooks the difference, not to say the opposition, between normality and pathology, excludes all possibility of determining once and for all the status and economy of a "normal" ego or of devising a psychic personality model having universal application. This is no doubt the aim of the ongoing controversy on the "subject". We must point out that Freud never used this term to designate the ego, the individual, the person. Moreover, the very fact of highlighting the concepts of object-choice, investment of the object and object-cathexis profoundly changes the meaning generally attributed to this term, correlated with the term *subject*. We know, of course, that ordinary language maintains that the "subject" cannot be treated like an "object", but psychoanalysis takes us into another sphere of signification. From the perspective of the psychic apparatus, which is in truth an intrapsychic apparatus, the subject is not an entity – rather, it is disseminated; it is plural. "I" is what designates the subject of a statement. This "I" must not be confused with an ideology of the ego, itself unrelated to psychoanalytic theorisation of the "ego".

Elements of a metapsychology of identification

In psychology, the term *identification* refers essentially to the change in behaviour of an individual influenced by someone he sees as a model; it belongs to a series of more or less interchangeable terms such as empathy, imitations, sympathy, compassion, emulation et cetera.

After scrutinising Freudian terminology, we are returning to the ordinary usage of the term to assess the modifications brought about by psychoanalytic exploration. These modifications originate in the discovery of a sphere at once foreign to "psychology" and belonging to it while excluding it from its own sphere. The analysis of the ego is not the psychology of the ego. It refers to a different sphere (that of the experience of analysis: that is, transference) from the sphere of psychology, which nevertheless nowadays claims to be "Freudian".[25]

A "metapsychological" examination of the identification process reveals the extent of this difference.

When consulting psychoanalytic dictionaries, it is surprising to see the effort deployed by different authors in attempting to classify the uses of the term *identification* as a way of establishing some order and creating distinctions. Interestingly, throughout our examination of the development of this term, we found no hint of any concern with classification on Freud's part. He did not emphasise the difference between the transitive form of the verb *to identify* (which encompasses the meanings found in the language of logic, of administration, of the law, of entomology, etc.) and the reflexive form *identify with* (which, in ordinary language, refers to love, imitation, mime or the theatre).

Relying solely on the materiality of words, we could say that the central problem of psychoanalysis can be found in this *with* of the second form of the verb. The logic of classification, the logic of the excluded third party and of non-contradiction, reveal what psychoanalysis, attentive to the "illogical" in the primary process, does not need and is not concerned with revealing. Under literal scrutiny, the term *gleichwie* (just like) reveals its unconscious elements. The peculiar "logic" of identification or, rather, of identifications (which we have seen to be frequently plural and contradictory) is the logic of like or the unconscious grammar governing the play of the presence or absence of this little *with* in *identify with*. The splitting in the active form – where a "subject" transports his action into an "object" – and in the reflexive form – where the same "subject" suffers the action whose agent he himself is – in unconscious identification (the sort psychoanalysis deals with) is no longer in effect because we are dealing with narcissism as a fundamental relationship, in which life and death impulses are present – a predominant space of primary masochism, where the verb has only an intermediary voice, we might say (lesser than the simple opposition between the active and the passive).

The desire motivating identifications and following their paths governs this logic of the intermediary of the "being like", in which the same is the other and – to add insult to injury – one equals two.

Let us go back to the difference between the psychology and the analysis of the ego. To draw its contours, let us adopt the perspective Freud succeeded in acquiring: the metapsychological perspective.

Identification models

Two models dominate the multiplicity of identifications: the hysterical model and the melancholic model – that is, a neurotic process and a quasi-psychotic process. The former was constructed in the first topographical model, with dream interpretation as its main axis – the dream being the pathological/psychotic nocturnal activity of all "normal" men. The latter model emerged from the analysis of disorders of the ego in the development of the "second topographical model" (id, ego, superego) in an attempt to solve the enigma of melancholia, guilt and masochism.

The difficulty posed by the hysterical identification model is its double version: the dream version and the symptomatic version. In dreams, regression to the primary process is massive, and unconscious wishes create very powerful and invasive identification. In the realm of the real, where the hysteric addresses the other in a partial imitation of the traits corresponding to his desire, the regression is more limited and restricted to secondary processes which intensify the work of distortion. There, desire only reveals itself through parapraxes, unfulfillable whims and refusals, which entrap the other (see the "beautiful butcher's wife" and "Dora"). Since hysterics are often witty, Freud takes advantage of the analysis of these patients to interpret the possibilities of jokes and parapraxes, more or less amusing or embarrassing, occurring in everyday life.

But Freud asserts that melancholic identification is nevertheless "better known and more important" than hysterical identification.

Melancholic or narcissistic identification is not an expression of rivalry or envy, like the hysterical form which involves an unconscious desire to be like someone and which only emerges at the preconscious level in the "strange" form of a partial, localised symptom that remains undecipherable. In the melancholic process, there is a frightening depth, a deadly atmosphere. The analysis of melancholia leads back to the origins of love, to its narcissistic nature, to the ambivalence of any relation with an object, to the origins of the ego and its unavoidable splitting. Melancholia makes it possible to understand the genesis of unconscious guilt associated with the function of a psychic agency whose discovery was decisive: the agency of the ideal. Melancholic identification, incorporation of the lost object and, with it, the repetition of the immensity of love and hate also provide a key and the necessary conditions for hysteria. Although the unconscious intent of the hysteric is to be like, to take the place of someone else, this "unifying" intent has a history and even a prehistory: the cannibalism of the oral stage, in which to love is to devour. In melancholia, the loss of the ego points to its origins, to original narcissism with no inside and not outside, no subject or object, but only auto-affection, auto-erotism, omnipotence, as well as total dereliction.

Melancholic identification, as destructive narcissistic regression, forces us to consider the instinctual aspect of the symptomatology and not only the psychic, conscious or unconscious "quality" of representations and repressed feelings. It is understandable that this genealogical element revealed by regression led Freud to postulate the existence of an "id" and to reconstitute the consolidation of the ego, based on the trajectory and accidents of its formation. Of course, the unconscious is the space of identification. But in this space, there is ego, ideal and impulse. The various scenarios of pathology show the servitudes of the "ego" in relation to reality, to the id (Eros and death) and to the ideal (superego). The second topographical model intersects with the first; this interlacing and its construction are described by identification theory, the same theory which explains the Oedipus complex. The opposing Oedipal instinctual currents are resolved (or should be, in theory, with the destruction of the Oedipus) by means of a complicated play of identifications of two kinds: hysterical (with the rival, with the ideal) and "melancholic" (replacement of a differentiation of the ego with the incorporation of abandoned love objects).

Thus, the destruction of this complex comes about through a narcissistic process of identification. The ego ideal or superego inherits the erotic, ambivalent investments and the links of affection that attached the child to his parents. Identification does more than repress the Oedipus complex since, theoretically, it replaces it by installing in the ego more or less conflictual agencies. But we know that it is this complex, insufficiently repressed, which produces the repetitions known as neuroses.

The construction of a double identification model (narcissistic investment of an ideal trait of the other, who is taken as a double and, at the same time, in whom there is real investment and regressive identification of the whole ego with the lost object) has caused certain commentators to ask, "Is all this not in the domain of pathology? Is there no type of identification that is constructive: progressive rather than regressive?"

Indeed, a third model has been proposed: a "maturity-promoting", "progressive" model exemplified by the introjection of the other's traits, which places the "subject" on a liberating path. Piera Aulagnier speaks of a sort of "identificatory project". This project would be, at the conscious level, the effect of unconscious identification mechanisms; it would illustrate these effects in concrete form, without demanding that a tribute of unawareness and repression be paid. Of course, the distinction between such a project (the ideal) and the ego would have to be preserved: psychosis consists of the annulment of this distinction, which guarantees the possibility of temporal delimitation, of historicisation.[26]

Such suggestions are made in response to the real difficulty of analytic practice and its therapeutic concerns, which are, at the same time, ethical. But this "third path", tending towards normalisation, seems to depart from Freudian theory.

Is it possible to leave aside unconscious, regressive modes of functioning, loving and desiring? What has been said so far, even in a sketchy manner, is enough to show that it is not easy to adopt a simple solution to the problem of the status, the origin and the functions of the ideal[27] without the risk of tending towards idealisation and normalisation.

Economy of identification

The identification process determines its economy based on the double imperative of the pleasure-unpleasure principle and its "beyond", the silent constraint of the death drive (return of the living to a dissociated, inorganic state).

The economic function of identification is to allow the transformation of instinctual energy in order to enable repression. It is the "royal" road to detachment of the libido from its objects.

Seen in this light, identification must be one of the most primitive forms taken by instinctual energy, existing prior to the repression observed in neuroses, which it no doubt makes possible because to repress means to withdraw investments from denied or prohibited objects. Identification is an alternative to another possible solution, which would be investing a new object; identification offers a portion of the ego as an object of the libidinal investment to be repressed. It appears to us that identification brings together two instinctual functions: the "turning round upon the subject's own self" and the "reversal into its opposite":[28] a repetition of the relation to the object in the initially auto-erotic, sado-masochistic setting of the emerging ego. As the locus for such an enactment, the ego offers itself as the place of choice for anxiety. Fear of castration, the prototype of all forms of anxiety, finds in all tensions between the ego and the superego, heir to the fantasised objects of the id, its obsessive reproductions.

By transforming sexual energy into ego-libido, identification brings about the desexualisation and sublimation of this energy. Since no libidinal investment is separate from the death instinct, the effect of desexualisation is to dissociate the instinctual combination. Thus, identification causes an instinctive defusion (*Ent-mischung*) having considerable consequences for the ego, which appears to benefit from identifications. The release of the death instinct triggers sadism directed at the ego, taken up by the superego against the ego, the place of masochism.

When ambivalence is successfully installed, sublimation uses ego processes and interests, particularly the ego's intellect, which, due to libidinal regression to narcissism, is filled with the energy withdrawn from objects.

The most obscure aspect of this play of metaphors is the "oral", cannibalistic dimension of the identification process, the original form of attachment to an object. This applies to primary identification, which Freud considers to be prior to any object-choice and to be an initial stage in which identification and object-choice cannot be separated or distinguished from each other. The double relation of the child to his parents, a narcissistic relation (he is heir to their "lost" narcissism) as well as an "anaclitic" relation (they are objects necessary to his survival and development), is an "oral" identification. The father, the mother, "the parents" (how can we designate these archaic "objects" whose contours are abolished by original narcissism?) are the objects or forerunners of what objects will be when there will be an "ego", a "someone". This double attachment, the place of inscription of the ideal, a point of the origin of desire always already fantasised requires an analytic investigation fraught with difficulties. Among them, the primary phantasies[29] haunting, in the unconscious, the desire to know the origins. Indeed, this mysterious primary identification, which concerns the origins of the psychic apparatus, is the primal scene of the emergence of desire.

This phantasmatic tissue of desire, born of immemorial identification with an undefinable but necessary object, brings to light the relation of identification to *imago* and to language. We know that Lacan's work finds its roots in an investigation which at once proved to be original on images and their "psychic reality", on the dimension of the imaginary concerned with the lure and with hallucination.

Using a totally different approach, Melanie Klein also founded her theory on the archaic phantasies of the origins.

Let us note in passing that these two authors started their work in the field of psychosis. Each of them, in his own brilliant way, immediately defined, together, the two processes of instinctual development and defence against the fear of death: projection and introjection, involved in identification. Freud examined these processes separately, except perhaps in *Totem and Taboo* and the analysis of Schreber. We see the Kleinian discussion of the paranoid-schizoid position on the one hand and the depressive position on the other as a possible reflection of this difficulty. Similarly, the Lacanian distinction between specular and symbolic identification (the imaginary is projected; a signifier is introjected) can be seen as an attempt to tackle this problem head on.

Dynamics of identification

From the start, identification has been recognised as a symptom-producing process and, therefore, a psychic compromise between opposing forces. Later, it was revealed to be the fundamental process involved in the formation of the agencies of the ego (ego, ego ideal, superego, ideal ego).

In any case, identification is a response to the urgent need to avoid the anxiety produced by conflict, an anxiety that endangers the ego.

For example, the identification of the homosexual, similar to that present in melancholia but without the destructive aspect associated with the intensity of ambivalence, consists of the introjection of an incestuous scene: the relation to the mother, which must be repressed, is not abandoned or sublimated; it is, rather, displaced onto the sphere of the psychic as a sexual relation. The ego, transformed into "the mother", now begins to seek libidinal objects on the model of what had previously been the mother's object: the ego itself. Here, we can clearly see the repressive function of identification, but this repression is not annihilation.

While *to repress* means to withdraw the investment made in an object, identification is an entirely beneficial narcissistic operation: it saves a portion of the investment and installs the object in the ego, which models itself on its image, partially or completely. In all neuroses, a portion of object libido resists this conversion to narcissism, to massive regression from object-cathexis to identification, which would make it "useless" to maintain a relation to the object, in reality or in phantasy. Object-cathexis can be maintained in the presence of identification to varying degrees.

Freud notes, without developing the idea, that the coexistence of these two types of object-relations is frequently seen in women. He writes:

> [Identification] is a very important form of attachment to someone else, probably the very first, and not the same thing as the choice of an object. The difference between the two can be expressed in some such way as this. If a boy identifies himself with his father, he wants to *be like* his father; if he makes him the object of his choice, he wants to *have* him, to possess him. In the first case the ego is altered on the model of the father; in the second case that is not necessary. Identification and object-choice are to a large extent independent of each other; it is however possible to identify oneself with someone whom, for instance, one has taken as a sexual object, and to alter one's ego on his

model. It is said that the influencing of the ego by the sexual object occurs particularly often with women and is characteristic of femininity.[30]

This text is another contribution to be added to the complicated body of analytic research on femininity. Identification could be seen as a sort of safeguard against the disappearance of the object, the threat of its loss. The fear of losing love could be the equivalent for women of fear of castration in men.

This relation between identification and object-choice is of paramount importance: it can be seen in children, in adults, in normal people as well as the "sick".

The phenomenon of mourning also deserves particular attention.

Mourning appears to be an inevitable task, a trial every man must face sooner or later. We know, since *Mourning and Melancholia*, that the seriousness and duration of mourning depend on the intensity of the emotional ambivalence the "survivor" harboured towards the lost object. Mourning is not a pathological process. But it is not altogether unrelated to what happens in melancholia, as Freud points out and, after him, Karl Abraham and Melanie Klein. Freud presents an interesting model of renouncing an object: the subject, in "revolt" against the object or against a mediator – the fate responsible for his disillusionment – compensates himself for this loss by setting up the object in his ego. Here, we can speak of "regression" from object-choice to identification or of passing from a sexual register to a narcissistic register. However, the mourning process, with this structurally regressive character (this word has never had a pejorative meaning for Freud), is the only way for the ego to survive: that is, to live and take responsibility for its survival.

Partial identification with the deceased completes the work of mourning. The ego is enriched, and the object is saved, in a manner of speaking. Could we not consider this work of mourning as the most general type of psychic working through of conflict?

In mourning, the conflict resides in the antagonism of love, which is suddenly "without a real object" and painfully attached to memories, to the traces of the deceased and of hate, unconscious in serious cases, provoked or revived by absence, by the failure, the deficiency of the object which is suddenly missing.

Is it not the case that the superego emerges from this work of mourning?

The ever-uncertain success of this enormous work of mourning, which involves abandoning Oedipal libidinal positions, is confirmed by the state of "health" of the ego. Identification in a context of mourning means repossessing what had to be lost. The ego is composed of lost objects. Failure of this transformative work, due to the strength of archaic attachments to objects, generates neuroses and psychoses.

To conclude, let us look at what takes place in psychoanalytic treatment.

Freud, who defined the conditions required for this therapy, says this about analytic work:

[T]he therapeutic efforts of psycho-analysis... its intention, is... to strengthen the ego, to make it more independent of the super-ego, to widen its field of perception and enlarge its organization, so that it can appropriate fresh portions of the id. Where id was, there ego shall be. It is a work of culture – not unlike the draining of the Zuider Zee.[31]

These famous words carry much of what identification theory teaches us. The superego, of which the ego must become more independent, can be supposed to be, given its genesis, the transformed remnant of fragments of the id, appropriated by the ego to escape narcissistic castration anxiety. Having originated in the matchless objects of the id, of which it was "bereaved", the superego still speaks, in more or less severe tones, for these "deceased".

Fear of the superego's demands, the primordial form of human anxiety, repeats the vicissitudes of the journey that led to the emergence of the "I".

It would be reasonable to ask if this "ideal" which pulls the ego forward is not the very thing which also holds it back. In other words, we might ask ourselves if the Oedipus complex, with its unfathomable prehistory, can really ever disappear.

It may be the case, as analytic work sometimes shows only too clearly, that to accept the inheritance of the Oedipus, to renounce Oedipal objects – extravagant, fantastic, intrusive objects, as intrusive as the instinctive forces rushing in upon them – is a never-ending task, just as an analysis is infinite, interminable.

Although analysis intends to enable the subject (*Ich*) to appropriate fragments of the id, it does not do so by providing a means of unburdening or release. Appropriating the id is a work of culture, a work of speech, a work of symbolic identification: not identification "with the analyst" but with the traits that can take hold of words which unlock the timeless id and carry them into time and into difference.

Notes

1 Freud, S., *Findings, Ideas, Problems*, S.E. 23: 299–300, London: Hogarth, 1941.
2 The language is borrowed from J. Lacan's text "Logical Time and the Assertion of Anticipated Certainty: A New Sophism", in *Écrits*, Fink, B. (Trans.), New York: W.W. Norton, 2002, pp. 161–175.
3 We have borrowed this language from a short technical text Freud wrote in 1914: "Remembering, Repeating and Working-Through", in *Papers on Technique*, S.E. 12: 147–156.
4 Freud, S., *The Origins of Psycho-Analysis: Letters to Wilhelm Fliess, Drafts and Notes, 1887–1902*, New York: Basic Books, 1954.
5 Freud, S., *The Interpretation of Dreams*, S.E. 4-5, London: Hogarth, 1900.
6 Freud, S., *New Introductory Lectures on Psycho-Analysis*, S.E. 22, London: Hogarth, 1932, p. 38.
7 Freud, S., *Jokes and Their Relation to the Unconscious*, S.E. 8, London: Hogarth, 1905.
8 Freud, S., *Group Psychology and the Analysis of the Ego*, S.E. 18: 67–143, London: Hogarth, 1921.
9 Freud, S., *Fragment of an Analysis of a Case of Hysteria*, S.E. 7: 1–122, London: Hogarth, 1905.
10 Freud, S., *From the History of an Infantile Neurosis*, S.E. 17, London: Hogarth, 1918.
11 Freud, S., *On an Autobiographical Account of a Case of Paranoia*, S.E. 12, London: Hogarth, 1911.

12 Freud, S., *On Narcissism: An Introduction*, S.E. 14: 67–102, London: Hogarth, 1914.
13 Freud, S., *Three Essays on the Theory of Sexuality*, S.E. 7: 198, London: Hogarth, 1915.
14 Freud, S., *Totem and Taboo*, S.E. 13, London: Hogarth, 1913.
15 Freud, S., *Leonardo da Vinci and a Memory of His Childhood*, S.E. 11, London: Hogarth, 1910.
16 Freud, S., *Analysis of a Phobia in a Five-year-old Boy*, S.E. 10, London: Hogarth, 1909a.
17 Freud, S., *Notes Upon a Case of Obsessional Neurosis*, London: Hogarth, 1909b.
18 Ibid.
19 Freud, S., *Mourning and Melancholia*, S.E. 14, London: Hogarth, 1917.
20 Freud, S., *Beyond the Pleasure Principle*, S.E. 18, London: Hogarth, 1920.
21 We can only suggest in passing the contrast between this *fort-sein* and the Heideggerian theme of the Dassein, whose being there has been the source of countless phenomenological developments on "presence".
22 Freud, S., "The Dissection of the Psychical Personality", in *New Introductory Lectures on Psycho-Analysis*, S.E. 22, London: Hogarth, 1932.
23 The debate between Freud and Melanie Klein left visible traces in Chapter VII of *Civilization and Its Discontents*.
24 For instance, Paul Ricoeur's hermeneutic essays: *Freud and Philosophy: An Essay on Interpretation*, New Haven, CT: Yale University Press, 1970; and *The Conflict of Interpretations*, Evanston, IL: Northwestern University Press, 1974.
    See also: Vergote, A., *Problèmes de psychanalyse*, Paris: Desclée de Brouwer, 1973.
    Other psychoanalysts compare the opposition between the (impure) "ego" and the (pure) "id" to the opposition between the unconscious and the conscious. For instance, Luquet, P., "Les idéaux du moi et les idéaux du je", *Revue française de psychanalyse*, nos. 5–6 (1973), pp. 1007–1013.
    We have not yet overcome the effects of a Platonian antinomy. We have the impression that we must take seriously the linguistic status of this "id" in order to free ourselves from philosophical misunderstanding. We believe Jacques Lacan has succeeded in doing this.
25 See Chapter 3, "The Anatomy of the Mental Personality", in *New Introductory Lectures on Psycho-Analysis*, S.E. 22, London: Hogarth, 1932.
26 See Donnet, J.-L., and Pinel, J.-P., "Le problème de l'identification chez Freud", *L'Inconscient*, no. 7 (1968), pp. 5–22; and Aulagnier, P., "Demande et identification", *L'Inconscient*, no. 7 (1968), pp. 23–65.
27 This question holds a strategic place in the dispute between Freud's heirs, divided into different "schools": Kleinian, Lacanian, American, "orthodox" et cetera. An overview of the situation among non-Lacanian practitioners can be found in "L'idéal du moi", by Jeanine Chasseguet-Smirgel, *Revue Française de Psychanalyse*, XXXVII (1973).
28 Freud, S., *Instincts and Their Vicissitudes*, S.E. 14, London: Hogarth, 1915.
29 See the remarkable essay by Laplanche, J., and Pontalis, J.-B., "Fantasy and the Origins of Sexuality", *The International Journal of Psychoanalysis*, 49, no. 1 (1968), pp. 1–18.
30 Freud, S., *New Introductory Lectures*, op. cit., p. 62. Note the peculiar "it is said" which introduces the last assertion.
31 Ibid., op. cit., p. 79.

References

Abraham, K. (1965). *Selected Papers of Karl Abraham M.D.*, Bryan, D., and Strachey, A. (Trans.). London: Hogarth.

Abraham, N. & Torok, M. (1972). "Article in Destins du cannibalisme". *Gallimard*.

Adler, A. (1964). *Individual Psychology*. New York: Harper Perennial.

Alexander, F. & Staub, H. (1956). *The Criminal, the Judge and the Public*. Glencoe, IL: The Free Press.

Anonymous. (1970). "Le Clivage du sujet et son identification". *Silicet*, nos. 2-3.

Anzieu, D. (1986). *Freud's Self-Analysis*. Madison, CT: International Universities Press.

Arban, D. (1962). *Dostoievski par Lui-Même, Écrivains de Toujours*. Paris: Editions du Seuil.

Arban, D. (1968). *Dostoievski le Coupable*. Paris: Julliard.

Aulagnier, P. (1968). "Demande et identification". *L'Inconscient*, no. 7: 23–65.

Aulagnier, P. (1976). "Le concept d'identification". Lecture at Sainte-Anne Hospital, Paris. Unpublished.

Aulagnier, P. (2001). *The Violence of Interpretation*. London: Routledge.

Bastide, R. (1968). *Sociologia das doenças mentais (Sociology and Psychoanalysis)*. Lisbon: Publicações Europa-América.

Bergson, H. (2014). *Laughter: An Essay on the Meaning of the Comic*. Eastford, CT: Martino Fine Books.

Castoriadis-Aulagnier, P. (1968). "Demande et identification". *L'inconscient*, no. 7 (July).

Chasseguet-Smirgel, J. (1973). "L'idéal du moi". *Revue Française de Psychanalyse*, XXXVII.

Chasseguet-Smirgel, J. (1976). "Some Thoughts on the Ego Ideal: A Contribution to the Study of the 'Illness of Reality'". *The Psychoanalytic Quarterly*, 45, no. 3.

Chastaing, M. (1951). *L'Existence d'autrui*. Paris: Presses Universitaires de France.

Clavreul, J. (1968). "Identification et complexe de castration". *L'inconscient*, no. 7 (July).

Deleuze, G. (1991). *Masochism: Coldness and Cruelty*. New York: Zone Books.

Deleuze, G. & Guattari, F. (2009). *Anti-Oedipus: Capitalism and Schizophrenia*. London: Penguin Classics.

De Waelhens, A. (2001). "Figures of the Unconscious". In *Phenomenology and Lacan on Schizophrenia*, Ver Eecke, W., and De Waelhens, A. (Eds.). Leuven: Leuven University Press.

De Wolf, M. (1973). *La Castration dans l'oeuvre et l'expérience freudienne* (Castration in the Freudian Oeuvre and Practice). Doctoral thesis, Louvain Catholic University, Faculty of Psychology.

Dolto, F. (1988). *Au jeu du désir – Essais cliniques*. Paris: Éditions Points.

Dolto, F. (1973). *Dominique: Analysis of an Adolescent*. New York: E. P. Dutton.

Dolto, F. (2013). *Psychoanalysis and Paediatrics*. London: Routledge.

Donnet, J.-L. & Pinel, J.-P. (1968). "Le problème de l'identification chez Freud". *L'Inconscient*, no. 7.

Duyckaerts, F. (1974). "Conscience et prise de conscience". *Éditions Mardaga*.

Falzeder, E. & Brabant, E. (eds.). (1993). *The Correspondence of Sigmund Freud and Sandor Ferenczi: 1908–1914*. Cambridge, MA: Harvard University Press. (Letter July 9, 1913).

Fedida, P. (1971). *L'inceste et le meurtre dans la généalogie, in Szondiana*, VIII. Paris: Nauwelaerts.

Fedida, P. (1972). "Article in Destins du cannibalisme". *Gallimard*.

Fenichel, O. (1945). *The Psychoanalytic Theory of Neurosis*. New York: W.W. Norton.

Foucault, M. (1988). *Madness and Civilization*. New York: Vintage Books.

Frazer, J. G. (1998). *The Golden Bough*. Oxford: Oxford University Press.

Freud, A. (1992). *The Ego and the Mechanisms of Defence*. London: Karnac Books.

Freud, S. (1900a). *An Outline of Psycho-Analysis*, S.E. 5. London: Hogarth.

Freud, S. (1900b). *The Interpretation of Dreams*, S.E. 4. London: Hogarth.

Freud, S. (1900c). *The Interpretation of Dreams*, S.E. 5. London: Hogarth.

Freud, S. (1904). *Psychopathic Characters on the Stage*, S.E. 7. London: Hogarth.

Freud, S. (1905a). *Fragment of an Analysis of a Case of Hysteria*, S.E. 7: 1–122. London: Hogarth.

Freud, S. (1905b). *Jokes and Their Relation to the Unconscious*, S.E. 8. London: Hogarth.

Freud, S. (1905c). *Three Essays on the Theory of Sexuality*, S.E. 7. London: Hogarth.

Freud, S. (1906). *Psycho-Analysis and the Establishment of the Facts in Legal Proceedings*, S.E. 9. London: Hogarth.

Freud, S. (1908a). *'Civilized' Sexual Morality and Modern Nervous Illness*, S.E. 8: 76–99. London: Hogarth.

Freud, S. (1908b). *Character of Anal Erotism*, S.E. 9. London: Hogarth.

Freud, S. (1908c). *Creative Writers and Day-Dreaming*, S.E. 9. London: Hogarth.

Freud, S. (1909a). *Analysis of a Phobia in a Five-year-old Boy*, S.E. 10. London: Hogarth.

Freud, S. (1909b). *Family Romances*, S.E. 9. London: Hogarth.

Freud, S. (1909c). *Notes Upon a Case of Obsessional Neurosis*, S.E. 8. London: Hogarth.

Freud, S. (1909d). *Some General Remarks on Hysterical Attacks*, S.E. 9. London: Hogarth.

Freud, S. (1910a, 1912, 1918). *Contributions to the Psychology of Love*, S.E. 11. London: Hogarth.

Freud, S. (1910b). *Five Lectures on Psycho-Analysis*, S.E. 11: 3–55. London: Hogarth.

Freud, S. (1910c). *Leonardo da Vinci and a Memory of His Childhood*, S.E. 11: 57–138. London: Hogarth.

Freud, S. (1911a). *Psycho-analytic Notes on an Autobiographical Account of a Case of Paranoia*, S.E. 12. London: Hogarth.

Freud, S. (1911b). *On an Autobiographical Account of a Case of Paranoia*, S.E. 12. London: Hogarth.

Freud, S. (1911c). *On the Mechanisms of Paranoia*, S.E. 12. London: Hogarth.

Freud, S. (1911d). *Formulations on the Two Principles of Mental Functioning*, S.E. 12: 218–226. London: Hogarth.

Freud, S. (1913a). *The Disposition to Obsessional Neurosis*, S.E. 12. London: Hogarth.

Freud, S. (1913b). *Totem and Taboo*, S.E. 13. London: Hogarth.

Freud, S. (1914a). *On Narcissism: An Introduction*, S.E. 14. London: Hogarth.

Freud, S. (1914b). "Remembering, Repeating and Working-Through". In *Papers on Technique*, S.E. 12: 147–156. London: Hogarth.

Freud, S. (1915a). *Instincts and Their Vicissitudes*, S.E. 14. London: Hogarth.

Freud, S. (1915b). *Repression*, S.E. 14. London: Hogarth.

Freud, S. (1915c). *The Unconscious*, S.E. 14. London: Hogarth.

Freud, S. (1916a). *Metapsychological Supplement to the Theory of Dreams*, S.E. 14. London: Hogarth.

Freud, S. (1916b). *Some Character-Types Met with in Psycho-Analytic Work*, S.E. 14. London: Hogarth.

Freud, S. (1916–17). *Introductory Lectures on Psycho-Analysis: The Libido Theory and Narcissism*, S.E. 16. London: Hogarth.

Freud, S. (1917a). *Mourning and Melancholia*, S.E. 14: 239–258. London: Hogarth.

Freud, S. (1917b). *On Transformations of Instinct as Exemplified in Anal Erotism*, S.E. 17. London: Hogarth.

Freud, S. (1918). *From the History of an Infantile Neurosis*, S.E. 17. London: Hogarth.

Freud, S. (1919a). *A Child Is Being Beaten*, S.E. 17. London: Hogarth.

Freud, S. (1919b). *The Uncanny*, S.E. 17. London: Hogarth.

Freud, S. (1920a). *A General Introduction to Psychoanalysis*. New York: Boni and Liveright, p. 205.

Freud, S. (1920b). *Beyond the Pleasure Principle*, S.E. 18. London: Hogarth.

Freud, S. (1920c). *The Psychoanalysis of a Case of Homosexuality in a Woman*, S.E. 18: 147–172. London: Hogarth.

Freud, S. (1921). *Group Psychology and the Analysis of the Ego*, S.E. 18. London: Hogarth.

Freud, S. (1923a). *Some Neurotic Mechanisms in Jealousy, Paranoia and Homosexuality*, S.E. 18. London: Hogarth.

Freud, S. (1923b). *The Ego and the Id*, S.E. 19. London: Hogarth.

Freud, S. (1923c). *The Infantile Genital Organization*, S.E. 19. London: Hogarth.

Freud, S. (1924a). *The Dissolution of the Oedipus Complex*, S.E. 19. London: Hogarth.

Freud, S. (1924b). *The Economic Problem of Masochism*, S.E. 19: 159–170. London: Hogarth.

Freud, S. (1925a). *An Autobiographical Study*, S.E. 20. London: Hogarth.

Freud, S. (1925b). *Psychogenesis of a Case of Homosexuality in a Woman*, S.E. 18. London: Hogarth.

Freud, S. (1925c). *Some Psychical Consequences of the Anatomical Distinction Between the Sexes*, S.E. 19: 243–258. London: Hogarth.

Freud, S. (1926). *Inhibitions, Symptoms and Anxiety*, S.E. 20. London: Hogarth.

Freud, S. (1927a). *Humour*, S.E. 21. London: Hogarth.

Freud, S. (1927b). *The Future of an Illusion*, S.E. 21. London: Hogarth.

Freud, S. (1928). *Dostoevsky and Parricide*, S.E. 21. London: Hogarth.

Freud, S. (1930). *Civilization and Its Discontents*, S.E. 19. London: Hogarth.

Freud, S. (1932). *Why War?* S.E. 22. London: Hogarth.

Freud, S. (1933). *New Introductory Lectures on Psychoanalysis*, S.E. 22. London: Hogarth.

Freud, S. (1937). *Analysis Terminable and Interminable*, S.E. 23. London: Hogarth.

Freud, S. (1938). *Splitting of the Ego in the Process of Defence*, S.E. 21. London: Hogarth.

Freud, S. (1939). *Moses and Monotheism*, S.E. 23. London: Hogarth.

Freud, S. (1941). *Findings, Ideas, Problems*, S.E. 23: 299–300. London: Hogarth.

Freud, S. (1954). *The Origins of Psychoanalysis: Letters to Wilhelm Fliess, Drafts and Notes, 1887–1902*. New York: Basic Books.

Freud, S. & Breuer, J. (1895). *Studies on Hysteria*, S.E. 2. London: Hogarth, 1955.

Graf, M. (1942). "Reminiscences of Professor Sigmund Freud". *Psychoanalytic Quarterly*, 11, no. 4.

Granoff, W. (1975). *Filiations: L'Avenir du complexed'Oedipe*. Paris: Les Éditions de Minuit.

Grasset, A. (1968). *L'Enfant épileptique*. Paris: Presses Universitaires de France.

Green, A. (1972). "Article in Destins du cannibalisme". *Gallimard*.

Green, A. (1999). *The Fabric of Affect in Psychoanalytic Discourse*. London: Routledge.

Groddeck, G. (1949). *The Book of the It*. New York: Vintage Books.

Hesnard, A. (1957). *Psychanalyse du lien interhumain*. Paris: Presses Universitaires de France.

Hook, D., Neill, C., & Vanheule, S. (eds.). (2019). *Reading Lacan's Écrits: From 'The Freudian Thing' to 'Remarks on Daniel Lagache'*. London: Routledge.

Jones, E. (1956). *The Life and Work of Sigmund Freud*, Vol. 2. London: Hogarth.

Jones, E. (1957). *The Life and Work of Sigmund Freud*, Vol. 3. London: Hogarth.

Jones, E. (1976). *Hamlet and Oedipus*. New York: Norton Library.

Jones, E. (ed.). (1989). *Selected Papers of Karl Abraham, M.D.* London: Routledge.

Jung, C. (2008). *Contributions to Analytical Psychology*. Milton Keynes: Read Books.

Kaufmann, P. (1967). *L'Expérience émotionnelle de l'espace*. Paris: Vrin.

Klein, M. (1928). "Early Stages of Oedipus Complex". *International Journal of Psychoanalysis*, 9.

Klein, M. (1935). "A Contribution to the Psychogenesis of Manic-Depressive States". *International Journal of Psychoanalysis*, 16: 145–174.

Klein, M. (1975). *The Writings of Melanie Klein*, Vol. I. Glencoe, IL: The Free Press.

Lacan, J. (1938). "Family Complexes: 'The Complex, a Concrete Factor in Familial Psychology.'" In *Autres Écrits: 2001*. Paris: Editions du Seuil.

Lacan, J. (1953). "The Neurotic's Individual Myth". Lecture at Philosophical College of Paris. Unpublished.

Lacan, J. (1961–1962). *The Seminar of Jacques Lacan, Book IX: Identification*, Gallagher, C. (Trans.). Unedited typescripts.

Lacan, J. (1973). "L'Étourdit". *Scilicet*, no. 4.

Lacan, J. (1976–77). "Seminar XXIV". www.lacaninireland.com.

Lacan, J. (1977a). "A Theoretical Introduction to the Functions of Psychoanalysis in Criminology". In *Écrits: A Selection*. London: Tavistock.

Lacan, J. (1977b). "Subversion of the Subject and the Dialectics of Desire". In *Écrits: A Selection*, Sheridan, A. (Trans.). London: Tavistock/Routledge.

Lacan, J. (1977c). "The Mirror Stage as Formative of the Function of the I as Revealed in Psychoanalytic Experience". In *Écrits: A Selection*. London: Tavistock.

Lacan, J. (1977d). "The Signification of the Phallus" (1958). In *Écrits: A Selection*. London: Routledge.

Lacan, J. (1989a). *Écrits: A Selection*, Sheridan, A. (Trans.). London: Routledge.

Lacan, J. (1989b). *Kant with Sade*, Swenson, J. B. (Trans.), October. Cambridge: Massachusetts Institute of Technology Press.

Lacan, J. (1996). "The Function and the Field of Speech and Language in Psychoanalysis". In *Écrits*, Fink, B. (Trans.). New York: W.W. Norton.

Lacan, J. (1998). *The Seminar of Jacques Lacan: Four Fundamental Concepts of Psychoanalysis*, Book XI. New York: W.W. Norton.

Lacan, J. (2002). "Logical Time and the Assertion of Anticipated Certainty: A New Sophism". In *Écrits*, Fink, B. (Trans.). New York: W.W. Norton.

Lacan, J. (2006). *Écrits: The First Complete Edition*, Fink, B. (Trans.). New York: W.W. Norton.

Lacan, J. (2015). *The Ethics of Psychoanalysis: The Seminar of Jacques Lacan*, Book VIII. London: Routledge.

Lagache, D. (1961). "La psychanalyse et la structure de la personnalité". *La psychanalyse*, no. 6. Presses Universitaires de France.

Laplanche, J. (1973). "Les normes morales et sociales, leur impact dans la topique subjective". *Bulletin de psychologie*, 26, no. 308.

Laplanche, J. (1973–4). "La castration, ses précurseurs et son destin". *Bulletin de psychologie*, XXVI.

Laplanche, J. (1985). *Life and Death in Psychoanalysis*. Baltimore, MD: Johns Hopkins University Press.

Laplanche, J. & Pontalis, J.-B. (1968). "Fantasy and the Origins of Sexuality". *International Journal of Psychoanalysis*, 49, no. 1: 1–18.

Laplanche, J. & Pontalis, J.-B. (1974). *The Language of Psycho-Analysis*. New York: W.W. Norton.

Laplanche, J. & Pontalis, J.-B. (1997). *Vocabulaire de la psychanalyse*. Paris: Presses Universitaires de France.

Lasch, C. (1974). "Freud and Women". *The New York Review of Books*, XXI, no. 15 (October 3).

Le Bon, G. (1895). *The Crowd: A Study of the Popular Mind*. New York: Dover Publications, 2002.

Levinas, E. (1969). *Totality and Infinity*. Pittsburgh, PA: Duquesne University Press.

Lévi-Strauss, C. (1971a). *The Elementary Structures of Kinship*. Boston, MA: Beacon Press.

Lévi-Strauss, C. (1971b). *Totemism*. Boston, MA: Beacon Press.

Luquet, P. (1973). "Les idéaux du moi et les idéaux du je". *Revue française de psychanalyse*, nos. 5–6.

Luquet, P. (2003). *Les Identifications*. Paris: Presses Universitaires de France.

Mannoni, M. (1973). *Education Impossible*. Paris: Editions du Seuil.

Mannoni, O. (1952). *Conditions psychologiques d'action sur les foules*. Nancy: Publications du Centre Européen Universitaire.

Mannoni, O. (1969a). "L'analyse originelle". In *Clés pour l'imaginaire*. Paris: Editions du Seuil, pp. 115–130.

Mannoni, O. (1969b). "L'Illusion comique ou le théâtre du point de vue de l'imaginaire". In *Clefs pour l'imaginaire*. Paris: Editions du Seuil.

Mélèse, L. (2001). *La psychanalyse au risque de l'épilepsie*. Toulouse: érès.

Mélèse, L. (2012). "Critical Transference in a Case of Severe Epilepsy". *American Journal of Psychoanalysis*, 72, no. 3 (August 31).

Nunberg, H. (1955). *Principles of Psychoanalysis*. New York: International Universities Press.

Ortigues, E. (1971). *Problèmes psychologiques et conventions sociales, in Szondiana*, VIII. Paris: Nauwelaerts.

Ortigues, E. (1973). "Les quiproquos du désir". In *Recherches et débats, No.78*. Paris: Desclée de Brouwer.

Ortigues, M.-C. & Ortigues, E. (1966). *L'Œdipe africain*. Paris: Plon.

Poncelet, C. (1974). *Les questions de l'épilepsie à travers la psychanalyse et la Schick-sanalyse*. Licentiate Dissertation in Psychology, University of Louvain. Unpublished.

Pontalis, J.-B. (1973). "Preface in His French Translation of Dostoevsky's 'Les Frères Karamazov'". *Gallimard*.

Rank, O. (1973). *The Trauma of Birth*. New York: Harper Collins.

Rank, O. (2011). *The Double: A Psychoanalytic Study*. Chapel Hill: University of North Carolina Press.

Rank, O. (2015). *The Myth of the Birth of the Hero*. Baltimore, MD: Johns Hopkins University Press.

Ricoeur, P. (1970). *Freud and Philosophy: An Essay on Interpretation*. New Haven, CT: Yale University Press.

Ricoeur, P. (1974). *The Conflict of Interpretations*. Evanston, IL: Northwestern University Press.

Rifflet-Lemaire, A. (1982). *Jacques Lacan*. London: Routledge and Kegan Paul.

Rogers, R. (1970). *A Psychoanalytical Study of the Double in Literature*. Detroit, MI: Wayne State University Press.

Safouan, M. (1968a). "De la structure en psychanalyse". In *Qu'est-ce que le structuralisme?* Paris: Editions du Seuil.

Safouan, M. (1968b). "Note sur le père idéal". *Lettres de l'École freudienne de Paris*, no.5.

Safouan, M. (1980). "Is the Oedipus Complex Universal". In *Power/Knowledge*, Foucault, M. (Ed.). Sussex: Harvester Press.

Sami-Ali, M. (1970). *De la projection*. Paris: Payot.

Simonis, Y. (1968). *Claude Lévi-Strauss ou La Passion de l'inceste*. Paris: Aubier Montaigne.

Staiger, E. (1991). *Basic Concepts of Poetics*. University Park, PA: Penn State University Press.

Todorov, T. (1975). *The Fantastic: A Structural Approach to a Literary Genre*. Ithaca, NY: Cornell University Press.

Todorov, T. (1984). *Theories of the Symbol*. Ithaca, NY: Cornell University Press.

Trotter, W. (1930). *Instincts of the Herd in Peace and War*. London: Ernest Benn.

Vergote, A. (1973). *Problèmes de psychanalyse*. Paris: Desclée de Brouwer.

Winnicott, D. (1953). "Transitional Objects and Transitional Phenomena". *International Journal of Psychoanalysis*, 34: 89–97.

Winnicott, D. (1971). *Playing and Reality*. London: Routledge.

Zenoni, A. (1973). *Analyse du moi et langage: Essai d'articulation des théories analytiques du moi* (Analysis of Ego and Language: An Attempt at Linking the Analytic Theories on Ego). Dissertation, Université Saint-Louis Library. Unpublished.

Zenoni, A. (1981). "Metaphor and Metonymy in Lacanian Theory". *Enclictic*, V, no. 1 (Spring).

Index

For Product Safety Concerns and Information please contact our EU
representative GPSR@taylorandfrancis.com
Taylor & Francis Verlag GmbH, Kaufingerstraße 24, 80331 München, Germany